Statistical Analysis
of Epidemiologic Data

Monographs in Epidemiology and Biostatistics
edited by Jennifer L. Kelsey, Michael G. Marmot,
Paul D. Stolley, Martin P. Vessey

Monographs in Epidemiology and Biostatistics

Volume 17

Statistical Analysis of Epidemiologic Data

Steve Selvin, Ph.D.
University of California, Berkeley

New York   Oxford
OXFORD UNIVERSITY PRESS
1991

Oxford University Press

Oxford   New York   Toronto
Delhi   Bombay   Calcutta   Madras   Karachi
Petaling Jaya   Singapore   Hong Kong   Tokyo
Nairobi   Dar es Salaam   Cape Town
Melbourne   Auckland

and associated companies in
Berlin   Ibadan

Library of Congress Cataloging-in-Publication Data
Selvin, S.
Statistical analysis of epidemiologic data / by Steve Selvin.
p.   cm. — (Monographs in epidemiology and biostatistics; V. 17)
Includes bibliographical references.   Includes index.
ISBN 0-19-506766-5
1. Epidemiology—Statistical methods.
I. Title.   II. Series. [DNLM: 1. Data Interpretation, Statistical
2. Epidemiologic Methods.   W1 M0567Lt 17 / WA 950 S469s]
RA652.2.M3S45   1991
614.4'072—dc20   DNLM/DLC
for Library of Congress

9 8 7 6 5 4 3 2 1

Printed in the United States of America
on acid-free paper

For Liz

Preface

Differences among the fields of statistics, biostatistics, vital statistics, and epidemiology are often emphasized. This text makes no real distinction among these disciplines and draws material from all four areas to examine the analysis of data collected to study human disease. A number of statistical methods are surveyed in a way that should be useful to researchers concerned with the application of statistics to epidemiologic data. Additionally, these methods are chosen to illustrate general principles. For example, "jackknife" estimation (Chapter 5) is an excellent way to estimate specific parameters from collected data but, at the same time, illustrates the application of a "computer-intensive" estimation method. Statistical procedures useful in epidemiologic analysis are scattered throughout the statistical literature, and the explanations of their properties are often couched in rather theoretical language. The aim of this textbook is to develop a clear understanding of issues important to epidemiologic data analysis without depending on sophisticated mathematics or advanced statistical theory. Running throughout the text is a "casebook theme" by which real data are used to address questions surrounding the analysis of epidemiologic data. Extensive use is made, for example, of a data set that relates the risk of coronary heart disease to behavior. The use of actual data exhibits both the strengths and the weaknesses of an analytic approach in the ultimate understanding of a disease process. With one exception, data are fully presented and therefore available to the reader to verify calculations or to try different approaches for purposes of comparison.

The level of this text is beyond introductory but short of advanced. Knowledge of elementary statistical methods, like that gained from a one-semester statistics course, is assumed, and an introductory course in epidemiology is also likely to be useful background. Statistical methods based on the normal and t distributions are reviewed briefly, while other basic techniques (e.g., correlation, simple linear regression, and χ^2 analysis) are used but not described in any detail. This text was developed from a one-semester course taught during the second year of a master's degree program in epidemiology and biostatistics. A number of common topics in statistical epidemiology such as measures of association, matching, and study design are purposely left to other texts so that the reader can focus on additional material particularly useful for the analysis of disease data (e.g., the analysis of cohort data, Chapter 3; spatial data analysis, Chapter 5; and the study of survival from follow-up data, Chapters 10 and 11).

The calculations needed to achieve estimates or summaries with the techniques described in this text vary from easy to hard. In an age of powerful computers with "user-friendly" programs, however, the hard calculations should present no major problems. The multivariate techniques (e.g., logistic and proportional hazard regressions) must be implemented with a computer program. The parameters of the logistic and the proportional hazards models were estimated by use of a specialized system named EGRET. Other computer programs that are useful for implementing the methods discussed are relatively simple and can be written on a case-by-case basis or found in popular package systems (e.g., SAS or STATA). A set of problems is found in the appendix. These problems explore a few mathematical details ignored in the text and are not part of the mainstream development. The exercises are not opportunities to use the methods under discussion on other "data" sets since data manipulation problems are more an issue of getting the computer program to do the "right thing"—a process necessary for analyzing data but not very enlightening.

All statistical techniques involve attributing to the sampled population some sort of mathematical structure. This structure is often referred to as a "statistical model." Even the simplest t test depends on the validity of a statistical model. This book makes explicit the models underlying specific analytic approaches. These statistical structures are useful for understanding the fundamental principles of a particular technique, and in many cases they make it possible to study the consequences of bias. Throughout this text the mathematical investigation of these models is presented as simply as possible with some loss of rigor, and rarely are concepts presented in full generality. Readers interested in pursuing any topic in more depth will find references to relevant textbooks and journal articles.

Berkeley, California   S. S.
October 1990

Acknowledgments

I would like to acknowledge the years of support from colleagues Richard J. Brand and Nicholas P. Jewell who patiently answered questions and engaged in numerous lunchtime conversations that resulted in a large number of contributions to the material in this text. This work was substantially improved by Mary Castle White and David F. Selvin who read the complete manuscript and also made valuable contributions. I am especially grateful to Dennis Tani who designed the cover, Patricia Charley, who drew the technical illustrations, and Bonnie Hutchings, who helped with the index. I would also like to acknowledge the Department of Energy, Office of Health and Environmental Research which funded part of this project. Finally, I wish to thank Nancy, my wife, who has contributed to this volume in many ways.

Contents

Appendices

Statistical Analysis
of Epidemiologic Data

1 Measures of Risk: Rates and Probabilities

A rate is calculated from epidemiologic data almost always to reflect risk. Probability is another widely used measure of risk, distinct from a rate but playing a similar role in epidemiologic analysis. A rigorous definition of these quantities will clarify the similarities and differences between these two fundamental epidemiologic measures.

A variety of measures of risk are used in epidemiology that originate from the formal definition of a rate. Some examples of these "rates" in different setting are:

(i) *Fetal death rate* =

$$\frac{\textit{Number of fetal deaths}}{\textit{Number of fetal deaths plus live births}};$$

(ii) *Food-specific attack rate* =

$$\frac{\textit{Number of persons who ate a specific food and became ill}}{\textit{Total number of persons who ate the specific food}};$$

(iii) *Generic rate* =

$$\frac{\textit{Number of events in a specific period}}{\textit{Population at risk for these events in a specified period}} \times \textit{Base};$$

(iv) *Life table mortality rate* =

$$\frac{\textit{Number of individuals dying in the age interval } (x_i, x_{i+1})}{\textit{Number of years lived in } (x_i, x_{i+1}) \textit{ by those alive at } x_i} \times \textit{Base};$$

(v) *Annual death rate from all causes* =

$$\frac{\textit{Total number of deaths during a specific year}}{\textit{Number of persons in the population at midyear}} \times \textit{Base}.$$

The five expressions are referred to as rates, but none has all the properties of a rate when the term is precisely and unambiguously defined. The fetal death rate (i) and the food-specific attack rate (ii) are proportions; the individuals in the numerator are found in the denominator, and time plays no direct role in the calculations. Both are unitless. The generic rate (iii) is more like a probability. The life table mortality rate (iv) defines the population at risk in terms of person-years and is an estimate of an average rate. The annual rate (v), under certain circumstances, is also an approximate average rate, but none of these quantities should be viewed as a definition of a rate.

Rates

In words, a rate is a measure of the rapidity of change associated with a phenomenon. More precisely, a rate is an instantaneous measure of change per unit of time. A familiar example of a rate is the speed of a car, measured "instantaneously" in miles per hour by the speedometer. Instantaneous change is a theoretical quantity borrowed from physics and requires special mathematics for its exact definition. Isaac Newton explored the measurement of instantaneous change three centuries ago and invented some of the basic tools of calculus to deal with the concept of a rate.

In symbols, the change in a continuous measure y per unit change in time t is

$$\frac{\text{change in } y}{\text{change in time}} = \frac{\delta y}{\delta t}. \tag{1.1}$$

Since y is a function of t, denoted $y(t)$, the term δy represents the difference in y at two different times or, in symbols, $\delta y = y(t + \delta t) - y(t)$. An instantaneous rate is the value of $\delta y / \delta t$ as δt approaches 0 [denoted dy/dt, which represents the derivative of the function $y(t)$ with respect to t]. An exact value of a rate can be calculated only when the form of the function $y(t)$ is known.

A richer definition of a rate emerges if dy/dt is measured relative to the value $y(t)$. Such a rate then becomes

$$\text{rate} = \frac{dy/dt}{y(t)}, \tag{1.2}$$

dividing by $y(t)$ yields a measure of change in the quantity represented by y relative to the magnitude of y at specific time t. For example, a rate of 10 cases per month is more meaningfully expressed as a function of the size of the population: The quantity 10 cases per month for each 1,000 persons is different from 10 cases per month for a population of 100,000. Making a rate relative to population size at a specific time more strongly emphasizes a change in a small group over the same change in a larger group producing a numeric value that reflects risk, the central purpose of a mortality or disease rate.

A mortality or disease rate is almost always defined in terms of units of time. Time is so intrinsic to the calculation that it is often considered part of the definition. This view is overly restrictive; other types of rates exist, for example, the amount of charge or payment with reference to a base (e.g., cost of insurance per unit coverage). Or, in terms of price, rates can be cost per unit of quantity (e.g., dollars per pound). Units of dollars are certainly the most meaningful for insurance or sales. For automobile accidents, risk of death should be measured as a function of miles traveled. For counts of deaths or cases of illness, however, the natural units, and certainly the traditional units of measurement, are time lived or time free of a disease. Again, this choice is made so that a mortality or disease rate reflects risk.

Average Rate

Another measure of risk is an average rate. An average rate results from "averaging" instantaneous rates over a period of time, giving

$$\text{average rate} = \frac{\delta y}{\int_t^{t+\delta t} y(u)\,du}. \tag{1.3}$$

The integral in expression (1.3) is easily interpreted geometrically. It represents the area under the curve defined by $y(t)$ between times t and $t + \delta t$. An average rate measures a total change in $y(t)$, the numerator, relative to the magnitude of $y(t)$ integrated over a period of time (δt), the denominator. Rather than an instantaneous value, the average rate is a measure of the general level of a rate from time t to time $t+\delta t$. An average mortality or disease rate is again a theoretical quantity reflecting risk but over a specified period of time. Like the instantaneous rate, the components of an average rate can be exactly calculated only when the functional form of $y(t)$ is known.

To be concrete, suppose that $y(x)$ represents the number of individuals alive at age x in some population. A more common notation is

$$y(x) = l_x \quad \text{and} \quad \delta y = l_x - l_{x+\delta x} = d_x, \tag{1.4}$$

where d_x is the number of deaths in the interval x to $x + \delta x$. In this context, the denominator of the expression for the average rate [expression (1.3)] is the total time at risk accumulated by the l_x individuals from age x to $x + \delta x$. When the exact form of $y(x)$ is not known, an approximation is achieved by considering $y(x)$ to be a

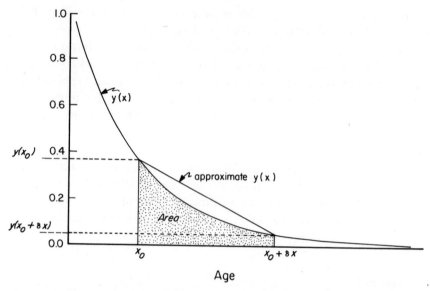

Figure 1-1. Survival curve and linear approximation over the period x_0 to $x_0 + \delta x$.

straight line (Figure 1.1). This linear approximation works best over short intervals. The area under the curve described by $y(x)$, in person-time units, is the cumulative time spent alive by those who survived the entire interval (x to $x + \delta x$) plus the total time spent by those who died during the interval before they died. If $y(x)$ is approximated by a straight line, the total time spent by those who died is half the interval length, giving

$$\text{area} = \int_x^{x+\delta x} y(u)\,du \approx \delta x\, l_{x+\delta x} + 0.5\,\delta x(l_x - l_{x+\delta x}) = \delta x(l_x - 0.5 d_x). \quad (1.5)$$

Often the interval studied is one year ($\delta x = 1$). Then, area $\approx$ $l_x - 0.5 d_x \approx P_x$, where P_x represents the midyear population of the age-specific group under study. That is, the midyear population is a readily available estimate of the person-years of risk for a 1-year interval, and therefore often serves as an estimate of the area under the curve. Since the midyear population P_x is commonly used as a denominator, rates are often stated as deaths or cases per number of individuals at risk (e.g., per 100,000), which, for intervals of one year, is equivalent to person-years of risk. The accuracy of P_x as an estimate of the person-years of risk also depends on the assumption that $y(x)$ is at least approximately a straight line.

Generically an average rate is

$$\text{average rate} = \frac{\delta y}{\text{area}}, \tag{1.6}$$

which in epidemiologic situations often translates to

$$\text{average rate} = \frac{\text{Events}}{\text{Time-at-risk}}. \tag{1.7}$$

For example, an approximate average mortality rate (R_x) is

$$\text{average mortality rate } (R_x) \approx \frac{d_x}{\delta x(l_x - 0.5 d_x)} \tag{1.8}$$

or sometimes, in the case where $\delta x = 1$ year,

$$\text{average mortality rate } (R_x) \approx \frac{d_x}{P_x}. \tag{1.9}$$

Rates are usually multiplied by a base value (e.g., 100,000) to produce a number greater than one strictly for aesthetic reasons.

The principal function of a rate is to provide a measure of risk that can be directly compared among a series of causes or for a series of groups. U.S. mortality data for a few selected causes are illustrated in Table 1.1.

Table 1-1. Death rates* for selected causes for white males and females (U.S., 1986)

Disease	Male	Female
All causes	954.4	840.7
Malignant neoplasms	218.8	185.6
Malignant neoplasms of breast	0.2	34.6
Malignant neoplasms of lung	77.8	35.9
Leukemias	8.7	6.7
Cardiovascular diseases	422.0	418.7
Ischemic heart disease	251.6	214.6
Cerebrovascular diseases	50.5	76.2
Pneumonia	29.3	30.0
Appendicitis	0.2	0.2
All accidents	55.0	24.4
Suicide	22.3	5.9
Homicide	8.6	3.0

*Average rate per 100,000 person-years of risk.

Probabilities

The probability of an event can be defined as the number of equally likely ways an event occurs divided by the total number of possible outcomes. Other definitions exist. The theory and philosophy surrounding the study of probabilities is subtle and complex, but this simple definition serves the present purpose. Again using mortality as an example, the probability of death is estimated by the number of deaths in a specific time interval divided by the number of individuals who could have died (alive at the start of the interval) or

$$P \text{ (death in the interval } x \text{ to } x + \delta x) = q_x = \frac{d_x}{l_x}. \tag{1.10}$$

A probability does not incorporate a direct reference to ,time, whereas a rate is a measure of change per unit of time. A probability is a unitless value between 0 and 1. Nevertheless, these two risk measures are related, because

$$\text{rate} = R_x = \frac{d_x}{\delta x(l_x - 0.5 d_x)} = \frac{q_x}{\delta x(1 - 0.5 q_x)}; \quad \text{then } q_x = \frac{\delta x \, R_x}{1 + 0.5 \, \delta x \, R_x}. \tag{1.11}$$

In most cases of death or disease, the rate R_x is small, so that

$$q_x \approx \delta x \, R_x. \tag{1.12}$$

Expression (1.12) clearly shows that the difference between a rate and a probability concerns primarily the role of time (δx). Confusion between the two arises since for many applications rates are small and based on a time interval of 1 unit (e.g., $\delta x = 1$ year) so that the values for a rate and a probability are more or less indistinguishable $(q_x \approx R_x)$. Even for a relatively large mortality rate, a rate and a probability are similar. If there are 10 deaths in a year producing an average mortality rate of $0.01 = 1$ deaths per 100 person-years, then the probability of death is 0.00995. Additionally, ratio measures of risk are common, and the difference between a ratio of probabilities and a ratio of rates is inconsequential when applied to the same time period, since

$$\text{risk ratio} = \frac{q_x}{q_x'} \approx \frac{\delta x \, R_x}{\delta x \, R_x'} = \frac{R_x}{R_x'}. \tag{1.13}$$

In generally unrealistic situations, a rate and a probability can be rather different. For example, if all but one person die in a population of 100 individuals during the first week over a period of 1 year, then

$$q_x = \frac{99}{100} = 0.99 \quad \text{but}$$

$$R_x = \frac{99}{1 + 0.5(99/52)} = 50.719 \text{ deaths per person-years.} \quad (1.14)$$

A rate can also be expressed as the probability of an event relative to the average time at risk. For the mortality example,

$$\text{mortality rate} = \frac{\text{Deaths}}{\text{Total time at risk}} = \frac{d}{\sum_{i=1}^{n} t_i} = \frac{q}{\bar{t}} = \frac{\text{Probability of death}}{\text{Average time}},$$

$$(1.15)$$

where t_i represents the time observed for the ith person [$\Sigma\, t_i$ is the total time-at-risk for l individuals and $\bar{t} = (1/l)\Sigma\, t_i$ is the average time-at-risk for these individuals]. Expression (1.15) is essentially another version of the previous expression (1.12) relating a rate and a probability.

Incidence and Prevalence

Two epidemiologic measures, often called rates, reflect the incidence and prevalence of a disease. Incidence is measured in two ways:

1. *Incidence rate* = number of new cases of illness over a period of time divided by the person time-at-risk; or more commonly,
2. *Incidence proportion* = number of new cases of illness over a period of time divided by the number of persons at risk at the beginning of the time period.

A disease incidence rate is usually measured in person-years (time accumulated), such as the number of new lung cancer cases in 1987 divided by the number of person-years of risk during that year. An incidence proportion is unitless and is a common measure of risk from prospective data, where the number of newly affected individuals are counted and divided by the number of individuals who could have become affected. Incidence proportion usually refers to a period of time. For example, the number of coronary events in the first six months of a study divided by the number of individuals under observation is an incidence proportion. Notice that the incidence rate, like all rates, explicitly depends on the element of time.

A point prevalence proportion (often called a prevalence "rate") is the number of affected individuals in a population at a specific point in time divided by the size of the population under consideration. For example, the point prevalence proportion of congenital heart defects among children under 10 years of age in a specific county is the number of existing cases divided by the number of children under 10 years of age residing in the county on a specified date. This measure of disease frequency is not a rate. Prevalence does depend on time in the sense that the cases are counted at a specific time, but it does not result in a value expressed per unit time. A point prevalence proportion, like all proportions, is unitless.

One final measure of prevalence is a period prevalence proportion (also usually called a "rate") which is the number of affected individuals in a population plus a count of new cases over a defined period of time divided by the size of the population under consideration. This measure is not commonly used since it combines both incidence and point prevalence into a single not very meaningful number.

Prevalence and incidence are related. If the incidence proportion is 10 new cases each month per 10,000 individuals and the duration of this disease is 5 months, then the prevalence in this population is 50 cases per 10,000 individuals. This simple relationship—that prevalence equals incidence multiplied by duration—holds under rather strict steady-state conditions. Steady-state conditions rarely occur in realistic situations since diseases generally have complex incidence/prevalence dynamics influenced by such factors as race, age and medical care. Expressions relating incidence and prevalence are discussed in detail elsewhere (see Ref. 1). It is useful, however, to note that when the duration of a disease is short, prevalence and incidence proportions are roughly equal; conversely, for conditions with long duration, prevalence and incidence measures likely provide information on different aspects of a disease.

Mortality is related to disease incidence through a measure called the case fatality proportion (sometimes called a case fatality "rate" or ratio). A case fatality proportion is the number of cases of a disease that end in death divided by the total number of cases of that disease within a defined population. Case fatality expresses mortality risk among those with a disease. A mortality rate is a function of the number of new cases that arise (incidence) in a population and the proportion of diseased individuals who die (case fatality). Like prevalence, when the case fatality proportion of a disease is near 1 (such as for pancreatic cancer), mortality and incidence measures are similar, and, if the case fatality rate is low (such as for some kinds of skin cancer), incidence and mortality rates will differ and probably measure different dimensions of the disease process (again, more discussion is found in [Ref. 1]).

It is occasionally desirable to estimate the duration of a disease—a sometimes deceptively difficult task. Under ideal conditions, duration is estimated by identifying and following every new case until death or the end of the disease period. The total amount of time ill, divided by the number of persons observed, is an estimate of expected disease duration. However, this complete follow-up is expensive, time consuming, and many times not possible. An alternative strategy is to identify a group of existing cases at a specific point in time and ascertain the amount of time each patient has been ill. Another is to identify and follow a number of patients with the disease for a specific period and record the observed duration for each individual. Although these two types of data collection patterns are efficient ways to sample duration data, the directly calculated mean values are "length biased." These sampling schemes yield direct estimates of duration that are probably too small, because short-lasting cases are likely to be overrepresented in the sample (see Figure 1.2) and long-lasting episodes are not entirely included (they are said to be censored—a future topic). To illustrate, consider the following data collected from a skilled nursing facility over a four-week sample period *(x =* length of stay recorded in complete weeks, which is the measure of duration of "illness"). The patients were observed for a maximum of 4 weeks, and the amount of time in the facility was recorded for each individual including both patients who

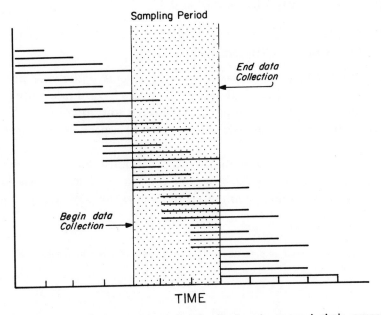

Figure 1–2. Representations of longitudinal cohorts and their associated lengths of stay for data collected over a specific time period.

were present at the beginning of the study period and patients who arrived during the period of observation (see Figure 1.2). The data are given in Table 1.2.

Lengths of stay in the facility of more than 4 weeks are recorded as four ($x = 4$) and the likely overrepresentation of short stays makes it probable that $\bar{x}$ is an underestimate of the true length of stay. The mean value calculated directly from these data is $\bar{x} = 1.190$ weeks. This "length-biased" mean can be adjusted by postulating a specific statistical structure [Ref. 2] and, with some algebra, yields:

$$\text{estimated mean duration} = \bar{x}(\text{correction factor}) = \bar{x}\left(\frac{1}{1 - (1 + \bar{x})/k}\right),$$
(1.16)

where k is the length of maximum possible observation ($k = 4$ for the nursing home data). The adjusted value of $\bar{x}$ gives a less biased estimated mean duration of stay $= 1.190(2.210) = 2.630$ weeks. Other sampling schemes and corrections are possible (e.g., [Ref. 2]). The central point is that a directly calculated mean duration is often "length biased" when complete follow-up is not possible but an improved estimate of duration can be computed. Correction for bias, a recurring issue in statistical analysis, is described in the following chapters, particularly Chapters 10 and 11.

Survival Probability and Hazard Rate

Two specialized measures based on the concepts underlying probabilities and rates are a survival probability and a hazard rate. Both play fundamental roles in describing data collected to study disease. These two quantities are related but reflect different aspects of the survival process.

A survival probability is simply the probability that an individual will survive or be disease free from one time to another. For example, the survival probability, symbolized by $S(t)$, is the probability that a

Table 1.2. Number of patients completing x weeks of stay during a 4-week interval

Week	0	1	2	3	4^+	Total
Patient	39	37	24	11	5	116

person alive at time 0 will survive to at least time t. A survival curve describes the relationship between the probability of survival and time.

A hazard rate is another frequently used measure of risk, sometimes called the force of mortality or failure rate. A hazard rate measures the instantaneous risk of developing a disease at a specific time when one has been free of the disease up until that time. When $S(t)$ represents the probability of not developing a disease in the interval time 0 to time t, then the hazard rate is

$$\text{hazard rate} = \lambda(t) = -\frac{dS(t)/dt}{S(t)}. \tag{1.17}$$

A hazard rate does not differ in principle from the general definition of a rate [expression (1.2)] and measures instantaneous mortality or disease (failure) risk relative to a survival probability. The survival probability and hazard rate are important elements in the study of disease data and will be reintroduced in the context of life tables and survival analysis in Chapters 9, 10, and 11.

The relationship among an average mortality rate, a survival probability, and a hazard rate is illustrated by a simple model. The probability of surviving up to time t (the survival probability) is given by the theoretical relationship

$$S(t) = 1 - \frac{t}{100}, \qquad \text{where } 0 \leqslant t \leqslant 100 \text{ weeks.} \tag{1.18}$$

The survival curve $S(t)$ describes the probability of surviving at least t weeks. For example, the probability a person survives beyond 40 weeks is $S(40) = 1 - 40/100 = 0.6$. Note that $S(0) = 1$, $S(100) = 0$ and that the probability of survival is linearly related to time (intercept $= 1$ and slope $= -1/100$; Figure 1.3, top). In terms of numbers of individuals (n), the number of persons expected to survive beyond time t is $n \times S(t)$ and the number of deaths occurring between two times $(t_0$ and t_1 with $t_0 < t_1)$ is

$$\text{deaths} = n[S(t_0) - S(t_1)] = \frac{n(t_1 - t_0)}{100}. \tag{1.19}$$

The number of person-weeks accumulated by n individuals between times t_0 and t_1 is

$$\text{time-at-risk} = n(t_1 - t_0)\{S(t_1) + 0.5[S(t_0) - S(t_1)]\}$$

$$= n(t_1 - t_0)\left(1 - \frac{0.5(t_0 + t_1)}{100}\right). \tag{1.20}$$

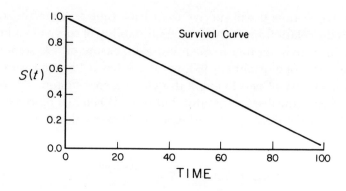

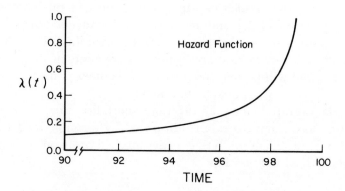

Figure 1–3. Survival curve and hazard function associated with the survival function $S(t) = 1 - t/100$.

Therefore, an average mortality rate between times t_0 and t_1 is

$$\text{average rate} = \frac{\text{number who died}}{\text{Time-at-risk}} = \frac{n(t_1 - t_0)/100}{n(t_1 - t_0)[1 - 0.5(t_0 + t_1)/100]}$$

$$= \frac{1}{100 - 0.5(t_0 + t_1)}. \qquad (1.21)$$

A hazard rate $\lambda(t)$ is an instantaneous rate at specific time t. An average mortality rate becomes a more precise approximation of the hazard rate as the time interval between t_0 and t_1 decreases. Ultimately, when $t_1 = t_0 = t$, the average rate becomes the hazard rate associated with the survival curve $S(t)$ and for the illustrative case is

$$\text{average rate} \approx \frac{1}{100 - t} = \text{hazard rate} = \lambda(t). \qquad (1.22)$$

This hazard rate is displayed in Figure 1.3 (bottom) for the weeks 90 to

99 since the curve is relatively flat for the first 90 weeks. Of course, directly applying the definition that the hazard rate as the derivative with respect to t of the survival curve divided by $S(t)$ (multiplied by -1) yields the same expression.

Statistical Properties of Probabilities Calculated from Mortality or Incidence Data

Statistical properties of an estimated value directly or indirectly arise from an underlying statistical model. A common model that is the source of many statistical properties of a probability calculated from mortality or disease data involves two assumptions. First, the probability of death or disease is assumed to be the same for each individual in a defined group; and second, the occurrences of death or disease are assumed to occur in a statistically independent manner. If these two assumptions are tenable, the observed number of deaths (D) in a sample of individuals is accurately described by a binomial distribution (see Appendix for more detail). In such a population, the expected number of deaths in a sample of n individuals is nq, and the variance associated with the observed number of deaths is: variance$(D) = nq(1 - q)$, where q represents the probability of death. The variance of an estimated value is the key to assessing statistical precision, an essential part of any conclusions drawn from data.

A number of other statistical properties follow from the binomial model. The probability of death is estimated by

$$\hat{q} = \frac{D}{n}, \quad \text{with variance}(\hat{q}) = \frac{q(1 - q)}{n} \approx \frac{\hat{q}}{n} \approx \frac{D}{n^2}, \qquad (1.23)$$

since for most mortality or disease data q is small (i.e., $1 - q \approx 1$). Other approximate measures of variability also follow, such as:

$$\text{standard error}(\hat{q}) \approx \frac{\hat{q}}{\sqrt{n}} \qquad (1.24)$$

and

$$\text{variance}(D) \approx n\hat{q} \approx D \quad \text{or} \quad \text{standard error}(D) \approx \sqrt{D}. \qquad (1.25)$$

These variances, generated from a binomial model, are used in many contexts to evaluate estimates made from mortality or disease data. The fact that the approximate standard error of an observed number of deaths is estimated by the square root of the number of deaths is an often-used "rule of thumb" for assessing isolated mortality counts. If 5 deaths occur in a specific county, for example, an estimated standard error associated with this observation is $\sqrt{5} = 2.236$. The binomial model is also used to derive expressions for the variances of more complicated measures of mortality such as the standardized mortality ratio and the direct adjusted standardized mortality rate (see [Ref. 3 or 4]).

The utility of the binomial model must be tempered by two issues. Variance is most easily interpreted when the situation addressed is related to a normal, or at least an approximately normal, distribution. When q is small the distribution of $\hat{q}$ becomes skewed so that the normal distribution will not represent accurately the distribution of $\hat{q}$. The phrase "plus or minus two standard deviations," often suggesting likely ranges of a statistic, has little meaning when q is small, particularly when the sample size is also small. William Cochran, who is responsible for many modern statistical techniques, produced a table to be used as a "working rule" for application of the normal approximation to estimated binomial probabilities [Ref. 5]. Table 1.3 is constructed so that approximate 95% confidence interval limits have less than a 5.5% error.

If n is large enough, then confidence limits based on a normal distribution approximation are an accurate assessment of the impact of random variation on the estimated value $\hat{q}$ [e.g., an approximate 95% confidence interval is $\hat{q} \pm 1.96\sqrt{\hat{q}(1 - \hat{q})/n}$]. When the sample size for a given value of q is smaller than the value in Cochran's table, the distribution associated with $\hat{q}$ is sufficiently skewed that alternatives to approximations based directly on the normal distribution should be used. Tables of exact confidence limits exist [Ref. 6] and more accurate approximations are also possible [Ref. 3]. Since q is small for most studies involving human data, exact methods are often required, or, at least, care is necessary in the application of approximate methods.

The second issue involves the assumption that the population of interest is homogeneous with respect to the probability q. Most disease data are divided into roughly homogeneous groups. It is common to form categories according to sex, age, and race to reduce the heterogeneity of q within groups. The reduction in heterogeneity aids in the statistical analysis but, more importantly, aids in the interpre-

Table 1-3. Sample sizes for accurate use of the normal approximation

q	0.50	0.40	0.30	0.20	0.10	0.05
Sample size	30	50	80	200	600	1,400

Table 1-4. Four hypothetical levels of risk

Population	q_1	q_2	q_3	q_4	$\bar{q}$
Homogeneous	0.09	0.09	0.09	0.09	0.09
Heterogeneous	0.20	0.10	0.05	0.01	0.09

tation. The statement that "the probability of breast cancer is 102 cases per 100,000 women" is meaningful only if the women sampled to estimate this probability have similar risks. If most women in the data set have a risk of 1 case per 100,000 while a few have a risk of 10 cases per 1,000 (1,000 cases per 100,000), a summary value of 102 cases per 100,000 is not very meaningful.

A consequence of the assumption of homogeneity of risk (constant q) is that it is conservative. By "conservative," it is meant that the variability is overestimated when heterogeneity of q is ignored. Overstating the actual variability makes it less likely that differences in disease frequencies will be detected when they exist. That is, treating a population that is heterogeneous for q as if it were homogeneous exaggerates variability, and the evaluations of measures of association tend to be biased toward the conclusion of no association. A simple and artificial model illustrates.

Two populations are considered, each with four subgroups; one population is completely homogeneous and the other heterogeneous with respect to q, as shown in Table 1.4.

First consider the homogeneous case. If four individuals are sampled, then the number of "deaths" can equal 0, 1, 2, 3, or 4 with binomial probabilities for the five possible outcomes, which are shown in Table 1.5. Then, the variance$(D) = 4(0.09)(0.91) = 0.328$, where D is the observed number of "deaths" among a sample of four.

For the heterogeneous case the calculation is not as simple. To account for the four levels of heterogeneity of q, a sample of one observation is taken from each of the four strata. Table 1.6 lists all possible outcomes of a sample of four and their associated probabilities.

Table 1-5. Distribution of possible outcomes

"Deaths"	0	1	2	3	4
Probability	0.68575	0.27128	0.04024	0.00265	0.00006

Table 1-6. All possible samples from the hypothetical heterogeneous population

i	1	2	3	4	D	Probability
1	1	1	1	1	4	0.00001
2	1	1	1	0	3	0.00099
3	1	1	0	1	3	0.00019
4	1	0	1	1	3	0.00009
5	0	1	1	1	3	0.00004
6	1	1	0	0	2	0.01881
7	1	0	0	1	2	0.00171
8	0	0	1	1	2	0.00036
9	1	0	1	0	2	0.00891
10	0	1	0	1	2	0.00076
11	0	1	1	0	2	0.00396
12	0	0	0	1	1	0.00684
13	0	0	1	0	1	0.03364
14	0	1	0	0	1	0.07524
15	1	0	0	0	1	0.16929
16	0	0	0	0	0	0.67716

These probabilities are calculated under the assumption that the four sampled observations are independent so that the probability of any one outcome is the product of the associated probabilities [e.g., number 10, $P(0101) = P(D = 2) = (0.80)(0.10)(0.95)(0.01) = 0.00076$]. The distribution of 0, 1, 2, 3, and 4 "deaths" is produced by summing the probabilities associated with each of these outcomes and is shown in Table 1.7. The variance associated with the observed number of "deaths" calculated for the heterogeneous population is variance$(D) = 0.307$.

The number of "deaths" (D) sampled from the heterogeneous population is less variable (0.307) than the variability (0.328) associated with the number of "deaths" sampled from a homogeneous population. The relationship between these two variances in general is

$$\text{variance}(D|q = \text{homogeneous}) \geqslant \text{variance}(D|q = \text{heterogeneous}) \qquad (1.26)$$

since

$$n\bar{q}(1 - \bar{q}) = \sum_{i=1}^{k} n_i q_i (1 - q_i) + (k - 1)\sigma_q^2, \qquad (1.27)$$

Table 1-7. Distribution of possible outcomes

"Deaths"	0	1	2	3	4
Probability	0.67716	0.28701	0.03451	0.00131	0.00001

where $\sigma_q^2 = [1/(k-1)] \sum n_i (q_i - \bar{q})^2$ measures the amount of variability among the subgroups (heterogeneity of q), n_i is the number of individuals sampled from each subgroup ($n = \sum n_i$) and k is the number of subgroups. The value $\bar{q}$ is the mean probability of death, where $\bar{q} = (1/n) \sum n_i q_i$. The variance based on this value, variance$(D) = n\bar{q}(1 - \bar{q})$, will always be greater than the variance$(D) = \sum n_i q_i (1 - q_i)$, when heterogeneity with respect to q exists within the population sampled. Only when the population is exactly homogeneous ($\sigma_q^2 = 0$) is the variance estimate based on the binomial model and $\bar{q}$ strictly correct; otherwise the estimated variance is biased (slightly biased in many cases) toward overstating the true variability.

Suppose that $D = 676$ deaths during a specific year were reported in a county among $n = 14,700$ residents at risk. An estimate of the probability of death is $\hat{q} = 676/14,700 = 0.046$, and, as mentioned, the standard error of this estimate is $\sqrt{\hat{q}(1 - \hat{q})/n} = 0.00173$ based on the assumption that all persons at risk have the same probability of death. However, it is likely that the 676 deaths result from combining heterogeneous subgroups such as the city residents, suburban residents, and rural residents, who undoubtedly have differing probabilities of death (i.e., the q_i values are in reality heterogeneous). Because $\hat{q}$ and its standard error are based on the assumption of homogeneous q (the usual choice when information is lacking on any heterogeneous subgroups), the estimated standard error is too large, giving an upper limit to the value that would be calculated if the heterogeneity of the q values was taken into account.

Special Case: Probability or Rate Equals Zero

The statistical properties of an estimated probability when the observed value is small require special considerations, as mentioned. The most extreme case occurs when a value of zero is observed. Confusion sometimes arises between an impossible event and a rare event. If the event is impossible, then an observed value of zero is exactly what is expected (no variance), but, when a zero value is observed for an event that is expected to be rare, a statistical evaluation of the estimate $\hat{q} = 0$ is called for. In the first case, the size of the sample is not relevant, but in the second case, it is the sample size, as always, that primarily determines the precision of the estimate.

Cancer incidence data for the city of Oakland, California, recorded as part of a community action project aimed at decreasing the stage-specific cancer incidence among black females, are given in Table 1.8.

Table 1-8. Rate of localized incidence of colon cancer, (Oakland, California, 1977)

Site	Number of cases	Population	Rate per 100,000
Colon	0	20,183	0.0

The "background" rate of localized colon cancer among black females was 15.5 per 100,000 for the San Francisco area over the decade 1970–80. Is there anything special about absence of cases of local colon cancer in Oakland (1977), or is this lack of cases expected for a rare disease? It is difficult to answer this question without further evaluation. One method used to evaluate the influence of chance fluctuations on a statistical estimate is a confidence interval. However, a confidence interval is typically developed in terms of a normal approximation (e.g., estimated parameter $\pm 2 \times$ standard error). If an estimated probability is zero, then a confidence interval based on the normal distribution is logically impossible, since the lower bound will be less than zero. As indicated earlier, the distribution of an estimated proportion near zero becomes skewed, further reducing the utility of the normal distribution as an approximation. However, it is entirely possible to develop an exact confidence interval for an observed value of zero without using a normal distribution approximation. The process begins with the fundamental concept underlying the construction of confidence intervals in general.

The 95% confidence interval limits are created from estimated values to have a probability of 0.95 of containing the true parameter. The interval is subject to random variation, but the parameter is not. To construct a confidence interval, the sample data are considered as fixed, and the likelihood associated with different parameters is considered. For the colon cancer example, if the probability of cancer is 5 per 100,000, then the probability of observing zero cases among 20,183 women is $(1 - 0.00005)^{20,183} = 0.365$. If the probability is 10 per 100,000, then the probability of observing zero cases decreases to $(1 - 0.0001)^{20,183} = 0.133$. Table 1.9 shows the probability of observing zero cases in a population of 20,183 individuals for a number of possible cancer probabilities.

Confidence limits are bounds for possible values of the true probability (q) for which the observed data are likely. For the case of zero observations among n individuals, these bounds are 0 and q_{upper}. For a 95% confidence interval the value of q_{upper} is the cancer probability

Table 1-9. Probability of zero cases for different rates of localized colon cancer

Probability of cancer	Probability of zero cases
1/100,000	0.817
3/100,000	0.546
5/100,000	0.365
10/100,000	0.133
15/100,000	0.048
20/100,000	0.018
25/100,000	0.006
30/100,000	0.002

such that the probability of observing zero cases among n individuals is 0.05 and is given by

$$(1 - q_{upper})^n = 0.05; \quad \text{then } q_{upper} = 1 - (0.05)^{1/n}. \quad (1.28)$$

Values of q greater than q_{upper} are considered inconsistent with the data since the observed result (zero cases) becomes "unlikely" (i.e., less than 0.05) for these larger cancer probabilities. For the colon cancer example, $q_{upper} = 1 - 0.05^{1/20,183} = 0.000148$. That is, the probability of observing zero cases is 0.05 for a probability of 0.000148. The probability of zero cases is less than 0.05 for any rate above 14.842 per 100,000. Rates that exceed q_{upper} are, somewhat arbitrarily, considered unlikely explanations of the observed data since they are unlikely candidates for a parameter producing no cases of disease. Note that since

$$x^{1/n} = 1 + \frac{\log(x)}{n} + \frac{[\log(x)]^2}{2!n^2} + \cdots \text{ an algebraic result}, \quad (1.29)$$

then, approximately

$$q_{upper} = 1 - (0.05)^{1/n} \approx 1 - \left(1 + \frac{\log(0.05)}{n}\right) = \frac{3}{n}. \quad (1.30)$$

An approximate 95% confidence interval for a zero rate is therefore $(0.0, \ 3/n \times 100,000)$ per 100,000. Other limits are $2.3/n$ for a 90% confidence interval, $4.6/n$ for a 99% confidence interval, and $5.3/n$ for a 99.5% confidence interval. For the localized colon cancer data, $(0.0, 0.000148)$ is almost equal to the exact 95% confidence interval based on the observed proportion of $\hat{q} = 0.0$.

A confidence interval indicates a set of likely parameters giving some idea of the range of possible values that could have produced the observed data. The "usual" rate of 15.5 cases of localized colon cancer per 100,000 black women is not a very plausible explanation of the Oakland data, since rates higher than 14.84 rarely produce zero cases (i.e., the 95% confidence interval does not contain the background rate). That is, the true and unknown rate for localized colon cancer in Oakland for the year 1977 likely differs from the rate 15.5 cases per 100,000 based on the observation of 0 cases among a population of 20,183 individuals.

ANALYSIS OF RATES: SMOOTHING, TRANSFORMING, AND ADJUSTMENT

Three techniques—smoothing, transforming, and adjusting—are ways to describe and evaluate a set of rates. Smoothing is a simple and useful descriptive tool. A logistic transformation is effectively used to test specific hypotheses. Adjustment procedures yield a summary "rate" that account for the influence of other variables, usually age. These methods apply not only to rates but also to a variety of data; they are only three possibilities among a large number of statistical strategies for analyzing rates of disease.

Smoothing

A sequence of rates can be viewed as a series of numbers with two components: an underlying pattern disrupted by nonsystematic fluctuations. These fluctuations are due to such things as random variation, bias, or outlier observations. Regardless of their nature, the fluctuations often obscure underlying patterns in a sequence. Smoothing techniques dampen the roughness in a sequence so that any underlying pattern is more clearly seen. Most smoothing techniques operate on a simple general principle. Each observation in the sequence is replaced by a more "typical value." A "typical" observation is established by combining adjacent values to produce a new value influenced to some extent by neighboring values. One "typical-value" calculation is called a running median. For a sequence of n values $\{y_1, y_2, y_3, \ldots, y_n\}$, each y_i is replaced by the median of the three consecutive values y_{i-1}, y_i, y_{i+1}. Consider the 20 consecutive observations in Table 1.10 (also see Figure 1.4).

The smoothed values (Smooth 1 in Table 1.10) represent a running-median smoothing of the data. For example, y_2 is replaced with the median of 1.71, -14.47, and 10.20, namely 1.71. This process is repeated for all observations except the first and the last. For this

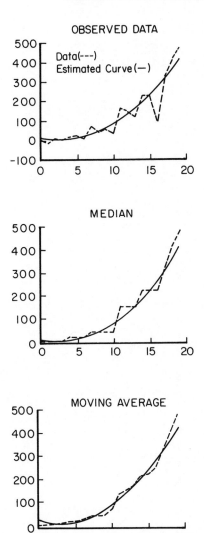

Figure 1–4. Illustration of median/average smoothing process and a fitted curve for data given in Table 1.10.

illustration the first and last observations are left unchanged, but other possibilities exist for smoothing these two end values (see [Refs. 7 or 8]). The resulting smoothed sequence is displayed in Figure 1.4 (middle). The immediate consequence of this process is the elimination of extreme values. For example, $y_{17} = 93.43$ no longer disproportionally influences the pattern since it is replaced by the locally more consistent value of 224.71.

Table 1–10. Data, median smoothed, moving average smoothed, and residual values

Data	1.71	−14.47	10.20	4.68	18.56	26.22	10.09	73.57	42.69	59.19
	37.35	168.01	152.86	127.23	227.44	224.71	93.43	331.17	415.17	471.02
Smooth 1	1.71	1.71	4.68	4.68	18.56	18.56	18.56	42.69	42.69	42.69
	42.69	152.86	152.86	152.86	224.71	224.71	224.71	331.17	415.17	471.02
Smooth 2	1.71	2.45	4.12	8.01	15.92	17.90	24.43	38.12	41.55	42.40
	70.16	132.18	147.69	169.53	210.92	221.26	250.48	331.99	408.34	471.02
Residual	—	−16.92	6.08	−3.33	2.64	8.32	−14.34	35.45	1.14	16.79
	−32.81	35.83	5.17	−42.30	16.52	3.45	−157.05	−0.82	6.83	—

An important feature of most smoothing techniques is that they are model free. The smoothed sequence of estimates in Table 1.10 comes from applying the running median, and no assumptions are made about the underlying form of the data. For contrast, a second-degree polynomial ($y = b_0 + b_1 x + b_2 x^2$) is estimated and fitted to the data (also displayed in Figure 1.4). The clear advantage of the median-smoothing approach is that it does not require the specification and estimation of a possibly complex mathematical form. Figure 1.4, however, indicates a feature of median smoothing that is not particularly desirable. A tendency towards level spots appears in the smoothed "data." Also, median smoothing has no influence on sequences of numbers that strictly increase. For example, the sequence 5, 10, 15, 30, 60, 100 is unaffected by applying the median-smoothing process.

A second smoothing improves the running-median approach. This iteration involves applying a moving average to the sequence of median-smoothed values. One version of a moving average is defined by $y_i = 0.25 y_{i-1} + 0.50 y_i + 0.25 y_{i+1}$ (called hanning after Julis von Hanning, an early scientist). Other versions of a moving average use different weights or different numbers of adjacent observations, but all work essentially in the same manner. Applying the hanning moving average to the illustrative data (Smooth 1) yields another set of smoother values (the median-smoothed "data" is again smoothed). For example, the once-smoothed second value $y_2 = 1.71$ is replaced by $0.25(1.71) + 0.50(1.71) + 0.25(4.68) = 2.45$. This process is also applied to all but the first and last observations, producing a second set of smoothed "data" (Smooth 2 in Table 1.10), which is shown in Figure 1.4. The estimated polynomial is included for comparison.

The median smoothing removes outlier observations, and the moving average is effective in smoothing increasing sequences and removing the level patterns that arise from the median smoothing. The combination produces a relatively smooth, model-free representation of the data, and, as seen from the example case, the sequence of smoothed values can be similar to fitting a mathematical function.

Median smoothing followed by moving-average smoothing can be applied to the already smoothed "data," producing yet a smoother curve. The median/averaging process can be applied a number of times (iteratively) until little or no difference is observed in the resulting smoothed "data." To illustrate, a series of multiply smoothed distributions of cancer incidence rates are given in Figure 1.5. These age-specific rates are from incidence cases collected routinely by series nine U.S. cancer registries (Surveillance Epidemiology End Results, SEER, see [Ref. 9]) for the years 1974 through 1983. Incidence rates of cancer

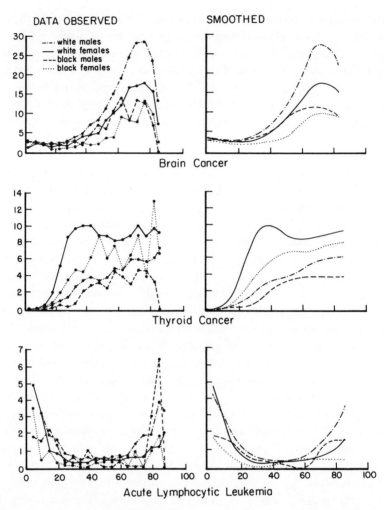

Figure 1-5. Incidence rates by age, by sex, and by race for selected sites of cancer from the SEER data (1974–83).

are given by age, sex, race, and site for both the observed data and the multiple smoothed "data." Clear age-specific patterns emerge from the smoothed race–sex groups. The smoothing process has the most pronounced effect on the cancer sites with the fewest cases (e.g., thyroid cancer and leukemia) because the extreme fluctuations associated with small numbers of observations are minimized. Sites with more stable rates (e.g., brain cancer) are less dramatically affected by the smoothing process.

Smoothing sacrifices detail for a clearer picture of the underlying pattern. This fact does not imply that detail is unimportant. In many cases the detailed characteristics of a sequence of rates are its most important feature. Once a smoothed pattern is established, it is possible to go back and investigate the detail eroded away by the smoothing process. One approach is to subtract the smoothed "data" points from the original values. An exploration of these differences, called residuals, is useful in understanding specific characteristics of a sequence of rates. For example, large residual values may identify unnoticed atypical values (outliers). Residual values for the illustrative data are given in Table 1.10. The analysis of residual values is a key statistical technique further explored in Chapter 4.

Logistic Transformation

Rates can be transformed to give them valuable statistical properties that allow easier and more accurate assessment of specific hypotheses. To illustrate, consider the 1980 colon cancer incidence data presented in Tables 1.11 to 1.13. Average rates are calculated from data collected in three communities (Oakland, the rest of the East Bay, and San Francisco), for two races (white and black) and both sexes (male and female).

Table 1–11. Cases of colon cancer (during 1980): Location by race by sex

Place	White		Black	
	Male	Female	Male	Female
Oakland	23	18	15	14
Other East Bay	112	98	6	13
San Francisco	58	60	5	12

Table 1–12. Population (at the beginning of 1980): Location by race by sex

Place	White		Black	
	Male	Female	Male	Female
Oakland	19,789	21,783	18,701	21,395
Other East Bay	172,074	182,596	11,933	13,271
San Francisco	63,356	63,681	12,214	13,423

Table 1–13. Rates of colon cancer per 100,000: Location by race by sex

Place	White		Black	
	Male	Female	Male	Female
Oakland	116.3	82.7	80.2	65.5
Other East Bay	65.1	53.7	50.3	98.0
San Francisco	91.6	94.3	40.9	89.4

Analysis of rates is enhanced by applying a logistic transformation, suggested and discussed by Cox [Ref. 10]. The data are transformed by use of the relationship

$$y_j = \log\left(\frac{x_j + 0.5}{l_j - x_j + 0.5}\right), \tag{1.31}$$

where x_j represents the observed cases and l_j represents the number at risk for the jth rate. The value 0.5 is added to both the number of cases and noncases, making the y_j less biased (again, see Cox [Ref. 10]). This transformation is actually applied to the probability of disease (x_j/l_j) and not strictly to the rates [e.g., for the Oakland white males $\log(y_1) = \log(23.5/19766.5) = -6.735 \approx \log(\text{rate}) = \log(116.3/100,000) = -6.757$]. The approximate variance of the transformed value y_j is

$$\text{variance}(y_j) = v_j \approx \frac{(l_j + 1)(l_j + 2)}{l_j(x_j + 1)(l_j - x_j + 1)}. \tag{1.32}$$

For disease data, x_j is almost always much less than l_j $(x_j \ll l_j)$; this variance is then simply estimated by

$$\text{variance}(y_j) = v_j \approx \frac{1}{x_j + 1}. \tag{1.33}$$

Applying the logistic transformation to the colon cancer data gives the values shown in Table 1.14, along with the estimated variances in Table 1.15.

Table 1–14. Logit transformed (y_j): Location by race by sex

Place	White		Black	
	Male	Female	Male	Female
Oakland	$y_1 = -6.73$	$y_2 = -7.07$	$y_3 = -7.09$	$y_4 = -7.30$
Other East Bay	$y_5 = -7.33$	$y_6 = -7.52$	$y_7 = -7.51$	$y_8 = -6.89$
San Francisco	$y_9 = -6.99$	$y_{10} = -6.96$	$y_{11} = -7.71$	$y_{12} = -6.98$

Table 1–15. Logit transformation variance (v_j): Location by race by sex

	White		Black	
Place	Male	Female	Male	Female
Oakland	$v_1 = 0.041$	$v_2 = 0.052$	$v_3 = 0.062$	$v_4 = 0.066$
Other East Bay	$v_5 = 0.009$	$v_6 = 0.010$	$v_7 = 0.143$	$v_8 = 0.071$
San Francisco	$v_9 = 0.017$	$v_{10} = 0.017$	$v_{11} = 0.167$	$v_{12} = 0.077$

These 12 transformed values are easily contrasted in terms of summaries (represented by c) that have approximate normal distributions. That is, a contrast is

$$c = \sum_{j=1}^{k} a_j y_j, \tag{1.34}$$

where the a_j values are chosen to identify specific issues, and k represents the number of cells in the table. The variance of c is estimated by

$$\text{variance}(c) = \text{variance}\left(\sum_{j=1}^{k} a_j y_j\right) = \sum_{j=1}^{k} a_j^2 \,\text{variance}(y_j) \approx \sum_{j=1}^{k} \frac{a_j^2}{x_j + 1} \tag{1.35}$$

when the values y_j are independent, which is the case for the colon cancer data and usually the case when rates are calculated from individuals classified into a series of categories. The test statistic $z = c/\sqrt{\text{variance}(c)}$ has an approximate standard normal distribution when the expected value of c is zero.

The construction of a contrast arises naturally from specific questions asked about the subject matter contained in a table of rates. Differences in the y_j values are weighted so they have expected value of zero when the logit transformed values (rates) do not systematically differ. For example, male and female transformed rates (i.e., $y_{\text{male}} - y_{\text{female}}$), contrasted for each community and each race in Table 1.14, yield six comparisons. These differences are then summed from the relevant parts of the table to form a contrast of c, which is used to evaluate observed differences between male and female rates from the entire table.

Specifically, the question of whether the colon cancer incidence rates differ by sex is addressed by calculating c from the 12 y_j values, forming 6 contrasts $y_i - y_{i+1}$, where

$$c_{\text{sex}} = y_1 - y_2 + y_3 - y_4 + y_5 - y_6 + y_7 - y_8 + y_9 - y_{10} + y_{11} - y_{12} \tag{1.36}$$

with

$$\text{variance}(c_{\text{sex}}) = v_1 + v_2 + v_3 + v_4 + v_5 + v_6 + v_7 + v_8 + v_9 + v_{10} + v_{11} + v_{12}$$

(1.37)

and $z = c_{\text{sex}} / \sqrt{\text{variance}(c_{\text{sex}})}$ has an approximately standard normal distribution when no systematic difference exists between male and female colon cancer rates (i.e., when the expected value of c_{sex} is 0). The contrast $c_{\text{sex}} = -0.651$ with $\text{variance}(c_{\text{sex}}) = 0.818$ produces $z = -0.720$ with a p-value $= 0.472$, showing no strong evidence of a difference between male and female colon cancer rates. Similarly, the difference between races can be investigated, where

$$c_{\text{race}} = y_1 + y_2 - y_3 - y_4 + y_5 + y_6 - y_7 - y_8 + y_9 + y_{10} - y_{11} - y_{12}$$

(1.38)

and the estimated variance has the same value as the contrast for sex. Again, if no systematic differences exist between white and black rates, the expected value of c_{race} is 0. Here, $c_{\text{race}} = 0.872$, giving $z = 0.965$ with p-value $= 0.334$, also showing little evidence of an important difference. A slightly more complicated contrast is illustrated by investigating the differences among the three communities:

$$c_{\text{places}} = y_1 + y_2 + y_3 + y_4 - 2(y_5 + y_6 + y_7 + y_8) + y_9 + y_{10} + y_{11} + y_{12}$$

(1.39)

and

$$\text{variance}(c_{\text{places}}) = v_1 + v_2 + v_3 + v_4 + 4(v_5 + v_6 + v_7 + v_8)$$
$$+ v_9 + v_{10} + v_{11} + v_{12}.$$

(1.40)

For this contrast, $c_{\text{places}} = 1.698$ with $z = 1.340$ producing a p-value $= 0.180$, again showing no strong evidence of a difference among the three communities. This contrast is also a sum of contrasts between two differences or

$$c_i = (y_i - y_{i+4}) - (y_{i+4} - y_{i+8}) = y_i - 2y_{i+4} + y_{i+8} \quad \text{and}$$
$$c_{\text{places}} = c_1 + c_2 + c_3 + c_4,$$

(1.41)

which has expected value zero when only random differences exist among the rates from the three communities. Other useful contrasts (with estimated variances) can be similarly formed from the logistic transformed rates to explore more complex issues and do not differ in principle from the contrasts illustrated by the colon cancer analysis.

The example data illustrate the ease with which specific issues are assessed, from just about any table containing a set of rates, by

contrasting a series of logit-transformed values. The logistic transformation, more formally referred to as the fully saturated logistic
model (discussed in Chapters 7 and 8), provides an introduction to a
general and important approach to the analysis of binary outcome data
(data with two outcomes: cancer case and not a cancer case).

Age Adjustment of Rates

The process of age adjustment is an integral part of the analysis of
mortality and incidence rates since age almost always strongly influences disease risk. The adjustment process seeks to produce a single
summary that compensates for differences in age distributions among
groups to be compared. Observed differences in adjusted rates are then
attributable to the influence of factors other than age. The two most
common approaches, called the direct and indirect methods, are
discussed extensively elsewhere; see [Refs. 3 and 4], for example.

The problem of relying on only a crude rate (total deaths per total
person-years of risk) for the comparison of disease mortality or
incidence among groups is seen from a simple hypothetical example.
Data from populations I and II are given in Table 1.16.

These two populations are constructed with identical age-specific
rates but with differing age structures. The larger number of older
individuals in population II leads to a higher crude mortality rate
[457.1 versus 586.1 deaths per 100,000 person-years at risk], where the
risk of death is clearly the same for populations I and II since the age-
specific rates are the same for both groups.

Crude rates furnish simple, direct summaries of a set of age-specific
disease data but fail to reflect risk exclusively. A mixture of the age-
specific risk and the age structure confounds observed differences in
crude rates. An ideal strategy is to compare directly the age-specific

Table 1-16. Hypothetical deaths and populations at risk

| | Population I | | | Population II | | |
Age	Deaths	Person-years	Rates	Deaths	Person-years	Rates
40—50	1	1,000	0.001	1	1,000	0.001
50—60	3	1,500	0.002	10	5,000	0.002
60—70	8	2,000	0.004	40	10,000	0.004
70—80	20	2,500	0.008	160	20,000	0.008
Total	32	7,000	0.00457	211	36,000	0.00586

rates or to construct a model summarizing the relationship between age and rates of disease. Many times directly comparing the age-specific rates does not provide sufficient summarization, and a modeling approach is usually complex. Although detail and potentially important characteristics of the groups being compared can be lost, a single summary is nevertheless useful.

Direct Method

Direct adjustment is achieved by using a standard population as a basis of comparison. Two populations that frequently serve as standards are the U.S. 1950 or 1970 populations (Table 1.17). An alternative to choosing a U.S. population or some other external standard is to use the total observed population as a standard. For example, the total population could serve as a standard for comparing populations I and II [i.e., age group totals: 2,000, 6,500, 12,000, and 22,500].

The direct method produces a single summary value for each of a series of groups "free" from the confounding influences of the age distribution. An age-specific number of deaths in each group is calculated as if all groups had the same population distribution, namely the standard. The numbers of "deaths" are computed by applying age-specific rates to the corresponding age groups of the standard population. The total number of these "deaths" divided by the total population of the standard is the direct age-adjusted rate. In symbols, if the ith age-specific category from the standard contains P_i individuals and the age-specific rate for the ith age category in the jth comparison group is r_{ij}, then

$$\text{direct adjusted rate} = \frac{\text{"deaths"}}{P} \times \text{base} = \frac{\sum_{i=1}^{k} r_{ij}P_i}{P} \times \text{base}, \quad (1.42)$$

where k is the number of age categories, and $P = \Sigma P_i$ is the total population of the standard.

Indirect Method

Indirect age adjustment is based on deriving an expected number of deaths from a standard population and contrasting this value to the number of deaths observed in a specific comparison group. The ratio of the total observed number of deaths to the number expected is called the standard mortality ratio (SMR). An indirect adjusted rate is found

Table 1–17. Standard million population of the United States for 1950 and 1970

Age	1950	1970	Age	1950	1970
0—4	107,258	84,416	45—49	60,190	59,622
5—9	87,591	98,204	50—54	54,893	54,643
10—14	73,785	102,304	55—59	48,011	49,077
15—19	70,450	93,845	60—64	40,210	42,403
20—24	76,191	80,561	65—69	33,199	34,406
25—29	81,237	66,320	70—74	22,641	26,789
30—34	76,425	56,249	75—79	14,725	18,871
35—39	74,629	54,656	80—84	7,025	11,241
40—44	67,712	58,958	85+	3,828	7,435

by multiplying the SMR by the crude rate from a standard population (denoted by R). In symbols,

$$\text{indirect adjusted rate} = \text{SMR} \times R = \frac{d_j}{e_j} R = \frac{\sum_{i=1}^{k} d_{ij}}{e_j} R, \qquad (1.43)$$

where d_j is the total number of deaths observed in the jth comparison group and d_{ij} represents the number of "deaths" occurring in the ith age-specific category of the jth group. The expected number of deaths is

$$e_j = \sum_{i=1}^{k} R_i p_{ij}, \qquad (1.44)$$

where R_i represents the rate from the ith age-specific category of the standard and p_{ij} represents the population of the ith age-specific category in the jth comparison group. The product $R_i p_{ij}$ is the expected number of "deaths" in the ith age category of the jth comparison group. The value e_j is then the total expected number of "deaths," based on the rates of the standard and the age-specific populations from the jth comparison group.

To illustrate, breast cancer incidence rates among women residents of the San Francisco Bay Area (1977–83) are compared between whites and blacks for two stages of cancer in Table 1.18. The race-, age-, and stage-specific incidence rates from these data are shown in Table 1.19. The age-adjusted incidence rates are given in Table 1.20.

The adjusted rates are based on the internal standard created by summing the populations at risk for all four categories to form a single standard population. An overall crude rate from the standard is $R = 92.02$ deaths per 100,000 for each age–stage group. The direct

Table 1–18. Breast cancer by race, age, and stage: Cases (1977–83)

Age	White			Black		
	Local	Regional	Person-years	Local	Regional	Person-years
40—49	1,429	1,082	1,625,812	1,006	999	1,767,995
50—59	1,825	1,394	1,437,511	809	913	996,536
60—69	1,048	667	565,078	258	212	235,442
70—79	484	273	229,203	245	162	171,292
79+	176	87	84,698	44	38	31,789
Total	4,962	3,503	3,942,302	2,362	2,324	3,203,054

Table 1–19. Breast cancer by race, age, and stage: Age-specific incidence rates/100,000 (1977–83)

Age	White		Black	
	Local	Regional	Local	Regional
40—49	87.89	66.55	56.90	56.50
50—59	126.96	96.97	81.18	91.62
60—69	185.46	118.04	109.58	90.04
70—79	211.17	119.11	143.05	94.58
79+	207.80	102.72	138.41	119.54
Crude rate	125.87	88.86	73.74	72.56

Table 1–20. Breast cancer by race, age, and stage: Age-adjusted incidence rates/100,000 (1977–83)

	White		Black	
	Local	Regional	Local	Regional
Direct adjusted	121.00	86.22	77.23	75.38
Deaths	4,962	3,503	2,362	2,324
Expected deaths	3,770.4	3,770.4	2,805.7	2,805.7
SMR	1.316	0.929	0.842	0.828
Indirect adjusted	121.11	85.50	77.49	76.24

and indirect age-adjusted rates are not appreciably different for the breast cancer data (Table 1.20). The highest mortality is found among the white, local-stage patients. The age-adjusted rate among whites for regional stage is somewhat lower. The age-adjusted rates for blacks show still lower values but are similar for the two stages.

Another example of age adjustment is provided by the question of whether cancer rates have increased since 1940. A relevant set of data and a series of summary values for U.S. cancer mortality among white males are given in Table 1.21 (extracted from *Vital Statistics of the U.S. 1940 and 1960*, published by the National Center for Health Statistics).

The crude rates [166.09 in 1960 and 119.53 in 1940) show an apparently important increase in cancer mortality (about 40%). However, the age distribution also changed over the 20-year period, 1940–60. Specifically, higher proportions of individuals are found in the older age categories in 1960, where the cancer mortality is highest. To assess more clearly the observed increase in cancer mortality, this difference in age distributions must be taken into account.

A natural standard is the 1960 population. That is, the number of "deaths" is computed by use of the rates from the 1940 data and the age-specific population counts from 1960. These "1940 deaths" are given in the table ("deaths"—direct; column 8 of Table 1.21). The crude rate based on these theoretically derived "deaths" (the direct adjusted rate) is $109,127/78,367,144 = 139.25$ per 100,000. Once the 1940 "rate" is based on the age distribution of the 1960 population, the difference in cancer mortality is less striking but not attributable to differences in age distributions. A large part of the remaining difference is undoubtedly due to the smoking-related cancers, which dramatically increased over the past 30 or so years.

An indirect adjustment produces essentially the same result. When the 1960 rates are applied to the 1940 age-specific population counts, a set of expected "deaths" is produced ("deaths"—indirect; column 9 of Table 1.21). The standard mortality ratio based on these "deaths" and the deaths observed in 1940 is $71,058/85,557 = 0.831$, and an indirect adjusted rate is $SMR \times 1940$ crude rate $= 0.831(166.09) = 137.94$ deaths per 100,000. Incidentally, direct standardization also can be viewed as a ratio of total expected "deaths" to observed deaths (i.e., $109,127/130,158 = 0.838$) multiplied by the 1960 crude rate, producing the direct adjusted rate of $0.838(166.09) = 139.25$, as before. Table 1.22 summarizes the data.

When a comparison group contains a small number of deaths or only the total number of deaths is known (i.e., d_j), then only indirect age adjustment is possible. However, since indirect standardization does not completely remove the influence of differences in population composition (see Ref. [3]), it is possible to construct contradictory examples. Two populations (A and B) can be constructed so that the age-specific rates in A are all larger than those of B, but the indirect age-adjusted rates show the opposite relationship. In applied situa-

Table 1–21. Comparison of U.S. cancer mortality for the years 1940 and 1960 (white males)

Age	1960			1940			"Deaths"	
	Deaths	Population	Rate*	Deaths	Population	Rate*	Direct	Indirect
<1	141	1,784,033	7.9	45	906,897	5.0	89	72
1—4	926	7,065,148	13.1	201	3,794,573	5.3	374	497
5—14	1,253	15,658,730	8.0	320	10,003,544	3.2	501	800
15—24	1,080	10,482,916	10.3	670	10,629,526	6.3	661	1,095
25—34	1,869	9,939,972	18.8	1126	9,465,330	11.9	1,182	1,780
35—44	4,891	10,563,872	46.3	3,160	8,249,558	38.3	4,047	3,819
45—54	14,956	9,114,202	164.1	9,723	7,294,330	133.3	12,149	11,970
55—64	30,888	6,850,263	450.9	17,935	5,022,499	357.1	24,462	22,647
65—74	41,725	4,702,482	887.3	22,179	2,920,220	759.5	35,715	25,911
75—84	26,501	1,874,619	1,413.7	13,461	1,019,504	1,320.3	24,751	14,412
85+	5,928	330,915	1,791.4	2,238	142,532	1,570.0	5,196	2,553
Total	130,158	78,367,144	166.09	71,058	59,448,516	119.53	109,127	85,557

*Rate per 100,000 person-years.

Table 1-22. Summary: 1940 and 1960 cancer rates per 100,000

	Crude	Direct	Indirect
1940	119.53	139.25	137.94
1960	166.09	166.09	166.09
Difference	46.56	26.84	28.15

tions, however, both the direct and the indirect adjustment procedures usually provide an effective measure of the average level of mortality and convey much of the essential information contained in the age-specific rates. The choice of a standard is not critical but can make a difference in certain situations (see Ref. [4]). The absolute values of both age-adjusted rates have little meaning; rather, the relative magnitude of an adjusted rate is a useful summary of a set of age-specific rates. A model-based age-adjustment procedure that does not depend on a standard population is discussed in Chapter 11.

2 Variation and Bias

A designed experiment typically begins with the random assignment of individuals to a series of groups. Each group then receives one of a series of treatments. Subsequent differences observed among these groups likely result from treatment effects since it is probable that the randomization process produced groups essentially equivalent with respect to all other factors. Or conversely, if the treatments under investigation have no influence, then comparisons among randomly assigned groups will show only random differences. The balancing of extraneous influences among groups to be compared is the essence of experimental data.

The analysis of nonexperimental data, often called observational data, also involves the comparison of a series of groups, but, for one reason or another, individuals are assigned to these groups in nonrandom ways. Individuals can select group membership themselves (e.g., smokers versus nonsmokers), and this self-selection tends to make groups different regardless of "treatment" influences. Others may assign group membership. For example, physicians may place patients on one versus another therapy. As with self-selection, the reasons for the choice of a particular therapy tend to make groups different for a range of characteristics. In other situations, groups are selected in some sort of natural way (e.g., low-weight infants versus normal-weight infants) and undoubtedly differ by other characteristics. The fact that non-randomized groups differ with respect to a number of variables makes isolation of a specific influence difficult and also makes direct comparisons of specific measures of association hard to interpret. The analysis and interpretation of observational data, therefore, are almost always complicated by potential biases arising from the lack of randomization.

Another important property of both experimental and observational data is the lack of uniformity in the study subjects. Variation tends to obscure systematic influences among groups, also making it difficult to isolate reasons for observed differences. In an experimental setting, individuals chosen to be as similar as possible are randomly assigned to comparison groups, diminishing the influence of extraneous variation. It is rare that observational data are controlled to the same extent. Observational studies rely on statistical techniques to deal with differences that result from lack of randomization and to minimize of extraneous variation. Such techniques as matching, stratifying, and statistical modeling are typical analytic approaches to observational data.

This chapter reviews several basic analytic methods by postulating a statistical model to justify the data analysis; at the same time, these statistical structures are employed to define and illustrate the possible consequences of specific biases associated with observational data.

Two types of mathematical structures are referred to as models. Both employ mathematical expressions to describe relationships within a set of data but with different goals. One attempts to reflect biological or physical reality, whereas the other is essentially a mathematical convenience to make predictions or to represent a set of relationships in a parsimonious way. Galileo postulated a mathematical explanation for the behavior of the solar system. His model described the paths of planetary movements around the sun. If his model had been simply a mathematical convenience to make predictions, presumably the Catholic Church would not have objected to such an exercise. Mendel's genetic model is another example of a mathematical structure postulated to reflect reality and ranks among the most important scientific theories because of its correspondence to the biological mechanisms underlying inheritance. Models used in most statistical analyses are carefully constructed to reflect the observed data, providing a mathematically convenient way to deal with complex issues without detailed knowledge of underlying mechanisms. The relationships surrounding the occurrence of disease, for example, are not governed by mechanisms with simple mathematical expressions. However, simple mathematical expressions are often useful for summarizing, analyzing, and, in general, understanding these relationships.

A Simple Model

In research situations, complete knowledge about the true relationships under study is generally not available. A statistical model provides a mathematical framework to make decisions, despite this lack of concrete knowledge, about how data might be collected and analyzed. Such models describe possible data structures, are used to choose among analytic strategies and allow estimation of relevant summary values. Although a statistical model describing the measurement of two pieces of string is not a critical element in epidemiologic analysis, it is a good place to start.

Suppose two lengths of string are to be measured with two measurements. Can one do better than making one measurement on each piece of string? A simple statistical model provides a justification for a specific approach. Assume that the lengths of these strings cannot be measured perfectly. That is, if a large number of independent measurements is made on the same piece of string, the mean value will approach the true length of the string (unbiased), but the individual measurements will differ (error variability: some too large and some too small). Let μ_1 represent the true length of piece 1, and μ_2 represent the true length of piece 2. Assume also that the measurement errors are not related to the length of the string. A mathematical structure describing this model is

$$\text{string 1: } y_1 = \mu_1 + e_1 \qquad \text{and} \qquad \text{string 2: } y_2 = \mu_2 + e_2, \qquad (2.1)$$

where y_1 and y_2 are the observed lengths and e_1 and e_2 represent the contribution of random measurement error (mean=0 and variance represented by σ^2). The variance of the observed length (σ^2) is the variability associated with the distribution of repeated independent measurements on a single length. This elementary model contains a systematic (μ_i) and a random (e_i) component—a property of statistical models in general.

Suppose the two lengths of string are measured first by laying them end to end and measuring the total length (L), then by laying the strings side by side and measuring the difference in lengths (D). On the average, the value

$$\frac{L+D}{2} \text{ estimates } \frac{(\mu_1 + \mu_2) + (\mu_1 - \mu_2)}{2} = \mu_1 \qquad \text{or} \qquad \hat{\mu}_1 = \frac{L+D}{2}$$

$$(2.2)$$

is an estimate of the true length of string 1 (μ_1) since the mean of the errors $(e_i$'s$)$ is zero. Similarly, $\hat{\mu}_2 = (L - D)/2$ estimates the length of string 2 (μ_2). The trick is to note that the variance of the estimated length $\hat{\mu}_1$ based on the combined measurements is

$$\text{variance}(\hat{\mu}_1) = \text{variance}\left(\frac{L+D}{2}\right) = \frac{\sigma^2 + \sigma^2}{4} = \frac{\sigma^2}{2}, \qquad (2.3)$$

which is half the variance of measuring each piece separately, given by σ^2. Similarly, the variance of $\hat{\mu}_2 = (L - D)/2$ is also $\sigma^2/2$. Since the error in measurement is the same for any length, it is possible to reduce the variability associated with the estimated lengths by an averaging process. Therefore, the averages $\hat{\mu}_1 = (L + D)/2$ and $\hat{\mu}_2 = (L - D)/2$

produce less variation, resulting in more precise estimates of the lengths of the two pieces of string by a factor of 2 over measuring each string separately. If the pieces of string vary in length and the measurement process is perfect (another model), then combining the strings does not produce gains in precision. The question of how to measure two strings becomes clearer when a statistical model is postulated and investigated. Also, a focused discussion on the measuring process can suggest important issues. Although this model is designed to be as simple as possible, the process has many of the characteristics of the more complex and certainly more useful situations.

A statistical model is, by and large, a conceptual process. It is derived from knowledge or speculation about how the data might behave rather than directly from the data itself. It is not costly, involves no risk, requires no experimentation, and is easily modified, making it a basic tool in the struggle to understand the complexities of the "real" world reflected by collected data.

t Test

The *t* test, sometimes called Student's *t* test, and the accompanying *t* distribution are fundamental to statistical analysis.

> Aside: The *t*-test procedure was pioneered by William Sealy Gosset (1876–1937), who used the pseudonym "Student." Around the turn of the century, Gosset developed several significant biometric solutions to problems in agriculture and genetics. His most important contribution, the *t*-test, was essentially contained in a 1908 paper entitled "The Probability Error of a Mean," which opened the door to the analysis of small samples of data. W. S. Gosset was not only a statistician but a master brewer. He worked for the famous Guinness brewing firm and ultimately became the chief brewer for the London branch. Gosset was part of a select group of scientists who came together during the first part of the twentieth century to "invent" statistical analysis. Others in this group were Karl Pearson, Ronald A. Fisher, J. B. S. Haldane, and later, Jerzy Neyman and E. S. Pearson.

A statistical model can justify and be used to study the *t*-test procedure employed to compare two groups (two-sample *t* test). Random assignment of individuals to treatment and control groups gives two samples of data, and a statistical model representing this two-sample situation is:

$$\text{control individual: } y_{1j} = \mu + e_{1j}$$

$$\text{treatment individual: } y_{2j} = \mu + \delta + e_{2j},$$

where y_{ij} is the observed response for the jth individual belonging to either control group $(i = 1)$ or treatment group $(i = 2)$. The value μ is the overall mean level of the variable being studied, and the term δ represents the influence of the treatment on the response variable. If there is no treatment effect, then δ is zero. The term e_{ij} symbolizes one of a series of independent random error terms assumed to have normal distributions with mean zero and with the same variance (σ^2) for both treatment and control groups. The response variables $(y$ values) are also normally distributed since the model requires that the contribution of μ and δ be constant (i.e., not affected by the probability distribution associated with the error contribution). A statistical analysis explores the magnitude of the treatment effect (δ) while accounting for the variation in response. This structure is called the "shift" model since the treatment shifts all participants in the treatment group δ units from the overall mean μ.

A natural comparison of treatment and control groups is the difference in mean values, or $\bar{y}_2 - \bar{y}_1$, where $\bar{y}_2$ is a mean value based on n_2 treatment responses and $\bar{y}_1$ is a mean value based on n_1 control responses. Under the conditions postulated by the "shift" model, the difference in mean values is an unbiased estimate of the treatment effect or $\hat{\delta} = \bar{y}_2 - \bar{y}_1$. The estimate $\hat{\delta}$ is unbiased because the random errors $(e_i\text{'s})$ balance each other (in the long run), producing no net effect. When the treatment does not influence the response variable, or, more formally, under the null hypothesis that no treatment effect exists $(H_0: \delta = 0)$, then

$$T = \frac{\hat{\delta} - 0}{S_{\hat{\delta}}} = \frac{\bar{y}_2 - \bar{y}_1}{\sqrt{\text{variance}(\bar{y}_2 - \bar{y}_1)}} \tag{2.4}$$

and the variable T has a t distribution with $n_1 + n_2 - 2$ degrees of freedom. Extreme (unlikely) values of T lead to the inference that the difference observed between two mean values is not due to random variation; evidence exists that δ is not zero. The test statistic T is judged extreme when it exceeds the point $t_{1-\alpha}$ selected from a t distribution so that the null hypothesis is mistakenly rejected with a specified probability α (more discussion follows in the next chapter).

> Aside: Note that the subscript on the t value refers to the area to the left of a specific point. For example, $t_{1-\alpha}$ is the point on the t distribution such that $1 - \alpha$ of the distribution is to the left of that point. Specifically for $\alpha = 0.025$, $t_{0.975} = 2.025$ for 38 degrees of freedom means that 97.5% of the t distribution is less than 2.025. In the case of a standard normal distribution, $z_{0.95} = z_{1-0.05} = 1.645$, for example, since 95% of all standard normal values are less than 1.645 (to the left).

The "shift" model explicitly states that the variance is unchanged by the treatment. This assumption, necessary for small sample sizes, is less important as the sample sizes in both groups increase. Properties of the variance produce three forms of the two-sample test statistic:

1. If the variances for the treatment and control groups are equal ($\sigma_1^2 = \sigma_2^2 = \sigma^2$), then for any sample size

$$\text{variance}(\bar{y}_2 - \bar{y}_1) = S_p^2 \left(\frac{1}{n_1} + \frac{1}{n_2} \right),$$
(2.5)

where S_p^2 is a pooled estimate of the variance (σ^2) given by

$$S_p^2 = \frac{\sum\limits_{j=1}^{n_1} (y_{1j} - \bar{y}_1)^2 + \sum\limits_{j=1}^{n_2} (y_{2j} - \bar{y}_2)^2}{n_1 + n_2 - 2}.$$
(2.6)

2. If the variances are not equal but the sample size is large (both n_1 and $n_2 > 30$ or so), then

$$\text{variance}(\bar{y}_2 - \bar{y}_1) = \left(\frac{S_2^2}{n_2} + \frac{S_1^2}{n_1} \right),$$
(2.7)

where S_1^2 and S_2^2 are the variances estimated separately from each group by

$$S_i^2 = \frac{\sum\limits_{j=1}^{n_i} (y_{ij} - \bar{y}_i)^2}{n_i - 1}.$$
(2.8)

The test statistic T no longer has a t distribution but an approximately normal distribution; a standard normal distribution (mean$=0$ and variance$=1$) under the hypothesis that the treatment has no influence ($\delta=0$).

3. If either n_1 or n_2 is small and the variances are unequal, then T has a complicated distribution requiring special tables or approximations (see [Ref. 1]).

Data from the Western Collaborative Group Study (WCGS) yield a concrete application of a t test (see Appendix for a complete description of this data set, which is repeatedly used in the following). Cholesterol determinations for the 40 heaviest men in the data set (all 225 pounds or more) are recoded along with a behavior-type measure (type A and type B; see again the Appendix), giving Table 2.1.

To assess the association between cholesterol and behavior type, the "shift" model is assumed appropriate, and a null hypothesis is postulated that there is no difference in cholesterol levels between the

Table 2-1. WCGS data: Cholesterol (mg/100 ml) and behavior type

Obs	Chol	A/B	Obs	Chol	A/B	Obs	Chol	A/B
1	344	B	15	148	B	28	183	B
2	233	A	16	268	A	29	234	A
3	291	A	17	224	A	30	137	B
4	312	A	18	239	A	31	181	A
5	185	B	19	239	A	32	248	A
6	250	A	20	254	A	33	252	A
7	263	B	21	169	B	34	202	A
8	246	A	22	226	B	35	218	A
9	246	B	23	175	B	36	202	B
10	224	B	24	276	A	37	212	A
11	212	B	25	242	B	38	325	A
12	188	B	26	252	B	39	194	B
13	250	B	27	153	B	40	213	B
14	197	A						

two behavior type groups (i.e., $\delta = 0$). Without prior knowledge of whether the type A individuals have higher cholesterol than the type B individuals or vice versa, large positive or negative values of $\hat{\delta}$ lead to the inference that cholesterol and behavior type are associated. The mean values are: $\bar{y}_A = 245.050$ for the $n_1 = 20$ type A individuals, $\bar{y}_B = 210.300$ for the $n_2 = 20$ type B individuals and $\hat{\delta} = \bar{y}_A - \bar{y}_B = 34.750$. Assuming that the variability in cholesterol levels is the same for both type A and type B individuals leads to a pooled estimate of variance, $S_p^2 = 1839.557$. Since $n_1 = n_2 = 20$, then $t_{0.975} = 2.025$ (degrees of freedom = 38) and the t statistic is

$$T = \frac{34.750}{\sqrt{1839.557(2/20)}} = 2.562. \tag{2.9}$$

A value of $T = 2.562 > 2.025$ indicates that type A individuals are likely to have higher cholesterol levels than type B individuals—behavior type is associated with cholesterol level among heavy men. The probability of observing a value of T more extreme when no difference exists in levels of cholesterol between type A and type B individuals is 0.014 (again from a t distribution with 38 degrees of freedom). A significance probability (p-value) of 0.014 indicates it is unlikely that a difference more extreme ($\hat{\delta}$ less than -34.750 or greater than 34.750) would have occurred by chance alone. However, this inference results from the analysis of a set of observational data. Individuals were not assigned to groups "A" and "B" at random, raising the possibility that influences (biases) from variables other than behavior type, which differ between these two groups, might account for all or part of the differences seen in cholesterol. Some of these biases are discussed in the next sections.

Another measure of the association between behavior type and cholesterol level is a correlation coefficient; that is, the correlation between behavior $(A=1$ and $B=0)$ and level of cholesterol is $r=0.384$.

Aside: The term correlation coefficient almost always refers to the measure of association originated by Karl Pearson in 1897 and more formally called the Pearson product-moment correlation coefficient. This important measure of linear association is defined by

$$r_{xy} = \frac{S_{xy}}{\sqrt{S_{xx}S_{yy}}} \quad \text{with} \quad S_{xy} = \sum_{i=1}^{n} (x_i - \bar{x})(y_i - \bar{y}), \quad S_{xx} = \sum_{i=1}^{n} (x_i - \bar{x})^2,$$

and

$$S_{yy} = \sum_{i=1}^{n} (y_i - \bar{y})^2 \qquad (2.10)$$

where n pairs of (x_i, y_i) values are observed. The value r is most often calculated for continuous variables x and y, where these pairs have a bivariate normal distribution. This case produces a rigorous and rich interpretation of the correlation r. However, the variables x and y can represent any sort of numeric variables, and the value of r remains a summary value between -1 and $+1$ that measures association within observed pairs. Specialized product-moment correlation coefficients are typically given specific names (e.g., when x and y are binary variables, r is called a "ϕ correlation"; when x and y are sets of ranks, r is called a rank correlation coefficient; when x and y are linearly adjusted, r is called a partial correlation coefficient). The correlation coefficient is only one of the numerous contributions to statistics made by Karl Pearson, who, many believe was the founder of modern statistical thought. Perhaps Karl Pearson's most significant contribution is the χ^2 goodness-of-fit test to compare a series of expected to observed values.

A correlation coefficient of 0.384 reflects the degree of association between the binary variable "A/B" and the continuous variable cholesterol in heavy men (r in this case is called a point biserial correlation coefficient). The value r produces a measure of association between -1 and 1, while the t test allows interpretation of the results in terms of a probability. A t test and a point biserial correlation are different ways an association between two variables is expressed but produce identical statistical significance tests (p-values) since they are related. Specifically,

$$T^2 = \frac{r^2}{1 - r^2}(n_1 + n_2 - 2) \qquad (2.11)$$

so that any probability associated with T is also associated with r [e.g., if the observed value of T is determined to be a rare event, then the corresponding value of r will be equally unlikely].

Another issue worth noting concerns the allocation of individuals to the two comparison groups. In experimental settings a total of $n = n_1 + n_2$ observations are assigned to either the treatment or control groups; but how are n_1 and n_2 best determined? If the variances in both groups are equal ("shift" model), using $n_1 = n_2 = n/2$ is best. Allocating equal numbers to both groups minimizes the variance of $\bar{y}_2 - \bar{y}_1$ (i.e., the term $1/n_1 + 1/n_2$ is minimized). Reducing the denominator of the t-test statistic increases the chances of detecting a difference in response in the numerator $\bar{y}_2 - \bar{y}_1$, when one exists. In general,

$$n_1 = \frac{n\sigma_1}{\sigma_1 + \sigma_2} \qquad \text{and} \qquad n_2 = n - n_1 \qquad (2.12)$$

will best allocate [for maximum reduction of the variance $(\bar{y}_2 - \bar{y}_1)$] the sample sizes for the comparison of two groups when the variances are known. Expression (2.12) shows the sensible result that the group with the most variability receives proportionally more observations. Observational studies, where control over allocation is rarely possible, often produce disproportionate values of n_1 and n_2, leading to a less effective comparison of mean values.

Test-Direction Bias

The selection of which t test—one-sided or two-sided—to use should be based only on prior knowledge about the influence of the treatment. If the treatment is known to increase the mean response $(\delta > 0)$, then a one-sided test is usually chosen; the null hypothesis is rejected if T is extreme, greater than $t_{1-\alpha}$. Likewise, if the treatment is known to decrease the mean response $(\delta < 0)$, then a one-sided test is also chosen; the null hypothesis of no treatment influence is rejected if T is less than $-t_{1-\alpha}$. However, if no *a priori* knowledge is available about the direction of the treatment response, then a two-sided test is used; the null hypothesis is rejected if T is either greater than $t_{1-\alpha/2}$ or less than $-t_{1-\alpha/2}$. The decision to use a one- or two-sided test must be made in advance of the data analysis. Basing this decision on information from the collected data incurs test-direction bias.

To illustrate, consider the following procedure: if $\hat{\delta} = \bar{y}_2 - \bar{y}_1 > 0$, then conduct a one-sided test but if $\hat{\delta} = \bar{y}_2 - \bar{y}_1 < 0$, then conduct a two-sided test. The probability of rejecting the null hypotheses is a combination of probabilities derived from a t distribution or normal distribution. It is

$$\alpha^* = P \, (\textit{reject } H_0 \textit{ when } H_0 \textit{ is true})$$
$$= P \, (\textit{one-sided} \, | \, \hat{\delta} > 0) P(\hat{\delta} > 0) + P(\textit{two-sided} \, | \, \hat{\delta} < 0) P(\hat{\delta} < 0).$$

If an "α level$=0.05$" test is based on the standard normal distribution, then the actual error rate is

$$\alpha^* = P(\mathcal{Z} > 1.645 \, | \, \delta > 0)(\tfrac{1}{2}) + P(\mathcal{Z} < -1.960 \, | \, \delta < 0)(\tfrac{1}{2})$$
$$= 0.10(1/2) + 0.05(1/2) = 0.075. \tag{2.13}$$

However, reporting this "options-open" test as an "$\alpha = 0.05$ level" procedure clearly will be test-direction biased.

Selection Bias

Implicit in the "shift" model is the assumption that all individuals sampled come from the same population. Consequently, all individuals have a common underlying mean level of the variable being studied (μ). If individuals are not randomly assigned to treatment and control groups, a selection bias occurs when individuals in the two comparison groups do not have the same underlying mean value. The "shift" model becomes

$$\text{``control'' individual: } y_{1j} = \mu_1 + e_{1j}$$
$$\text{``treatment'' individual: } y_{2j} = \mu_2 + \delta + e_{2j}.$$

A t statistic based on this model is

$$T = \frac{(\bar{y}_2 - \bar{y}_1) - (\mu_2 - \mu_1) - \delta}{\sqrt{\text{variance}(\bar{y}_2 - \bar{y}_1)}}, \tag{2.14}$$

and when there is no treatment effect, $\delta = 0$, then

$$T = \frac{(\bar{y}_2 - \bar{y}_1) - (\mu_2 - \mu_1)}{\sqrt{\text{variance}(\bar{y}_2 - \bar{y}_1)}}. \tag{2.15}$$

The probability of rejecting the null hypothesis ($H_0: \delta = 0$) in the presense of this specific selection bias depends on the values of μ_1 and μ_2 and is approximately [based on expression (2.15)]

$$\alpha^* = 1 - P(-z_{1-\alpha/2} + b < \mathcal{Z} < z_{1-\alpha/2} + b), \tag{2.16}$$

where $\mathcal{Z}$ has a standard normal distribution with percentiles represented by $z_{1-\alpha}$. The bias b is

$$\text{bias} = b = \sqrt{n/4} \left(\frac{\mu_2 - \mu_1}{\sigma} \right), \tag{2.17}$$

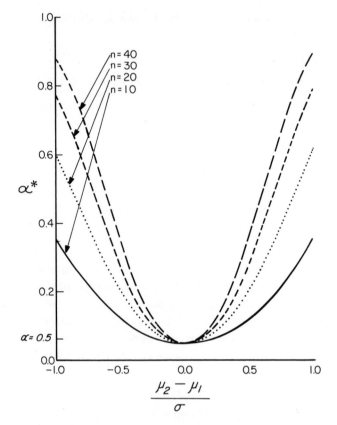

Figure 2–1. Selection bias α^* for $n = 10$, 20, 30, and 40 observations for an α-level test of 0.05.

where $n_1 = n_2 = n/2$ is the number of observations in each group. Some selected values of α^* are shown in Table 2.2.

Figure 2.1 shows the considerable impact of this bias on a t test. The actual probability α^* is always greater than or equal to the nominal level of α (0.05 in the illustration). The biased test inflates the probability of falsely declaring a difference. Furthermore, this bias

Table 2–2. Selection-biased values α^*

$(\mu_1 - \mu_2)/\sigma$	-1.0	-0.5	0.0	0.5	1.0
$n = 10$	0.352	0.124	0.05	0.124	0.352
$n = 20$	0.609	0.201	0.05	0.201	0.609
$n = 30$	0.782	0.278	0.05	0.278	0.782
$n = 40$	0.885	0.352	0.05	0.352	0.885

increases as the sample size increases, a not uncommon property of bias. The assumption that no selection bias exists ($\mu_1 = \mu_2 = \mu$) is clearly critical for a valid two-sample t test.

Comparison of k Groups

A natural extension of the two-sample t test is the comparison of more than two groups. Envision k groups, where one or more of the groups, for example, could receive no treatment producing a control group. A basic model for describing the k-sample situation is

$$\text{observed individual: } y_{ij} = \mu + \delta_i + e_{ij},$$

where $i = $ group and $j = $ observation within the group. The parameters of this statistical structure are analogous to those of the two-sample "shift" model. Comparison among k groups using a t test can detect which, if any, of the treatments have important influences on the outcome variable (e.g., $\delta_1 \neq \delta_2$?). Each group produces a sample mean ($\bar{y}_i$) based on n_i observations, where the total number of observations is $n = \Sigma n_i$. Parallel to the two-sample t test, hypotheses are generated concerning the values of the δ_i's. These hypotheses take the form of contrasts. A contrast, as before, is a weighted sum of values (e.g., $\Sigma a_i \bar{y}_i$ or $\Sigma a_i \delta_i$), where the sum of the coefficients is zero ($\Sigma a_i = 0$). For example, if group 1 is a treatment group and groups 2, 3, ..., k are various kinds of control groups, then

$$\bar{y}_1 - \frac{1}{k-1} (\bar{y}_2 + \bar{y}_3 + \cdots + \bar{y}_k) \tag{2.18}$$

is a contrast of the mean of the treatment group with the mean level among $k - 1$ control groups.

If interest is focused on a contrast of m mean values ($\Sigma a_i \bar{y}_i$), then

$$T = \frac{\sum_{i=1}^{m} a_i \bar{y}_i - \sum_{i=1}^{m} a_i \delta_i}{\sqrt{\text{variance} \left(\sum_{i=1}^{m} a_i \bar{y}_i \right)}} \tag{2.19}$$

has a t distribution with $n - k$ degrees of freedom. When the groups contrasted have the same level of treatment effect, then $\delta_i = \delta$, giving $\delta \Sigma a_i = 0$. The variance of a contrast is estimated by

$$\text{variance} \left(\sum_{i=1}^{m} a_i \bar{y}_i \right) = S_p^2 \sum_{i=1}^{m} \frac{a_i^2}{n_i} \tag{2.20}$$

Table 2–3. Mean disease severity scores

	Diet	Nondiet
Treatment	$\bar{y}_1$	$\bar{y}_2$
Control	$\bar{y}_3$	$\bar{y}_4$

when all k groups have the same associated variance. When the variability in response (y_{ij}) is the same for all k groups (not influenced by the treatments), an estimate of the common variance (σ^2) is derived by pooling the k sample variances [expression (2.8)] using a weighted average (weights $= n_i - 1$) or

$$S_p^2 = \frac{\sum_{i=1}^{k} (n_i - 1)S_i^2}{n - k}, \qquad (2.21)$$

which is alternatively expressed as

$$S_p^2 = \frac{\sum_{i=1}^{k} \sum_{j=1}^{n_i} (y_{ij} - \bar{y}_i)^2}{\sum_{i=1}^{k} (n_i - 1)}. \qquad (2.22)$$

A set of illustrative data comes from a clinical trial concerning the efficacy of a caffeine-free diet in reducing the severity of benign breast disease (adapted from Ernster [Ref. 2]). Participating women with the disease were assigned randomly to a control group (regular diet) or a treatment group (caffeine-free diet). These women were measured at the beginning and at the end of the trial to produce a score reflecting changes in severity of the disease. Compliance with the diet also was determined by biochemical analysis, producing four groups of participants as shown in Table 2.3. The symbol $\bar{y}_i$ represents the mean

Table 2–4. Benign breast disease summary data

Group	Status	Biochemical	$\bar{y}_i$	n_i	S_i^2
1	Treatment	Diet	−5.0	62	12.44
2	Treatment	Nondiet	0.6	7	13.65
3	Control	Diet	−2.0	15	16.34
4	Control	Nondiet	1.0	48	17.41
1+3	—	Diet	−4.416	77	—
2+4	—	Nondiet	0.949	55	—
1+2	Treatment	—	−4.432	69	—
3+4	Control	—	0.286	63	—

response score for each group, and negative scores indicate a decrease in severity of disease. Summary data from the trial are shown in Table 2.4. Two simple contrasts are of interest:

1. The difference in mean scores between those who followed the diet and those who did not based on biochemical evidence; and
2. The difference in mean scores between those assigned to the treatment versus those assigned to the control group.

Two issues with regard to bias are important in the interpretation of these clinical trial data. The nurse examiner knew whether a patient had been assigned to the diet or the control group and whether the patient complied or not with the diet. The "nonblind" aspect of this study leads to the possibility of observer bias. The disease severity score could be influenced (consciously or unconsciously) by the examining nurse.

> Aside: A study is usually called blind when the person measuring the outcome is unaware of the treatment/control status of the individual being measured. A trial is called double blind if additionally the patient is unaware of his or her own treatment/control status. The purpose of a blinded study is so far as possible to reduce bias introduced by the tendency of the patient or the investigator to report results based on preconceived notions. This type of bias is referred to as observer bias. A placebo effect is the tendency to report favorable results from a treatment regardless of its efficacy and is an example of observer bias. The ability to conduct a double-blind study depends on the treatment and the control being similar. In many cases, it is not possible to carry out a double-blind study since the treatment is clearly distinguishable from the control. For example, a caffeine-free diet cannot be concealed from the participants. In this situation the strength of a clinical trial is diminished, and observer bias is an issue.

Also present in the breast disease data is misclassification bias. That is, individuals assigned to the treatment group did not conform to the diet (7 individuals), potentially diluting any impact of the diet on the differences in mean response. Also some members of the control group voluntarily conformed to the diet causing the nondiet group to contain some (15 individuals) dieters, also diluting differences between groups in mean response.

It is tempting to argue that patients who complied to the diet should be compared with those who did not comply (based on the biochemical analysis), ignoring the original treatment/control categories. This approach restricts analysis to those actually receiving and not receiving the treatment, eliminating misclassification bias. The difference in mean scores between those who followed the diet and those who did not is -5.365. A t test to assess this difference is

$$T = \frac{\bar{y}_{1+3} - \bar{y}_{2+4}}{\sqrt{S_p^2 \left(\dfrac{1}{n_1 + n_3} + \dfrac{1}{n_2 + n_4}\right)}} = \frac{-5.365}{\sqrt{14.748 \left(\dfrac{1}{77} + \dfrac{1}{55}\right)}} = -7.913. \qquad (2.23)$$

The estimate of the variance in scores (σ^2) is based on the assumption that all four groups are subject to the same variability and the pooled estimate is

$$S_p^2 = \frac{\sum\limits_{i=1}^{k} (n_i - 1)S_i^2}{n - k} = \frac{1887.739}{128} = 14.748. \qquad (2.24)$$

The t test provides sufficient evidence (p-value < 0.001) that the observed difference is not likely a result of random variation and is likely due to systematic influences differing between groups. This result, however, is potentially biased. Compliance or noncompliance with the diet is voluntary, and comparing these two groups no longer maintains the original randomization. Analyzing the difference between compliers and noncompliers avoids the misclassification bias at the cost of introducing a possible selection bias. The experimental data (randomized) become observational data (nonrandomized).

The comparison between the treatment and the control groups can be evaluated with a t test despite the misclassification bias. The difference in mean scores between treatment and controls is -4.718, and the t test to assess this difference produces

$$T = \frac{\bar{y}_{1+2} - \bar{y}_{3+4}}{\sqrt{S_p^2 \left(\dfrac{1}{n_1 + n_2} + \dfrac{1}{n_3 + n_4}\right)}} = \frac{-4.718}{\sqrt{14.748 \left(\dfrac{1}{69} + \dfrac{1}{63}\right)}} = -7.050.$$

$$(2.25)$$

This difference between mean responses (-4.718) is also likely due to systematic differences between the treatment and control groups (p-value < 0.001). Even though misclassification exists, a comparison that maintains the original randomization is still useful as long as the misclassification of data is not large (less than 20 or 30%). The presence of two misclassified subgroups will generally dampen observed effects, but any remaining difference is not caused by selection bias because there is none. Maintaining randomization by contrasting the original treatment and control groups produces a meaningful measure of the treatment effect, the primary goal of statistical analysis in general.

The contrast, however, of treatment and control mean values does not discriminate between observer bias and an effect from the diet. The observed mean decrease in scores could be due to a combination of bias introduced by the examiner and the influence of a caffeine-free diet.

One last note: The statistical analysis indicates that the diet is associated with a reduction in the severity of the disease (not likely a random reduction). The reduction observed, however, is not clinically important. A reduction in the severity score of 5.0 or so was judged by both physician and patient to have no important consequence. Statistical significance does not always lead to biologically important results. Statistical analyses are limited to questions as to whether an observed phenomenon is or is not likely a result of chance variation.

Interaction Contrast

Combining sets of data is governed by a simple principle: *Data that differ with respect to the quantity being studied should not be combined.* Forming larger groups by combining smaller sets of data improves precision of an estimated quantity that is free of bias only when the combined groups provide estimates of the same quantity. Data collected on levels of hypertension in the white and black populations of part of Alameda county, California, illustrate this principle (adapted from [Ref. 3]). Each individual is classified by race (white or black) and whether the census tract of residence is predominately white or black in racial composition ("white" or "black" neighborhood). The average diastolic blood pressures for a sample of females, ages 35—49, are shown in Table 2.5.

When interest is focused on a comparison of the white versus black levels of blood pressure, a natural contrast is achieved by comparing the mean from groups 1 and 2 to the mean from groups 3 and 4 or $(\bar{y}_1 + \bar{y}_2)/2 - (\bar{y}_3 + \bar{y}_4)/2$. This contrast produces a measure of racial

Table 2-5. Hypertension summary data

Group i	Race	Neighborhood	$\bar{y}_i$	n_i	S_i^2
1	White	"White"	77.2	167	62.4
2	White	"Black"	78.9	47	74.6
3	Black	"White"	83.3	45	86.4
4	Black	"Black"	98.4	245	87.8

differences in blood pressure only if $(\bar{y}_1 - \bar{y}_3) - (\bar{y}_2 - \bar{y}_4)$ is small. That is, $\bar{y}_1 - \bar{y}_3$ (the difference between races in "white" neighborhoods) and $\bar{y}_2 - \bar{y}_4$ (the difference between races in "black" neighborhoods) must reflect the same quantity. If, however, these two quantities substantially differ, then summary values are not easily interpreted. Failure to reflect the same relationship at different levels of another variable is called an interaction. Interactions limit the "combinability" of data.

A contrast measuring the magnitude of an interaction for the case of four mean value is $(\bar{y}_1 - \bar{y}_3) - (\bar{y}_2 - \bar{y}_4)$ and is readily evaluated with a t statistic under the conditions of the k-sample "shift" model where the t statistic

$$t_I = \frac{(\bar{y}_1 - \bar{y}_3) - (\bar{y}_2 - \bar{y}_4)}{\sqrt{S_p^2 \left(\frac{1}{n_1} + \frac{1}{n_2} + \frac{1}{n_3} + \frac{1}{n_4} \right)}} \tag{2.26}$$

has a t distribution with $\sum n_i - 4$ degrees of freedom when the observed difference between the differences is due to random variation. For the blood pressure data

$$T_I = \frac{13.400}{\sqrt{78.030 \left(\frac{1}{167} + \frac{1}{45} + \frac{1}{47} + \frac{1}{245} \right)}} = 6.554. \tag{2.27}$$

The value of T_I indicates (p-value < 0.001) that the differences between races differ within each neighborhood type. Combining the white/black levels of blood pressure without regard to neighborhood type obscures the fact that the observed difference is almost entirely associated with the "black" neighborhoods. In the "white" neighborhoods the difference between blacks and whites (6.1) is substantially smaller than the same difference (19.5) occurring in the "black" neighborhoods. The differences in mean blood pressure levels differ depending on which neighborhood is considered. The mean difference, averaged over "neighborhoods," is 12.8, which does not accurately reflect the black/white differences in either neighborhood. In the presence of an interaction, measures from combined data are the average of differing quantities and in some cases produce entirely spurious results (an example appears in Chapter 6, Table 6.28). The issue of interaction is central to a number of statistical methods and will appear in several forms in the remainder of the text, particularly Chapters 6, 7, and 8.

Figure 2.2 shows the mean diastolic blood pressures plotted for both

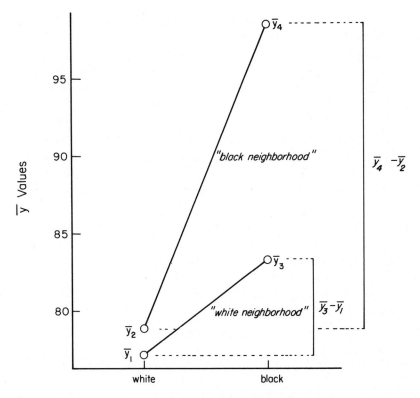

Figure 2-2. Mean diastolic blood pressure levels by neighborhoods and by race

races within each type of neighborhood (one line for "white" and one line for "black" neighborhoods). The differences between mean blood pressure values for white and black women in the survey are clear (6.1 in "white" and 19.5 in "black" neighborhoods). If no interaction were present, then these differences would be the same or nearly the same in each neighborhood type, making the lines reflecting the influence of race approximately parallel.

Two-Way Analysis

To reduce variation and control bias, a simple approach is to classify data into a series of groups, simultaneously stratified by levels of another variable. For example, individuals could be classified by exposure to air pollution (e.g., high, medium, low, and no exposure), while at the same time classified by the number of years they have lived at a specific location (e.g., less than a year, 1–5 years, and more than 5 years). Data of this sort form a two-way or a two-dimensional table.

The cells of the table could be counts of a discrete variable or measured values of a continuous variable. Continuing the air pollution example, the categories formed by a two-way classification could contain the numbers of individuals with respiratory problems or the cells of the table could contain specific measurements such as exposure levels to household nitrous oxide. The analysis of discrete tabular data is a topic in itself (partially covered in Chapters 6 and 7). A brief look at the analysis of continuous data classified into a two-way table continues to illustrate the way statistical models guide the analytic approach to specific types of data.

Data classified into a two-way table are displayed in Table 2.6. Each cell contains a continuous outcome measure represented by y_{ij} (ith row and jth column of the table, where r is the number of rows and c is the number of columns). The row means are represented by $\bar{y}_{i.}$ and equal $(1/c)(\Sigma_{j=1}^{c} y_{ij})$; similarly, the column means are $\bar{y}_{.j}$ and equal $(1/r)(\Sigma_{i=1}^{r} y_{ij})$ and $\bar{y}$ equals $(1/rc)(\Sigma_{i=1}^{r} \Sigma_{j=1}^{c} y_{ij})$.

To examine the properties of an $r \times c$ two-way table a useful statistical model is

$$y_{ij} = \mu + \gamma_i + \delta_j + e_{ij}, \tag{2.28}$$

and, as before, μ represents a constant underlying mean value. The term γ represents the influence of the row variable, and δ represents the contribution of the column variable ("treatment"). The data are sometimes said to be stratified on the row variable. The error terms e_{ij}, as in the previous sections, are assumed to be independent and have normal distributions with the same variance (σ^2) for all levels of the categorical variables (for all cells in the table). This model is referred to as an additive model since the observed values of y_{ij} result from the addition of an overall, row, and column influence plus a random component.

A specific example of an additive model, with the column variable at

Table 2-6. Observed values

	1	2	$\cdots$	c	$\bar{y}_{i.}$
1	y_{11}	y_{12}	$\cdots$	y_{1c}	$\bar{y}_{1.}$
2	y_{21}	y_{22}	$\cdots$	y_{2c}	$\bar{y}_{2.}$
3	y_{31}	y_{32}	$\cdots$	y_{3c}	$\bar{y}_{3.}$
$\vdots$	$\vdots$	$\vdots$	$\vdots$	$\vdots$	$\vdots$
r	y_{r1}	y_{r2}	$\cdots$	y_{rc}	$\bar{y}_{r.}$
$\bar{y}_{.j}$	$\bar{y}_{.1}$	$\bar{y}_{.2}$	$\cdots$	$\bar{y}_{.c}$	$\bar{y}$

three levels ($c = 3$) and a row variable at two levels ($r = 2$), produces the expected values for a 2×3 table given in Table 2.7. The mean values from the rows, columns, and total of a two-way table reflect the parameters of the additive model [expression (2.28)] or, in symbols,

$$\text{columns means: } \bar{y}_{.j} \text{ estimates } \mu + \bar{\gamma} + \delta_j, \tag{2.29}$$

$$\text{row means: } \bar{y}_{i.} \text{ estimates } \mu + \gamma_i + \bar{\delta}, \text{ and} \tag{2.30}$$

$$\text{total mean: } \bar{y} \text{ estimates } \mu + \bar{\gamma} + \bar{\delta}. \tag{2.31}$$

The additive nature of the postulated model allows the influence of the column variable to be estimated free from the influence of the row variable. Specifically, note that the column mean minus the overall mean value

$$\bar{y}_{.j} - \bar{y} \text{ estimates } \delta_j - (\delta_1 + \delta_2 + \delta_3)/3, \text{ or, in general,}$$

$$\bar{y}_{.j} - \bar{y} \text{ estimates } \delta_j - \bar{\delta}. \tag{2.32}$$

Also, for the row variable

$$\bar{y}_{i.} - \bar{y} \text{ estimates } \gamma_i - (\gamma_1 + \gamma_2)/2, \text{ or, in general,}$$

$$\bar{y}_{i.} - \bar{y} \text{ estimates } \gamma_i - \bar{\gamma}. \tag{2.33}$$

Expression (2.32) shows that the influences from the column variable are estimated without interference from the row variable. The influence of the row variable is "removed." For example, contrasting the means of columns j and k produces an estimate of specific column variable effects, and the row variable plays no role in this estimate since

$$\bar{y}_{.j} - \bar{y}_{.k} \text{ estimates } \delta_j - \delta_k. \tag{2.34}$$

Also, contrasts of the row means are not biased by influences from the variable used to construct the columns of the table.

When two factors fail to have additive effects, the factors are said to interact, and the direct comparison of column mean values, for example, does not measure the effect of the column variable free from the influence of the row variable. Again, the presence of an interaction inhibits the "combinability" of the data. Specifically, the "column" effect, averaged over the row variable $\bar{y}_{.j} - \bar{y}_{.k}$ is no longer an unbiased estimate of $\delta_j - \delta_k$.

The estimated variance of a contrast constructed from m mean values from a two-way table is given, as before, by

$$\text{variance}\left(\sum_{j=1}^{m} a_j \bar{y}_{.j} \right) = \frac{S^2}{r} \left(\sum_{j=1}^{m} a_j^2 \right). \tag{2.35}$$

where S^2 is the estimated variability calculated from the $r \times c$ table. The

Table 2-7. Model values

	1	2	3	$\bar{y}_{i.}$
1	$y_{11}: \mu + \gamma_1 + \delta_1$	$y_{12}: \mu + \gamma_1 + \delta_2$	$y_{13}: \mu + \gamma_1 + \delta_3$	$\bar{y}_{1.}: \mu + \gamma_1 + (\delta_1 + \delta_2 + \delta_3)/3$
2	$y_{21}: \mu + \gamma_2 + \delta_1$	$y_{22}: \mu + \gamma_2 + \delta_2$	$y_{23}: \mu + \gamma_2 + \delta_3$	$\bar{y}_{2.}: \mu + \gamma_2 + (\delta_1 + \delta_2 + \delta_3)/3$
$\bar{y}_{.j}$	$\bar{y}_{.1}: \mu + (\gamma_1 + \gamma_2)/2 + \delta_1$	$\bar{y}_{.2}: \mu + (\gamma_1 + \gamma_2)/2 + \delta_2$	$\bar{y}_{.3}: \mu + (\gamma_1 + \gamma_2)/2 + \delta_3$	$\bar{y}: \mu + (\gamma_1 + \gamma_2)/2 + (\delta_1 + \delta_2 + \delta_3)/3$

variability associated with a variable classified into a two-way table involves two issues: the lack of fit of the additive model and the background variation. The deviation between an observed data value and the corresponding value from the model [i.e., $e_{ij} = y_{ij} - (\mu + \gamma_i + \delta_j)$] measures this variability. Using the data to estimate the values of the parameters μ, γ_i, and δ_j gives

$$\hat{e}_{ij} = y_{ij} - (\hat{\mu} + \hat{\gamma}_i + \hat{\delta}_j) = y_{ij} - [\bar{y} + (\bar{y}_{i.} - \bar{y}) + (\bar{y}_{.j} - \bar{y})]$$

$$= y_{ij} - \bar{y}_{i.} - \bar{y}_{.j} + \bar{y}. \tag{2.36}$$

Each cell produces a residual $\hat{e}_{ij}$ value. If these residual values are all zero, then the additive model fits the data perfectly. The degree to which the residuals values are not zero measures the "lack of fit" of the additive model and/or the background variation intrinsic in the table. A summary estimate of these two sources of variability is

$$S^2 = \frac{\sum\limits_{i=1}^{r} \sum\limits_{j=1}^{c} \hat{e}_{ij}^2}{(r-1)(c-1)} = \frac{\sum\limits_{i=1}^{r} \sum\limits_{j=1}^{c} (y_{ij} - \bar{y}_{i.} - \bar{y}_{.j} + \bar{y})^2}{(r-1)(c-1)}. \tag{2.37}$$

The sum of the $\hat{e}_{ij}^2$ divided by $(r-1)(c-1)$ is an estimate of the background variability when the data conform to the additive model. The reason for dividing by $(r-1)(c-1)$ is beyond the scope of this presentation, except to note that by doing so S^2 becomes an unbiased estimate of the background variation of the tabled data.

If the variables used to form the rows and the columns of the table do not behave in the additive way postulated by the model, the variance estimate S^2 is biased by influences not described by the model. When only one observation per cell is available, the random error and the "nonadditivity bias" cannot be separated. If more than one observation per cell is available, then a separate estimate of the variation σ^2 can be made and the impact of the "nonadditivity bias" assessed (see [Ref. 1]).

In a clinical laboratory experiment three different methods to determine serum lead levels were examined. Data collected on six individuals, each blood sample was tested by three methods, are shown in Table 2.8. The estimate of the variance of serum lead levels assuming an additive model is $S^2 = 9.122$ [Expression (2.37)]. A summary of three contrasts $\bar{y}_{.i} - \bar{y}_{.j}$ using a t test is given in Table 2.9. Note that the estimated variance of the contrast $\bar{y}_{.j} - \bar{y}_{.k}$ is variance$(\bar{y}_{.j} - \bar{y}_{.k}) = 2S^2/r = 3.041$. Again assuming that an additive model describes the patient–method relationship to the serum lead tests, the differences among patients do not influence the contrasts among the three laboratory methods.

Table 2–8. Three methods for determining serum lead: Data

Patient	Method 1	Method 2	Method 3	$\bar{y}_{i.}$
1	20	26	28	24.67
2	34	32	38	34.67
3	54	61	68	61.00
4	38	40	46	41.33
5	19	25	31	25.00
6	40	38	54	44.00
$\bar{y}_{.j}$	34.17	37.00	44.17	38.44

Table 2–9. Three methods for determining serum lead: Contrast

	$\bar{y}_{.2} - \bar{y}_{.1}$	$\bar{y}_{.3} - \bar{y}_{.1}$	$\bar{y}_{.3} - \bar{y}_{.2}$
Mean	2.833	10.000	7.167
Variance	3.041	3.041	3.041
t test	1.625	5.735	4.110
p value	0.135	<0.001	0.002

The variability of the difference between mean values (the denominator of the t-test statistic) is considerably reduced by taking into account the variation among the individual patients. If the data were treated as a simple one-way classification (ignoring the distinctions among the six patients), then the estimated variability would be $S_p^2 = 192.644$ [expression (2.21) or (2.22)] rather than $S^2 = 9.122$. The reduction in variability increases the resolution power of the t test applied to contrasts between means from a two-way table. The two-way classification allows isolation of the effects of the three laboratory methods while removing the variability associated with differences in lead levels among patients. A two-way table in general allows removal of influences associated with a confounding variable and usually produces a reduction in variability. However, these two properties of a two-way classification, like many statistical approaches, depend on the adequacy of the model to represent the relationships in the data, particularly the assumption that the row and column effects are additive (no interaction).

A special case of a two-way classification is a matched pair design. Each row is a pair of similar or matched observations, and the two columns result from the presence or absence of a treatment producing an $r \times 2$ table. In the matched pair case the variance of the contrast $\bar{y}_{.2} - \bar{y}_{.1}$ is

$$\text{variance}(\bar{y}_{.2} - \bar{y}_{.1}) = \frac{2\sigma^2(1 - \rho)}{r}, \tag{2.38}$$

where ρ measures the correlation between values of y (i.e., between y_{1j} and y_{2j}) within the matched pairs [technical note: $\sigma^2(1 - \rho)$ is estimated by S^2, Expression (2.37)]. This correlation is caused by purposely using similar observations in each row of the table. A high value of ρ (near 1) indicates that the pairs within strata (rows) are similar, making treatment differences more easily detected. The increase in the ability to detect a difference within pairs is directly related to the decrease in variance. The decrease is proportional to $1 - \rho$. To the extent that observations in the rows of a two-way table are made as similar as possible, gains result in the likelihood of detecting differences among the columns.

Crossover Design

The way data are collected can lead to increased efficiency in detecting treatment influences. A crossover design, useful in comparative clinical studies, provides an example of manipulating the data collection process to produce elegant and powerful analyses. A crossover design involves a treatment given in one time period followed by a different treatment given in a second time period to the same individual. This pattern of collecting data is sometimes described as "using a person as his/her own control."

One version of a crossover design involves two time periods, two treatments, and a series of paired study participants. Suppose one "treatment" is a placebo (control) and the other treatment contains the agent under investigation. Two types of patients are distinguished: patient type 1, who receives the placebo during the first period and then the treatment during the second period, and patient type 2, who receives the treatment during first period and the placebo during the second period. Both patients are subject to a time-period effect, which can cause the first response to differ from the second regardless of whether the patient receives the treatment or placebo. A statistical model describing the parameters of a crossover design for each pair of patients, where a placebo is evaluated against an experimental treatment, is given in Table 2.10. The term δ represents the treatment influence, the term τ the influence from time (period effect), and the term μ is again the common underlying mean value. Data from each of

Table 2–10. Crossover design: Model

	Time 1	Time 2
Patient 1	μ	$\mu + \tau + \delta$
Patient 2	$\mu + \delta$	$\mu + \tau$

a series of pairs of patients collected in a crossover pattern would look like those in Table 2.11. Each patient is measured twice, producing n differences (D_i values) for each patient type (total $2n$ observations). Again, the response (y) is assumed to have a normal distribution with constant variance. A critical assumption (to be explored further) is that no "carry-over" effect exists. In other words, the order of the treatments has no importance. In terms of the model parameters, the value δ is the same for type 1 and type 2 patients. Furthermore, only the time period effect (τ) influences the mean response in time period 2 for those who received the treatment in time period 1. The "recovery" time between treatment and placebo is an important element for a successful (unbiased) estimate of the treatment effect and must be considered carefully when employing a crossover design.

The efficiency of a crossover design comes from the property that all subjects are used to evaluate the treatment. If individuals were simply assigned to treatment and control groups, typically more subjects would be necessary to achieve the same precision associated with detecting a treatment effect. The increased efficiency is purchased at the cost of the no "carry-over" assumption.

The key to the analysis of the crossover design is the differences in observed values between time periods within each patient (D_i). These differences form a basis to estimate and evaluate the treatment and time parameters of the model. To evaluate the treatment note that

$$y_{\tau\delta} - y_0 = D_1 \text{ estimates } \tau + \delta \text{ and } y_\delta - y_\tau = D_2 \text{ estimates } \delta - \tau. \quad (2.39)$$

The mean values of the differences ($\bar{D}_i$), each based on n individuals, produce an estimate of δ where

$$(\bar{D}_1 + \bar{D}_2)/2 \text{ estimates } \delta \text{ or } \hat{\delta} = (\bar{D}_1 + \bar{D}_2)/2, \quad (2.40)$$

Table 2–11. Crossover design: Observed data

	Time 1	Time 2	Difference
Patient 1	y_0	$y_{\tau\delta}$	$D_1 = y_{\tau\delta} - y_0$
Patient 2	y_δ	y_τ	$D_2 = y_\delta - y_\tau$

which is the estimated average change within subjects. A null hypothesis that the treatment has no effect is postulated ($H_0: \delta = 0$) and assessed with the t-test statistic

$$T_{\delta} = \frac{\hat{\delta} - \delta}{S_{\hat{\delta}}} = \frac{(\bar{D}_1 + \bar{D}_2)/2 - 0}{S_{(\bar{D}_1 + \bar{D}_2)/2}} = \frac{\bar{D}_1 + \bar{D}_2}{\sqrt{(S_{D_1}^2 + S_{D_2}^2)/n}}, \qquad (2.41)$$

which has a t distribution with $2(n-1)$ degrees of freedom when the null hypothesis is true. The estimated variance $S_{D_i}^2$ is calculated in the usual way using the D_i values for each patient type [Expression (2.8)].

It may be also of interest to investigate the difference between time periods. Again, the mean differences provide the key since

$$(\bar{D}_1 - \bar{D}_2)/2 \text{ estimates } \tau \text{ or } \hat{\tau} = (\bar{D}_1 - \bar{D}_2)/2. \qquad (2.42)$$

The null hypothesis that there is no difference in response between time periods is postulated ($H_0: \tau = 0$) and assessing the estimate $\hat{\tau}$ with a t statistic gives

$$T_{\tau} = \frac{\hat{\tau} - \tau}{S_{\hat{\tau}}} = \frac{(\bar{D}_1 - \bar{D}_2)/2 - 0}{S_{(\bar{D}_1 - \bar{D}_2)/2}} = \frac{\bar{D}_1 - \bar{D}_2}{\sqrt{(S_{D_1}^2 + S_{D_2}^2)/n}}, \qquad (2.43)$$

which also has a t distribution with $2(n-1)$ degrees of freedom when the null hypothesis is true.

Data adapted from Rivard [Ref. 4] illustrate the analysis of a crossover design. An experiment was conducted to assess the influence of noise (treatment) on a person performing a stressful task. The task was a computer video game, and the treatment was an elevated level of noise (94 dBA) versus background noise (control). The outcome was a performance score on the computer game. The data for 20 participants are shown in Table 2.12.

To evaluate the influence of an elevated noise level, the null hypothesis is $H_0: \delta = 0$ and the corresponding t test statistic is

$$T_{\delta} = \frac{0.140 + (-0.220)}{\sqrt{(1.163 + 1.024)/10}} = -0.171. \qquad (2.44)$$

The t statistic indicates that noise is not a significant factor in the performance of the task (null hypothesis not rejected—p-value 0.866). To assess the period effect, the t test statistic is

$$T_{\tau} = \frac{0.140 - (-0.220)}{\sqrt{(1.163 + 1.024)/10}} = 0.770, \qquad (2.45)$$

again indicating that no evidence exists that the participant's performance score on the computer game changed during the two time periods (p-value = 0.452).

Table 2–12. Data from a crossover experiment on the effects of noise

Obs	Participant 1		Participant 2		Difference		Sums	
	y_0	$y_{\delta\tau}$	y_δ	y_τ	D_1	D_2	C_1	C_2
1	2.3	3.0	2.3	3.0	0.7	−0.7	5.3	5.3
2	3.0	2.0	1.3	1.3	−1.0	0.0	5.0	2.6
3	3.3	3.0	3.3	3.0	−0.3	0.3	6.3	6.3
4	2.0	2.7	3.3	5.7	0.7	−2.4	4.7	9.0
5	3.0	3.0	4.5	3.0	0.0	1.5	6.0	7.5
6	2.3	3.0	4.6	4.3	0.7	0.3	5.3	8.9
7	1.3	1.3	0.3	1.0	0.0	−0.7	2.6	1.3
8	3.3	3.0	2.0	2.7	−0.3	−0.7	6.3	4.7
9	3.3	5.7	2.7	2.7	2.4	0.0	9.0	5.4
10	4.5	3.0	3.7	3.5	−1.5	0.2	7.5	7.2
Means	2.83	2.97	2.80	3.02	0.140	−0.220	5.80	5.82
S^2	0.789	1.251	1.871	1.811	1.163	1.024	2.918	6.340

Crossover design: Residual Effect

As mentioned, the valid analysis of a crossover design depends on the absence of a "carry-over" effect. If the treatment leaves residual effects that influence the patient receiving the placebo in time period 2, a biased estimate of the treatment influence results. A term to represent this bias can be incorporated into the statistical model (Table 2.10) and assessed. Such a model is given in Table 2.13. The additional parameter π represents residual effects from the treatment given in time period 1. The data collected for each pair of individuals has the same form as before. A series of the sums (C_i's) are calculated to estimate and test the magnitude of the residual effect (π) prior to an investigation of the treatment influences. The data and the corresponding sums are represented in Table 2.14.

The sums of the observations for time periods 1 and 2 for each patient produce an estimate of the residual effect. Note that

$$C_1 \text{ estimates } 2\mu + \tau + \delta \text{ and } C_2 \text{ estimates } 2\mu + \tau + \delta + \pi. \qquad (2.46)$$

Table 2–13. Crossover design: Residual model

	Time 1	Time 2
Patient 1	μ	$\mu + \tau + \delta$
Patient 2	$\mu + \delta$	$\mu + \tau + \pi$

Table 2-14. Crossover design: Observed data

	Time 1	Time 2	Sum
Patient 1	y_0	$y_{\tau\delta}$	$C_1 = y_{\tau\delta} + y_0$
Patient 2	y_δ	y_τ	$C_2 = y_\delta + y_\tau$

The means of the C_i values ($\bar{C}_i$ based on n within patient sums) estimate the amount of residual effect since

$$\bar{C}_2 - \bar{C}_1 \text{ estimates } \pi \text{ or } \hat{\pi} = \bar{C}_2 - \bar{C}_1, \qquad (2.47)$$

which is the estimated difference in total mean response of type 1 and type 2 patients. The magnitude of this estimate is again evaluated with a t test and when $\pi = 0$ the test statistic

$$T_\pi = \frac{\hat{\pi} - \pi}{S_{\hat{\pi}}} = \frac{(\bar{C}_2 - \bar{C}_1) - 0}{S_{\bar{C}_2 - \bar{C}_1}} = \frac{\bar{C}_2 - \bar{C}_1}{\sqrt{(S_{\bar{C}_2}^2 + S_{\bar{C}_1}^2)/n}} \qquad (2.48)$$

has a t distribution with $2(n-1)$ degrees of freedom. Using the crossover design data from the noise experiment (Table 2.12) gives

$$T_\pi = \frac{5.800 - 5.820}{\sqrt{(2.918 + 6.340)/10}} = -0.02. \qquad (2.49)$$

Clearly the value of T_π indicates no evidence (p-value $= 0.982$), from the 20 sampled individuals, of a "carry-over" effect.

If the null hypothesis is accepted ($\pi = 0$), then it is common to behave as if no residual effect exists and use the "no-carry-over" model to analyze the data (Table 2.10). If the null hypothesis is rejected ($\pi \neq 0$), it is recommended that only time period 1 be used in the analysis [Ref. 5]. This strategy is not ideal, since the sample size is cut in half and no advantage is gained by the design. On the other hand, the time period 1 data yield an unbiased estimate of the treatment effect.

An issue that occurs in a number of statistical analyses arises in connection with a crossover design. A bias results from using a preliminary statistical test to make decisions about further analyses. The test for a residual effect determines how the analysis of the treatment will be conducted. Formal statistical tests (with some exceptions) require that decisions regarding the conduct of the test be made without knowledge derived from the collected data. Without employing special techniques, decisions based on the data at hand introduce bias into subsequent test procedures. That is, a test with a nominal level of α is no longer an α-level test. This test-direction bias was discussed earlier in a slightly simpler context. However, if analyses are used without investigating the underlying assumptions, then potentially greater errors can occur. One solution, in the case of a crossover design, is to conduct both tests (for residual and treatment effects) at an $\alpha/2$ level and then the overall error rate for both tests will not exceed α. The complicated question of conducting multiple tests on a single set of data is an extensive topic (see [Ref. 6]), and, other than pointing out the possibility of a bias, the topic will not be pursued further.

The crossover design illustrates a common approach to measuring and evaluating bias associated with the relationship under investigation. A model is formulated that describes the relationship of the bias to the outcome variable. Based on the postulated statistical structure, the magnitude of the bias is estimated, and the analysis adjusted to be "free" of the biasing influence if its impact is found to be substantial.

Confounder Bias: A basic Description

The term confounder bias is widely used in epidemiologic analysis and will be described in several contexts, particularly Chapter 6. A simple model which provides an illustration of this bias is

$$\text{control individual: } y_{1j} = \mu + bx_{1j} + e_{1j},$$

$$\text{treatment individual: } y_{2j} = \mu + \delta + bx_{2j} + e_{2j}.$$

The value y_{ij}, as before, represents the response of the variable of interest in the absence (y_{1j}) and presence (y_{2j}) of a treatment effect (δ). The symbol x_{ij} represents values of a variable related to y, which interferes with directly evaluating the treatment effect, sometimes called a confounder (i.e., producing confounder bias). This statistical model is an extension of the previous "shift" model where, again, the e_{ij} values are a series of independent normally distributed error terms (mean $= 0$, variance $= \sigma^2$). If x_{1j} differs from x_{2j}, then the difference $y_{2j} - y_{1j}$ does not exclusively reflect the influence of the treatment (δ), except under special conditions. The difference in response values is a combination of influences from both the x variable and the treatment. The inability to isolate and measure δ directly is, in a narrow sense, confounder bias. If the mean values of treatment and control groups are contrasted, then

$$\bar{y}_2 - \bar{y}_1 \text{ estimates } \delta + b(\bar{x}_2 - \bar{x}_1) \tag{2.50}$$

for this linear model. Clearly, if x_{ij} is unrelated to y $(b = 0)$, the variable x_{ij} does not play a role in measuring δ. There is no confounder bias.

Also, if the x variable is equally distributed between treatment and control groups, $\bar{x}_2 = \bar{x}_1$, then no confounder bias occurs. Otherwise, the x variable distorts the difference between two means as an assessment of the influence represented by δ. The magnitude of the confounder bias is $b(\bar{x}_2 - \bar{x}_1)$.

Three fundamental methods to remove this confounder bias are:

1. Randomization to eliminate confounder bias.

The purpose of randomization is to balance between treatment and control groups extraneous variables associated with the response y so that the differences observed between groups are predominately due to any treatment effect. Assigning observations randomly to the groups to be compared makes it likely that mean values of the x variates in each group are similar. If $\bar{x}_1$ is approximately equal to $\bar{x}_2$, then the confounding influence of the x variable is reduced. In terms of the model, when $\bar{x}_2 - \bar{x}_1$ has a difference of zero, $\bar{y}_2 - \bar{y}_1$ is an unbiased estimate of δ (no confounding from the value represented by x). Most epidemiologic data do not result from randomized experiments, and issues of confounder bias are dealt with using other approaches.

2. Matching to eliminate confounder bias.

Another way to balance the x_{ij} values between treatment and control groups is to match each treatment individual with a control individual so that each pair has the same value of the x variable. A difference in the mean values of y for a series of matched pairs then directly estimates δ free of confounder bias since $\bar{x}_1$ must equal $\bar{x}_2$. For example, if x_{ij} represents age and each pair of subjects is matched for age, then the mean age for both the treatment and control groups is identical. A difference in the mean responses measured by $\bar{y}_2 - \bar{y}_1$ directly estimates δ since it will not be biased by the influence of age, even though age is related to y ($b \neq 0$ but $\bar{x}_1 - \bar{x}_2 = 0$).

A series of matched pairs can be statistically analyzed using a t test applied to a sample of n within-pair differences such that

$$d_j = y_{2j} - y_{1j} \quad \text{and} \quad T = \frac{\bar{d}}{S_{\bar{d}}} = \sqrt{n}\,\frac{\bar{d}}{S_d}, \qquad \text{where } S_d^2 = \frac{1}{n-1} \sum_{j=1}^{n} (d_j - \bar{d})^2.$$

$$(2.51)$$

The resulting value T has a t distribution with $n - 1$ degrees of freedom when δ is 0.

A matched pair strategy is conceptually easy and leads to a simple analysis. However, there are some important disadvantages. Matches for individuals with unusual values for the confounder variable are sometimes hard to find, and imperfect matching removes only some of the confounder bias. A sample of matched pairs is not usually representative of any specific population, which may reduce the general application of the analytic results. Also, in some situations a statistical adjustment procedure is possible that avoids the sometimes considerable logistical problems of collecting matched data.

3. Statistical adjustment to eliminate confounder bias.

Adjustment is based strictly on a statistical model, and its success depends on whether the model accurately describes the underlying relationships in the data. For the present model, two adjusted mean values estimate and, if necessary, are used to remove the confounding bias of the x variable. The adjusted mean values are

$$\bar{y}'_1 = \bar{y}_1 - \hat{b}(\bar{x}_1 - \bar{x}) \quad \text{and} \quad \bar{y}'_2 = \bar{y}_2 - \hat{b}(\bar{x}_2 - \bar{x}), \tag{2.52}$$

then

$$\bar{y}'_2 - \bar{y}'_1 \text{ estimates } \delta + (b - \hat{b})(\bar{x}_2 - \bar{x}_1). \tag{2.53}$$

Since it is likely, particularly for large samples of data, that $\hat{b}$ is essentially equal to b, then the difference between the adjusted mean values directly reflects the treatment effect or

$$\text{since } b \approx \hat{b}, \text{ then } \bar{y}'_2 - \bar{y}'_1 \text{ estimates } \delta \text{ or } \hat{\delta} = \bar{y}'_2 - \bar{y}'_1 \tag{2.54}$$

regardless of the values of $\bar{x}_1$ and $\bar{x}_2$.

When the confounding variable is linearly related to y, application of simple linear regression techniques produces an estimate of b. The coefficient b among the controls (b_1) is estimated by

$$\hat{b}_1 = \frac{S_{x_1 y_1}}{S_{x_1 x_1}} = \frac{\Sigma (x_{1j} - \bar{x}_1)(y_{1j} - \bar{y}_1)}{\Sigma (x_{1j} - \bar{x}_1)^2}, \tag{2.55}$$

and the coefficient b among the treatment individuals (b_2) is similarly estimated by

$$\hat{b}_2 = \frac{S_{x_2 y_2}}{S_{x_2 x_2}} = \frac{\Sigma (x_{2j} - \bar{x}_2)(y_{2j} - \bar{y}_2)}{\Sigma (x_{2j} - \bar{x}_2)^2}. \tag{2.56}$$

Since the model postulates a single value for the parameter b, these two estimates are combined to give a single estimate $(\hat{b})$ as

$$\hat{b} = \frac{(w_1 \hat{b}_1 + w_2 \hat{b}_2)}{(w_1 + w_2)} = \frac{S_{x_1 y_1} + S_{x_2 y_2}}{S_{x_1 x_1} + S_{x_2 x_2}} \text{ with } w_i = S_{x_i x_i}. \tag{2.57}$$

Therefore, $\bar{y}'_1$ and $\bar{y}'_2$ can be derived from the data, and the difference between these two adjusted mean values is an unbiased ("free" from confounding bias from x_{ij}) estimate of the treatment influence when the postulated model adequately represents the relationships between treatment, confounder, and outcome. The value $\bar{y}'_2 - \bar{y}'_1$ is the distance between two straight lines with common slopes b (parallel) and is a special case of a general approach to adjusting mean values called the analysis of covariance. Expressions for the variance and confidence interval for these adjusted mean values are found in [Ref. 7] along with an extensive discussion of confidence intervals in general.

Ecologic Bias

The fact that certain summary measures derived from grouped data rarely reflect the behavior of the individuals who make up the group was noted by Robinson [Ref. 8] and subsequently called the ecologic fallacy or ecologic bias. In one form the ecologic fallacy appears as a bias in correlation and regression coefficients.

Correlation

To illustrate ecologic bias the following statistical structure is useful. Let $X_{1i} = U_i + cV_i$ and $X_{2i} = U_i + cW_i$, where U, V, and W are independent, random variables and their distributions have means $= 0$ and variances $= 1$. It follows that

$$\text{variance}(X_1) = \text{variance}(X_2) = 1 + c^2 \text{ with covariance}(X_1, X_2) = 1.0,$$
(2.58)

giving the correlation between X_1 and X_2 as ρ when $c = \sqrt{(1 - \rho)/\rho}$. That is,

$$\text{correlation}(X_1, X_2) = \frac{1}{1 + c^2} = \rho.$$
(2.59)

This general structure generates a series of pairs (X_1, X_2) of "data" with a specific level of correlation ρ. To model the behavior of X_1 and X_2 in the context of grouped data (sometimes called an ecologic study), envision a total of N pairs (X_{1i}, X_{2i}) distributed into k groups with n pairs per group ($N = nk$). These k groups are summarized by k pairs of mean values $(\bar{X}_{1j}, \bar{X}_{2j})$ calculated for each group based on n observations.

When the k groups are formed without regard to the values of X_1 or X_2, the estimate of the correlation coefficient $\bar{r}$, calculated employing the k pairs of means, directly reflects ρ or, in other words, $\bar{r}$ is approximately equal to ρ for large values of k and n. Note that $\bar{r}$ is based on a sample of size k (grouped data), reducing its precision compared to a correlation coefficient based on sample of size N (ungrouped data) but, nevertheless, $\bar{r}$ is a consistent estimate of the correlation within individual pairs of observations.

If the grouping of the N pairs is based, at least to some extent, on the values of X_1 or X_2, a different picture emerges. Consider the following special and unrealistically extreme case. Suppose k groups are formed on the basis of X_1. The N pairs (X_{1i}, X_{2i}) are ordered from high to low according to values of X_1 and then formed into k groups. Again each group is summarized by $(\bar{X}_{1j}, \bar{X}_{2j})$. For this situation,

$$\text{variance}(\bar{X}_1) \approx \text{variance}(X_1) = 1 + c^2 = 1/\rho \text{ (almost unchanged)}, \qquad (2.60)$$

$$\text{covariance}(\bar{X}_1, \bar{X}_2) \approx \text{covariance}(X_1, X_2) = 1.0 \text{ (also almost unchanged)},$$

$$(2.61)$$

but

$$\text{variance}(\bar{X}_2) \approx \frac{\rho^2 + (1 - \rho^2)/n}{\rho}, \qquad (2.62)$$

which is less than the variance(X_2) for $n > 1$. Therefore, the correlation coefficient based on the grouped data is approximately

$$\text{correlation}(\bar{X}_1, \bar{X}_2) = \bar{\rho} \approx \rho[\rho^2 + (1 - \rho^2)/n]^{-1/2}, \qquad (2.63)$$

which is greater than ρ $(n > 1)$. The ecologic bias is $\bar{\rho} - \rho > 0$.

Figure 2.3 shows the relationship between ρ and $\bar{\rho}$. The bias is clearly large $(\bar{\rho} \gg \rho)$ for even moderate values of ρ and increases as n increases. For example, if $\rho = 0.3$ and $n = 20$, then $\bar{\rho} = 0.815$. Note that, when n is large, the variance of $\bar{X}_2 \approx \rho$ making $\bar{\rho} = \text{correlation}(\bar{X}_1, \bar{X}_2) \approx 1$ for all values of ρ $(\rho \neq 0)$. The influence of this type of ecologic bias has been noted in correlations calculated from grouped data, where coefficients exceeding 0.9 have been regularly observed [Ref. 9]. The central point is that the way data are formed into groups produces an influence on the estimate of the correlation coefficient.

Regression

Ecologic bias can also influence regression analysis. Consider the variables X_1 and X_2 entered as predictor variables into a linear bivariate regression analysis or

$$Y_i = a + b_1 X_{1i} + b_2 X_{2i} + e_i, \qquad (2.64)$$

where e_i again represents a series of independent and normally distributed error terms with the same variance.

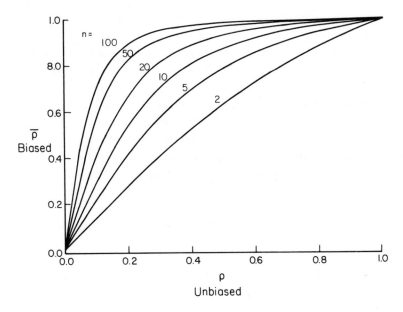

Figure 2–3. Ecologic bias in a correlation coefficient (unbiased ρ plotted against biased value $\bar{\rho}$) for $n = 2, 5, 10, 20, 50,$ and 100 observations.

If k groups of size n are randomly formed from a set of N values (Y_i, X_{1i}, X_{2i}), then estimates of the regression coefficients are not biased by the grouping process. In other words, an regression analysis based on mean values $(\bar{Y}_i, \bar{X}_{1i}, \bar{X}_{2i})$ from randomly grouped data consistently reflects, with loss of precision, the underlying linear relationship. Even if, as before, the data are ordered into k groups based on X_1, the regression analysis employing means calculated from each group produces consistent estimates of the parameters of the linear model. However, if the variable used to form the groups is not included in the analysis, the resulting estimate of the remaining regression coefficient is biased. If X_1 is again used to order the data, for example, but not included in the regression analysis, then employing k pairs of mean values $(\bar{Y}_j, \bar{X}_{2j})$ gives a biased estimate of the regression coefficient associated with X_2, where the bias is approximately $b_1\bar{\rho}^2/\rho$ or b_1/ρ for large sample sizes ($\bar{\rho} \approx 1$). As in the case of the correlation coefficient, this bias can be considerable.

The statistical model of ecologic data illustrates that a correlation coefficient calculated from grouped data is usually misleading when interpreted as the measure of the correlation that would have resulted if the nonaggregated data were employed. A similar bias in the regression coefficients occurs when the coefficients are estimated from grouped data and the analytic model fails to include measures that reflect the grouping process. The "ecologic fallacy" in terms of a regression coefficient can be considered as a special case of incomplete model bias [Ref. 10]. From another point of view, the grouping process is a confounding influence on the relationships under investigation, and failure to account for this influence in the analysis produces confounder bias. Therefore, a fundamental question associated with applying linear regression analysis to grouped data is whether the process underlying the formation of the groups is measured and included in the model. If the answer is yes, the estimated regression equation may be of value (no ecologic bias). If the answer is no, the estimated regression equation has little value with respect to understanding the relationships among the individuals who make up the sampled groups (ecologic bias).

3 Statistical Power and Sample Size Calculations

A primary goal of statistical analysis is to detect systematic influences in the presence of random variation. The likelihood that a statistical technique correctly detects nonrandom effects is called power. Statistical power is rigorously defined by two specific hypotheses, the null and the alternative. The null hypothesis asserts that all observed variation is due to the variability intrinsic in the material under investigation. The alternative hypothesis states that a systematic (nonrandom) influence explains at least some part of the observed results. Power is measured by the probability of rejecting the null hypothesis when the alternative is true. That is, power is the probability of identifying a systematic effect when it exists.

Technical Details

To explore the concept of power, a statistical structure is postulated consisting of a null and alternative hypothesis. A statistical summary represented by X, with a normal or approximately normal distribution, will be used to choose between these two hypotheses. When the null hypothesis is true, this summary has mean $= \mu_0$ and variance $= \sigma_0^2$. When the alternative hypothesis is true, X also has a normal distribution but with mean $= \mu$ and variance $= \sigma^2$. In symbols,

null hypothesis—H_0: mean of $X = \mu_0$ with variance $(X) = \sigma_0^2$

alternative hypothesis—H_1: mean of $X = \mu > \mu_0$ with variance $(X) = \sigma^2$.

An observed value of X leads to a decision to accept or reject H_0 (reject or accept H_1). The first step in deciding between these two hypotheses is to define a decision rule. The usual rule is: If the summary statistic X exceeds a specific point (called the α-level critical point and represented as $c_{1-\alpha}$), then the null hypothesis is rejected in favor of the alternative hypothesis, and, conversely, if X is less than $c_{1-\alpha}$, then the null hypothesis is accepted. In other words, if X is sufficiently greater than μ_0, then it is inferred that H_1 is a better description of the distribution that generated the data than H_0. The critical point is determined so that the null hypothesis is mistakenly rejected with a predetermined probability, called a type I error rate or level of significance and symbolized as α. That is,

$$P(X > c_{1-\alpha}) = \alpha \tag{3.1}$$

is the probability of rejecting the null hypothesis when it is true. Since X is assumed to have a normal distribution, then

$$P\left(Z > \frac{c_{1-\alpha} - \mu_0}{\sigma_0}\right) = \alpha, \tag{3.2}$$

where Z represents a variable with a standard normal distribution. Therefore, the α-level critical point is

$$c_{1-\alpha} = z_{1-\alpha}\sigma_0 + \mu_0. \tag{3.3}$$

The symbol $z_{1-\alpha}$ represents the $(1 - \alpha)$-th percentile of the standard normal distribution. The value $c_{1-\alpha}$ is determined solely on the basis of H_0 and a selected value for α.

Since the power of the test statistic X is measured by the probability of rejecting the null hypothesis H_0 when the alternative hypothesis H_1 is true, then

$$\text{power} = 1 - \beta = P(X > c_{1-\alpha}) = P(X > z_{1-\alpha}\sigma_0 + \mu_0), \tag{3.4}$$

and, again, since X is assumed to have at least an approximate normal distribution, then

$$\text{power} = P\left(Z > \frac{z_{1-\alpha}\sigma_0 + \mu_0 - \mu}{\sigma}\right) = P(Z > z_\beta), \tag{3.5}$$

where

$$z_\beta = \frac{z_{1-\alpha}\sigma_0 + \mu_0 - \mu}{\sigma}. \tag{3.6}$$

When the null hypothesis, the alternative hypothesis, and the type I error rate are known or postulated, the power of the test statistic X is the probability $P(Z > z_\beta) = 1 - \beta$. The symbol β represents the probability of rejecting the alternative hypothesis when it is true, called a type II error. A type II error occurs when sampling variation causes X to be less than $c_{1-\alpha}$ when the alternative hypothesis is true, leading to a mistaken acceptance of the null hypothesis. Expression (3.6) for z_β relates the null hypothesis, the alternative hypothesis, and the α level to the power of the test statistic X and is a key element in assessing the likelihood of identifying systematic influences in a data set. The expression for z_β also leads to sample-size calculations (following sections).

The power of a test statistic X does not depend in any way on sampled data. It is entirely determined by H_0, H_1, and α. Figure 3.1 illustrates a distribution of X under the null hypothesis H_0: $\mu_0 = 2$ with variance $= \sigma_0^2 = 2$ and under the alternative hypothesis H_1: $\mu = 5$ with variance $= \sigma^2 = 2$, where $\alpha = 0.05$. For this case $c_{1-\alpha} = c_{0.95} = 4.326$. This hypothetical structure produces a type II error of $\beta = 0.317$, and the power to discriminate between random (H_0) and systematic (H_1) effects on the basis of an observed value of X is $1 - \beta = 0.683$.

A summary of the hypothesis testing notation is shown in Table 3.1,

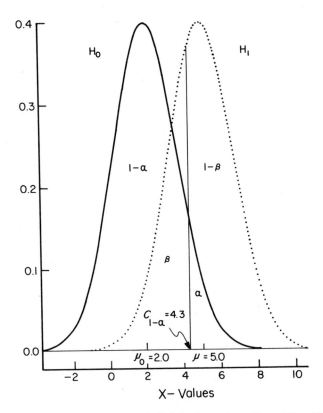

Figure 3–1. Two illustrative normal distributions ($\mu = 2$ and 5 with $\sigma^2 = 2$) generated under null and alternative hypotheses.

Table 3-1. Summary of the hypothesis testing notation

	H_0 is true H_1 is false	H_0 is false H_1 is true
Accept H_0 (reject H_1)	$1 - \alpha$	Type II error $= \beta$
Reject H_0 (accept H_1)	Type I error $= \alpha$	Power $= 1 - \beta$

and, specifically, the example values of type I and type II errors are summarized in Table 3.2.

This section describes the power of a test statistic X where large values of X lead to rejecting the null hypothesis. The situation where small values of X lead to rejecting H_0 does not differ in principle and is similarly developed with only minor changes. The calculation of the power for a two-sided test is a bit more complicated and is not presented.

Normal Distribution: Sample Mean

A potentially toxic material found in the workplace is benzene. The federal government has established a safety standard of 1.0 part benzene per million (ppm). The question arises: Is it likely that a company with a mean level of 1.5 ppm will be detected in violation of this standard using a sample of $n = 10$ measured exposures? The benzene exposure values have an approximate normal distribution; therefore the sample mean $\bar{x}$ also has an approximately normal distribution. The summary statistic $\bar{x}$ (i.e., $X = \bar{x}$) is used to discriminate between the null hypothesis that the workplace mean is at the standard versus the alternative hypothesis that the workplace mean exceeds the standard by 0.5 ppm or

meets standard—H_0: expectation of $\bar{x} = \mu_0 = 1.0$ with

$$\text{variance}(\bar{x}) = \sigma_0^2 = 1.4/10$$

exceeds standard—H_1: expectation of $\bar{x} = \mu = 1.5$ with

$$\text{variance } (\bar{x}) = \sigma^2 = 1.4/10.$$

Table 3-2. Specific example of the hypothesis testing notation

	H_0 is true H_1 is false	H_0 is false H_1 is true
Accept H_0 (reject H_1)	0.95	0.317
Reject H_0 (accept H_1)	0.05	0.683

Using the values generated by H_0 and H_1 and choosing $\alpha = 0.05$ gives

$$z_\beta = \frac{1.645\sqrt{1.4/10} + 1.0 - 1.5}{\sqrt{1.4/10}} = 0.309 \qquad (3.7)$$

and

$$P(\mathcal{Z} > z_\beta) = P(\mathcal{Z} > 0.309) = 0.379. \qquad (3.8)$$

Companies with workplace means in violation of the standard by more than 0.5 parts per million will be detected at least 38% of the time when a sample of 10 workers is used.

Perhaps the weakest link in the argument that produces a power calculation is the determination of the variance. In most situations it is difficult and sometimes impossible to get reliable estimates of the background variation. The variance for the benzene example is $\sigma_0^2 = \sigma^2 = 1.4/10$ based on a large quantity of previously collected data and assumed equal for both the null and alternative hypotheses. Occasionally, reasonable values are available from relevant literature or pilot studies, but, by and large, it is rare that σ_0^2 and σ^2 are known with any degree of certainty.

Poisson Distribution: Relative Risk

A power calculation is often revealing in the investigation of an environmental exposure. Suppose a region is exposed to a toxic material suspected of causing a birth defect, such as an area in a county exposed to a water supply contaminant. Interest is focused on the probability that an infant born in the contaminated area will have a birth defect compared to the probability for unexposed newborns (e.g., the rest of the county). Such a comparison can be summarized by a relative risk; the ratio of the probability of the event in the exposed group divided by the same probability in the unexposed group.

When a rare event such as a birth defect is under consideration, a Poisson distribution is often used to describe the distribution of the number of occurrences of these events.

Aside: The Poisson distribution can be derived from basic considerations [Ref. 1], or it can be viewed as an approximation for the binomial distribution where the probability of a specific event (p) is small and the number of all possible events (n) is large (see Appendix). The expected value for both distributions is np, which in the context of a Poisson distribution is often symbolized by λ (i.e., $np = \lambda$). The assumptions underlying these two distributions are the same, namely each of a series of n binary events occur independently with constant probability p. Both probability distributions describe the number of specific occurrences X

among n such events. For example, if $p = 0.03$ and $n = 100$, then the probability that $X = 2$ specific occurrences will occur among $n = 100$ possible events is

$$P(X = 2) = \binom{100}{2} p^2 (1 - p)^{98} = 0.2252 \tag{3.9}$$

based on the binomial distribution or

$$P(X = 2) = \frac{e^{-\lambda} \lambda^2}{2!} = \frac{e^{-3} 3^2}{2} = 0.2240 \tag{3.10}$$

based on the Poisson distribution. A feature of the Poisson distribution is that only the expected number of events λ needs to be specified to determine the probability distribution of X while values for both n and p are necessary to calculate binomial probabilities.

The mean and the variance of the Poisson distribution have the same value, namely the expected number of events in the population under consideration (see Appendix). For pregnant women exposed to toxic material in the water supply, the expected number of newborn with malformations is represented by np, where n is the number of exposed mothers and p is the probability of a birth defect among those mothers. If a toxic material has no adverse effects on pregnancy outcome, then the expected number of cases in the contaminated area is np_0, where p_0 is the probability of a birth defect among unexposed mothers (the null hypothesis). The relative risk is defined as $r = p/p_0$. When p_0, the "background" incidence, is known or postulated, power calculations show the likelihood of detecting specific increases in relative risk for different numbers of exposed individuals for chosen error rates α and β.

The observed number of birth defects $(X = \hat{M})$ will be used to discriminate between the null hypothesis that no difference exists in frequency of birth defects in exposed and unexposed areas (i.e., $p = p_0$, then $r = 1$) and the alternative hypothesis that the exposed area has a greater frequency of birth defects (i.e., $p > p_0$, then $r > 1$). Applying the Poisson structure to describe the number of birth defects gives

no excess risk—H_0: expected number of defects = np_0 with

variance$(\hat{M}) = np_0$

excess risk—H_1: expected number of defects = $np = nrp_0$ with

variance$(\hat{M}) = np$

and, as before,

$$P(Z > z_\beta) = 1 - \beta \tag{3.11}$$

is the probability of detecting an excess of birth defects in the exposed area when the contaminant is associated with an increase (H_1 true: $p > p_0$). Applying expression (3.6) gives

$$z_\beta = \frac{z_{1-\alpha} + \sqrt{np_0}(1-r)}{\sqrt{r}} \qquad (3.12)$$

for this special Poisson case. It is postulated that $\hat{M}$, the observed number of birth defects, has an approximately normal distribution which in many cases (np not too small) is a realistic assumption. That is, the normal distribution serves as an approximation to the Poisson distribution to facilitate the calculation of the power of the test. A direct calculation is also possible. When $r = 1$, then $z_\beta = z_{1-\alpha}$ so that the null hypothesis will be mistakenly rejected with probability α, P(type I error) $= \alpha$. Figure 3.2 shows four power curves associated with different relative risks and sample sizes (number of exposed pregnancies) when $p_0 = 0.01$ and $\alpha = 0.05$. It can be seen, for example, that about an 86% chance exists of detecting a relative risk of 2.5 when 500 individuals are exposed but only a 46% chance when 100 individuals are exposed.

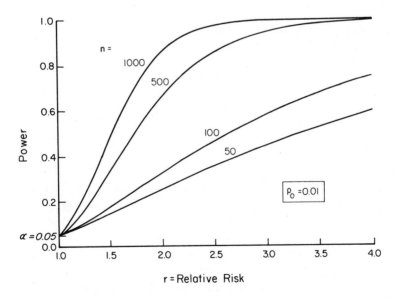

Figure 3–2. Power for detecting an excess relative risk r for sample sizes $n = 50$, 100, 500, and 1000 for $p_0 = 0.01$.

Sample Size: One-Sample Test of a Proportion

Power considerations can be used to calculate the sample size necessary to meet selected levels of type I and type II errors. The test of a single proportion illustrates the pattern for this sample size calculation. For a series of binary outcomes, the proportion of a specific result is commonly calculated (represented by $\hat{p}$). The statistic $\hat{p}$ could, for example, be the proportion of male infants in a series of births, the proportion of times the white pieces win a chess match in a series of games, or the proportion of recessive genetic traits in a series of individuals. The test statistic $\hat{p}$ is used to discriminate between two hypotheses. The null hypothesis states that the observed proportion differs only because of chance variation from a specified proportion p_0. For example, playing the white or black chess pieces produces no difference in the probability of winning ($p = p_0 = 0.50$). The alternative hypothesis states that $\hat{p}$ differs only by chance from another population value, p_1. That is, the observed difference between $\hat{p}$ and p_0 is due to a systematic effect—white pieces, for example have an advantage ($p = p_1 > 0.50$, or say $p_1 = 0.60$). The test statistic $X = \hat{p}$ is used to choose between p_0 and p_1 as a description of the sampled population. In symbols,

$$H_0: \text{proportion} = p_0 \text{ with variance}(\hat{p}) = p_0(1 - p_0)/n$$

$$H_1: \text{proportion} = p_1 > p_0 \text{ with variance}(\hat{p}) = p_1(1 - p_1)/n$$

where n represents the number of samples collected. Using these proportions and variances along with the expression for power [expression (3.6)] produces an approximate sample size n of

$$n = \frac{p(1 - p)(z_{1-\alpha} + z_{1-\beta})^2}{(p_1 - p_0)^2}, \tag{3.13}$$

where $p = (p_0 + p_1)/2$. The value n is the sample size necessary to attain the specified error probabilities α and β. It is assumed, for the sake of simplicity, that $p_0(1 - p_0) \approx p_1(1 - p_1) \approx p(1 - p)$, which is approximately true for proportions between 0.3 and 0.7. Specifically, the expression for sample size n is derived from the values $\mu_0 = p_0$, $\mu = p_1$, and $\sigma_0^2 \approx \sigma^2 \approx p(1 - p)/n$ substituted into the expression (3.6), which is then solved for n. The resulting value for n is approximate since $\hat{p}$ has only an approximately normal distribution. Therefore, when p is small (<0.3) or large (>0.7) the approximation works less well. For p in the neighborhood of 0.0 or 1.0, alternative methods should be employed (see [Ref. 2 or 3]). Analogous to the Poisson case, the normal distribution is used to approximate a binomial distribution to calculate sample size easily.

The sample size n can be found for specified values p_0, p_1, α, and β. For example, if α is set at 0.05 ($z_{1-\alpha} = 1.645$), β at 0.10 ($z_{1-\beta} = 1.282$), $p_0 = 0.5$, and $p_1 = 0.6$, then $n = 213$ using $p = 0.55$. A sample, therefore, of about 213 observations will correctly discriminate between population proportions 0.5 and 0.6 with a probability of 0.90 (power) and, at the same time, the probability of falsely declaring a difference exists is 0.05 (type I error—level of significance).

To get an idea of the relationship between the difference ($p_1 - p_0$) and sample size, consider the case where p_0 and p_1 are in the neighborhood of 0.5 with α and β set at 0.02. The sample size to attain these error rates is approximately

$$n \approx \frac{4}{(p_1 - p_0)^2}. \tag{3.14}$$

If $p_0 = 0.50$ and $p_1 = 0.51$, then $n \approx 4/0.01^2 = 40,000$ or if $p_0 = 0.50$ and $p_1 = 0.55$, then $n \approx 4/0.05^2 = 1600$. These calculations show the obvious underlying principle that as the distance between p_0 and p_1 increases (for specific levels of α and β), then smaller, sometimes considerably smaller, sample sizes are required to detect reliably which value, p_0 or p_1, best represents the "true" proportion in the population sampled.

Sample Size: Two-Sample Test of Proportions

A two-sample situation occurs when two proportions, each sampled from a different source, are compared. A difference between these observed proportions indicates one of two possibilities—the difference occurred by chance (null hypothesis) or a systematic difference exists between the two sources of data (alternative hypothesis). For example, $\hat{p}_1$ could be the proportion of *in situ* cervical cancer cases in a specific community observed in 1980 and $\hat{p}_2$ the proportion observed in 1985. These two values will undoubtedly differ, but is this difference due to the natural fluctuation of sampled values or due to a change in the cancer staging distribution? The test statistic $X = \hat{p}_2 - \hat{p}_1$ is used to discriminate between H_0 and H_1, where $\hat{p}_1$ and $\hat{p}_2$ are the sample proportions from each of two sources of data. The formal hypotheses are:

no change in proportion—H_0: $p_1 = p_2 = p$

with variance $(\hat{p}_1 - \hat{p}_2) = 2p(1 - p)/n$

increase in proportion—H_1: $p_2 > p_1$

with variance $(\hat{p}_1 - \hat{p}_2) = p_1(1 - p_1)/n + p_2(1 - p_2)/n$.

Table 3–3. Sample size: Two-sample situation illustration

p_2	0.15	0.20	0.25	0.30	0.35	0.40	0.45	0.50	0.55	0.60	0.65	0.70	0.75	0.80	0.85	0.90
n	748	217	109	67	46	34	26	21	17	14	12	10	8	7	6	5

Again using the expression (3.6), solving for n yields

$$n = \frac{[z_{1-\alpha}\sqrt{2p(1-p)} + z_{1-\beta}\sqrt{p_1(1-p_1) + p_2(1-p_2)}]^2}{(p_2 - p_1)^2}, \quad (3.15)$$

where $p = (p_1 + p_2)/2$. Again, the implicit assumption is that $X = \hat{p}_1 - \hat{p}_2$ has an approximately normal distribution.

The value n is the approximate number of sample observations necessary from each source (assumed equal here but similar calculations can be made for the case of unequal sample sizes). If $p_1 = 0.10$ and $p_2 = 0.15$, then a sample of $n = 748$ observations from each population is necessary to achieve a type I error of 0.05 and a type II error of 0.10 (a total of $n = 1496$ observations). Table 3.3 gives a series of sample sizes associated with $\alpha = 0.05$, $\beta = 0.10$, and $p_1 = 0.10$. Figure 3.3 shows plots of the sample size curves (two versions of the same curves) associated with detecting a difference between two proportions.

If p_1 and p_2 are again about 0.5 with α and β set at 0.02, then

$$n \approx \frac{8}{(p_1 - p_2)^2} \quad (3.16)$$

for each of the two samples. Comparing this result with the previous one-sample result shows, not surprisingly, a fourfold increase in total sample size to detect the same difference between two proportions. Like before, this sample-size calculation is approximate and only applies to restricted values of p; nevertheless, it indicates that the two-sample situation requires about four times as many observations to achieve the same error rates as the one-sample case.

The odds are the ratio of the probability that an event occurs divided by the probability an event does not occur. The odds ratio is simply the ratio of two sets of odds (see Appendix for a more complete description). A number of texts completely describe the odds ratio measure of association (see, for example, [Refs. 4 and 5]). Occasionally it is desirable to calculate the sample size necessary to detect an elevated odds ratio (represented as *or*) given the probability of disease among those without a risk factor (p_0). To estimate a sample size, the

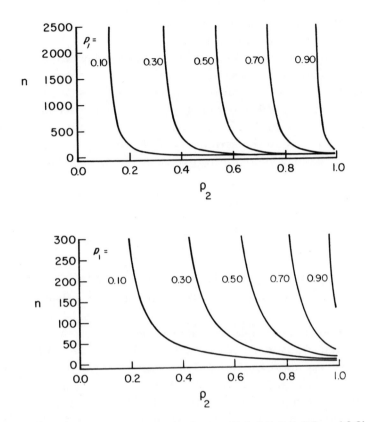

Figure 3–3. Sample sizes (n) for comparing p_1 (0.1, 0.3, 0.5, 0.7, and 0.9) to p_2 with type I error $= \alpha = 0.05$ and type II error $= \beta = 0.10$ (one set of curves plotted on different scales).

values or and p_0 are used to generate the probability of disease among those with the risk factor (p_1). That is, since

$$or = \frac{p_1/(1 - p_1)}{p_0/(1 - p_0)} \quad \text{then} \quad p_1 = \frac{p_0(or)}{1 + p_0(or - 1)}, \qquad (3.17)$$

and the values p_0 and p_1 can be used in expression (3.15) for computing the sample size (n) necessary to detect specific differences in two proportions for selected error rates (α, β). Note that the value of n is the number of individuals in each group compared (a total of $2n$ observations is necessary, as before). For example, if the "background" frequency of a disease is $p_0 = 0.02$ and sufficient data must be collected to detect an odds ratio of 3.0, then

$$p_1 = \frac{0.02(3.0)}{1 + 0.02(3.0 - 1)} = 0.058, \qquad (3.18)$$

implying that a sample size of approximately $n = 567$ must be collected from each sampled population for $\alpha = 0.05$ and $\beta = 0.05$; that is, 567 individuals with the risk factor and the same number without the risk factor. Although this sample-size calculation gives some idea of the required number of observations, the estimate is not accurate in all situations. When the difference in proportions is in the neighborhood of -1 or $+1$, for example, the normal distribution fails to be a good approximation due to the asymmetry of the distribution of estimated value $\hat{p}_1 - \hat{p}_0$. A few more illustrative values for $p_0 = 0.02$ are given in Table 3.4.

Two comments: The two earlier expressions for sample size [(3.13) and (3.15)] are special cases of the general expression

$$n = \frac{(z_{1-\alpha}\sigma_0 + z_{1-\beta}\sigma_1)^2}{(\mu_1 - \mu_0)^2}, \qquad (3.19)$$

which is used in a variety of situations where the null and the alternative hypotheses defined the properties of other statistical measures.

Applied power or sample size calculations based on the assumption that the test statistic X is normally distributed are approximate (sometimes very approximate) and in certain cases can be "fine tuned" to be more accurate (e.g., [Ref. 3]). However, it is rarely possible to define the alternative hypothesis or the required variances with sufficient precision so that this "fine tuning" is worthwhile. These calculations should be motivated by the desire to get a rough idea of the range of sample sizes (power) associated with a series of analytic strategies at the study design stage. The description of this range is an important part in planning an approach to data collection.

Table 3-4. Illustration of the odds ratio sample sizes ($\alpha = \beta = 0.05$ and $p_0 = 0.02$)

Odds ratio	p_1	n
1.5	0.030	5,572
2.0⁻	0.039	1,682
2.5	0.049	877
3.0	0.058	567
3.5	0.067	410
4.0	0.075	318
4.5	0.084	258
5.0	0.093	216

Additional power considerations

The question: How can the power to detect an association be increased? is easily answered. Increase the number of sampled observations. Power can also be increased, however, without collecting more data, by changing the α level of a statistical test. The tradition of setting α (type I error rate) at 0.05 is almost universal and rarely altered. A "5%" test is not usually required; in fact, the level of significance can be set at any level. Increasing the level of significance increases the power of a test.

For example, if $\mu_0 = 2(H_0)$ and $\mu_1 = 5(H_1)$ are mean values from two normal distributions with equal variances ($\sigma_0^2 = \sigma^2 = 2$), then increases in significance levels α produce increases in the power $1 - \beta$. Specifically, see the values in Table 3.5.

If the null hypothesis is rejected more often, then a direct consequence is that the alternative hypothesis will be accepted more often, when it is true. When it is important to detect effects if they exist and not so important that effects are declared if they do not exist, increasing the type I error is sometimes a useful strategy for increasing the power associated with a statistical procedure (see notes on interaction in Chapter 9).

Loss of Statistical Power from Grouping Data

For generally unclear reasons, investigators occasionally judge that, when a continuous observation is not measured precisely, grouping data into categories and using contingency table techniques is superior to analyses based directly on the continuous measures themselves. A statistical model gives some idea of the consequences of this decision in terms of loss of power. Assume that a continuous variable labeled Y, used to measure the disease under investigation, has a normal distribution. For example, Y could represent the level of an individual's systolic blood pressure. Further, assume that a dichotomous risk factor exists such as educational level— no college education ($E = 0$) versus college education ($E = 1$). The variables Y and E define a population model where Y is normally distributed with mean μ_0 when $E = 0$ and with

Table 3–5. Illustration of the relationship between α and $1 - \beta$

α	0.005	0.010	0.025	0.050	0.100	0.150	0.200	0.250	0.300
$1 - \beta$	0.325	0.419	0.564	0.683	0.799	0.861	0.900	0.926	0.945

mean μ_1 when $E = 1 (\mu_0 < \mu_1)$. Both normal distributions are assumed to have the same variance, say $\sigma^2 = 1.0$ for convenience. If a sample of k individuals is randomly selected from this population, the expected data would produce a 2×2 contingency table with cell probabilities P_{ij}, shown in Table 3.6, where the symbol $\bar{D}$ represents all observations with blood pressure $\Upsilon \leqslant 0.5(\mu_0 + \mu_1)$ and D represents blood pressure $\Upsilon > 0.5(\mu_0 + \mu_1)$. The dichotomous variable (D and $\bar{D}$) results from grouping the continuous variable Υ into diseased and nondiseased categories. A familiar example of such a practice is defining individuals as nonhypertensive (say, $\Upsilon \leqslant 140$) and hypertensive ($\Upsilon > 140$) based on systolic blood pressure. The prevalence of the risk factor E is represented as p [i.e., $p = P(E = 1)$] and

$$\Phi = P(\Upsilon \leqslant 0.5(\mu_0 + \mu_1)|E = 0) = P(\Upsilon > 0.5(\mu_0 + \mu_1)|E = 1)$$

$$= \frac{1}{\sqrt{2\pi}} \int_{-\infty}^{0.5(\mu_1 - \mu_0)} e^{-(1/2)t^2} \, dt. \tag{3.20}$$

This statistical structure is depicted in Figure 3.4.

To compare two risk groups ($E = 0$ versus $E = 1$), the odds ratio is

$$\text{odds ratio} = or = \frac{P_{00}/P_{01}}{P_{10}/P_{11}} \tag{3.21}$$

and the odds ratio expected from data sampled from these two normal populations classified into a 2×2 table is $or = [\Phi/(1 - \Phi)]^2$ or $\log(or) = 2\log[\Phi/(1 - \Phi)]$. The variance of $\log[or]$ is approximately [applying expression (A.15) given in the Appendix]

$$\text{variance}[\log(or)] = [kp(1 - p)\Phi(1 - \Phi)]^{-1}, \tag{3.22}$$

where k is the total number of sampled individuals.

A typical α-level test of the hypothesis of no association between risk factor and disease is

$$H_0: or = 1.0 \text{ versus } H_1: or > 1.0,$$

and can be used to assess the role of the risk factor E.

Table 3–6. Expected frequencies

	$\bar{D}$ (no disease)	D (disease)
No college ($E=0$)	$kP_{00}=k(1-p)\Phi$	$kP_{01}=k(1-p)(1-\Phi)$
College ($E=1$)	$kP_{10}=kp(1-\Phi)$	$kP_{11}=kp\Phi$

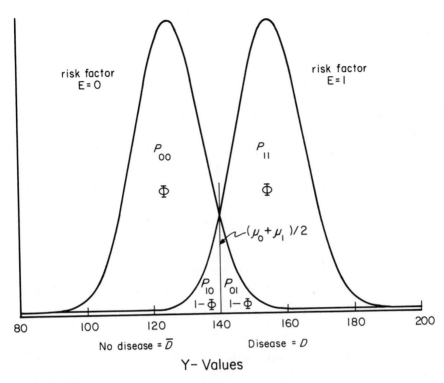

Figure 3-4. Model of a continuous variable grouped into four categories where two levels of a risk factor are investigated for a normally distributed outcome variable.

If the power of this test is set at a level $1 - \beta$ or $P(\text{reject } H_0 | H_1) = 1 - \beta$, then the necessary sample size k to achieve a power of $1 - \beta$ is approximately

$$k = \frac{\left(2z_{1-\alpha} + \dfrac{z_{1-\beta}}{\sqrt{\Phi(1-\Phi)}} \right)^2}{p(1-p)\,[\log(or)]^2} \qquad (3.23)$$

from the expression (3.19) for sample size.

For continuous rather than dichotomous data, the comparison of two mean values each based on a sample from a normal distribution is a classic problem in statistics. For example, to compare two mean values of blood pressure ($\bar{y}_1$ for $E = 1$ and $\bar{y}_0$ for $E = 0$), the test statistic $\bar{y}_1 - \bar{y}_0$ is a common and statistically efficient choice. When sampling is conducted without knowledge of the risk factor (E) or disease status

(D), the approximate variance of the difference between these two mean values is

$$\text{variance}(\bar{y}_1 - \bar{y}_0) \approx [np(1 - p)]^{-1}, \tag{3.24}$$

where n represents the total sample size.

An α-level test of the hypothesis that no difference exists between the two sampled populations is

$$H_0: \mu_0 = \mu_1 \text{ versus } H_1: \mu_0 < \mu_1.$$

The sample size necessary for an α-level test with statistical power of $1 - \beta$ is then

$$n = \frac{(z_{1-\alpha} + z_{1-\beta})^2}{p(1 - p)(\mu_1 - \mu_0)^2}, \tag{3.25}$$

again from expression (3.19) for sample size.

An efficiency ratio (k/n), contrasting the dichotomous and the continuous approaches, is given by (for the special case of $\alpha = \beta$)

$$k/n = \frac{[2 + 1/\sqrt{\Phi(1 - \Phi)}\,]^2/[\log(or)]^2}{4/(\mu_1 - \mu_0)^2} > \frac{\pi}{2}. \tag{3.26}$$

Furthermore, if the odds ratio is less than 7.0, or $0 < \mu_1 - \mu_0 < 1.2$, then, approximately, $k/n \approx \pi/2 = 1.571$ (i.e., <1.71). For this range, the efficiency ratio implies that if $n = 100$ observations are necessary to achieve a specific level of α and β, then at least 50% more observations are required when continuous data are dichotomized and analyzed with an odds ratio. When $(\mu_1 - \mu_0) > 1.2$, the efficiency ratio increases, and the odds ratio approach becomes more costly compared to the two-sample test in terms of additional data to maintain specified error rates or less powerful for a fixed sample size.

Using an odds ratio to analyze dichotomized continuous data reduces the probability of detecting an influence from a risk factor. On occasions, grouping continuous data into a table protects the analysis against effects of outliers. Outliers (out and out outliers) should be eliminated from a data set and should not dictate the analytic approach. Presentation and simplicity of measurement are other motivations for an odds ratio approach but again should not be the primary reason for choosing a specific analytic strategy. Certain groupings have medical or public health importance but again should not dictate a less than fully efficient statistical analysis. Lack of accuracy in outcome measures introduces additional variation into the analysis, but whether the effects are decreased by the analysis of continuous data with contingency table techniques is a question that has not been fully explored, and, clearly, the presence of measurement error hurts any analytic approach. The best that can be said for using a 2×2 table instead of a continuous outcome variable is that equivocal gains are paid for by a definite loss of statistical power. One last point: If a continuous variable is divided into more than two categories, the power loss decreases as the number of categories increases [Ref. 6].

Sample Size: Estimation

Sample sizes necessary to estimate a particular quantity with a specified precision can be derived from a confidence interval. The precision of an estimate is first described in terms of the length or width of an α-level confidence interval. The length is then used to calculate the number of observations necessary to obtain this desired degree of precision. No need exists to specify a null or an alternative hypothesis, but the results do not guarantee a specific significance level or level of power.

Generically, consider a parameter represented by θ. The estimate of θ is $\hat{\theta}$, based on a sample size of n observations. When the estimate is known or assumed to have at least an approximately normal distribution, the 95% confidence interval (95% will be used here but any significance level can be used) is approximately

$$(\theta_{\text{lower}}, \theta_{\text{upper}}) = \left(\hat{\theta} - 1.96\frac{\sigma}{\sqrt{n}}, \hat{\theta} + 1.96\frac{\sigma}{\sqrt{n}} \right) \tag{3.27}$$

where σ^2 represents the variation associated with the sampled population. Such an interval has approximately a 0.95 probability of containing the population parameter θ. The length of this 95% confidence interval is

$$\text{length} = \theta_{\text{upper}} - \theta_{\text{lower}} = \left(\hat{\theta} + 1.96\frac{\sigma}{\sqrt{n}} \right) - \left(\hat{\theta} - 1.96\frac{\sigma}{\sqrt{n}} \right) = 3.92\frac{\sigma}{\sqrt{n}} \tag{3.28}$$

or

$$\text{width} = w = 1.96\frac{\sigma}{\sqrt{n}}. \tag{3.29}$$

Therefore, if a width (w) and a variance (σ^2) are specified, then the approximate sample size n to obtain a confidence interval of width w follows as

$$n = \frac{3.84\sigma^2}{w^2}. \tag{3.30}$$

The translation of a width of a confidence interval into a sample size is used in a number of situations to achieve a specific level of precision associated with the estimate $\hat{\theta}$.

Example: Sample mean

The sample mean $\bar{x}$ (i.e., $\hat{\theta} = \bar{x}$) has variance σ^2/n. For $w = 0.5$ units and $\sigma^2 = 10$, then from expression (3.30)

$$n = \frac{3.84(10)}{0.5^2} = 154. \tag{3.31}$$

A sample size of 154 observations is necessary to achieve an approximate 95% confidence interval of width 0.5 units (length = 1.0). That is, there is an approximate 0.95 probability that the interval centered at the sample mean based on $n = 154$ ($\bar{x} \pm 0.5$ units) contains the population mean.

Example: Sample proportion

An estimated proportion $\hat{p}$ has variance $p(1-p)/n$, and the necessary sample size to achieve an approximate 95% confidence interval of width 0.1 for this estimate is

$$n = \frac{3.84(0.4)(0.6)}{0.1^2} = 93 \tag{3.32}$$

when p is equal to 0.4.

Example: Difference between two sample proportions

The estimated difference between two sample proportions $\hat{p}_2 - \hat{p}_1$ has associated variability $[p_1(1-p_1) + p_2(1-p_2)]/n$ when the same number of observations is sampled from the two populations. The sample size necessary to produce an approximate 95% confidence interval of length 0.5 ($w = 0.25$) is

$$n = \frac{3.84[(0.1)(0.9) + (0.4)(0.6)]}{0.25^2} = 21; \tag{3.33}$$

a total of 42 observations when p_1 is 0.1 and p_2 is 0.4.

Some basic properties of this process are: (1) for a confidence interval with a lower level of α, increased numbers of observations will be needed, (2) increases in the variability associated with the sampled variable cause increases in the sample size required to achieve a specified width; and (3) if a smaller width is chosen, then a larger sample size will be necessary.

Using a confidence interval to specify the level of precision for an estimate requires the knowledge or the assumption that the estimate has at least an approximately normal distribution. This is a reasonable assumption for many estimates or functions of estimates. More critically, the confidence interval approach to finding an approximate sample size requires two somewhat subjective decisions. First, a choice of an acceptable width w (or precision) is required. This choice is usually made on nonstatistical grounds. Second, a choice must be made for a value of the variance σ^2. In the preliminary stages of an investigation it is not usual that an accurate assessment of this quantity is available. Therefore, sample-size calculations for estimation are only approximate and, like the hypothesis testing case, best serve as guidelines rather than hard and fast determinations.

4 Cohort Data: Description and Illustration

The term cohort often describes a group of individuals collected to investigate a specific disease. For example, one type of cohort involves following a group over a period of time and observing the number of new cases of disease. Another type of cohort arises in the analysis of mortality data, also observed over a period of time, and is the topic of this chapter.

Two basic elements of cause-specific mortality data are age at death and year of death. Of course, many other pieces of information are usually available, such as the place of residence and the sex of the person who died, but the focus here is on age at death and year of death as elements that provide a special perspective on the description of the factors associated with specific causes of death. Using these two quantities, deaths can be classified into a two-way table where rows, for example, consist of different age categories and columns contain different calendar years of death. This simple table becomes more complex when it is realized that a third factor is present. Mortality data analyzed by calendar year do not directly account for the fact that individuals who died during a specific year were born at different times. This almost trivial fact has important implications in the study of certain diseases. Individuals born about the same time, a birth cohort, potentially have similar types and intensity of experiences throughout their lives. For example, individuals born around 1900 were in their late teens and early twenties during the influenza pandemic of 1919, while persons born after 1920 had no such "exposure." If an event occurring at a specific point in time puts certain individuals at increased risk of a disease throughout the rest of their lives, a related increase in mortality is often not apparent in data displayed in an age by calendar year tabulation. Increased risk associated with a group born on or near the same year is called a cohort effect. It was not until 1939 that tuberculosis mortality was noted (Frost [Ref. 1]) to be influenced by a strong cohort effect. Other diseases, such as lung cancer

(Levin [Ref. 2]), Parkinson's disease (Poskanzer [Ref. 3]), and prostatic cancer among nonwhites (Ernster [Ref. 4]), have cohort influences that are now recognized to be part of their mortality pattern.

Cohort effect: Model

To define and understand a cohort effect, consider the following hypothetical situation (statistical model). Suppose the influence of calendar time produces the mortality rates per 100,000 person-years of risk shown in Table 4.1. If age is not an influence on the cause-specific mortality rates, then these rates are constant over age and an age—year tabulation of this mortality data is given in Table 4.2. However, most causes of death are strongly influenced by age (older individuals die at higher rates). Suppose these rates are as listed in Table 4.3. If age is the only factor influencing mortality, then these rates are constant over time and the age—year tabulation of this mortality data is given in Table 4.4.

Both age and time, for most diseases, simultaneously influence mortality. Age and time effects can be combined to illustrate a mortality pattern for a cause of death where both influences produce an

Table 4–1. Mortality by time

Year	1935	1945	1955	1965	1975	1985
Rate	100	200	300	400	500	600

Table 4–2. Mortality by year and age: Time effect only

Age	1935	1945	1955	1965	1975	1985
35–44	100	200	300	400	500	600
45–54	100	200	300	400	500	600
55–64	100	200	300	400	500	600
65–74	100	200	300	400	500	600
75–84	100	200	300	400	500	600
85+	100	200	300	400	500	600

Table 4–3. Mortality by age

Age	35–44	45–54	55–64	65–74	75–84	85+
Rate	50	200	350	500	650	800

Table 4–4. Mortality by year and age: Age effect only

Age	1935	1945	1955	1965	1975	1985
35–44	50	50	50	50	50	50
45–54	200	200	200	200	200	200
55–64	350	350	350	350	350	350
65–74	500	500	500	500	500	500
75–84	650	650	650	650	650	650
85+	800	800	800	800	800	800

additive increase on top of a background rate of 50 deaths per 100,000 person-years, producing the rates shown in Table 4.5.

This age—year mortality table is strictly the sum of three influences. That is, the data are generated so that the age and time effects are additive; no interaction exists between age and time for the fictional cause of death under investigation (see Figure 4.1). For example, the age 55—64/year 1965 rate is $50 + 350 + 400 = 800$ deaths per 100,000. Additivity of age and time effects produces a pattern where plots of the row rates (or column rates) are parallel lines. In this artificial case, the lines are also straight lines, since both age and time have linearly increasing influences.

Suppose an exposure occurred around 1900 that subsequently increased the risk of death to individuals born about that time. Suppose further that the exposure around 1890 was moderate, by 1900 was at its strongest and by 1910 this exposure was again moderate. Assume also that the exposure did not exist prior to or following these 20 years. Such an exposure could produce the mortality pattern shown in Table 4.6 when no other influences are present.

Notice that this cohort effect is associated with the diagonal cells of an age—year tabulation of mortality data. Individuals on the diagonals of this age—year tabulation were born on or near the same year

Table 4–5. Mortality by year and age: Age and time influence

Age	1935	1945	1955	1965	1975	1985
35–44	200	300	400	500	600	700
45–54	350	450	550	650	750	850
55–64	500	600	700	800	900	1,000
65–74	650	750	850	950	1,050	1,150
75–84	800	900	1,000	1,100	1,200	1,300
85+	950	1,050	1,150	1,250	1,350	1,450

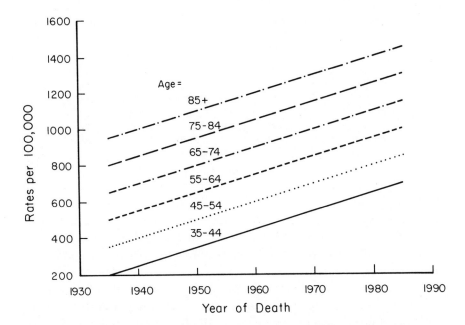

Figure 4–1. Age-specific curves for hypothetical data showing nortality rates per 100,000 population by year of death with no cohort effect.

and thus form a birth cohort. Combining the age, time, and cohort effects, Table 4.7 emerges.

The cohort effect is seen in Figure 4.2 as an increase and then a decrease in the mortality rate at some point on each of the six age-specific mortality curves (in this artificial case, straight lines). These areas of increased mortality occur at different points of calendar time for each age group. A cohort effect is a specific type of age–time nonadditivity. In other words, the influence of age is not the same for all calendar years, and, conversely, the calendar time influence is not

Table 4–6. Mortality by cohort influence only

Age	1935	1945	1955	1965	1975	1985
35–44	100	30	0	0	0	0
45–54	30	100	30	0	0	0
55–64	0	30	100	30	0	0
65–74	0	0	30	100	30	0
75–84	0	0	0	30	100	30
85+	0	0	0	0	30	100

Table 4–7. Mortality by age and time: Age, time, and cohort influence

Age	1935	1945	1955	1965	1975	1985
35–44	300	330	400	500	600	700
45–54	380	550	580	650	750	850
55–64	500	630	800	830	900	1,000
65–74	650	750	880	1,050	1,080	1,150
75–84	800	900	1,000	1,130	1,300	1,330
85+	950	1,050	1,150	1,250	1,380	1,550

the same for all ages. Geometrically, it is no longer possible to depict these rates by parallel lines. Figure 4.3 shows the same rates as Figure 4.2, but plotted by year of birth rather than year of death, which causes the cohort influence to appear directly above the years associated with the effect.

The view that a cohort influence is a specific type of age–time interaction suggests a statistical model to evaluate possible cohort influences on the pattern of mortality. An often postulated model states that a cause-specific mortality rate for a specific age and calendar time

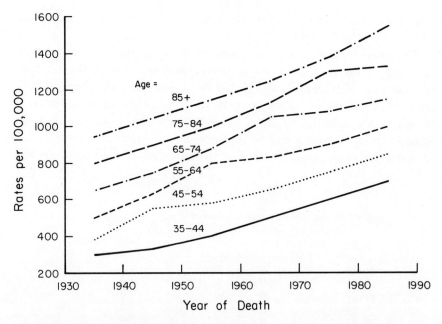

Figure 4–2. Age-specific curves for hypothetical data showing mortality rates per 100,000 population by year of death with a cohort effect present.

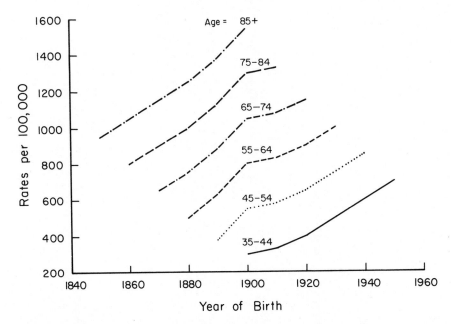

Figure 4-3. Age-specific curves for hypothetical data showing mortality rates per 100,000 population by year of birth with a cohort effect present.

is proportional to the product of a background rate, an age influence, a time influence, and a cohort influence. In terms of the logarithm of the rate which produces a linear model, the symbolic representation is

$$\log(\text{rate}) = \mu + a_i + t_j + c_{(k)} \tag{4.1}$$

where μ = the background rate, a_i = the age effect (ith row), t_j the time effect (jth column), and $c_{(k)}$ the effect associated with the kth cohort (the diagonal cells in the age–year table). For example, the birth cohort influence in the hypothetical data is $c_{(5)} = c_{(7)} = 30$, $c_{(6)} = 100$ and otherwise $c_{(k)} = 0$. Also note that, when $c_{(k)} = 0$, no cohort influence exists and the age and time effects are additive (no interaction).

Cohort Effect: Prostatic Cancer (Applied Example)

Ernster [Ref. 4] demonstrated a cohort influence on the pattern of rates of prostatic cancer among nonwhites in the United States. The data (rates/100,000) are given in Table 4.8.

The logarithms of the rates are displayed in Figure 4.4 for the eight age categories (rows) by birth date and median/average smooth values are also shown.

Table 4–8. Prostatic cancer mortality rates by age and time among U.S. nonwhites

Age	1930	1935	1940	1945	1950	1955	1960	1965	1970	1975	1980
45–49	3.5	4.9	6.6	7.2	4.7	4.7	2.7	2.4	3.5	2.1	2.2
50–54	5.4	11.4	16.0	15.7	23.3	16.3	15.8	13.4	12.0	10.9	10.4
55–59	18.8	22.4	32.1	41.4	39.0	44.4	30.9	32.4	29.9	28.2	28.0
60–64	24.0	45.9	50.2	60.4	77.7	84.2	81.4	77.4	68.2	71.5	71.5
65–69	35.1	60.2	72.3	74.1	74.1	141.1	147.4	177.1	149.0	143.7	164.6
70–74	60.7	66.5	90.1	126.0	148.0	168.5	224.7	235.9	276.7	282.8	271.3
75–79	47.5	90.6	151.4	130.0	219.2	234.4	299.6	304.2	399.9	388.8	403.5
80+	56.7	124.5	152.1	155.6	299.1	328.6	371.6	359.1	471.3	557.9	673.6

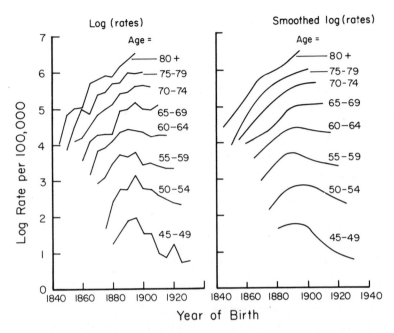

Figure 4-4. Age-specific curves for prostatic cancer mortality among nonwhites by year of birth, logarithm of the rates per 100,000 population. Also shown are the same curves median/average smoothed.

Aside: The analysis of the logarithm of a rate, rather than dealing directly with the rate itself, is traditional and has some justification in the empiric behavior of risk. A wide range of studies of cancer and to a lesser extent other diseases show that influences on age-specific rates often act multiplicatively. For example, smoking appears to increase the risk of coronary heart disease in a multiplicative pattern (as will be seen in subsequent analyses) and, therefore, produces a linear relationship among the logarithms of the incidence rates. Certainly, no hard and fast reason exists to analyze disease data in terms of logarithms of the rate, and the choice of scales (multiplicative, additive, or others) is an issue in the description and analysis of disease data.

The cohort influence on prostatic cancer rates associated with individuals born around 1900 is most pronounced in the five younger age groups (<70 years old). Each age group has a maximum (or near maximum) mortality rate associated with individuals born near the beginning of the twentieth century. A quantitative description will better delineate this apparent cohort effect and provides an assessment of its magnitude.

Methods exist to estimate and to evaluate analytically the parameters from a set of mortality data based on cohort models such as expression (4.1) (see [Ref. 5], for example). These model-based approaches are not easily implemented and possess computational difficulties. One method, however, designed to deal with two-way tables in general, is useful in the analysis of mortality data with particular emphasis on the description of a cohort effect. The method is called a median polish (see [Ref. 6 or 7] for a complete development). This approach to analyzing a two-way contingency table makes no assumptions about the distribution or structure of the sampled data (distribution-free) and is effective when the tabled data are rates or logarithms of the rates.

The median polish involves computing a residual value for each cell in a table by removing from each observation the additive influence of the row variable and the additive influence of the column variable. In symbols, for each cell in the table, the residual is

$$\text{residual} = r_{ij} = (\text{tabled value}) - (\mu + a_i + t_j), \tag{4.2}$$

where, as before, a_i represents the row influence and t_j represents the column influence. The residual values measure the failure of an additive model to reflect the values contained in each cell of the table. In a cohort analysis this lack of additivity can come from the influence of a cohort effect that is typically assumed constant for each birth cohort. However, these residual values reflect nonadditivity in general and are meaningful indications of any type of interaction associated with data classified into a two-way table.

The median polish calculation produces a set of residual values by an iterative process. First the median value is found for each row. Each row median is then subtracted from each cell value in the same row of the table, producing a revised value for each cell. Then, column medians are found for each column of the revised table. Lilewise each column median is subtracted from each corresponding cell value in the same column. The process is then repeated a number of times (usually five or so) until the residual values no longer appreciably change (i.e., until all medians ≈ 0). When the values remaining in the table become stable, they reflect the nonadditive component for each cell. The differences between these residual values and the original data produce a set of "data" that have an exactly additive relationships. The process divides the data into an additive piece and a residual piece (data = "additive data" + residual). The cells with large residual values show the areas of the lack of fit of the additive structure that are potentially important in understanding the joint effects of the row and column variables.

Data:

	col 1	col 2	col 3	col 4
row 1	12	18	44	55
row 2	17	28	52	65
row 3	22	48	66	85
row 4	35	55	75	100

Step 1

	col 1	col 2	col 3	col 4
row 1	7.5	-2.0	2.0	-2.5
row 2	3.5	-1.0	1.0	-1.5
row 3	-8.5	2.0	-2.0	1.5
row 4	-3.5	1.0	-1.0	8.5

Step 3

	col 1	col 2	col 3	col 4
row 1	7.5	-2.0	2.0	-2.66
row 2	3.5	-1.0	1.0	-1.66
row 3	-8.18	2.31	-1.66	1.66
row 4	-3.5	1.0	-1.0	8.34

Step 2

	col 1	col 2	col 3	col 4
row 1	7.5	-2.0	2.0	-2.625
row 2	3.5	-1.0	1.0	-1.625
row 3	-8.25	2.25	-1.75	1.625
row 4	-3.5	1.0	-1.0	8.375

Step 4

	col 1	col 2	col 3	col 4
row 1	7.50	-2.00	2.00	-2.67
row 2	3.50	-1.00	1.00	-1.67
row 3	-8.17	2.33	-1.67	1.67
row 4	-3.50	1.00	-1.00	8.33

Figure 4-5. Illustrative data and iterative steps in the "median polish" process.

A simple demonstration of the way a median polish works for a 4×4 table is given in Figure 4.5. The data that demonstrate the mechanics of the median polish are shown in Table 4.9. The "median polish" produces the residual values after four iterations, as given in Table 4.10. Subtracting the stable residual values (Table 4.10) from each value in the original table (Table 4.9) produces a no-interaction table—strictly additive effects of the rows and the columns. The perfectly "additive data" are displayed in Table 4.11.

Note that the difference between rows is constant for all columns of Table 4.11, and, similarly, the difference between columns is

Table 4-9. Data

	Col 1	Col 2	Col 3	Col 4
Row 1	12	18	44	55
Row 2	17	28	52	65
Row 3	22	48	66	85
Row 4	35	55	75	100

Table 4-10. Residuals

	Col 1	Col 2	Col 3	Col 4
Row 1	7.50	−2.00	2.00	−2.67
Row 2	3.50	−1.00	1.00	−1.67
Row 3	−8.17	2.33	−1.67	1.67
Row 4	−3.50	1.00	−1.00	8.33

Table 4-11. "Additive data": No interaction

	Col 1	Col 2	Col 3	Col 4
Row 1	4.50	20.00	42.00	57.67
Row 2	13.50	29.00	51.00	66.67
Row 3	30.17	45.67	67.67	83.33
Row 4	38.50	54.00	76.00	91.67

constant for all rows. If the median polish technique were to be applied to this table, no changes would occur and the residual values would be exactly zero. Geometrically, a plot of the rows in Table 4.11 (or columns) produces four parallel lines.

The "median polish" technique is one of several ways a set of observations can be split into meaningful pieces. The median polish arbitrarily starts with determining the medians of the rows. If the residual estimation process starts with the median of each column, the final residual table can differ but, in most cases, not dramatically. If the median polish technique is applied using the mean value instead of the median value, stable residual values emerge after one iteration. These estimated residuals are identical to the e_{ij} values estimated from the additive model used to analyze continuous data in a two-way table [i.e., $e_{ij} = y_{ij} - \bar{y}_{i.} - \bar{y}_{.j} + \bar{y}$; Chapter 2, expression (2.36)]. Whether the process begins with rows or columns or uses medians or means, the data are partitioned into perfectly additive and residual components.

Before returning to the prostatic cancer cohort analysis, consider a set of cell-type-specific leukemia data that provide an opportunity to use a "median polish" to describe the mortality pattern associated with myeloid leukemia for both acute and chronic forms. The rates and the logarithms of the rates (in parentheses) for leukemia mortality in the U.S. during the years 1969—77 [Ref. 8] are given in Table 4.12. A plot of the logarithms of the rates is shown in Figure 4.6 (top). Applying a "median polish" to the logarithms of the rates produces a set of perfectly "additive data" which are shown in Table 4.13.

Table 4–12. Myeloid leukemia mortality by sex and type (U.S. whites 1969–77): Rates per 100,000 and logarithms of the rates

Age	Acute		Chronic	
	Male	Female	Male	Female
0–4	0.40 (−0.92)	0.41 (−0.89)	0.07 (−2.66)	0.06 (−2.81)
5–9	0.33 (−1.11)	0.27 (−1.31)	0.06 (−2.81)	0.04 (−3.22)
10–14	0.41 (−0.89)	0.36 (−1.02)	0.06 (−2.81)	0.04 (−3.22)
15–24	0.69 (−0.37)	0.55 (−0.60)	0.15 (−1.90)	0.04 (−3.22)
25–34	0.87 (−0.14)	0.77 (−0.26)	0.42 (−0.87)	0.10 (−2.30)
35–44	1.27 (0.24)	1.14 (0.13)	0.70 (−0.36)	0.26 (−1.35)
45–54	2.22 (0.80)	1.74 (0.55)	1.06 (0.06)	0.73 (−0.31)
55–64	4.66 (1.54)	2.98 (1.09)	1.89 (0.64)	1.24 (0.22)
65–74	9.98 (2.30)	5.59 (1.72)	4.00 (1.39)	2.26 (0.82)
75–84	16.47 (2.80)	9.98 (2.30)	8.00 (2.09)	4.46 (1.50)
85+	18.39 (2.91)	10.29 (2.33)	10.82 (2.38)	5.94 (1.78)

Table 4–13. Myeloid mortality leukemia by sex and type (U.S. whites 1969–77): Additive model rates per 100,000 and the logarithms of the rates

Age	Acute		Chronic	
	Male	Female	Male	Female
0–4	0.38 (−0.97)	0.28 (−1.28)	0.15 (−1.87)	0.06 (−2.76)
5–9	0.28 (−1.27)	0.21 (−1.58)	0.11 (−2.17)	0.05 (−3.06)
10–14	0.31 (−1.16)	0.23 (−1.47)	0.13 (−2.06)	0.05 (−2.95)
15–24	0.51 (−0.68)	0.37 (−0.99)	0.20 (−1.59)	0.08 (−2.47)
25–34	0.95 (−0.05)	0.70 (−0.36)	0.38 (−0.96)	0.16 (−1.84)
35–44	1.55 (0.44)	1.14 (0.13)	0.63 (−0.46)	0.26 (−1.35)
45–54	2.49 (0.91)	1.83 (0.60)	1.01 (0.01)	0.42 (−0.88)
55–64	4.66 (1.54)	3.42 (1.23)	1.89 (0.64)	0.78 (−0.25)
65–74	18.03 (2.89)	13.22 (2.58)	7.31 (1.99)	3.02 (1.10)
75–84	9.92 (2.30)	7.28 (1.99)	4.02 (1.39)	1.66 (0.51)
85+	22.15 (3.10)	16.25 (2.79)	8.98 (2.19)	3.71 (1.31)

Comparison of these "data" (also shown in Figure 4.6, bottom) with the observed data shows that the additive model produces a useful structure to examine the relationship of age, leukemia type, and sex to mortality. The "additive data" indicate that death from acute myeloid leukemia occurs about 2.5 times more frequently than the chronic form in males (differences in logarithms 0.90) and about 4.4 times more frequently in females (difference in logarithms of 1.48). The influence of age is also easily summarized from the "additive data." For example,

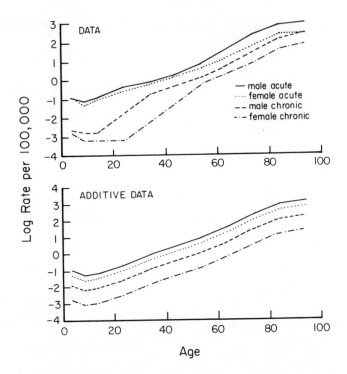

Figure 4-6. Age-specific curves for cell- and sex-specific myeloid leukemia mortality by age, logarithm of the rates per 100,000 population. Also shown are the same curves for strictly "additive data."

the rates of both forms of leukemia for both sexes increases about 6.5-fold between the ages 40 to 80 (difference in logarithms 1.86).

The strength of an additive model is demonstrated by these median-polished leukemia "additive data." The effect of each variable is summarized without reference to the other. The difference in mortality associated with the acute and chronic forms is the same at all levels of age for both sexes. Similarly age effects are described uninfluenced by leukemia type or sex. An additive model implies a type of independence among the variables under investigation, allowing a succinct description of the collected data based on separate assessments of each variable. The validity of assessing separately each influence results from the parallel relationships among the sex-, cell-type-specific curves (Figure 4.6, bottom). For example, the geometric distance between acute and chronic types of leukemia is the same for all ages within each sex since the logarithms of the rates for these two diseases form parallel lines for the "additive data." That is, the influence of cell-type is constant for both sexes and all ages. When the data are not adequately represented by an additive model (nonparallel lines), at least some of the residual values (r_{ij}) will be large indicating more intricate relationships among the risk variables and disease outcome.

A cohort effect, as previous stated, can be viewed as a specific type of nonadditivity in a table of mortality rates. This nonadditivity is likely to be reflected by the residual values. The median polish technique applied to the prostatic cancer data produces an estimate of the magnitude of the observed cohort effect (nonadditivity). Residual values for the prostatic cancer mortality rates (converted to a multiplier of the rates—$e^{-\text{residual}}$) are given in Table 4.14.

The tabled values are proportional to the lack of additivity of age and time in determining the logarithm of the prostatic cancer rate; that is, dividing each rate by the corresponding value in the table removes the cohort effect. For example, the mortality rate for ages 45–49 in 1930 is 3.5, and when the cohort effect is removed it becomes $3.5/2.4 = 1.5$. A residual value greater than 1 indicates higher than additive influence and less than 1 indicates lower than additive influence from age–time effects on the logarithm of the mortality rates.

Table 4–14. Age, time, and cohort influences on prostatic cancer: Residual

Age	1930	1935	1940	1945	1950	1955	1960	1965	1970	1975	1980
45–49	2.4	2.2	2.2	2.2	1.1	1.0	0.5	0.5	0.8	0.5	0.5
50–54	1.1	1.5	1.5	1.4	1.6	1.0	0.9	0.8	0.8	0.7	0.6
55–59	1.4	1.1	1.2	1.4	1.0	1.0	0.7	0.7	0.7	0.7	0.7
60–64	1.0	1.2	1.0	1.1	1.1	1.1	1.0	1.0	1.0	0.9	0.9
65–69	0.8	0.9	0.8	0.7	0.6	1.0	1.0	1.2	1.1	1.1	1.1
70–74	1.0	0.7	0.7	0.9	0.8	0.9	1.1	1.2	1.5	1.5	1.3
75–79	0.6	0.8	1.0	0.8	1.0	1.0	1.2	1.2	1.7	1.7	1.6
80+	0.6	0.8	0.7	0.7	1.0	1.0	1.1	1.0	1.5	1.8	2.0

Table 4–15. Age, time, and cohort influence on prostatic cancer: Residuals $(+, -)$

Age	1930	1935	1940	1945	1950	1955	1960	1965	1970	1975	1980
45–49	+	+	+	+	+	1	−	−	−	−	−
50–54	+	+	+	+	+	1	−	−	−	−	−
55–59	+	+	+	+	1	1	−	−	−	−	−
60–64	1	+	1	+	+	+	1	1	−	−	−
65–69	−	−	−	−	−	1	1	+	+	+	+
70–74	1	−	−	−	−	−	+	+	+	+	+
75–79	−	−	1	−	1	1	+	+	+	+	+
80+	−	−	−	−	1	1	+	1	+	+	

If no age–time interaction exists (no cohort influence), then the table of residual values will contain only small and essentially random values making $e^{-\text{residual}}$ near 1.0 for all cells in the table. A simple summary table using plus and minus signs clearly shows the systematic effect from the birth cohorts born around 1880 to 1900 on the pattern of prostatic cancer mortality.

The plus values indicate an excess of mortality over that expected from additive age and time effects. Inspired by the cohort model [expression (4.1)], Figure 4.7 quantifies the influence of the observed cohort effect on the prostatic cancer rates using the average of the diagonal elements from the table of residual values (Table 4.14). These mean values estimate the nonadditive and constant component associated with each birth cohort (each diagonal of the age–time table). These average residual values consistently rise for the cohorts born before 1895, then rapidly and consistently fall for subsequent cohorts, indicating a definite cohort effect influencing the prostatic cancer mortality rates among nonwhites.

Figure 4.8 shows the logarithm of the mortality rates by year of death

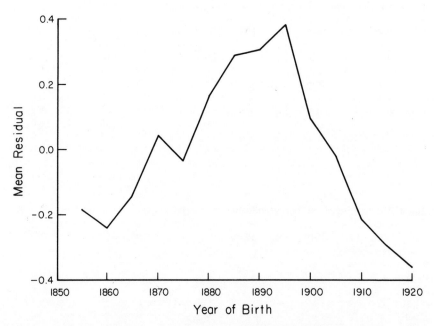

Figure 4–7. Average of the estimate residuals (the diagonal values in the age–time array) quantifying a specific nonadditive effect from the prostatic cancer data.

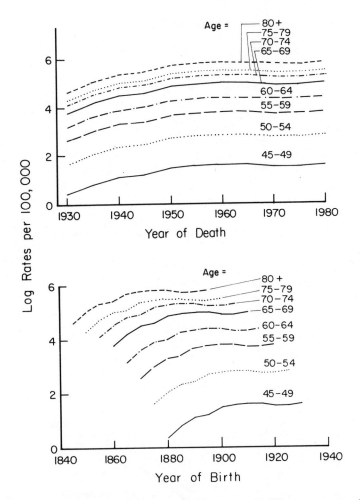

Figure 4–8. Age-specific curves for prostatic cancer mortality among nonwhites by year of death and by year of birth with the cohort effect removed (1969–77), logarithm of the rates per 100,000 population.

and by year of birth where the estimated cohort influence has been statistically removed. That is, an "additive rate" is calculated by

$$\text{additive rate} = \frac{\text{observed rate}}{e^{\text{residual}}} \text{ or}$$

$$\log(\text{additive rate}) = \log(\text{observed rate}) - \text{residual}. \quad (4.3)$$

The "additive rates" are given in Table 4.16.

The age–time interaction is no longer present, and the logarithms of these "rates" are a perfect additive function of age and calendar time effects; the curves representing the logarithm of the rates for each age

Table 4–16. Prostatic cancer mortality "data" by age and time among U.S. nonwhites

Age	1930	1935	1940	1945	1950	1955	1960	1965	1970	1975	1980
45–49	1.5	2.2	3.0	3.3	4.3	4.7	4.9	4.9	4.5	4.5	4.8
50–54	5.0	7.7	10.4	11.5	15.0	16.3	17.0	17.0	15.7	15.7	16.9
55–59	13.8	20.2	27.2	30.0	39.0	42.5	44.4	44.3	40.9	41.1	44.0
60–64	24.1	36.9	47.8	55.0	71.4	77.8	81.4	81.1	74.9	75.3	80.6
65–69	43.5	66.9	90.1	99.6	129.4	141.0	147.4	146.9	135.7	136.4	146.0
70–74	60.5	93.0	125.3	138.4	179.8	195.9	204.8	204.2	188.6	189.6	202.9
75–79	73.8	113.3	152.7	168.7	219.7	238.9	249.7	249.0	229.8	231.1	247.3
80+	101.5	155.9	210.1	232.1	301.6	328.6	343.6	342.5	316.2	317.9	340.3

Table 4–17. Age-adjusted prostatic cancer rates (with and without a cohort effect)

	1930	1935	1940	1945	1950	1955	1960	1965	1970	1975	1980
Cohort	7.2	11.8	15.6	17.6	23.0	26.8	29.7	30.6	34.1	35.4	38.2
No cohort	8.5	13.0	17.4	19.3	25.1	27.3	28.5	28.5	26.3	26.4	28.3

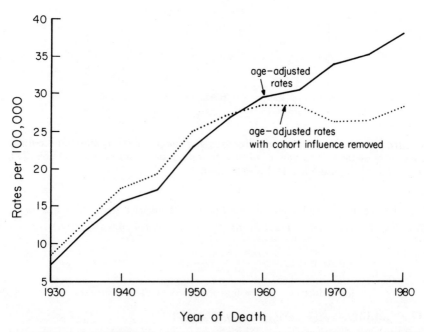

Figure 4–9. Age-adjusted curves for prostatic cancer mortality among non-whites rates by year of death with the cohort effect present and removed, rate per 100,000 population.

group are parallel. The "additive rates" produce a pattern of prostatic cancer mortality where no special "exposure" was experienced by any birth cohort ($c_{(k)} = 0$ for all k).

The non-white prostatic cancer data produce an essentially linear increase in the age-adjusted rates of disease over the period 1930 to 1980. Age-adjusted rates per 100,000, using the U.S. 1970 standard population and based on the original data (Table 4.8), are shown in Table 4.17. These age-adjusted rates are shown in Figure 4.9 solid line, labeled "cohort" in Table 4.17. Also shown are the age-adjusted "rates" of prostatic cancer among non-whites with the observed cohort effect removed (based on the "additive data" from Table 4.16). The "additive rates" allow the calculation of a set of age-adjusted "rates" without a cohort influence (plotted in figure 4.9 as the dotted line, labeled "no cohort" in table 4.17). The linearly increasing pattern seen in the prostatic cancer data levels off about 1950 when the cohort effect is "removed." These "rates" then remain fairly constant after 1950, even decreasing slightly. Comparison of the patterns of these two sets of age-adjusted prostatic cancer mortality rates leads to the inference that the cohort effect in the non-white population is the principal reason for increases in mortality since 1950.

5 Clustering: Space and Time Analysis

The distribution of disease in a population is fundamental to epidemiology, as noted by Abraham Lilienfeld [Ref. 1], who began his basic text:

> Epidemiology may be defined as the study of the distribution of disease or a pathological condition in human populations and the factors that influence this distribution.

Although Lilienfeld had in mind distribution in a broad sense, initial successes in epidemiology can be traced to the study of the spatial distribution of disease. John Snow identified the source of cholera in the nineteenth century primarily from the spatial distribution of cases in London.

> Aside: British Physician John Snow utilized what became the classic epidemiologic approach to study cholera in 1854. He postulated that cholera was caused by a contaminant in the water supply when bacterial disease was an unknown phenomenon. Dr. Snow then proceeded to collect data on customers of two water companies where one of these companies provided water that was relatively free of sewage. He also plotted the locations of deaths from cholera in central London on a map. By comparing the rates of death between groups served by the two companies and examining the spatial distribution of cases, he concluded that an "impurity" in the water was associated with an increase in cholera cases. The complete account of this remarkable "natural experiment" is given in Snow's book *On the Mode of Communication of Cholera*.

Burkitt [Ref. 2] published geographic distributions of cases of malignant lymphoma in Africa that led to a hypothesis that an insect vector was important in the etiology. Geographic distributions have played a central role in the epidemiology of a number of other diseases and are essential to evaluate data on exposures to environmental pollutants. This chapter explores a few analytic techniques for identifying nonrandom spatial patterns of disease.

Poisson Model

The Poisson probability distribution (see Appendix) is an effective tool for the description of objects distributed spatially at random. The spatial distribution of such things as stars, weeds, bacteria, and even flying-bomb strikes are described, sometimes quite accurately, by Poisson probabilities. A Poisson probability distribution applied to study spatial patterns begins by dividing the area of interest into a series of nonoverlapping subdivisions with equal area, so that the probability that a single random point falls within any one subdivision is small. In many cases this is easily done by creating a large number of subdivisions. If the probability that a specific random point is found in a single subdivision is small and constant, then the number of subdivisions containing 0, 1, 2, 3, ... points follows a Poisson probability distribution. Random means that each point has a probability of falling into a specific subdivision proportional to the area of that subdivision. The size of each subdivision but not the location influences the probabilities associated with each of point. More formally, if k represents the number of random points in a subdivision, then the number of subdivisions with k points is given by

$$\text{Number of subdivisions with } k \text{ points} = mP(X = k) = m\frac{\lambda^k e^{-\lambda}}{k!}, \quad (5.1)$$

where m is the total number of subdivisions and $P(X = k)$ is a Poisson probability. The parameter λ represents the expected number of points in each subdivision. The Poisson distribution as a description of random points on a plane is rigorously justified on theoretical grounds (see [Ref. 3]). Without going into the mathematical details, two conditions must hold to justify the Poisson distribution: (1) The probability (p) that each point falls in a specific subdivision must be small, and (2) the probability p must be constant.

If spatial clustering exists, then p differs among the subdivisions; for some areas p will be large where data cluster, and for other areas p will be relatively small where data are sparse. The Poisson distribution is synonymous with the null hypothesis that p is constant. Rejection of the null hypothesis provides evidence that p is heterogeneous, implying that at least some points are not randomly distributed across the region of interest.

Figure 5.1 displays $n = 200$ computer generated random points on a unit square. There are $m = 100$ subsquares with area $= 0.01$, so that every random point has a probability of $p = 1/m = 0.01$ of falling in a specific subsquare. The expected number of points per subsquare is

200 RANDOM POINTS

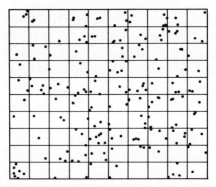

Figure 5–1. Two hundred random points distributed over a unit square divided into 100 equal subsquares.

$\lambda = np = 200(0.01) = 2$. The Poisson probabilities associated with an expected value of $\lambda = 2$ as well as the observed frequency of subareas with k points per subsquare (Figure 5.1) are shown in Table 5.1.

A classic study [Ref. 3] of spatial distributions occurred during World War II, in which records of flying-bomb strikes in south London were analyzed. It was critical to know if the German bombs were falling at random or if these bombs possessed a guidance system. South London was divided into $m = 576$ small subdivisions of equal area, each about 0.25 square kilometers. The number of flying bomb hits is recorded in Table 5.2.

The Poisson model cannot be applied without a value of the parameter λ. An estimate of this parameter comes from using the observed mean number of hits per area $(\hat{\lambda})$ as an estimate of the unknown expected number of hits per area (λ). That is,

$$\hat{\lambda} = \frac{\text{Total number of hits}}{\text{Number of subdivisions}} = \frac{n}{m}$$

$$= \frac{0(229) + 1(211) + 2(93) + 3(35) + 4(7) + 5(1)}{576} = 0.929 \qquad (5.2)$$

Table 5–1. Count of subareas with k points per square

k	0	1	2	3	4	5	6	7	Total
Areas	15	25	25	22	8	3	1	1	100
Probability	0.135	0.271	0.271	0.180	0.090	0.036	0.012	0.005	1.00
Frequency	0.150	0.250	0.250	0.220	0.080	0.030	0.010	0.010	1.00

Table 5-2. Flying-bomb hits in south London: Data

k	0	1	2	3	4	5^+	Total
Areas	229	211	93	35	7	1	576

is the observed mean number of hits per square among the 576 squares (a bit less than one per square). Note that 5^+ was set to 5 to estimate λ. An estimate of λ makes it possible to estimate the Poisson probabilities and expected number of random hits distributed among 576 areas, as shown in Table 5.3.

A χ^2 statistic or some other goodness-of-fit procedure to test the accuracy of the Poisson distribution as a model for the London data is hardly necessary. This example is classic because of the extraordinarily good fit of the observed to the theoretically derived values. The conclusion some 50 years ago would have been that the data from south London indicated no evidence that these weapons were guided with any accuracy.

Situations certainly arise where it is not obvious whether a Poisson distribution can serve as a description of a set of observations. Then, a summary statistic and a significance test are useful. Such a summary statistic is developed from the fact that the mean and the variance are identical for the Poisson distribution. Therefore, the sample mean and the sample variance from a set of Poisson distributed data should be about equal, give or take random variation. In other words, the sample mean value $\bar{x}$ and the sample variance S^2 should be approximately equal under the conditions that the data are a random sample from a Poisson distribution or

$$\frac{S^2}{\bar{x}} \approx 1. \tag{5.3}$$

The ratio $S^2/\bar{x}$ multiplied by $(n - 1)$ has an approximate χ^2 distribution when the population sampled has a Poisson distribution, where n is the total number of observed values. The degrees of freedom are the

Table 5-3. Flying-bomb hits in south London: Probabilities and expected hits

k	0	1	2	3	4	5^+	Total
Probability	0.395	0.367	0.170	0.053	0.012	0.003	1.0
Expected areas	227.53	211.34	98.15	30.39	7.06	1.54	576
Observed areas	229	211	93	35	7	1	576

number of observations minus one $(n - 1)$. This test statistic, sometimes called the test of variance for obvious reasons, can be justified from the common expression for the χ^2 statistic,

$$X^2 = \sum \frac{(\text{Observed} - \text{Expected})^2}{\text{Expected}}. \tag{5.4}$$

For the test of variance the observed value is represented by x_i and the expected value, represented as λ, is estimated by $\hat{\lambda} = \bar{x} = \sum x_i/n$. Substituting this estimate into the χ^2 expression gives

$$X^2 = \sum_{i=1}^{n} \frac{(x_i - \bar{x})^2}{\bar{x}} = (n - 1)\frac{S^2}{\bar{x}}. \tag{5.5}$$

To illustrate, the mean value of the data displayed in Figure 5.1 (also given in Table 5.1) is $\bar{x} = 2.010$, and the variance is $S^2 = 2.091$. Then, $X^2 = 199(2.091)/2.010 = 207.0$, which has a χ^2 distribution with $n - 1 = 199$ degrees of freedom when the 200 points are distributed at random over the unit square. The associated p-value of 0.334 indicates that the deviations from the expected values are typical when no spatial pattern of points exists.

The test of variance approach is effective even for fairly small samples of data $(n \approx 20$ or so) and is not restricted to the assessment of spatial distributions but is also useful in most contexts to evaluate the goodness-of-fit of a Poisson distribution.

Nearest Neighbor

Employing the Poisson distribution to detect clustering has a weakness. Distance is a continuous measure. As discussed earlier, employing a set of counts is not an efficient method for dealing with continuous phenomena, particularly for small numbers of observations. One method to investigate spatial randomness, which utilizes the actual distance between points, is a nearest-neighbor analysis. A nearest neighbor is basically what the name implies. For n points, distances to all other points under consideration are calculated. The nearest neighbor is the minimum distance among these $n - 1$ measurements. The collection of these n distances constitutes a set of nearest-neighbor data. The expected mean distance and the variance of the distribution for a set of nearest-neighbor values can be derived under the conditions that the spatial distribution is random. A test of randomness results from the comparison of the mean from a set of observed nearest-neighbor distances to the mean expected when no spatial pattern exists.

Suppose, as before, that a sample of points is distributed at random over a specified area. For a specific point let the probability that no other points occur within d units be symbolized by $P_0(d)$. The probability that no points are within an additional small distance δ can then be expressed as

$$P_0(d + \delta) \approx P_0(d)(1 - \lambda\delta), \qquad (5.6)$$

where λ is the expected number of points per unit area. Then,

$$\frac{P_0(d + \delta) - P_0(d)}{\delta} \approx -\lambda P_0(d) \qquad (5.7)$$

and a bit of mathematical manipulation, or noting that exponential growth (decay) occurs when the rate of change of a variable is proportional only to the level of that variable, gives

$$P_0(d) = e^{-\lambda d}. \qquad (5.8)$$

Aside: This same expression, in an entirely different context, results from probably the most famous single differential equation. Thomas Malthus (1798) used this exponential relationship to support his view that populations tend to increase faster than the resources needed to sustain them. This theory, published in his famous work, *Essay on the Principle of Populations* has had substantial impact on many fields and, perhaps, was the beginning of the field of demography.

When interest lies in the distance from a specified point to its nearest neighbor in any direction, a circle with radius r is an appropriate measure of area with the parameter λ equal to n/A, where A represents the total area under consideration and n the total number of observed points. The value $\lambda = n/A$ is the frequency of points per unit area (density) on the x-y plane.

The probability that one or more points is found in a circle of radius r is

$$F(r) = 1 - e^{-n\pi r^2/A} \qquad (5.9)$$

as long as the spatial distribution of the n points is random. The same probability applies to the nearest neighbor (the minimum distance). That is, the probability of finding one or more points within a circle with radius r is the same as the probability of finding the minimum distance point within the same circle. The distribution function $F(r)$ relates the distance r to probabilities associated with nearest-neighbor values when points are spatially random. More precisely, P (nearest-neighbor distance $< r$ units) $= 1 - e^{-n\pi r^2/A}$.

Knowledge of the probability function $F(r)$ allows the calculation of various summary parameters associated with nearest-neighbor distances for a sample of randomly distributed points. For example, the expected median distance associated with a sample of n nearest-neighbor distances is

$$F(r) = 0.5, \text{ which implies that median } (r) = 0.470\sqrt{A/n}. \quad (5.10)$$

Along the same lines, using a calculus argument, the expected mean distance and variance of the mean are

$$\text{mean } (r) = 0.5\sqrt{A/n}, \text{ with variance } (\bar{r}) = 0.068\frac{A}{n^2} \quad (5.11)$$

when the n points are distributed randomly over the region of interest. Additionally, the probability distribution $F(r)$ provides a basis for a χ^2 goodness-of-fit test when large amounts of data are available. That is, the expected number of nearest-neighbor values between any two distances r_i and r_j $(r_i < r_j)$ is

$$\text{Expected number} = nP(r_i < \text{nearest-neighbor distance } < r_j)$$
$$= n[F(r_j) - F(r_i)] \quad (5.12)$$

where, as before, n is the total number of points observed. The expected numbers can be compared to the observed numbers with the usual χ^2 test (i.e., Σ (Observed − Expected)^2/Expected).

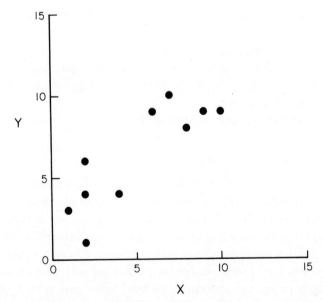

Figure 5–2. Ten hypothetical data points distributed over a square 15 units on a side to illustrate nearest-neighbor calculations.

Table 5–4. Nearest-neighbor example

	Point		Nearest		Distance*	
i	X	Y	X'	Y'	r_i^2	r_i
1	1	3	2	4	2	1.414
2	2	1	1	3	5	2.236
3	2	4	1	3	2	1.414
4	2	6	2	4	4	2.000
5	4	4	2	4	4	2.000
6	6	9	7	10	2	1.414
7	7	10	6	9	2	1.414
8	8	8	9	9	2	1.414
9	9	9	10	9	1	1.000
10	10	9	9	9	1	1.000

$*r_i = \sqrt{(x_i - x_i')^2 + (y_i - y_i')^2}$

To illustrate, ten hypothetical points are plotted in Figure 5.2 contained in a total area $A = 15^2 = 225$ square units. These points and their nearest neighbors are given in Table 5.4.

Figure 5.3 shows the cumulative probability distribution $F(r) = 1 - e^{-0.140r^2}$ associated with these 10 hypothetical points. The

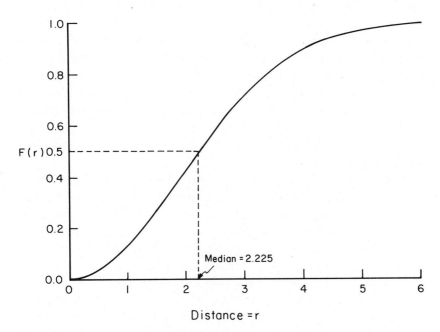

Figure 5–3. The cumulative distribution function from the hypothetical nearest-neighbor data.

expected mean value and variance of the mean calculated for the $n = 10$ nearest-neighbor distances, under the conjecture that the points occur randomly over the 225 square units of the x-y plane, are

$$\text{mean } (r) = 0.5 \sqrt{\frac{225}{10}} = 2.372 \quad \text{and}$$

$$\text{variance } (\bar{r}) = 0.068 \frac{225}{100} = 0.153. \tag{5.13}$$

The observed mean of the ten nearest-neighbor distances $\bar{r}$ has an approximately normal distribution even for moderate sample sizes ($n > 6$ or so; [Ref. 4]) and from Table 5.4 is

$$\bar{r} = \Sigma\, r_i/n = 15.307/10 = 1.531, \tag{5.14}$$

giving

$$z = \frac{\bar{r} - \text{mean } (r)}{\sqrt{\text{variance } (\bar{r})}} = \frac{1.531 - 2.372}{\sqrt{0.153}} = -2.150. \tag{5.15}$$

The test statistic z is an observation from a standard normal distribution when no spatial pattern exists. The one-sided p-value associated with $z = -2.150$ is 0.016, indicating that it is not likely that the ten points represent a random distribution over the 225 square units of area.

The nearest-neighbor analysis applied to the data shown in Figure 5.1 and given in Table 5.1 confirms the previous Poisson analysis. For 200 random points distributed on a unit square, the expected mean nearest-neighbor distance is $0.5\sqrt{1/200} = 0.0354$ with a standard deviation of 0.00130. The observed mean calculated from the nearest-neighbor distances among the 200 points is $\bar{r} = 0.0351$, producing a $z = (0.0351 - 0.0354)/0.00130 = -0.196$, and the associated one-sided p-value is 0.422.

A general problem encountered in spatial analyses is illustrated by the nearest-neighbor data. The determination of the total area (A) is critical to the analysis, but rarely are clear, unequivocal boundaries available to define the relevant area of interest. Boundary determination is complicated since extending boundaries is likely to include noninformative points, which reduces the likelihood of detecting a cluster (decreases power). If an apparent "cluster" occurs in a specific town, it is likely that, when these data are combined with the distribution over the county, the importance of the "cluster" will be reduced; further, if the state is included, the "cluster" may disappear altogether. The opposite is also true. If the area of interest is made sufficiently small, only a few cases becomes a "cluster." Clearly, the boundaries of the area considered, to a large extent, determine whether points cluster. Sometimes "natural" boundaries are appropriate, but, by and large, the determination of the total area is fairly subjective. A less important issue that applies to nearest-neighbor analysis also concerns boundary influences. Implicit in the development of the expressions for the expected mean and variance is the assumption, which clearly is violated in practice, that a circle of radius r surrounding a point never intersects a boundary of the study area. Last, note that nearest-neighbor distances are not independent. Lack of independence has been studied and shown to have little effect on the significance levels of statistical tests. Adjustments to the expected mean and variance that partially correct for the problems of edge influences and nonindependence are available [Ref. 4].

Transformed Maps

Poisson and the nearest-neighbor approaches are not effective in the direct study of spatial distributions of human disease. The spatial pattern of human disease is dominated by the influence of the distribution of the population at risk. For example, Figure 5.4 shows

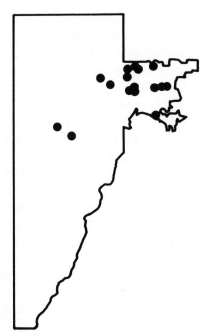

Figure 5–4. Lung cancer incidence cases (adenocarcinoma) among white females aged 55 years or older for Jefferson and Denver counties, Colorado (1970), displayed on a geopolitical map.

the cases of lung cancer (adenocarcinoma) among white females, 55 years and older, in Jefferson and Denver counties, Colorado (1970). A cluster of cases occurs in the northeast because the vast majority of the population of these two counties lives in the city of Denver, which is located in the northeast. Most maps of human disease are so strongly affected by the distribution of the residential population that a direct plot of cases is useless. In other words, humans tend to concentrate in specific areas, causing a high frequency of disease in those areas regardless of other factors.

Underlying the Poisson and nearest-neighbor approaches to the analysis of spatial data is the assumption that, if the phenomenon under study occurs at random, the spatial distribution has no pattern. For human populations, a disease can occur at random with respect to risk (every individual is equally likely to contract the disease), but clusters will continue to appear when plotted on a geopolitical map. The reason for this clustering, as mentioned, is a nonuniform distribution of the population at risk over the area of interest.

One method of depicting and analyzing the spatial distribution of disease, without the interfering influence of the nonuniform population density, involves redrawing the geopolitical boundaries of a map (for a complete description see [Ref. 5]). Redrawing a map to equalize population density allows the potential identification of other factors that influence risk since the confounding effect of the population distribution is removed. One such transformed map, called a cartogram, is produced by first dividing the total area into a series of small subdivisions (e.g., census tracts). A computer algorithm is then used to expand the densely populated subareas and contract the sparsely populated subareas until all areas have the appropriate sizes so that they reflect identical densities of persons at risk.

Figure 5.5 is a cartogram of Jefferson and Denver counties constructed with equal population density of white women, aged 55 and over, among 179 census tracts. The fundamental feature of this redrawn map is that, when a disease occurs with equal probability among the individuals who make up the population at risk, the distribution of cases on a transformed map will be spatially random. That is, the distribution of the locations of cases will not differ in a systematic way from the distribution of the population at risk on a transformed map; only random differences will exist. For example, when a disease has no spatial pattern, the location of the population centroid (the center or mean of a two-dimensional distribution) and the centroid of the cases will differ only by chance when placed on a density-equalized map (see Figure 5.5). The 16 lung cancer cases

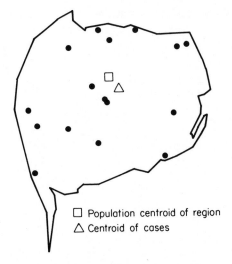

□ Population centroid of region
△ Centroid of cases

Figure 5-5. Lung cancer incidence cases (adenocarcinoma) among white females aged 55 years or older for Jefferson and Denver counties, Colorado (1970), displayed on a density-equalized transformed map.

plotted in Figure 5.5 on a density-equalized map show no visual evidence of a spatial pattern. The clustering caused by the high-density population of the city of Denver is no longer present, and no other spatial pattern appears to remain. Poisson or nearest-neighbor analysis could be used in conjunction with a transformed map to evaluate statistically the distribution of cases of disease for evidence of nonrandomness.

To illustrate the nearest-neighbor approach using a map transformed to equalize the density of the population at risk, the locations (x_i, y_i) of incidence cases of lymphatic cancer from the city of San Francisco (1973–86) among white residents under the age of 20 are given in Table 5.5.

These 26 cases include both sexes and are located at the centroid of the census tract of residence on a map of San Francisco transformed so that all individuals under the age of 21 are uniformly distributed over the map (Figure 5.6). Each case generates a nearest-neighbor distance (r_i) also given in the Table 5.5. The nearest-neighbor distances of zero are an artifact resulting from considering the location of all cases as occurring at the centroid of the census tract of residence since cases in the same tract are placed at the same location. The expected mean nearest-neighbor distance among 26 points distributed at random on the San Francisco transformed map is $0.5\sqrt{A/n} =$

Table 5-5. Locations of cases of lymphatic cancer cases, San Francisco (1977-86)

i	x_i	y_i	r_i	i	x_i	y_i	r_i
1	3.563	4.250	0.880	15	2.742	3.935	0.880
2	−4.640	−1.317	1.551	16	2.769	−1.877	1.852
3	−3.974	4.083	1.635	17	−2.308	−2.536	0.000
4	−2.506	−0.530	1.269	18	1.095	3.028	1.880
5	−2.075	−5.288	1.305	19	−3.549	0.192	0.000
6	−0.998	4.031	1.393	20	−0.934	2.329	1.534
7	−2.368	3.779	1.189	21	4.331	−0.883	1.852
8	−2.250	−3.994	1.054	22	−2.308	−2.536	0.000
9	0.711	−2.470	2.142	23	−2.308	−2.536	0.000
10	−2.668	2.628	1.189	24	−3.549	0.192	0.000
11	−2.308	−2.536	0.000	25	−3.918	−3.729	1.002
12	−0.826	−0.666	1.685	26	−0.013	1.102	1.534
13	−4.001	−2.730	1.002				
14	−1.207	−3.840	1.054				

$0.5\sqrt{111.444/26} = 1.035$ kilometers with a variance of $0.068A/n^2 = 0.068(111.444)/26^2 = 0.011$, where A (the area) = 111.444 square kilometers. The observed mean calculated from the 26 nearest-neighbor distances is $\bar{r} = 1.072$ kilometers. The comparison of the expected

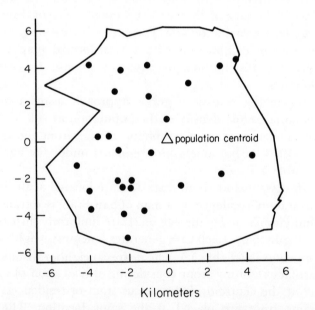

Figure 5-6. Lymphatic cancer incidence cases among white males and females aged 20 years or younger displayed on a density-equalized transformed map (San Francisco, California, 1977-86).

and observed values yields a value $z = (1.072 - 1.035)/\sqrt{0.011}$ $= 0.352$ and a one-sided p-value of 0.637. The nearest-neighbor analysis shows no evidence of spatial clustering of lymphatic cancer among individuals under 21 years old.

Spatial distribution about a point

An important question concerning spatial distributions arises in a variety of contexts: Is there an excess of disease associated with a point source of exposure? For example, chemical waste dumps and nuclear facilities are often suspected as a cause of local increases in disease incidence. If a point source is associated with a disease, then the observed average distance between the source and the cases is likely to be smaller than a distance calculated under the hypothesis that no spatial association exists. This null hypothesis can be stated in two ways: Disease occurs at random on a density-equalized map, or all individuals are at equal risk of disease regardless of their location on a geopolitical map. In the first case clustering may be apparent from cases displayed on a transformed map, but the analysis is somewhat complicated (see [Ref. 6 or 7]). In the second case the analysis is not complicated, but the cases displayed on a geopolitical map are confounded by the distribution of the population at risk and do not accurately reflect the disease risk from a point-source exposure.

Spatial disease data are often collected for a specific area where the geographic area can be subdivided into a series of subareas such as census tracts. If the population for each subarea is known and the distance to a point source of exposure calculated, then it is relative easy to assess statistically the degree of association between a spatial pattern of cases of disease and a specific geographic location, even though a geopolitical map will not accurately depict any association. Suppose the point source of exposure is located at (x_0, y_0). Under the hypothesis that no spatial pattern exists among the n cases, the expected distance from the location of a randomly selected person (x_i, y_i) to the point (x_0, y_0) on a geopolitical map is approximately

$$\text{Expected mean distance} = ED \approx \frac{\sum\limits_{i=1}^{k} p_i d'_i}{\sum\limits_{i=1}^{k} p_i}, \tag{5.16}$$

where p_i is the number of persons at risk the ith subarea, d'_i is the distance from the centroid of the ith subarea to the point of exposure and k is the number of these areas. The variance of the distribution of observed distances, again calculated under the assumption that the cases are distributed randomly, is estimated by

$$\text{variance } (D) \approx \frac{\sum\limits_{i=1}^{k} p_i (d_i' - ED)^2}{\sum\limits_{i=1}^{k} p_i}. \tag{5.17}$$

The average distance $[\bar{d} = (1/n) \Sigma d_i$, where $d_i = \sqrt{(x_i - x_o)^2 + (y_i - y_0)^2}$ is the distance from the location of the ith case to the point (x_0, y_0) on a geopolitical map] can be calculated from the location of the n observed cases. A statistical test of the hypothesis of no association between the location (x_0, y_0) and the spatial distribution of disease results from the comparison of this observed mean value with the null hypothesis generated expectation or

$$z = \frac{\bar{d} - ED}{\sqrt{\text{variance } (D)/n}}, \tag{5.18}$$

where z has an approximate standard normal distribution when the null hypothesis is true. The test statistic z is an accurate assessment of observed spatial patterns associated with a specific point when the number of cases is not extremely small (greater than 10 or 15) and a

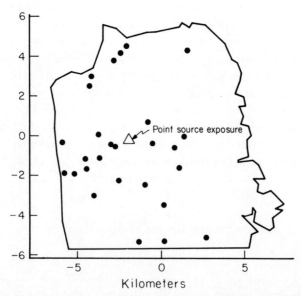

Figure 5–7. Brain cancer incidence among white males and females aged 20 years or younger displayed on a geopolitical map (San Francisco, California, 1977–86).

large number of subareas are used to calculate ED and variance (D).

A possible point source of exposure is a large microwave tower located near the center of the city of San Francisco (see Figure 5.7). The location and the distance in kilometers to the tower for 27 cases of brain cancer found in white individuals less than 21 years old are shown in Figure 5.7 and given in Table 5.6.

The expected distance to the microwave tower for a random white person less than 21 years old living in San Francisco is $ED = 3.735$ kilometers, and the variance associated with the distribution of random "cases" is 2.115 [from expressions (5.16) and (5.17), respectively] based on 148 San Francisco census tracts. The observed mean distance among the 27 brain cancer cases is $\bar{d} = 3.379$ kilometers, where the microwave tower is located at $(x_0 = -2.0, y_0 = 0.2$; see Figure 5.7). The 27 cancer cases exhibit an average distnce to the point source of about 0.5 kilometers less than the distance expected for a noncase. Comparing this observed mean to the expected value yields a standard normal statistic, when the location of the tower is unrelated to the spatial pattern of disease, of $z = -1.270$ with a one-sided p-value of 0.102. The p-value indicates that the pattern of disease observed is somewhat unlikely to have occurred by chance; that is, the spatial distribution of cases (Figure 5.7) in proximity to the microwave tower may be associated with factors other than the nonuniform distribution of the population at risk.

Nonrandom spatial patterns of disease do not unequivocally identify specific causes. Such factors as differential smoking patterns, socioeconomic differences, and access to medical care are examples of possible

Table 5-6. Locations of cases of brain cancer cases, San Francisco (1977–86)

i	x_i	y_i	d_i	i	x_i	y_i	d_i
1	−1.136	0.718	1.406	15	−4.865	−1.154	2.831
2	−0.163	−3.429	3.818	16	−6.156	−1.854	4.288
3	−2.718	4.185	4.415	17	1.036	−0.013	3.241
4	−3.090	−0.532	0.950	18	0.474	−0.568	2.699
5	−4.103	0.111	1.928	19	−0.141	−5.267	5.470
6	−4.664	2.567	3.705	20	−2.741	4.196	4.429
7	−5.528	−1.899	3.736	21	−2.865	−2.249	2.154
8	−0.842	−0.363	1.367	22	−4.036	−1.093	2.042
9	2.330	−5.074	6.654	23	−4.513	3.042	3.983
10	−1.393	−2.411	2.353	24	−4.849	−1.142	2.812
11	−1.636	−5.274	5.105	25	−6.267	−0.282	4.067
12	−2.732	4.177	4.410	26	1.257	4.304	5.678
13	−3.055	−0.513	0.911	27	0.748	−1.574	3.253
14	−4.346	−3.017	3.541				

explanations of observed spatial patterns. For analyses based on a density-equalized map or a geopolitical map, evidence of a nonrandom spatial pattern of disease remains subject to the same limitations in interpretation as most pairwise associations.

Time-Space Analysis

A time—space analysis is characterized by the absence of a population at risk. Data on the nondiseased population or data on the disease rates are not necessary. All that is needed is the time of occurrence and the location of each case for a defined geographic region. Time differences (absolute value) and distance between disease cases form the basis of a time–space analysis. The sample of n observed times and locations is used to generate a series of all possible unsigned differences in time and distance between cases producing $\mathcal{N} = n(n-1)/2$ pairs of time–distance "data." The following hypothetical set of eight cases occurring at time t_i and located at (x_i, y_i), shown in Figure 5.8, are recorded in Table 5.7. These eight cases generate $8(7)/2 = 28$ possible different pairs of time–distance observations. They are shown in Table 5.8, and, as before, the distance between (x_i, y_i) and (x_j, y_j) is

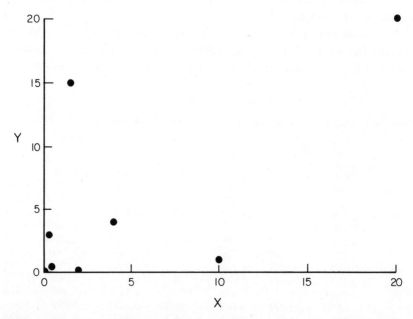

Figure 5–8. Eight hypothetical points distributed over a square 20 units on a side to illustrate time–space clustering calculations.

Table 5–7. Data: Time–Space

	Time	Location	
i	t_i	x_i	y_i
1	1.0	0.1	0.1
2	1.4	2.0	0.2
3	2.0	0.3	3.0
4	2.6	4.0	4.0
5	5.0	0.5	0.5
6	7.0	10.0	1.0
7	10.0	1.5	15.0
8	13.0	20.0	20.0

$d_{ij} = \sqrt{(x_i - x_j)^2 + (y_i - y_j)^2}$. A plot of the time–distance pairs is shown in Figure 5.9.

The principle underlying the time–space approach is that cases of disease with common underlying factors will be close in both time and location, while unrelated cases will tend to be separated by typical differences in time or space. Clustering in space only or time only does not provide evidence of an association between cases of disease. For example, cases clustering because of unequal population densities are not likely to cluster with respect to time when no relationship exists among cases of disease. Figure 5.4 shows a cluster of lung cancer cases due to the high population density of the city of Denver. When all individuals are at equal risk, no reason exists for cases within Denver city limits to occur at times different from those cases that occur outside the city in the less populated areas. Also, in the absence of an association, cases that cluster in time (e.g., a seasonality) will not occur closer in distance than would be expected by chance. It is only when

Table 5–8. All pairs: Time–Space

Obs	$|t_i - t_j|$	d_{ij}	Obs	$|t_i - t_j|$	d_{ij}	Obs	$|t_i - t_j|$	d_{ij}
1	0.4	1.90	11	5.6	8.04	21	7.4	11.28
2	1.0	2.91	12	8.6	14.81	22	10.4	22.63
3	1.6	5.52	13	11.6	26.76	23	2.0	9.51
4	4.0	0.57	14	0.6	3.83	24	5.0	14.53
5	6.0	9.94	15	3.0	2.51	25	8.0	27.58
6	9.0	14.97	16	5.0	9.90	26	3.0	16.38
7	12.0	28.14	17	8.0	12.06	27	6.0	21.47
8	0.6	3.28	18	11.0	26.02	28	3.0	19.16
9	1.2	4.29	19	2.4	4.95			
10	3.6	1.53	20	4.4	6.71			

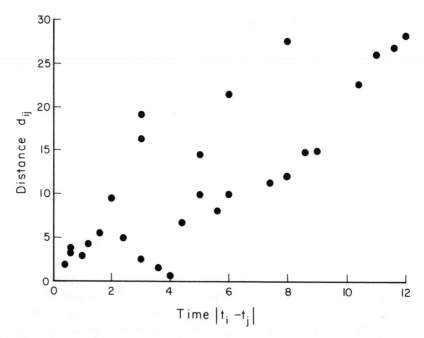

Figure 5–9. The 28 possible pairs of time–space "data" for the eight hypothetical data points.

cases occur in proximity in both time and location that excess pairs of small time differences and relatively short distances appear together. Infectious disease exhibits classic time–space clustering where cases arise at similar times and in similar places because of the contagious nature of the disease. Infectious disease serves as a biological model for the time–space approach.

A difficulty in analyzing time–distance pairs is the increased variability incurred by creating the $n(n-1)/2$ data values. A simple analysis of time–space data using a 2×2 table reduces the impact of this variation [Ref. 8]. Critical values for time and for distance are used to classify time—distance pairs into four categories. Suppose the critical difference for time is t_0 and the critical distance between cases is d_0, then the time–distance pairs form a typical 2×2 table represented by Table 5.9, where $N = n(n-1)/2$ pairs. A two-way table treats all values exceeding the critical distance or time values as equivalent, thereby reducing the variability induced by the formation of the time–distance pairing. Using a 2×2 table approach implicitly makes the assumption that most cases occurring beyond t_0 or d_0 are not related and at least some cases occurring with time and distance measurements less than both t_0 and d_0 provide information on clustering. This approach can be

Table 5–9. 2×2 table of time–distance pairs

	$t < t_0$	$t \geqslant t_0$	Total
$d < d_0$	a	b	$a + b$
$d \geqslant d_0$	c	d	$c + d$
Total	$a + c$	$b + d$	N

applied to most sets of spatial data and makes a 2×2 table an effective way to assess clustering in time and space.

In a study of possible clustering among 96 cases of leukemia [Ref. 9], the critical distance was set a 1 kilometer $(d_0 = 1)$ and the critical time set at 60 days $(t_0 = 60)$, producing $96(95)/2 = 4560$ time–distance pairs distributed as shown in Table 5.10.

The expected number of pairs of cases "clustering" by chance is estimated from the expression $(a + b)(a + c)/N = (25)(152)/4560 = 0.833$, where time and distance are postulated as unrelated (independent); that is, the expected number of random "close" pairs $= N$ $P(\text{time} < t_0 \text{ and distance} < d_0) = NP(\text{time} < t_0P(\text{distance} < d_0)$, which is estimated by

$$\text{estimate expected number} = N\frac{a + b}{N}\frac{a + c}{N}. \tag{5.19}$$

Aside: The Poisson distribution is often used to investigate the likelihood of rare events among a series of unrelated individual outcomes. Rare events, under the null hypothesis that each event in the series under investigation occurs independently with equal probability, are assigned Poisson distribution probabilities (approximate binomial probabilities). In this time–space context, the question is: How likely is the occurrence of five or more "close" pairs among the 4,560 "events" when all "events" occur at random with an expected number of "close" pairs of 0.833? The Poisson distribution gives

$$P(X \geqslant k) = \sum_{i=k}^{\infty} \frac{e^{-\lambda}\lambda^i}{i!} = 1 - \sum_{i=0}^{k-1} \frac{e^{-\lambda}\lambda^i}{i!} \tag{5.20}$$

Table 5–10. 2×2 table of time–distance pairs for leukemia data

	$t < t_0$	$t \geqslant t_0$	Total
$d < d_0$	5	20	25
$d \geqslant d_0$	147	4,388	4,535
Total	152	4,408	4,560

and, specifically,

$$P(X \geqslant 5) = 1 - (0.4346 + 0.3622 + 0.1509 + 0.0419 + 0.0087)$$
$$= 1 - 0.9983 = 0.0017$$

(λ is estimated by $\hat{\lambda} = 0.833$) as the answer. That is, five or more "close" pairs will rarely occur when time and distance are unrelated. The Poisson-derived p-value is useful in evaluating results associated with rare events and provides an alternative to the more common χ^2 test for independence, which is not accurate when the expected values per cell become small (less than 3 or so).

Using a Poisson distribution, the observed result from the leukemia data is unlikely under the hypothesis of no association between time and distance. Five pairs with both time and distance less than the critical values (t_0 and d_0), when 0.833 pairs are expected, occur with probability 0.0017 when time and distance are unrelated.

Application of the Poisson distribution is not strictly correct. Time–distance pairs are not perfectly independent since the formation of the N time–space pairs introduces some interdependency. This lack of independence is slight and has little impact on the results. More important issues involve the loss of information from categorizing two continuous variables and the lack of clear-cut choices for the critical values. A number of other approaches to time–space data have been proposed that avoid these two problems. For example, a regression analysis using the reciprocal of the time and the reciprocal of the distance has been suggested [Ref. 10], emphasing "close" time-distance pairs. Another approach involves a permutation test to evaluate time–distance measures [Ref. 10], which is the topic of the next section.

Permutation Tests

A permutation test is a statistical procedure that applies to numerous situations as well as the study of time–space data. The application of this technique does not require sophisticated statistical distributions (e.g., t distribution or F distribution) but does require the use of a computer when the sample size is more than 10 or so. Before applying a permutation test to the time–space problem, the permutation test analogous to the two-sample t test illustrates the approach.

Analyzing cholesterol levels from the WCGS individuals classified as type A and type B with a permutation test allows comparison with previous t test results for the same data (Chapter 2). The data (repeated from Table 2.1) on the 40 heaviest WCGS mean are given in Table 5.11. The observed mean cholesterol level of the 20 type A

Table 5–11. WCGS data: Cholesterol and behavior type

Obs	Chol	A/B	Obs	Chol	A/B	Obs	Chol	A/B
1	344	B	15	148	B	28	183	B
2	233	A	16	268	A	29	234	A
3	291	A	17	224	A	30	137	B
4	312	A	18	239	A	31	181	A
5	185	B	19	239	A	32	248	A
6	250	A	20	254	A	33	252	A
7	263	B	21	169	B	34	202	A
8	246	A	22	226	B	35	218	A
9	246	B	23	175	B	36	202	B
10	224	B	24	276	A	37	212	A
11	212	B	25	242	B	38	325	A
12	188	B	26	252	B	39	194	B
13	250	B	27	153	B	40	213	B
14	197	A						

individuals is $\bar{y}_A = 245.050$ and $\bar{y}_B = 210.300$ for the 20 type B individuals.

The null hypothesis that behavior type is unrelated to cholesterol level is equivalent to considering the data as if 20 individuals were chosen at random and labeled A while the remaining 20 were labeled B. In fact, when 20 individuals are selected at random from the group of 40, the mean level of cholesterol for 20 randomly chosen individuals then estimates the cholesterol level in the group and the mean of the remaining 20 observations also estimates the same mean. Differences between these two mean values result from the random sampling process. Individuals with behavior types A and B will be, in the long run, balanced among a series of comparisons of the means from the two randomly chosen groups. In principle, all possible samples of 20 could be selected from the 40 measured cholesterol levels and used to calculate all possible meana values for 20 sampled and 20 nonsampled individuals. The set of differences between these means is the distribution of the test statistic $\bar{y}_A - \bar{y}_B$ under the null hypothesis that behavior type is unrelated to cholesterol level. The number of all such differences is too large even for a fast computer (1.4×10^{11} samples) to make this simple calculation. However, it is possible to program a computer to take a series of random samples of 20 observations from the data set and calculate the mean differences in cholesterol values between the sampled and nonsampled groups. Such a series of estimates reflects the distribution of differences uninfluenced by any systematic effects that may exist, called a null distribution.

Table 5-12. Summary of a permutation sample from the WCGS cholesterol–behavior-type data

Number of samples	5000
Mean value	−0.013
Variance	211.300
Standard deviation	14.536
Minimum value	−45.150
Maximum value	58.250

Percentiles	1%	5%	10%	90%	95%	99%
Observed value	−33.650	−23.450	−18.550	18.950	23.450	32.750

A set of 5,000 random samples of 20 from the 40 WCGS individuals (Table 5.11) produces the summary statistics for the values of "$\bar{y}_A - \bar{y}_B$" given in Table 5.12.

This null distribution is determined entirely by the empirical process of repeatedly sampling 20 values from the 40 WCGS observations (5,000 times). A histogram of the observed frequencies of mean differences is shown in Figure 5.10. The null distribution is essentially

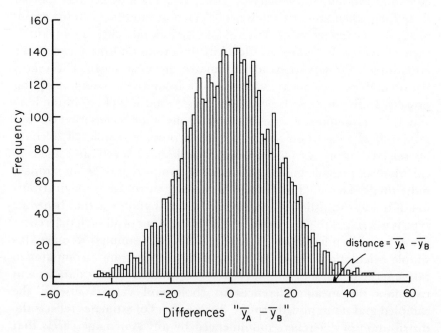

Figure 5-10. The histogram of the null distribution of "$\bar{y}_A - \bar{y}_B$."

symmetric with mean almost zero (-0.013). This empirical distribution accurately reflects a t distribution. For example, the t distribution predicts a 95th percentile of 23.927, and the observed percentile is 23.450. The observed mean difference between type A and type B individuals is $\bar{y}_A - \bar{y}_B = 245.050 - 210.300 = 34.75$. Again using the computer, it is a simple matter to count the more extreme values in the sample of 5,000. Only 35 randomized mean differences exceeded 34.75, showing that observed differences larger than 34.75 are not likely when no association exists between behavior type and cholesterol level. The p-value from the permutation test is then estimated by $35/50000 = 0.007$, which almost exactly agrees with the previous p-value of 0.00725 ($T = 2.562$) found using the t distribution and the "shift" model [expression (2.9)].

Of course, when the assumptions underlying a t test hold, it is easily and directly applied. But when the assumptions do not hold, t-test results become suspect while the permutation test continues to give an accurate p-value under almost all conditions. If, for example, the ratio of two mean cholesterol levels is a sensitive measure of the association between behavior type and cholesterol, then a t test is somewhat complicated (ratios do not often have simple distributions), but a permutation test follows the same pattern. Instead of a sample of random differences, a series of random ratios is constructed, and the observed ratio of $\bar{y}_A/\bar{y}_B$ is evaluated against this series (e.g., the number random ratios that exceed the observed ratio estimates a one-sided p-value). The simplicity and the general applicability of the permutation test makes the approach an important analytic tool.

Time-Space: Permutation Test

A permutation test is well suited to investigate possible patterns of disease in time and space. Since most measures of clustering are statistically complex, a repeated sampling scheme avoids difficult mathematical issues and, at the same time, produces a rigorous evaluation of the degree of time–space clustering found in a data set.

Parallel to the t test illustration, the hypothesis of no clustering is equivalent to postulating that the time–distance pairs are formed at random. A total of $N = n(n-1)/2$ observed pairs occur, where each pair contains a time and a distance measurement. There are $N!$ possible sets or permutations of time–distance "data," which are the basis for describing probabilities under the null hypothesis since each set is equally likely when no time–space association exists. For samples of seven or more pairs, complete enumeration of all possible $N!$ sets of time–distance "data" is impractical, but again a computer can be programmed to select sets of random pairings. The repeated calculation of a statistical measure of clustering from these randomized sets of "data" forms an estimate of the null hypothesis generated distribution.

One effective measure of time—space clustering is

$$c = \sum_{i=1}^{N} (t_i - \bar{t})(d_i - \bar{d}), \tag{5.21}$$

where, as before, t_i is the unsigned difference in time and d_i is the distance between the location of two cases. The means, $\bar{t}$ and $\bar{d}$, reduce the magnitude of the product $t_i d_i$ for ease of computation. The value c is no more than a function of the correlation between time and distance [i.e., $c = S_t S_d r_{td}$, where r_{td} is the product-moment correlation coefficient between time and distance; see expression (2.10)]. The measure c is large when an excess of "close" time–distance pairs occurs. That is, a large value of c indicates a positive association between time and distance where a value in the neighborhood of zero indicates no association. The distribution of c, under the null hypothesis, is estimated by forming random sets of the N time–distance pairs and calculating a series of randomized values "c." The distribution of "c" (estimated null distribution) is then used to assign a significance probability to the $\hat{c}$ calculated from the observed data.

In 1981, chemical solvents were detected in the drinking water supplied to a portion of Santa Clara county, California. A likely source of this contamination was leakage from underground storage tanks connected with the electronics manufacturing industry. It was thought that this contamination might be associated with an increase in the number of cardiac defects among newborn infants. The data in Table 5.13 (adapted from Shaw [Ref. 11]) gives the time (months) and the location (geographic coordinates modified to protect confidentiality) of the occurrence of 48 cardiac defects among births during the years 1981, 1982, and 1983 for Santa Clara county.

These 48 observations produce $48(47)/2 = 1128$ time–distance pairs. The observed value $\hat{c}$ calculated from the 1,128 pairs is $\hat{c} = -1715.06$. To evaluate formally this observed measure of time–space clustering of cardiac defects cases a series of 5,000 samples of 1,128 randomly paired time–distance observations was computer generated. A value of "c" was calculated for each set, forming an estimated null distribution. Estimated percentiles from the computer generated null distribution are given in Table 5.14.

The mean of the null distribution is 11.8 with a median value of

Table 5–13. Time–space: Santa Clara data

Time t_i	Location x_i	y_i	Time t_i	Location x_i	y_i	Time t_i	Location x_i	y_i	Time t_i	Location x_i	y_i
1	156.20	31.43	1	154.25	31.37	2	157.99	30.74	3	157.28	29.07
3	159.55	27.02	1	161.20	31.60	5	162.07	28.65	6	162.26	26.45
2	156.60	29.45	6	156.55	31.68	6	161.75	27.26	6	162.98	27.45
2	158.96	28.84	6	170.14	16.62	6	161.73	29.26	2	159.12	30.75
2	161.77	25.48	4	163.34	29.53	2	160.44	26.97	2	157.90	29.96
4	159.94	27.95	4	162.03	32.30	4	161.78	29.56	4	168.23	21.31
4	156.48	28.35	6	160.67	27.89	4	170.72	17.40	6	159.83	28.03
6	155.85	31.44	2	159.47	29.77	6	168.28	21.30	8	164.29	25.96
12	157.64	30.98	27	163.30	28.69	3	162.93	29.59	12	161.68	26.42
12	162.65	29.14	36	157.69	31.05	33	153.59	31.79	27	157.94	29.92
30	163.10	29.81	6	161.43	33.40	9	162.05	30.33	24	162.10	31.24
2	159.34	28.18	30	165.17	28.01	18	163.32	28.36	24	161.54	26.30

Table 5–14. Estimated percentiles of the null distribution of c generated from the Santa Clara data

Percentile	1%	5%	10%	90%	95%	99%
Observed value	−3,336.3	−2,344.9	−1,803.9	1,851.9	2,375.2	3,409.7

−14.9, which indicates a symmetric distribution of values of "c" (see Figure 5.11). If all possible samples were used, then the null distribution would be perfectly symmetric with mean and median equal to zero. The number of null distribution values of "c" greater than the observed $\hat{c} = -1,715.06$ is 4,447, giving an estimated p-value of $4,447/5,000 = 0.889$. Therefore, a more extreme (greater) value of c than the one observed is estimated to occur with a frequency of about 90% when no time–space association exists. A further analysis of these data would utilize the location of the cases in relation to the contamination. For example, the previously suggested population density-equalized map could be employed (again, see [Ref. 11 or 12]).

To summarize, some advantages and disadvantages of a permutation test approach are:

Advantages: For a permutation test approach

1. No assumptions are necessary about the sampled population,
2. The process is conceptually simple even for complex measures of associations,

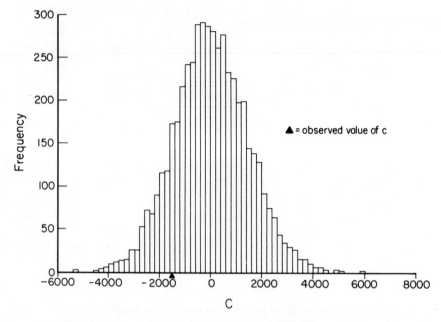

Figure 5–11. The histogram of the null distribution of "*c*."

3. Permutation tests apply to a wide range of analytic situations (*t* test, correlation analysis, analysis of variance, etc.), and
4. Permutation tests are valid for any sample size.

Disadvantages: If all possible permutations can not be enumerated, then

1. The results are not consistent—the test statistic depends on a series of random samples of observations, meaning that different analyses can produce differing *p*-values from the same set of data, and
2. The permutation test will require a special computer programs for most applications.

Jackknife Estimation: Distance

A permutation test usually requires a computer to provide a null distribution and statistical test. The jackknife estimation procedure is also designed to use a computer to produce an estimate and its variance. Estimating a quantity and at the same time evaluating its precision commonly involves the assumption that the population sampled has a particular structure. An assumption often made, for example, is that the sample of observations comes from a population with a normal distribution. Clearly data do not always come from populations with normal distributions or even symmetric distributions, which complicates the process of calculating a summary estimate. A distribution-free method called a jackknife estimate, because it is so handy, is one way to estimate a quantity and its variance for a wide range of situations. The payment for this flexibility is that the procedure generally requires computer implementation.

A jackknife estimate is calculated from a sample of n independent observations by creating a series of n truncated subsamples. Each subsample consists of $n - 1$ observations formed by deleting a different observation from the sample. The jackknife estimate and its variance are then calculated from these truncated subsamples.

If a summary statistic represented by θ is estimated by $\hat{\theta}$, then n estimates $\hat{\theta}_{(i)}$ are derived in the identical manner as the estimate $\hat{\theta}$, but with the ith value deleted from the sample. The mean of the $\hat{\theta}_{(i)}$ values is the jackknife estimate of θ or, in symbols,

$$\hat{\hat{\theta}} = \frac{\sum\limits_{i=1}^{n} \hat{\theta}_{(i)}}{n} \qquad (5.22)$$

and the variance of this estimate is estimated by

$$\text{variance } (\hat{\hat{\theta}}) = \frac{(n-1) \sum\limits_{i=1}^{n} (\hat{\theta}_{(i)} - \hat{\hat{\theta}})^2}{n}. \qquad (5.23)$$

Another feature of the jackknife estimate is that an estimate of bias, if any, is also available and given by the expression

$$\text{estimated bias} = (n-1)(\hat{\hat{\theta}} - \hat{\theta}), \qquad (5.24)$$

where $\hat{\theta}$ is the estimated quantity based on the complete set of n observations.

Consider the example of the mean and standard deviation of nine observations (2, 6, 10, 34, 66, 4, 8, 22, 45). The nine truncated subsamples are shown in Table 5.15.

The jackknife mean and its estimated variance are derived from the next to last column in Table 5.15 ($\bar{x}_{(i)}$). That is,

$$\bar{\bar{x}} = \frac{24.375 + \cdots + 19.000}{9} = 21.889, \qquad (5.25)$$

and the variance of this estimate is estimated by

$$\text{variance } (\bar{\bar{x}}) = \frac{8[(24.375 - 21.889)^2 + \cdots + (19.000 - 21.889)^2]}{9} = 54.568. \qquad (5.26)$$

Table 5–15. The nine subsamples used in the jackknife estimate of the mean and the standard deviation

Subsample	1	2	3	4	5	6	7	8	Sum	$\bar{x}_{(i)}$	$\hat{\sigma}_{(i)}$
1	6	10	34	66	4	8	22	45	195	24.375	22.309
2	2	10	34	66	4	8	22	45	191	23.875	22.818
3	2	6	34	66	4	8	22	45	187	23.375	23.207
4	2	6	10	66	4	8	22	45	163	20.375	23.188
5	2	6	10	34	4	8	22	45	131	16.375	15.767
6	2	6	10	34	66	8	22	45	193	24.125	22.580
7	2	6	10	34	66	4	22	45	189	23.625	23.026
8	2	6	10	34	66	4	8	45	175	21.875	23.691
9	2	6	10	34	66	4	8	22	152	19.000	21.804

The estimates of the mean and variance in this simple situation are the same as the usual estimates of mean and variance (i.e., $\bar{x} = \Sigma x_i/n = 21.889$ and variance $(\bar{x}) = \Sigma (x_i - \bar{x})^2/[n(n-1)] = 54.568$). Therefore, the estimated bias will always be zero [i.e., $(n-1)(\bar{\bar{x}} - \bar{x}) = 0.0$].

The jackknife estimate of the standard deviation, using the last column of Table 5.15 $(\hat{\sigma}_{(i)})$, follows the same pattern:

$$\hat{\hat{\sigma}} = \frac{22.309 + \cdots + 21.804}{9} = 22.043, \qquad (5.27)$$

and the variance of this estimate is estimated by

$$\text{variance } (\hat{\hat{\sigma}}) = \frac{8[(22.309 - 22.043)^2 + \cdots + (21.804 - 22.043)^2]}{9} = 41.578.$$

$$(5.28)$$

The usual estimate of a standard deviation is easily calculated from the nine observations $(\hat{\sigma} = \sqrt{\Sigma (x_i - \bar{x})^2/(n-1)} = 22.161)$, but estimates of the variance and the bias of this estimate are not as simple. However, an estimate of the variance for the jackknife-estimated standard deviation is easily calculated (41.578), and, additionally, an estimate of the bias is $8(22.043 - 22.161) = -0.941$. Jackknife estimation applies in the same manner to many situations where expressions for an estimate and its variance are either complicated or unknown.

Applied Illustration

A map showing incidence cases of oral/pharyngeal cancer in Contra Costa county, California suggests the possibility that the spatial distribution is more clustered among females than males (Figure 5.12).

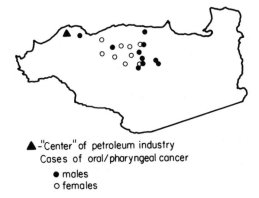

▲-"Center" of petroleum industry
Cases of oral/pharyngeal cancer
● males
o females

Figure 5–12. Oral/pharyngeal cancer incidence cases among white males and females ages 35 to 55 for Contra Costa county, California (1978–81).

The data in terms of the longitude and latitude coordinates of the observed cases are given in Table 5.16.

Several investigators have noted (e.g., [Refs. 13 and 14]) an excess of lung cancer that might be associated with the oil refining industry located in the northern part of Contra Costa county. Suppose for simplicity that the concentration of refining activity is located at a specific point (longitude $x_0 = 122.3$ and latitude $y_0 = 38.1$; see Figure 5.12). The distance from the point (x_0, y_0) to each case of oral/pharyngeal cancer can be calculated (symbolized by d_i). Mantel [Ref. 10] suggests that the sensitivity to detect clusters of observations is increased by measuring the reciprocal of distance $(1/d_i)$ rather than

Table 5–16. Longitude and latitude location of oral/pharyngeal cancer cases in Contra Costa county (1978–81) among individuals ages 35 to 54

	Females		Males	
i	Longitude	Latitude	Longitude	Latitude
1	121.91	38.15	121.60	38.02
2	121.90	37.88	121.25	38.20
3	122.05	37.93	122.01	37.95
4	122.10	37.95	122.04	37.91
5	122.00	37.85	122.05	37.88
6	122.15	37.88	122.08	37.98
7	122.12	37.80	122.01	37.81
8	122.25	37.78	122.11	38.15
9	122.20	37.95	122.32	37.83
10	—	—	122.31	37.84

Table 5–17. Harmonic mean distances $\bar{h}_{(i)}$ in kilometers

Deleted	1	2	3	4	5	6	7	8	9	10
Female	29.339	28.722	29.936	30.722	28.997	30.061	29.076	29.147	32.137	—
Male	29.694	29.164	31.458	31.361	31.161	32.590	30.503	34.462	31.425	31.570

using distance (d_i) directly. The transformation $1/d_i$ is a simple function of distance, which emphasizes the short distances observed in the data set. Following this suggestion, the distance from the "source" of pollution to a cancer case can be examined for both males and females with a harmonic mean. A harmonic mean is defined as

$$\bar{h} = \frac{1}{\dfrac{1}{n}\sum_{i=1}^{n}\dfrac{1}{d_i}},\qquad (5.29)$$

where n is the number of cases ($n = 9$ for females and $n = 10$ for males). A complicated expression such as the harmonic mean $\bar{h}$ is easily evaluated with a jackknife estimate, since its accompanying variance is readily calculated. Each truncated sample using the data from Table 5.16 produces an estimated harmonic mean $\bar{h}_{(i)}$ based on deleting the ith longitude—latitude pair from the n observations, giving Table 5.17.

Using the series of the $\bar{h}_{(i)}$ values to calculate the jackknife-estimated harmonic mean and the jackknife variance allows an approximate 95% confidence interval to be constructed for each sex. The summary statistics are displayed in the Table 5.18.

Comparison of the jackknife estimates ($\bar{h}$ values) shows a smaller mean distance for female cases compared to males. The variability associated with these estimates, however, is considerable, and, since the confidence intervals almost completely overlap, no strong statistical

Table 5–18. Summary statistics from the jack-knife estimates

Statistic	Female	Male
Sample size	9	10
Mean $(\bar{h})$	29.793	31.339
Variance $(\bar{h})$	8.327	17.604
SE $(\bar{h})$	2.886	4.195
Bias	−0.269	−0.548
Upper limit (95%)	35.450	39.562
Lower limit (95%)	24.136	23.116

evidence exists that the proximity to the center of the oil refining industry has differing effects on the spatial patterns of risk for oral/pharyngeal cancer between females and males for the age group 35—54.

Jackknife estimation and permutation tests are two examples of a class of modern computer-intensive statistical techniques that have two fundamental features. They free the user from employing sometimes unverifiable assumptions, but, more importantly, these techniques work for many complex statistical measures and not just the handful of measures employed the past. Most applied statistical methods in use today were developed before 1950, when computation was done almost exclusively by hand. Mathematically tractable approaches are no longer necessary, since mathematical tractability has been replaced by high-speed electronic computation, which continues to become less expensive and easier to apply. Thus computer-intensive approaches allow the user to explore complicated issues with methods dictated by epidemiology, unrestricted by traditional methods and measures. More extensive descriptions of computer-intensive methods are found in Refs. [15] and [16].

6 The Two × K Table and Two × Two × Two Table

The 2 × *K* contingency table

A basic tool of an epidemiologic investigation is the 2 × 2 table. Practically all epidemiologic data can be classified by the presence or absence of a disease and by two levels of a risk factor forming a 2 × 2 table. A number of texts fully develop the analysis and interpretation of data classified in a 2 × 2 table (e.g., [Refs. 1, 2, and 3]). An important extension is the 2 × *K* table where the presence or absence of a disease is recorded at *k* levels of a risk factor. The 2 × *K* contingency table can be viewed from the perspective of a *k*-level variable (risk factor) or from the perspective of a binary variable (disease)—in other words, a regression or two-sample approach. In terms of analytic questions these perspectives are:

1. Regression: What is the relationship between a *k*-level risk factor variable and a binary disease outcome variable?
2. Two-sample: Does the mean level of the risk factor differ between two disease outcome groups?

These two questions generate rather different analytic techniques but, as will be seen, produce the same statistical test. Ridit analysis is another technique for analyzing a 2 × *K* table. All three methods are "distribution-free" in that no knowledge or assumptions about the distribution that generates the data are required.

Data on coffee consumption and pancreatic cancer [Ref. 4] provide a concrete example for the discussion of a 2 × *K* table. Individuals ($n = 523$) were classified as cases ($Y = 0$; row 1) or controls ($Y = 1$; row 2) and by consumption of 0, 1, 2, and 3 or more cups of coffee per day ($X = j, j = 0, 1, 2,$ or 3; columns). For simplicity, three or more cups per day were scored as 3. The data are (also given in Figure 6.1) shown in Table 6.1.

The analysis of a 2 × *K* table will be addressed from three points of view. First, a general technique to evaluate the hypothesis of independence or homogeneity is described (Is coffee drinking related in any way to pancreatic cancer?). Second, the relationship between a

2 by K table: data

	X=0	X=1	X=2	X=3	total
Y=0	9	94	53	60	216
Y=1	32	119	74	82	307
total	41	213	127	142	523

Independence and homogeneity 2 by K table: notation n_{ij}

	X=1	X=2	X=3	X=4				X=k	total
Y=0	n_{11}	n_{12}	n_{13}	n_{14}	·	·	·	n_{1k}	$n_{1.}$
Y=1	n_{21}	n_{22}	n_{23}	n_{24}	·	·	·	n_{2k}	$n_{2.}$
total	$n_{.1}$	$n_{.2}$	$n_{.3}$	$n_{.4}$	·	·	·	$n_{.k}$	n

2 by K table: notation p_{ij}

	X=1	X=2	X=3	X=4				X=k	total
Y=0	p_{11}	p_{12}	p_{13}	p_{14}	·	·	·	p_{1k}	$p_{1.}$
Y=1	p_{21}	p_{22}	p_{23}	p_{24}	·	·	·	p_{2k}	$p_{2.}$
total	$p_{.1}$	$p_{.2}$	$p_{.3}$	$p_{.4}$	·	·	·	$p_{.k}$	1.0

2 by K table: null hypothesis generated values

	X=1	X=2	X=3	X=4				X=k	total
Y=0	$np_{1.}p_{.1}$	$np_{1.}p_{.2}$	$np_{1.}p_{.3.}$	$np_{1.}p_{.4}$	·	·	·	$np_{1.}p_{.k}$	$np_{1.}$
Y=1	$np_{2.}p_{.1}$	$np_{2.}p_{.2}$	$np_{2.}p_{.3.}$	$np_{2.}p_{.4}$	·	·	·	$np_{2.}p_{.k}$	$np_{2.}$
total	$np_{.1}$	$np_{.2}$	$np_{.3}$	$np_{.4}$	·	·	·	$np_{.k}$	n

2 by K table: expected values under the hypothesis of independence

	X=0	X=1	X=2	X=3	total
Y=0	16.93	87.97	52.45	58.65	216
Y=1	24.07	125.03	74.55	83.35	307
total	41	213	127	142	523

Figure 6–1. Notation for a 2 × *K* table.

Table 6-1. Pancreatic cancer and coffee consumption

X	0	1	2	3	Total
$Y = 0$	9	94	53	60	216
$Y = 1$	32	119	74	82	307
Total	41	213	127	142	523

Table 6–2. Notation n_{ij}

X	1	2	3	4		k	Total
$Y = 0$	n_{11}	n_{12}	n_{13}	n_{14}	$\cdots$	n_{1k}	$n_{1.}$
$Y = 1$	n_{21}	n_{22}	n_{23}	n_{24}	$\cdots$	n_{2k}	$n_{2.}$
Total	$n_{.1}$	$n_{.2}$	$n_{.3}$	$n_{.4}$	$\cdots$	$n_{.k}$	n

numeric or coded variable and the binary outcome is explored (Does pancreatic cancer risk increase as coffee consumption increases?). Last, the mean values of the numeric variable are compared for the two outcomes (Does the amount of coffee consumed differ between cases and noncases of pancreatic cancer?).

Independence and Homogeneity

A $2 \times K$ contingency table is represented in general notation (also given in Figure 6.1) in Table 6.2. The symbol n_{ij} represents the count of observations falling into the ith row and the jth column (e.g., cell frequency $n_{23} = 74$ for the pancreatic cancer data). The marginal frequencies (sums of the columns or the rows) are represented as $n_{.j}$ and $n_{i.}$. More precisely,

$$n_{.j} = n_{1j} + n_{2j} \quad \text{and} \quad n_{i.} = n_{i1} + n_{i2} + \cdots + n_{ik} = \sum_{j=1}^{k} n_{ij}. \quad (6.1)$$

Underlying a $2 \times K$ contingency table are several sets of probabilities: the probabilities that an observation falls in a specific cell (p_{ij}), the probabilities that $X = j$ ($p_{.j}$, column $= j$), the probability that $Y = 0$ ($p_{1.}$, row $= 1$), and the probability that $Y = 1$ ($p_{2.}$, row $= 2$). In tabular form these probabilities are shown in Table 6.3. Note that n_{ij} represents an observed quantity while p_{ij} represents an unobserved population (theoretical) probability.

The most basic question asked about data classified into a $2 \times K$

Table 6–3. Notation p_{ij}

X	1	2	3	4		k	Total
$Y = 0$	p_{11}	p_{12}	p_{13}	p_{14}	$\cdots$	p_{1k}	$p_{1.}$
$Y = 1$	p_{21}	p_{22}	p_{23}	p_{24}	$\cdots$	p_{2k}	$p_{2.}$
Total	$p_{.1}$	$p_{.2}$	$p_{.3}$	$p_{.4}$	$\cdots$	$p_{.k}$	1.0

contingency table concerns the statistical independence of the row variable (Y) and the column variable (X). If X and Y are independent, then the cell probabilities in the table are completely determined by the marginal probabilities. That is, X has no influence on Y and vice versa, implying that there is no reason to display the data in a two-way table. If variables represented by X and Y are independent, then the probability that $Y = 0$ and $X = j$ simultaneously is $p_1.p_{.j}$ and similarly, $P(Y = 1$ and $X = j) = p_2.p_{.j}$. Under the hypothesis of independence, the cell probabilities based on the marginal probabilities become those given in Table 6.4, where the expected number of observations in the ith, jth cell is $np_{i.}p_{.j}$.

Since the cell probabilities (p_{ij}) are theoretical quantities (population parameters), estimates of these values are almost always derived from the collected data. This is accomplished under the hypothesis of independence since the estimates for p_{ij} are then based on the marginal frequencies, where

$$\hat{p}_{i.} = \frac{n_{i.}}{n} \quad \text{and} \quad \hat{p}_{.j} = \frac{n_{.j}}{n}, \quad \text{giving } \hat{p}_{ij} = \hat{p}_{i.}\hat{p}_{.j}. \tag{6.2}$$

The estimated cell frequency is then $\hat{n}_{ij} = n\hat{p}_{ij} = n\hat{p}_{i.}\hat{p}_{.j}$, which is more succinctly written as $\hat{n}_{ij} = n_{i.}n_{.j}/n$. These estimates are typically calculated for each cell and compared to the observed values using a χ^2 statistic to assess the likelihood that variables X and Y are independent. For the pancreatic cancer data the estimated cell frequencies $(\hat{n}_{ij})$ generated under the hypothesis of independence are given in Table 6.5.

A χ^2 test statistic summarizes the fit of the estimated values to the observed data. Specifically,

$$X^2 = \sum_{i=1}^{2} \sum_{j=1}^{k} \frac{(n_{ij} - \hat{n}_{ij})^2}{\hat{n}_{ij}} = \sum_{i=1}^{2} \sum_{j=1}^{k} \frac{(n_{ij} - n_{i.}n_{.j}/n)^2}{n_{i.}n_{.j}/n} = 7.100. \tag{6.3}$$

The value of X^2 has an approximate χ^2 distribution with $k - 1$ degrees of freedom when applied to independent variables classified into a $2 \times K$ contingency table. For the cancer–coffee data the degrees of

Table 6–4. Values generated under the hypothesis of independence

X	1	2	3	4		k	Total
$Y = 0$	$np_1.p_{.1}$	$np_1.p_{.2}$	$np_1.p_3.$	$np_1.p_{.4}$	$\cdots$	$np_1.p_{.k}$	$np_1.$
$Y = 1$	$np_2.p_{.1}$	$np_2.p_{.2}$	$np_2.p_3.$	$np_2.p_{.4}$	$\cdots$	$np_2.p_{.k}$	$np_2.$
Total	$np_{.1}$	$np_{.2}$	$np_{.3}$	$np_{.4}$	$\cdots$	$np_{.k}$	n

freedom are three and the significance probability (p-value) is 0.069. The estimated values generated under the hypothesis that the amount of coffee consumed and pancreatic cancer risk are unrelated do not reflect the observed data extremely well (Table 6.5 versus Table 6.1), which supports the inference that some sort of systematic relationship exists between the risk factor and disease.

Sometimes data classified into a $2 \times K$ table are assessed for homogeneity. The basic issue is the consistency of the probabilities p_j, where p_j is the probability that $Y = 0$ for a specific value of X or $p_j = P(Y = 0 | X = j)$. A null hypothesis is imposed stating that the data come from a series of populations where the probabilities p_j are the same regardless of the level of X and, therefore, the estimates $\hat{p}_j$ differ only because of random variation, or

Homogeneity hypothesis—$H_0: p_1 = p_2 = p_3 = \cdots = p_k = p.$

To evaluate H_0 the common value p is estimated from the data ($\hat{p} = n_1./n$) and compared to each p_j, also estimated from the data ($\hat{p}_j = n_{1j}/n_{.j}$). Again a χ^2 statistic is used to assess the deviations of the estimated probabilities ($\hat{p}_j$) from the single overall estimated probability ($\hat{p}$) generated under the hypothesis of homogeneity. That is,

$$X^2 = \sum_{j=1}^{k} \frac{(\hat{p}_j - \hat{p})^2}{\text{variance}(\hat{p}_j)} = \frac{\sum_{j=1}^{k} n_{.j}(\hat{p}_j - \hat{p})^2}{\hat{p}(1 - \hat{p})} \tag{6.4}$$

has an approximate χ^2 distribution with $k - 1$ degrees of freedom when the null hypothesis is true. For the pancreatic cancer data $X^2 = 7.100$. It is not coincidental that the χ^2 value for independence and the χ^2 value for homogeneity are identical. A little algebra shows that the test for homogeneity and the test for independence produce the same χ^2 statistic. If p_j is constant for all levels of X, then the variable Y is not influenced by the variable X, which is another way of saying that X and Y are independent.

Table 6–5. Expected values under the hypothesis of independence

X	0	1	2	3	Total
$Y = 0$	16.93	87.97	52.45	58.65	216
$Y = 1$	24.07	125.03	74.55	83.35	307
Total	41.00	213.00	127.00	142.00	523

Regression

When the categorical variable represented as X is an ordered numeric variable, a regression approach more sensitively identifies any linear association between X and Y in a 2 × K contingency table. The previous χ^2 analysis of independence [expression (6.3)] does not require the X-values to be numeric, or even ordered, and applies to most 2 × K tables. However, considerable gains (increased power) are achieved by forming and testing specific hypotheses about the data. One such opportunity occurs when the X-variable is numeric or characterized by meaningful numeric values. In this setting, a 2 × K contingency table can be viewed as a set of k pairs of values. One proportion is generated for each value of X, producing k pairs $(x_j, \hat{p}_j)$. For example, the pancreatic cancer data yield the four pairs of values $(0, 0.220)$, $(1, 0.441)$, $(2, 0.417)$, and $(3, 0.423)$ (See Figure 6.2), where $\hat{p}_j$ is the proportion of cases for each amount of coffee consumed (x_j).

One approach to analyzing these k pairs of values is to fit a straight line to the $\hat{p}_j$ values and use the slope of the estimated line as a summary of the relationship between X and Y. Analogous to simple linear regression applied to continuous variables, three quantities are necessary to derive the basic statistical measures: the sum of squares for X (S_{xx}), the sum of squares for Y (S_{yy}), and the sum of cross-products for X and Y (S_{xy}). These expressions calculated from a 2 × K contingency table are:

$$S_{xx} = \sum_{j=1}^{k} n_{.j}(x_j - \bar{x})^2, \qquad \text{where } \bar{x} = \sum_{j=1}^{k} n_{.j}x_j/n, \qquad (6.5)$$

$$S_{yy} = n_{1.}n_{2.}/n, \qquad \text{and} \qquad (6.6)$$

$$S_{xy} = (\bar{x}_2 - \bar{x}_1)S_{yy}, \qquad \text{where } \bar{x}_i = \sum_{j=1}^{k} n_{ij}x_j/n_i. \qquad (6.7)$$

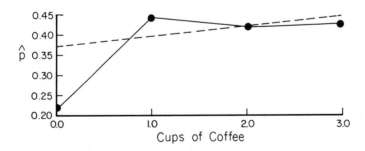

Figure 6–2. Proportion of cases of prostatic cancer for 0, 1, 2, and 3 cups of coffee consumed per day.

The same sums of squares are used in standard simple linear regression, but these expressions simplify somewhat due to the simpler structure of the data (i.e., Y takes on only two values, and there are only k different X values). The values for the pancreatic cancer data are: $S_{xx} = 474.241$, $S_{yy} = 126.792$, and $S_{xy} = 11.189$. Also the quantity $\bar{x}_1$ is the mean for the X values for which $Y = 0$ based on n_1 values (row 1) and $\bar{x}_2$ is the mean of the X values for which $Y = 1$ based on n_2 observations (row 2) with $n = n_1 + n_2$ total observations. It is not necessary to consider the data in terms of a $2 \times K$ contingency table. The means and the sums of squares are the same when the data are viewed as n pairs of values (x_i, y_j), where the cell frequencies are the numbers of identical pairs.

The estimated slope of the line summarizing the observed proportions, analogous to the case of simple linear regression, is given by

$$\hat{b}_{y|x} = \frac{S_{xy}}{S_{xx}}, \tag{6.8}$$

and an estimate of the variance of the estimated regression coefficient (the estimated slope) $\hat{b}_{y|x}$ is

$$\text{variance}(\hat{b}_{y|x}) = \frac{S_{yy}}{(n-1)S_{xx}}. \tag{6.9}$$

To evaluate the magnitude of the estimated slope, a χ^2 criterion is typically used. The ratio of the squared slope to its variance has an approximate χ^2 distribution with one degree of freedom when a linear function of X is unrelated to p_i. In other words, for the null hypothesis $b_{y|x} = 0$, the test statistic

$$X_L^2 = \frac{\hat{b}_{y|x}^2}{\text{variance}(\hat{b}_{y|x})} \qquad \text{(L for linear—see appendix)} \tag{6.10}$$

has an approximate χ^2 distribution with one degree of freedom. These quantities for the pancreatic cancer data are: $\hat{b}_{y|x} = 0.0236$ and variance$(\hat{b}_{y|x}) = 0.000512$, giving a χ^2 value $X_L^2 = 1.087$ (p-value $= 0.297$). No strong evidence exists that coffee consumption has a linear dose–response relationship with the proportion of cases of pancreatic cancer (see Figure 6.2).

A further refinement of this regression approach is achieved by dividing the total χ^2 statistic X^2 [expression (6.3) or (6.4)] into two parts:

1. Linear $= X_L^2$ has an approximate χ^2 distribution with 1 degree of freedom;

2. Nonlinear $= X_{NL}^2 = X^2 - X_L^2$ (NL for nonlinear) has an approximate χ^2 distribution with $k - 2$ degrees of freedom;

and, clearly, $X_{NL}^2 + X_L^2 = X^2$. The quantity X_{NL}^2 measures the lack of linearity in the relationship between X and p_i. Large values of X_{NL}^2 indicate a possible nonlinear association. The partitioning of a χ^2 statistic into two meaningful pieces is developed more rigorously in the appendix.

For the pancreatic cancer data the previous X^2 value is 7.100 and the linear component is $X_L^2 = 1.087$ (p-value $= 0.297$) giving the nonlinear component as $X_{NL}^2 = 7.100 - 1.087 = 6.013$ (p value $= 0.049$). This moderately large nonlinear χ^2 value (of borderline significance at the 5% level) suggests a nonlinear relationship between cancer risk and the consumption of coffee (note a potential thresholdlike effect of coffee consumption in Figure 6.2). A summary of this χ^2 analysis is given in Table 6.6.

It is possible that the test of the total χ^2 value (X^2) is not significant while the test for linearity (X_L^2) indicates a linear relationship. This apparent contradiction occurs because the total χ^2 test is not extremely powerful and can fail to show heterogeneity of response among the levels of X. A failure to reject this null hypothesis does not mean that X and Y are unrelated, and a more powerful approach, such as a test for linearity, may detect a specific relationship.

Two additional properties of a regression approach are worth noting. First, for regression analysis with the roles of X and Y reversed, the estimated slope and estimated variance of the slope will be different from the previous values, expressions (6.8) and (6.9). However, the χ^2 statistic is the same. That is, with the roles of X and Y reversed, the linear χ^2 statistic remains unchanged;

$$X_L^2 = \frac{\hat{b}_{x|y}^2}{\text{variance}(\hat{b}_{x|y})}. \tag{6.11}$$

From the illustrative data $\hat{b}_{x|y} = 0.088$ and variance$(\hat{b}_{x|y}) = 0.00717$, but $X_L^2 = 1.087$ is identical.

Table 6–6. Summary of partitioned χ^2

	χ^2	Degrees of freedom	p-value
X_L^2	1.087	1	0.291
X_{NL}^2	6.013	2	0.049
X^2	7.100	3	0.069

Second, a correlation coefficient measuring the degree of linear association between X and Y calculated in the usual way is

$$r_{xy} = \frac{S_{xy}}{\sqrt{S_{xx}S_{yy}}} \qquad (6.12)$$

based on all n pairs of observations [expression (2.10)]. This point biserial correlation coefficient r_{xy} is a number between -1 and $+1$ that expresses the degree of linear association between X and Y. The correlation between the case-control status and coffee consumption is $r_{xy} = 0.046$. One would expect the correlation coefficient to relate to the test of significance of $\hat{b}_{y|x}$, which also measures the degree of linear association between X and Y. The exact relationship between the two measures is $X_L^2 = (n-1)r_{xy}^2$.

The statistical measure r_{xy} summarizes the association between X and Y by a standardized value. The test statistic X_L^2 reflects the regression coefficient in terms of a probability calculated under specific conditions. These two approaches are complimentary. The measure of association assesses the strength of a relationship, while a statistical test gives an idea of the likelihood that such an association occurs by chance. The t test and the point biserial correlation coefficient have an analogous relationship for the continuous case, as noted earlier [expression (2.11)].

A primary goal of analyzing a $2 \times K$ table for trend is to evaluate a dose–response relationship. When risk increases steadily as the dose increases, strong evidence is produced of a direct relationship, even a causal relationship, between a dose variable and an outcome. When risk more or less smoothly increases with increasing dose, it is less plausible that the association results from bias or artifact and more likely that the observed relationship between risk factor and outcome is "real." The example of coffee consumption and pancreatic cancer shows a threshold response. This relationship is less easy to justify from a biological perspective. Threshold situations, like the one illustrated by the coffee-drinking data, can be indications of bias, particularly bias from some confounding variable.

Two-Sample: Comparison of Two Means

Another logical way to address the question of a relationship between a binary variable and a quantitative variable is the comparison of the mean values of the quantitative variable calculated at each of the two levels of the binary variable. This two-sample approach to a $2 \times K$ table is based on a t-test style comparison of the mean levels of X for the two values of Y. As before, the mean $\bar{x}_1$ is calculated for all values where

$Y = 0$, and $\bar{x}_2$ is calculated for all values where $Y = 1$. The obvious measure of the influence of Y is the difference between the two means, $(\bar{x}_2 - \bar{x}_1)$. In terms of the pancreatic cancer example, the mean level of coffee consumption among cases is $\bar{x}_1 = 1.759$ cups per day, and the mean level among the controls is $\bar{x}_2 = 1.671$. The natural question arises as to the importance of the observed difference and whether it indicates a nonrandom increase in coffee drinking among pancreatic cancer patients.

An estimate of the variance of the difference in the mean values is necessary for evaluating $\bar{x}_2 - \bar{x}_1$ and is calculated two ways (parallel to the t-test reviewed in Chapter 2). The first makes no assumptions about variance of the X values. The variance of each mean value is estimated by

$$\text{variance}(\bar{x}_i) = \frac{\sum_{j=1}^{k} n_{ij}(x_j - \bar{x}_i)^2}{n_{i.}(n_{i.} - 1)} \tag{6.13}$$

and the variance of $(\bar{x}_2 - \bar{x}_1)$ is $\text{variance}(\bar{x}_2) + \text{variance}(\bar{x}_1)$. This variance estimate is used, for example, to construct confidence intervals.

The second method is based on the conjecture or knowledge that the variances in each group are equal. The variance of the difference between two means is then

$$\text{variance}(\bar{x}_2 - \bar{x}_1) = V_p^2\left(\frac{1}{n_{2.}} + \frac{1}{n_{1.}}\right) \tag{6.14}$$

where V_p^2 is a pooled estimate of the variability of the X values and is estimated from the sum of squares of the X values by

$$V_p^2 = \frac{S_{xx}}{n - 1}. \tag{6.15}$$

A t-like statistical test of the difference between mean values is given by

$$z = \frac{\bar{x}_2 - \bar{x}_1}{\sqrt{\text{variance}(\bar{x}_2 - \bar{x}_1)}} = \frac{\bar{x}_2 - \bar{x}_1}{\sqrt{V_p^2\left(\frac{1}{n_{1.}} + \frac{1}{n_{2.}}\right)}} \tag{6.16}$$

where z has an approximate standard normal distribution (mean $= 0$ and variance $= 1$) when $\bar{x}_1$ and $\bar{x}_2$ differ only because of random variation. For the pancreatic cancer data, $\bar{x}_1 = 1.759$, $\bar{x}_2 = 1.671$ and variance $(\bar{x}_2 - \bar{x}_1) = 0.00717$, giving $z = -1.042$ with p-value $= 0.297$. Note that the value $z^2 = 1.087$ is identical to X_L^2 calculated previously; the regression approach and the comparison of two mean values lead to identical tests of significance in general (i.e., $X_L^2 = z^2$).

The point biserial correlation coefficient (r_{xy}), the regression coefficient ($\hat{b}_{y|x}$), and the mean difference ($\bar{x}_2 - \bar{x}_1$) are interrelated when calculated from a $2 \times K$ table. For example, each has an expected value of zero when the variables X and Y are unrelated. The three statistics measure the association between a risk factor and a disease in different ways but, in terms of probability, lead to the same inference.

In the discussion so far the coding of the X variable has been ignored. The determination of the values of X is important, and careful thought should be given to their determination. Some fields almost always use the logarithm of the dose as the measure of X. In yet other situations natural units arise, such as the number of cups of coffee consumed per day. In other cases, rather complicated polynomial expressions are used to determine the values of the "dose variable" [Ref. 5]. Even a series of zeros and ones can be employed to analyze a threshold response model. The analysis of a dose–outcome relationship will differ, sometimes considerably, depending on the choice of scale for the X values. This choice is essentially nonstatistical and rests primarily on subject-matter considerations. It should be noted, however, that when choices for the X values differ only by their measurement units (i.e., new $- X = aX + b$, where a and b are constants), then no changes occur in the χ^2 statistic or the p-value.

(Additional Example) Childhood cancer risk from prenatal x-ray exposure

The Oxford Survey of Childhood Cancer [Ref. 6] provides data on malignancies in children under 10 years of age and information on the mother's exposure to x-rays. The data in Table 6.7 (a small part of a large study containing data collected since 1953) show the numbers of prenatal x-rays received by mothers of children with a malignant disease and a series of controls (healthy children of the same age, sex, and similar areas of residence). The proportion of cases whose mothers were prenatally x-rayed 0, 1, 2, 3, 4, or 5^+ times (x_i) are 0.489, 0.546,

Table 6–7. Numbers of cases and controls by recorded number of x-ray films

Films	0	1	2	3	4	5^+	Unk	Total
Cases	7,332	287	199	96	59	65	475	8,513
Controls	7,673	239	154	65	28	29	325	8,513
Total	15,005	526	353	161	87	94	800	17,026
Proportion	0.489	0.546	0.564	0.596	0.678	0.691	—	—
Expected*	0.489	0.530	0.572	0.613	0.655	0.696	—	—

*Based on an estimated linear response.

0.564, 0.596, 0.678, and 0.691 ($\hat{p}_i$), respectively (Table 6.7 and shown in Figure 6.3).

The average number of x-rays received by mothers of cases is $\bar{x}_1 = 0.191$ and for the controls $\bar{x}_2 = 0.122$ (for simplicity, the value 5^+ was coded as 5 for these calculations). The test statistic

$$z = \frac{0.122 - 0.191}{\sqrt{0.415\left(\frac{1}{8188} + \frac{1}{8038}\right)}} = -6.805 \tag{6.17}$$

indicates that the difference between cases and controls in mean number of maternal x-ray exposures is not likely a result of chance variation (p-value < 0.001).

An additional assessment of the dose–response relationship is accomplished by partitioning the total χ^2 value. The χ^2 statistic that measures homogeneity (H_0: the proportion of cases is the same regardless of the degree of maternal exposure) is $X^2 = 47.286$. A χ^2 value of this magnitude indicates the presence of some sort of nonhomogeneous pattern of response in the data (p-value < 0.001). Postulating a linear response to x-ray exposure and fitting a straight line to the proportion of cases yields an estimated slope of $\hat{b}_{y|x} = 0.0415$ with an estimated standard deviation of 0.00609. The χ^2 test to evaluate the null hypothesis that $b_{y|x} = 0$ is

$$X_L^2 = \left(\frac{0.0415}{0.00609}\right)^2 = 46.311, \tag{6.18}$$

which produces the same result as the previous comparison of mean values ($z^2 = (-6.805)^2 = 46.311$). The striking feature of these data is the almost perfect linearity of the response. This property is formally assessed by partitioning the total χ^2 value into linear and nonlinear pieces ($X_{NL}^2 = X^2 - X_L^2 = 47.286 - 46.311 = 0.975$; p-value $= 0.914$).

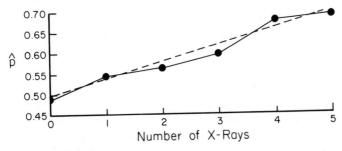

Figure 6–3. Proportion of cases of childhood cancer for exposure to 0, 1, 2, 3, 4, and 5 maternal x-rays during pregnancy.

Table 6–8. Summary of partitioned χ^2

	χ^2	Degrees of freedom	p-value
X_L^2	46.311	1	<0.001
X_{NL}^2	0.975	4	0.914
X^2	47.286	5	<0.00

The extremely small χ^2 value measuring nonlinearity verifies the impression of linearity of response clearly seen from the plotted data (Figure 6.3). A summary is given in Table 6.8. The linear response provides convincing evidence of strong risk from prenatal x-rays and the subsequent development of cancer in children.

Ridit Analysis

A χ^2 analysis applied to a $2 \times K$ table to investigate independence or homogeneity places no requirements on the k column values (X). To assess a dose–response relationship, the column variable must take on a sequence of increasing numeric values. An intermediate approach involves the analysis of a $2 \times K$ table, where the column variables are ordered but not necessarily numeric. For example, injuries from car accidents can be ordered as none, minor, moderate, severe, critical, and fatal without depending on a numeric value. The impact of such a variable is effectively explored with a statistical summary called a ridit. The rather strange name comes from using the initials "r" for relative, "i" of identified, and "d" for distribution along with "it" to resemble other terms in statistical use, such as logit or probit. Ridit analysis compares one group or a series of groups to a "baseline" distribution. The ridit was first presented by Bross in an analysis of car seat-belt safety [Ref. 7] but is not different from the well-known nonparametric Wilcoxon or Mann–Whitney procedures [Ref. 8 and 9]. A ridit analysis capitalizes on the fact that the columns in the $2 \times K$ table are ordered, producing a more powerful approach than a χ^2 test for independence but without the necessity of assigning specific numeric values to levels of X. Additionally, the ridit approach produces a probabilistic-based measure, reflecting the magnitude of the differences between compared groups.

A ridit is the estimated probability that a random individual from a comparison group is "to the right" of a person selected at random from a reference group. In terms of car accident injuries, if a ridit probability is large, a person is likely to be "worse off" and if the ridit is small, a person is likely to be "better off" than a random person selected from the reference group. If a ridit value is $\hat{P} = 0.25$, for example, the probability is 0.25 that a random individual from the comparison group has a more severe injury than a random individual from the reference group, inplying that the comparison group is "better off" than the reference group (less likely to be "to the right"). The magnitude of $\hat{P}$ reflects "how much" a specific sample differs from the reference group. A ridit probability of 0.5 implies that no difference exists between the two compared groups. It is equally likely that a random person from the comparison group has a value less or greater than a random person from the reference group—it makes no difference from which group the person is chosen. A ridit value greater than 0.5 implies that the comparison groups is "to the right," and a value less than 0.5 implies that the comparison groups is "to the left" of the reference group.

To estimate a ridit probability, the number of values in the reference group that are less than each value in the comparison group is counted. This number is related to $\hat{P} = P(X_{reference} < X_{comparison})$, where $X_{reference}$ is a random value selected from the reference group and $X_{comparison}$ is a random value selected from the comparison group. A simple example illustrates. Two sets of samples values are

$$\text{Comparison group: } 0, 4, 12, 24, 62$$

$$\text{Reference group: } 8, 32, 46, 81.$$

No value in reference group is less than 0, no value in the reference group is less than 4, one value in the reference group is less than 12, one value in the reference group is less than 24, and three values in the reference group are less than 62. These counts, symbolized by U_i, are summarized in Table 6.9.

The total count is 5 values in the reference group $(U = \Sigma U_i)$ less than each of the members of the comparison group or 5 of $(5)(4) = 20$

Table 6-9. U_i counts

i	8	32	46	81	U_i
0	0	0	0	0	0
4	0	0	0	0	0
12	1	0	0	0	1
24	1	0	0	0	1
62	1	1	1	0	3
U_i	3	1	1	0	5

possible paired comparisons. These values could also be counted as the number of times values in comparison group exceed values in the reference group; the answer is still 5. The ridit estimate is then $\hat{P} = 5/20$ or 0.25. The estimated probability that a random selection from the reference group is less than a random selection from the comparison group is 0.25. The comparison group is largely "to the left" of the reference group $(\hat{P} < 0.5)$. In general, a ridit probability is $\hat{P} = U/(n_1 n_2)$, where n_1 and n_2 are the respective group sizes. The process of determining a value of U is the basis of the Mann–Whitney nonparametric two-sample test [Ref. 8].

The same process applies to a $2 \times K$ table. A set of data from a 1975 health survey illustrates the application of a ridit analysis of a $2 \times K$ table. Surveyed individuals $(n = 165)$ were asked whether they thought that exercise increases life expectancy (reply: yes or no). The same individuals were also asked to report their exercise activities in terms of four categories (none, occasionally, regularly/moderate, and regularly/strenuous), producing Table 6.10.

In terms of the ridit analysis: Is a person selected at random from the "yes" group likely to exercise more than a person selected at random from the "no" group? The amount of exercise is considered an ordinal variable since it is unlikely that a more accurate measure of physical activity could be obtained with a questionnaire. For the ridit analysis of a $2 \times K$ table, it must be assumed that all individuals within the same column of the table, having the same values of X, do not differ. That is, the probability that one value is greater than another within each column is the same (i.e., 0.5) regardless of reference–comparison group status. Then, parallel to the previous example, the counts of the numbers of individuals in the reference group ("no" group) whose values are less than each member of the comparison group ("yes" group) leads to an estimate of the ridit probability.

In general, the estimated ridit from a $2 \times K$ table is expressed as

$$\hat{P} = \frac{\sum_{i=1}^{k} [n_{21} + n_{22} + n_{23} + \cdots + (n_{2i}/2)]n_{1i}}{n_1 . n_2 .} = \sum_{i=1}^{k} w_i \left(\frac{n_{1i}}{n_1 .}\right), \qquad (6.19)$$

Table 6–10. Life expectancy response by reported exercise activity

	None	Occasionally	Moderate	Strenuous	Total
Yes: $Y = 0$	7	7	8	20	42
No: $Y = 1$	25	34	32	32	123
Total	32	41	40	52	165

where $[n_{21} + n_{22} + n_{23} + \cdots + (n_{2i}/2)]$ is the number of individuals in the reference group whose values are less than each of the n_{1i} members of the comparison group ("to the left") and

$$w_i = \frac{[n_{21} + n_{22} + n_{23} + \cdots + (n_{2i}/2)]}{n_{2.}}. \tag{6.20}$$

The value w_i is the reference weight. If other groups are to be compared to the same reference group, the reference weights are the same and apply to any number of comparisons.

Specifically, for the survey data, the ridit calculation is shown in Table 6.11. The ridit $\hat{P} = \Sigma w_i(n_{1i}/n_{1.}) = 0.604$. The interpretation of this ridit probability is that a random person from the "yes" group is likely to exercise a greater amount than a random person from the "no" group. Notice, as expected, that the ridit weights applied to the reference group itself gives a ridit value of exactly 0.5 ($\Sigma w_i n_{2i}/n_{2.} = 0.5$).

Like all estimates, an estimate of the variance allows a statistical evaluation of an observed ridit $\hat{P}$. The estimated variance of an estimated ridit is

$$\text{variance}(\hat{P}) = \frac{1}{12n_{1.}} + \frac{1}{12n_{2.}}. \tag{6.21}$$

A test statistic is then

$$z = \frac{\hat{P} - 0.5}{\sqrt{\text{variance}(\hat{P})}}, \tag{6.22}$$

which has an approximate standard normal distribution when there is no difference between the comparison and the reference groups (H_0: $P = 0.5$). For the survey data,

$$z = \frac{0.604 - 0.5}{\sqrt{\dfrac{1}{12(42)} + \dfrac{1}{12(123)}}} = 2.020. \tag{6.23}$$

Table 6–11. Ridit for health survey data: Summary

	$n_{1i}/n_{1.}$	"Number to the left"	w_i	$w_i(n_{1i}/n_{1.})$
None	0.167	25/2	0.102	0.017
Occasionally	0.167	25 + 34/2	0.341	0.057
Moderate	0.190	25 + 34 + 32/2	0.610	0.116
Strenuous	0.476	25 + 34 + 32 + 32/2	0.870	0.414
Ridit	—	—	—	0.604

The ridit value of $\hat{P} = 0.604$ is unlikely to have arisen by chance (p-value = 0.043).

Comparison of several groups

An effective comparison of several groups is achieved by plotting a series of statistical summaries along with their confidence intervals. This graphic technique applies to ridit analysis as well as most situations where a number of summary values are compared. The end points of a confidence interval indicate a likely range of a summary value and are an informal way to assess differences among several groups or to compare results from a series of groups to a specific value. The confidence interval for a ridit is approximately

$$\hat{P} \pm 1.96\sqrt{\text{variance}(\hat{P})}. \qquad (6.24)$$

This confidence interval is the usual 95% interval derived under the assumption that $\hat{P}$ has at least an approximate normal distribution. The distribution of the $\hat{P}$ values is not normal, but an approximate confidence interval is still useful for the comparison of a series of ridit values [Ref. 7].

A data set consisting of counts of white women classified by age, smoking pattern, and socioeconomic status (adapted from [Ref. 9]) illustrates the use of ridits and confidence intervals as a way to compare a series of $2 \times K$ tables. These data are given in Table 6.12.

The "relative identified distribution" or reference group is arbitrarily chosen as nonsmokers, age 55 or older (column 1, Table 6.12). Using the previous expression (6.19) for $\hat{P}$ gives five ridit values, one for each comparison group. These ridit probabilities, along with their approximate 95% confidence intervals are given in Table 6.13.

Table 6–12. Numbers of white females by age, smoking pattern, and economic status (I = low)

	Nonsmoker		Past smoker		Present smoker	
Status	Age $\geqslant 55$	<55	Age $\geqslant 55$	<55	Age $\geqslant 55$	<55
I	37	9	2	1	15	14
II	129	77	6	10	22	84
III	41	38	3	3	12	44
IV	51	17	6	5	17	26
V	14	13	7	6	14	17
Total	272	154	24	25	80	185

Table 6–13. Ridit values for white females classified by age and smoking pattern

	Nonsmoker		Past smoker		Present smoker	
	Age ⩾ 55	< 55	Age ⩾ 55	< 55	Age ⩾ 55	< 55
Ridit	0.5	0.536	0.683	0.639	0.570	0.547
$\sqrt{\text{variance}}$	—	0.029	0.061	0.060	0.037	0.028
P_{lower}	—	0.479	0.562	0.521	0.498	0.493
P_{upper}	—	0.593	0.803	0.757	0.642	0.601

The ridits values and confidence intervals are plotted in Figure 6.4. The five comparison groups do not appear to differ from each other (confidence intervals overlap), but there is some evidence that two and perhaps four of the five groups differ from the reference group (*ridit* = P = 0.5). That is, several groups show statistical evidence that individuals from these groups are likely to have higher socioeconomic status than individuals from the older, nonsmoking reference group (confidence intervals do not contain 0.5 for two age groups and almost excluded 0.5 in two others). The most striking difference occurs for the

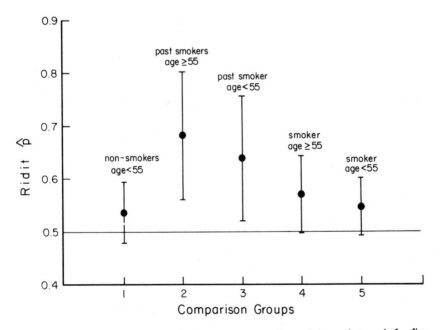

Figure 6–4. Ridit values and their approximate 95% confidence intervals for five smoking and age status comparison groups.

older, past smokers who have an estimated probability of $\hat{P} = 0.683$ of being in a higher socioeconomic class than a random member of the reference group.

THE 2 × 2 × 2 CONTINGENCY TABLE

Another important extension of the 2 × 2 table occurs when a third binary variable is added to the analysis to form a 2 × 2 × 2 table. Classification of three variables, each with two levels, into a 2 × 2 × 2 contingency table is the simplest possible case to study the analysis of an association between a disease and a risk factor in the presence and absence of another variable, often a confounding influence. Even this simplest case is somewhat complex. Each variable has two possibilities [disease (D)—no disease $(\bar{D})$, risk factor (F)—no risk factor $(\bar{F})$ and potential confounder present (C)—potential confounder absent $(\bar{C})$] producing eight combinations. The eight combinations reflect five different relationships among the three variables. These relationships have a variety of names, but will be referred to as:

1. Complete independence,
2. Partial independence,
3. Conditional independence,
4. No interaction, and
5. Interaction.

The following sections discuss these five relationships. Much of the development for the 2 × 2 × 2 table applies to three variables with any number of levels; furthermore, the principles discussed are important for understanding the analysis of categorical data in general. A multivariate logistic regression approach (next chapter) can also be applied to multidimensional categorical data. The 2 × 2 × 2 case, therefore, serves as a foundation to more general approaches.

Complete Independence

The frequency of the eight possible combinations of disease, risk factor, and a potential confounding variable, each represented by n_{ijk} (i = row, j = column, and k = identifier for each subtable), are displayed in Table 6.14.

If the variables measuring the disease, the risk factor, and the possible confounding influence are completely independent, then the expected counts are a function of the proportions of each of the

Table 6–14. Notation: Disease by risk factor by $C/\bar{C}$

	C			$\bar{C}$			Total		
	D	$\bar{D}$	Total	D	$\bar{D}$	Total	D	$\bar{D}$	Total
F	n_{111}	n_{121}	$n_{1.1}$	n_{112}	n_{122}	$n_{1.2}$	$n_{11.}$	$n_{12.}$	$n_{1..}$
$\bar{F}$	n_{211}	n_{221}	$n_{2.1}$	n_{212}	n_{222}	$n_{2.2}$	$n_{21.}$	$n_{22.}$	$n_{2..}$
Total	$n_{.11}$	$n_{.21}$	$n_{..1}$	$n_{.12}$	$n_{.22}$	$n_{..2}$	$n_{.1.}$	$n_{.2.}$	n

three variables in the sampled population. Table 6.15 contains a set of hypothetical data displaying three completely independent binary variables.

Each cell frequency is exactly determined by the marginal frequencies since the variables are completely independent. For example, the probability associated with the presence of the risk factor is estimated by P(factor present) $= n_{1..}/n = 100/1000$, the probability of the disease is given by P(disease present) $= n_{.1.}/n = 200/1000$, and the probability associated with the presence of the C variable is estimated by $P(C$ present) $= n_{..1}/n = 400/1000$. An estimate of the cell frequency n_{111} is the product of these probabilities multiplied by the total sample size, or specifically

$$\hat{n}_{111} = 1000 \left(\frac{100}{1000}\right)\left(\frac{200}{1000}\right)\left(\frac{400}{1000}\right) = 8. \tag{6.25}$$

The estimated value is identical to the observed value because these artificial data exhibit exact complete independence.

> Aside: An important and, perhaps, subtle issue should be noted. The P(disease) $= 0.2$, for example, does not imply that the chance of acquiring a disease is 2 out of 10 for each person in the population. Disease occurrence behaves in a far more complex fashion. One does not remain free of a disease or become ill by a simple random mechanism

Table 6–15. Complete independence: Disease by risk factor by $C/\bar{C}$

	C			$\bar{C}$			Total		
	D	$\bar{D}$	Total	D	$\bar{D}$	Total	D	$\bar{D}$	Total
F	8	32	40	12	48	60	20	80	100
$\bar{F}$	72	288	360	108	432	540	180	720	900
Total	80	320	400	120	480	600	200	800	1,000

analogous to flipping a biased coin $[P(\text{heads}) = 0.2 = P(\text{disease})]$. A useful interpretation of the phrase "probability of disease" is that, if 20% of the randomly sampled population has the disease, then the probability a sampled individual will have the disease is 0.2. The disease is present or absent (not subject to chance). Probability enters the picture because the data are a subset of the population and are subject to sampling variation, which can often be accurately described in terms of probabilities. Chance plays a role in the study of disease because of the nature of the sampling process and is, therefore, part of the foundation underlying the application of statistical models (analyses) to the study of disease–risk relationships.

In general, for three-variable table the estimated cell frequency under the hypothesis of complete independence is given by

$$\hat{n}_{ijk} = n \left(\frac{n_{i..}}{n}\right)\left(\frac{n_{.j.}}{n}\right)\left(\frac{n_{..k}}{n}\right). \tag{6.26}$$

The values estimated under the hypothesis of complete independence can be compared to the observed values with the usual χ^2 statistic

$$X^2 = \sum_{i=1}^{2} \sum_{j=1}^{2} \sum_{k=1}^{2} \frac{(n_{ijk} - \hat{n}_{ijk})^2}{\hat{n}_{ijk}} \tag{6.27}$$

to evaluate the conjecture of complete independence (an application follows at the end of the chapter; see Table 6.29). A consequence of complete independence is that a three-way table serves no useful purpose. All information from completely independent variables is contained in three separate binary classifications, which means that no new information is obtained by the study or analysis of the tabled frequencies. In the example, the $P(\text{disease})$ is 0.2 in all parts of the table, uninfluenced by either the presence or absence of the other two variables. No reason, therefore, exists to include the risk factor or the variable C in the study a disease when the three variables are completely independent.

Partial Independence

Partial independence occurs when a suspected confounding variable is unrelated (statistically independent) to both disease and risk factor, but an association exists between the disease and the risk factor. Hypothetical data that exhibit perfect partial independence are shown in Table 6.16.

Partial independence of the variable $C/\bar{C}$ means that the joint distribution of the risk factor and disease is the same at both levels of the

Table 6–16. Partial independence: Disease by risk factor by $C/\bar{C}$

	C			$\bar{C}$		
	D	$\bar{D}$	Total	D	$\bar{D}$	Total
F	45	60	105	255	340	595
$\bar{F}$	15	30	45	85	170	255
Total	60	90	150	340	510	850

C variable. When the potential confounder is not relevant to the relationship between the disease and the risk factor, the subtables formed for each level of the variable labeled C are simply multiples of the table formed by ignoring the variable C, aside from the influence of random variation. For the hypothetical data, summing over the two levels of the C variable gives the values in Table 6.17.

An estimate of the probability that the potential confounding variable is present (C), from Table 6.16, is $P(C \text{ present}) = P(C) = n_{..1}/n = 150/1000$. The estimated probability $P(\text{C})$ and the values in the summary Table 6.17 (the C variable ignored) generate the expected values for each cell in the $2 \times 2 \times 2$ table under the conjecture of partial independence. For example, the estimated frequency where all three variables are present (n_{111}) is

$$\hat{n}_{111} = 1000\left(\frac{300}{1000}\right)\left(\frac{150}{1000}\right) = 45. \tag{6.28}$$

Again, the fit is perfect for this artificial data since the variable represented by C is perfectly independent of both risk factor and disease.

In general, for a three-way table the estimated values under the conditions of partial independence of variable C are

$$\hat{n}_{ijk} = n\left(\frac{n_{ij.}}{n}\right)\left(\frac{n_{..k}}{n}\right). \tag{6.29}$$

Table 6–17. C variable ignored: Disease by risk factor

	D	$\bar{D}$	Total
F	300	400	700
$\bar{F}$	100	200	300
Total	400	600	1,000

As before, these estimated frequencies can be compared to those observed (n_{ijk} to $\hat{n}_{ijk}$) with a χ^2 statistic (again see Table 6.29). The inference drawn from evidence of partial independence is that the variable suspected of being a confounder is not a confounder and can be ignored without biasing the analysis of the risk-factor–disease relationship. That is, the table created by summing the data over the levels of the C variable accurately reflects the disease–risk relationship.

Conditional Independence

When a disease and a potential confounding variable are conditionally independent, the disease is unrelated (statistically independent) to the C variable at each level of the risk factor. In this case, the risk factor and disease as well as the risk factor and the suspected confounder are associated. A $2 \times 2 \times 2$ table displaying a set of hypothetical data that exhibit perfect conditional independence is shown in Table 6.18.

Rearranging these data shows directly that the disease and the variable labeled C are exactly independent in each of two C-variable–disease subtables (one where the risk factor is present and the other where the risk factor is absent). Specifically, see the values in Table 6.19.

Table 6–18. Conditional independence: Disease by risk factor by $C/\bar{C}$

	C			$\bar{C}$		
	D	$\bar{D}$	Total	D	$\bar{D}$	Total
F	30	120	150	10	40	50
$\bar{F}$	45	255	300	75	425	500
Total	75	375	450	85	465	550

Table 6–19. Conditional independence: Disease by risk factor by $C/\bar{C}$

	F			$\bar{F}$		
	C	$\bar{C}$	Total	C	$\bar{C}$	Total
D	30	10	40	45	75	120
$\bar{D}$	120	40	160	255	425	680
Total	150	50	200	300	500	800

For example, the estimated value of the cell frequency where all variables are present (n_{111}) is

$$\hat{n}_{111} = 200\left(\frac{40}{200}\right)\left(\frac{150}{200}\right) = 30, \tag{6.30}$$

which equals the observed value, since the data again are constructed to have exact conditional independence between the C variable and the disease.

In general, the estimated cell frequencies under the hypothesis of conditional independence of a disease and a third variable are

$$\hat{n}_{ijk} = n_{i..}\left(\frac{n_{ij.}}{n_{i..}}\right)\left(\frac{n_{i.k}}{n_{i..}}\right). \tag{6.31}$$

Parallel to the partial independence case, the table formed by summing over the potential confounder in the conditional independence case also does not disrupt the risk-factor–disease relationship. To illustrate, the table of conditionally independent values (Table 6.18) summed over the C variable gives Table 6.20, and the probability of disease with the factor present is the same for potential confounder present, absent, or ignored. That is, $P(\text{disease} | FC) = 30/150 = P(\text{disease} | F\bar{C}) = 10/50 = P(\text{disease} | F) = 40/200 = 0.2$, showing that the suspected confounder does not influence the calculation of the probability of disease. Consequently, measures of association relating the risk factor and disease will have identical expected values in both the subtables and the summary table $(C + \bar{C})$. Again the variable $C/\bar{C}$ is not a confounding influence on the risk–disease relationship.

For a 2 × 2 × 2 contingency table, complete independence, partial independence, and conditional independence with respect to a third variable $(C/\bar{C})$ imply that the variable can be ignored in the study of the risk factor and the disease. Under these conditions a three-variable analysis reduces to, at least, two variables (potential confounder eliminated) allowing a clearer and more powerful description of the disease–risk relationship.

Table 6–20. *C* variable ignored: Disease by risk factor

	D	$\bar{D}$	Total
F	40	160	200
$\bar{F}$	120	680	800
Total	160	840	1,000

Confounder Bias in a 2 × 2 × 2 Table

Factors influencing disease are also usually related to each other. The interrelationships among these variables have consequences in the assessment of a risk–disease association. One consequence is confounder bias. Similar to the previous definition, confounder bias is the distortion in the risk–disease relationship caused by ignoring one or more relevant variables. A variable must be related to the risk variable and also related to the disease outcome to have a confounding influence. It is often assumed that a confounding variable is a risk factor and, therefore, by definition related to the disease outcome. However, the exact way that a variable influences the disease outcome determines whether the variable is a confounder. The potential confounding variable must be related to the disease after adjustment for all other influences under investigation. That is, the confounding variable must have a direct and entirely separate association with the disease not measured by other risk variables. The case of conditional independence illustrates. The potential confounder and risk factor are associated; also the potential confounder and the disease are associated when the risk factor is ignored. But when the confounder–disease association is assessed at each level of the risk factor (i.e., adjusted for the risk factor influence), the association disappears. The variable labeled C is then seen to be related to the disease only because of its association with the risk factor (F) and is not related to the disease after adjustment and, therefore, is not a confounder.

The amount confounding bias is easily expressed by comparing two measures of the risk–disease association, one taking into account the confounding variable and the other with the confounding variable removed from consideration. The difference measures confounder bias. If this bias is small, then the confounding variable has little or no effect on the study of the disease in question and can be dropped from the analysis. When this bias is large, the confounding variable must be included in the analysis to produce unbiased estimates of the risk–disease association.

A simple case of confounder bias in a 2 × 2 × 2 table is illustrated by the hypothetical data in Table 6.21. If the confounder is ignored, then these data would appear in a summary (summed over the values of the confounder) 2 × 2 table as shown in Table 6.22.

A number of measures of association are available to reflect the risk–disease association and the amount of confounder bias will differ depending on the measure chosen. Here the odds ratio illustrates the influences of a confounding variable.

Table 6-21. Disease by risk factor by $C/\bar{C}$

	C			$\bar{C}$		
	D	$\bar{D}$	Total	D	$\bar{D}$	Total
F	10	10	20	40	20	60
$\bar{F}$	5	20	25	5	10	15
Total	15	30	45	45	30	75

Note that the odds ratios in Table 6.21 are equal in each subtable, when the confounder is present and when it is absent (odds ratios = 4). If a risk–disease association substantially differs in each subtable, then the issue of whether the potential confounding variable can be ignored is answered. Ignoring the variable will distort the risk–disease relationship regardless of whether the variable is a confounder or not, and no need exists to consider a summary table combining the two sets of data (subtable C and subtable $\bar{C}$).

The odds ratios taking into account the confounding variable are $\hat{or}_{FD|C} = \hat{or}_{FD|\bar{C}} = 4.0$ (separate sub-tables), and ignoring the confounding variable, the odds ratio is $\hat{or}_{FD} = 5.0$ (summary table). The confounder bias associated with the variable labeled C is then $(5.0 - 4.0) = 1.0$. In terms of the logarithm of the odds ratio, another often-used measure of association, the confounder bias is $\log(5) - \log(4) = 0.223$.

It is instructive to emphasize two situations for which a variable is not a confounding influence in a 2 × 2 × 2 table:

1. If a variable is unrelated to the risk factor at both levels of the disease, it will not confound the risk-factor–disease association, or
2. If a variable is unrelated to the disease at both levels of the risk factor, it will not confound the risk-factor–disease association.

Note that (1) and (2) are no more than statements of conditional independence (conditional independence of the risk factor and the C

Table 6-22. Disease by risk factor

	D	$\bar{D}$	Total
F	50	30	80
$\bar{F}$	10	30	40
Total	60	60	120

variable and conditional independence of the disease and the C variable). Whenever either of these conditions holds, the data are "combinable" with respect to the $C/\bar{C}$ variable, thus producing a more efficient, simpler, and unbiased description of the risk-factor–disease relationship when no interaction exists—the topic of the next section. The issue of when a variable is a nonconfounder is introduced here, and general considerations exist elsewhere, in Ref. [10] or [11]. More detail will be added to this concept in the context of logistic regression (the next two chapters).

Interaction

Interaction, in the context of a $2 \times 2 \times 2$ table, is the failure of a measure of association between disease and risk factor to be the same at both levels of the third variable. Hypothetical data with essentially no interaction as measured by an odds ratio are given in Table 6.23.

The odds ratio was chosen as the measure of association and $or_{FD|C} = or_{FD|\bar{C}} = 1.675$, showing the same value in both subtables, no interaction. Additionally, if no interaction between risk factor and disease exists, then the confounder–risk-factor and the confounder–disease subtables will also show no interaction. Specifically, for the odds ratio,

if $or_{FD|C} = or_{FD|\bar{C}},$ then $or_{FC|D} = or_{FC|\bar{D}}$ and $or_{CD|F} = or_{CD|\bar{F}}.$ (6.32)

A useful view of interaction comes from calculating a value δ where $+\delta$ or $-\delta$ is added to each data value in a $2 \times 2 \times 2$ table so that the marginal frequencies are unchanged, explicitly shown in Table 6.24. A value of δ can be determined so that no interaction exists and, thereby, becomes a measure of the magnitude of the interaction. If $\delta = 0$, then no interaction is present (which is the case for the hypothetical data in Table 6.23). The degree to which δ differs from zero measures the amount of interaction in a $2 \times 2 \times 2$ table.

Table 6–23. No interaction: Disease by risk factor by confounder

	C			$\bar{C}$		
	D	$\bar{D}$	Total	D	$\bar{D}$	Total
F	69	68	137	107	109	216
$\bar{F}$	91	150	241	150	256	406
Total	160	218	378	257	365	622

Table 6–24. Role of δ: Disease by risk factor by confounder

	C			$\bar{C}$		
	D	$\bar{D}$	Total	D	$\bar{D}$	Total
F	$n_{111}+\delta$	$n_{121}-\delta$	$n_{1.1}$	$n_{112}-\delta$	$n_{122}+\delta$	$n_{1.2}$
$\bar{F}$	$n_{211}-\delta$	$n_{221}+\delta$	$n_{2.1}$	$n_{212}+\delta$	$n_{222}-\delta$	$n_{2.2}$
Total	$n_{.11}$	$n_{.21}$	$n_{..1}$	$n_{.12}$	$n_{.22}$	$n_{..2}$

Rather than treat the calculation of δ in general, a set of data from an Alameda county survey (1975) concerning the knowledge of hypertension illustrates the interaction measure δ. Data were collected on answers to two questions along with the race of the respondent:

Risk factor: Answer to the question—Do you think you have elevated blood pressure? ("hypertension"—H or $\bar{H}$);
"Disease": Answer to the question—Can the symptoms of hypertension be detected without a medical examination and a blood pressure reading? (yes or no);
Confounder: Race of the respondent (white or black).

The data are shown in Table 6.25 and the odds ratios for each sub-table are $or_{FD|C} = 1.943$ and $or_{FD|\bar{C}} = 3.176$. A calculation of the factor δ quantifies the amount of interaction (failure of the odds ratio to be identical for the white and black respondents); a value of δ is such that there is no interaction in the data. Specifically, see Table 6.26.

To find the δ value so that the measure of association is identical for both whites and blacks, the odds ratio when the confounder is present (white) is equated to the odds ratio when the confounder is absent (black) or

$$\frac{(17 + \delta)(12 + \delta)}{(7 - \delta)(15 - \delta)} = \frac{(26 - \delta)(27 - \delta)}{(13 + \delta)(17 + \delta)}. \tag{6.33}$$

A bit of trial-and-error iterations yields the solution for the value of δ that must be added to or subtracted from the values in each of the eight

Table 6–25. Perceived hypertension by answer by race

	White			Black		
"Hypertension"	17	7	24	26	17	43
No "hypertension"	15	12	27	13	27	40
Total	32	19	51	39	44	83

Table 6-26. Perceived hypertension by answer by race

	White			Black		
	Yes	No	Total	Yes	No	Total
"Hypertension"	$17+\delta$	$7-\delta$	24	$26-\delta$	$17+\delta$	43
No "hypertension"	$15-\delta$	$12+\delta$	27	$13+\delta$	$27-\delta$	40
Total	32	19	51	39	44	83

cells to produce a set of "data" with exactly no interaction as measured by the odds ratio. For the survey data $\delta = 0.866$. The estimated "data" and summary odds ratio under the no interaction hypothesis are then given in Table 6.27 where now the odds ratios for each sub-table are $or_{FD|C} = 2.651$ and $or_{FD|\bar{C}} = 2.651$.

The estimated values in Table 6.27 $\hat{n}_{ijk}$ can be compared to n_{ijk} with the usual χ^2 statistic to assess the fit of the no-interaction conjecture (see Table 6.29). Also the estimate of an odds ratio from these no interaction "data" (i.e., $\hat{or}=2.651$) is an excellent summary value under the hypothesis that the disease–risk relationship is the same in both subtables. Further development of the statistical assessment of the odds ratio $\hat{or}$ will be taken up in the next chapter. If measures of association other than the odds ratio were used, the value of δ would differ, but the process of finding δ would be similar and produce an analogous interpretation.

If no interaction exists (or nearly so), then it is meaningful to assess the influence of a possible confounding variable on the measure of association chosen. Continuing the "hypertension" example, the summary odds ratio when race (confounder) is considered is 2.651. The odds ratio calculated from the table where white and black respondents are combined (ignoring the confounder) is 2.496. The comparison of these two odds ratios directly shows the amount of confounder bias

Table 6-27. No interaction: Perceived hypertension by answer by race

	White			Black		
	Yes	No	Total	Yes	No	Total
"Hypertension"	17.866	6.134	24	25.134	17.866	43
No "hypertension"	14.134	12.866	27	13.866	26.134	40
Total	32	19	51	39	44	83

associated with these data when no interaction is present. Whether this bias occurred by chance is not much of an issue, and a statistical test is not a relevant addition to the analysis. When confounder bias exists in the collected data and if it is substantial, strategies must be adopted to provide an unbiased description of the influence of a risk factor regardless of whether the bias is "real" or "random." For the perceived hypertension data, the race variable confounds the relationship between "hypertension" and the answer to the question about symptoms (2.651 versus 2.496). The summary table (ignoring race) is not very useful, and whether or not this bias arose by chance is unimportant.

Like confounding, interaction basically addresses the question of "combinability." If no interaction exits and a variable is a nonconfounder, then a summary table generally increases power and simplifies the analysis. If interaction and/or confounding are present in a data set, then ignoring this fact (adding the frequencies over the levels of another variable when interactions or confounding is present) will produce a table that, at best, is not very meaningful and, at worst, deceptive. Examples of "data" have been developed to show that rather anomalous results can occur when interaction or confounding variables are ignored. A famous example is called Simpson's paradox [Ref. 13]. A simple example concerns two baseball players who bat against both left-handed and right-handed pitching with the results shown in Table 6.28.

Player A's batting average is $90/300 = 0.300$, where player B's batting average is $48/150 = 0.320$. Is B a better hitter than A? Note that player A hits better than player B against left-handed pitching ($50/200 = 0.250$ versus $10/50 = 0.200$). Player A also out-hits player B against right-handed pitching ($40/100 = 0.400$ versus $38/100 = 0.380$). The true worth of the two players is reflected in the subtables rather than the summary table. This example serves as a reminder that, when interaction is present, summary tables or measures of association derived from summary tables are not likely to reflect accurately the

Table 6–28. Hits against left- and right-handed pitching

	Player A			Player B			Summary		
	Left	Right	Total	Left	Right	Total	Player A	Player B	Total
Hits	50	40	90	10	38	48	90	48	138
Outs	150	60	210	40	72	102	210	102	312
Total	200	100	300	50	100	150	300	150	450

issues under study. The concept of interaction takes on more precise meaning in the context of a logistic regression analysis and will be discussed further in the next two chapters.

Summary

The hierarchal ordering of the five statistical relationships among a potential confounding variable, a risk factor, and a disease outcome is worth noting. If the values classified into a $2 \times 2 \times 2$ table are completely independent, then necessarily the variables are partially independent, conditionally independent, and no interaction exists in all subtables. Additionally, if the data are partially independent, then the data also must be conditionally independent and no interaction exists. Last, conditional independence implies that no interaction exists. In other words, complete independence is a special case of partial independence, partial independence is a special case of conditional independence, and conditional independence is a special case of no interaction.

An important issue pertaining to a $2 \times 2 \times 2$ table remains: Which of the four possible models is the "right" description of the sampled data? The perceived hypertension data will be used to explore possible statistical structures to describe the disease, risk factor, and confounder variable relationships. The χ^2 statistic $\Sigma\Sigma\Sigma (n_{ijk} - \hat{n}_{ijk})^2 / \hat{n}_{ijk}$ serves to summarize the fit of four models, where $\hat{n}_{ijk}$ is estimated under complete independence, partial independence, conditional independence, and no interaction structures. The data and the estimated cell frequencies as well as a χ^2 goodness-of-fit statistic for each statistical model are given in Table 6.29.

The four descriptions of the data from a $2 \times 2 \times 2$ table produce specific patterns of any measure of association. The odds ratio, for example, applied to the expected values (Table 6.29) derived from the Alameda health survey data for the four basic models produces Table 6.30. This table emphasizes that a choice of a model to represent the data is also a choice of a pattern of the measures of association.

The more complex the model (fewer degrees of freedom), the better the fit of the estimated values to the data. These four analyses, like most statistical investigations, involve a tradeoff between simplicity of the statistical structure and increasing "goodness" of fit (the χ^2 values get smaller). For statistical models in general, increased complexity leads to greater flexibility of the mathematical structure, which, in turn, leads to less unexplained variation. Although the χ^2 measure is useful in the process of deciding on an optimum statistical structure, it does not

Table 6–29. Perceived hypertension by answer by race

C	F	D	Count	Complete	Partial*	Conditional**	No interaction	Data
White	"yes"	H	n_{111}	13.511	16.366	19.380	17.866	17
	"yes"	$\bar{H}$	n_{211}	13.511	10.657	12.620	14.134	15
	"no"	H	n_{121}	11.989	9.134	7.238	6.134	7
	"no"	$\bar{H}$	n_{221}	11.989	14.843	11.762	12.866	12
Black	"yes"	H	n_{112}	21.989	26.634	23.620	25.134	26
	"yes"	$\bar{H}$	n_{212}	21.989	17.343	15.380	13.866	13
	"no"	H	n_{122}	19.511	14.866	16.762	17.866	17
	"no"	$\bar{H}$	n_{222}	19.511	24.157	27.238	26.134	27

Summary

	Complete	Partial*	Conditional**	No interaction
X^2	10.745	4.582	1.367	0.430
DF	4	3	2	1
p-value	0.030	0.205	0.505	0.512

*Partial independence of race.

**"Hypertension" and race independent conditional on answers "yes" and "no."

Table 6–30. The odds ratios for the five descriptions of data in a $2 \times 2 \times 2$ table

Model	$or_{FD|C}$	$or_{FD|\bar{C}}$	or_{FD}	$or_{DC|F}$	$or_{DC|\bar{F}}$	or_{DC}	$or_{FC|D}$	$or_{FC|\bar{D}}$	or_{FC}
Complete	1.00	1.00	1.00	1.00	1.00	1.00	1.00	1.00	1.00
Partial	2.50	2.50	2.50	1.00	1.00	1.00	1.00	1.00	1.00
Conditional	2.50	2.50	2.50	1.00	1.00	1.15	1.90	1.90	1.90
No interaction	2.65	2.65	2.50	0.70	0.70	0.83	2.07	2.07	1.90
Data	1.94	3.18	2.50	0.57	0.93	0.83	1.59	2.60	1.90

provide an unequivocal answer. The primary role of the χ^2 criterion is to identify those statistical structures that are incompatible with the data. The ultimate choice of the "right" model to represent the relationships among the variables in collected data should be based on biological–physical considerations supported by statistical analysis.

7 The Analysis of Contingency Table Data: Logistic Model I

Epidemiologic data often occur as a series of counts resulting from tabulating discrete variables or tabulating continuous variables made discrete. Converting continuous variables to categorical variables simpifies the interpretation and is usually based on traditional cut points (at a cost of statistical power, as already noted). For example, individuals are considered hypertensive or not hypertensive depending on whether their systolic blood pressure exceeds 140 mm Hg, and smokers are categorized into a series intervals based on 0, 1–20, 21–30, and 30+ cigarettes reported smoked per day. The end result is a multidimensional table of counts. Tables are themselves a useful summary of collected data, but, in addition, it is important to explore further the sometimes complex relationships found in a table.

An example of a multidimensional table describing three risk factors and a disease outcome from the WCGS data is shown in Table 7.1.

This table consists of counts of coronary heart disease (CHD) events and the number of individuals at risk classified by blood pressure, smoking, and behavior type. Clearly increased risks are incurred by increasing amounts smoked, by being in a high blood pressure category, and by having a type A behavior pattern. However, a number of questions are not easily answered. Among them are:

1. Does smoking have a threshold influence or does risk increase more or less consistently as the number of cigarettes smoked increases?
2. What is the influence of blood pressure and smoking on the behavior–disease relationship?
3. Do these three risk factors influence the frequency of CHD events in an independent way?
4. If these risk factors are not independent, how do they act together to influence the probability of a coronary event? and
5. What is the relative influence of each of these factors on the risk of coronary heart disease?

The inability to answer elementary questions about the risk–disease relationships in a satisfactory way stems, to a large extent, from lack of

Table 7–1. Coronary disease by A/B by systolic blood pressure by smoking: A Summary

Blood Pressure (mm Hg)	Behavior Type	Smoking frequency–cigarettes per day			
		0	1–20	21–30	30+
≥140	A	29/184 = 0.158	21/97 = 0.213	7/52 = 0.135	12/55 = 0.213
≥140	B	8/179 = 0.045	9/71 = 0.127	3/34 = 0.088	7/21 = 0.333
<140	A	41/600 = 0.068	24/301 = 0.080	27/167 = 0.162	17/133 = 0.128
<140	B	20/689 = 0.029	16/336 = 0.048	13/152 = 0.086	3/83 = 0.036

data. If hundreds of thousands of individuals were classified into a table with perhaps more categories, the answer to most questions about the role of the risk factors and CHD would be clear. The "thiness" of the data requires a more sophisticated approach in the form of a statistical model. When a large number of variables is investigated, a table often fails to summarize the data adequately, and a need arises to deal yet more efficiently with the relationships among the categorical variables. Additionally, human disease is, by and large, a rare event causing sparse cell frequencies in most tabulated data (e.g., only three events occur in the low blood pressure, heavy smoking, type B category), making it vital that any analytic procedure account for the impact of sampling variation. The logistic model is one way to describe succinctly and efficiently, as well as analyze quantitatively, the associations between a set of risk factors and a disease outcome. The use of a multivariate model to analyze data classified into a multidimensional table is the topic of this chapter; the extension to include continuous risk variables is discussed in the following chapter. Logistic regression is by no means the only approach to the analysis of risk–disease relationships but is frequently used and demonstrates both the strengths and weaknesses of multivariate data analysis techniques applied to epidemiologic data.

The Simplest Case

A 2×2 table provides the simplest application of a logistic model to the relationships among contingency table variables. To start, the variables to be analyzed are the presence $(D = 1)$ or absence $(D = 0)$ of a disease investigated at two levels of a risk factor $(F = 1$, risk factor present, or $F = 0$, risk factor absent). The general notation (repeated) for a contingency table applies and is specifically shown in Table 7.2.

There are many ways to analyze such tables. The common χ^2

Table 7-2. 2×2 contingency table

	Disease: $D=1$	No disease: $D=0$	Total
Factor present: $F=1$	n_{11}	n_{12}	$n_{1.}$
Factor absent: $F=0$	n_{21}	n_{22}	$n_{2.}$
Total	$n_{.1}$	$n_{.2}$	n

technique is the most powerful approach. A χ^2 statistic will detect an association between risk factor and disease with the highest possible probability when an association exists. Other methods based on conditional probabilities such as $P(D|F)$ and $P(\bar{D}|F)$ are also used to describe the risk-factor–disease relationship.

Yet another choice is to employ the odds as a measure of association between a risk factor and a disease for data recorded in a 2×2 table. The odds of disease among those individuals without the risk factor is the ratio of $P(D|F = 0)$ to $P(\bar{D}|F = 0)$ and can be compared to the odds among those with the disease, $P(D|F = 1)/P(\bar{D}|F = 1)$. A statistically strategic measure is the logarithm of the odds, called the log-odds or logit. One motivation for employing a log-odds measure of risk is its utility for detecting multiplicative effects among risk factors.

A baseline measure of disease risk on a log-odds scale is the estimated log-odds when the risk factor is absent, or

$$\hat{a} = \log\left(\frac{\hat{P}(D|F = 0)}{\hat{P}(\bar{D}|F = 0)}\right) = \log\left(\frac{n_{21}/(n_{21} + n_{22})}{n_{22}/(n_{21} + n_{22})}\right) = \log(n_{21}/n_{22}) \quad (7.1)$$

so that

$$\hat{a} \text{ is an estimate of } a = \text{log-odds} = \log\left(\frac{P(D|F = 0)}{P(\bar{D}|F = 0)}\right). \quad (7.2)$$

A measure of particular interest is the estimated increase or decrease in the log-odds due to the presence of the risk factor measured relative to the baseline value or

$$\hat{b} = \log(n_{11}/n_{12}) - \log(n_{21}/n_{22}) \quad (7.3)$$

so that

$$\hat{b} \text{ is an estimate of } b = \log\left(\frac{P(D|F = 1)}{P(\bar{D}|F = 1)}\right) - \log\left(\frac{P(D|F = 0)}{P(\bar{D}|F = 0)}\right) \quad (7.4)$$

and also note that

$$e^b = \frac{P(D|F = 1)/P(\bar{D}|F = 1)}{P(D|F = 0)/P(\bar{D}|F = 0)} = \text{or} \quad (7.5)$$

is the odds ratio associated with a 2×2 table. The two quantities (a, b) form the simplest possible linear model. That is, log-odds $= a + bF$, where $F = 0$ or $F = 1$ and

$$\text{when } F = 0, \text{ then log-odds} = \log(n_{21}/n_{22}) = \hat{a} \qquad (7.6)$$

and

$$\text{when } F = 1, \text{ then log-odds} = \log(n_{11}/n_{12}) = \hat{a} + \hat{b}. \qquad (7.7)$$

The value $\hat{b}$ measures, on the log-odds scale, the estimated change in risk of disease associated with the presence of the risk factor (F) relative to the absence of the same factor $(\bar{F})$. The risk factor in the context of a linear model has other names—sometimes called the predictor variable, the explanatory variable, or the independent variable. The log-odds measure is not a particularly intuitive way to assess the risk-factor disease association, but it has tractable mathematical properties and relates directly to the odds ratio measure of risk, which is the natural measure of association when data are analyzed using a logistic regression model.

Consider a 2×2 table (Table 7.3) from the WCGS data describing the relationship between behavior type (risk factor) and a coronary event (disease outcome). From these data, $\hat{a} = \log(79/1486) = -2.934$ and $\hat{a} + \hat{b} = \log(178/1411) = -2.070$, giving the change in the log-odds of CHD associated with type A individuals (risk factor present) relative to type B individuals (risk factor absent—baseline) as $\hat{b} = -2.070 - (-2.934) = 0.864$ (see Figure 7.1). Since $\log(or) = \hat{b} = \log(n_{11}n_{22}/n_{12}n_{21})$, then $e^{\hat{b}} = n_{11}n_{22}/n_{12}n_{21}$, which is the usual estimate of the odds ratio calculated from a 2×2 table. For the behavior type data (Table 7.3) the odds ratio estimate is $\hat{or} = e^{0.864} = 2.373$. The odds of a coronary event is, therefore, 2.373 times greater for a type A individual than for a type B individual. This odds ratio can also be calculated directly from the tabled data where $\hat{or} = (178)(1486)/(79)(1411) = 2.373$.

When the number of parameters estimated is equal to the number of observed log-odds in a table of data, the results of using a logistic model

Table 7–3. CHD by A/B

	CHD	No CHD	Total
Type A	178	1,411	1,589
Type B	79	1,486	1,565
Total	257	2,897	3,154

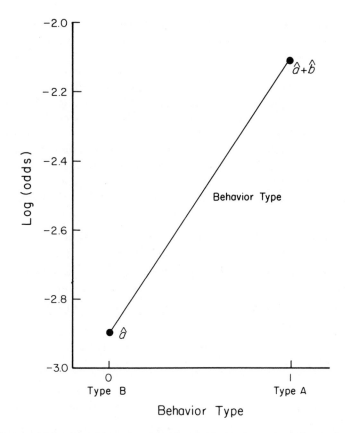

Figure 7-1. Log-odds associated with CHD risk by behavior type.

to describe associations and making direct calculations are identical. When a model approach and direct calculations produce identical results, the model is said to be saturated. The two-parameter logistic model applied to a 2×2 table is an example of a saturated model.

The two primary ways to evaluate the influence of sampling variation on the estimate $\hat{b}$ are a significance test and a confidence interval (or both).

> Aside: The relative merits of a confidence interval versus a significance test have been occasionally discussed, even debated (e.g., [Refs. 1, 2, and 3]). The confidence interval and the two-sided significance test are in reality similar and rarely give contradictory results. The confidence interval conveys more information in the sense that the interval width gives some idea of the range of parameter possibilities (power). A confidence interval is expressed in the same units as the estimated quantity, which is sometimes helpful. A significance test reported in

isolation tends to reduce conclusions to two choices ("significant" or "not significant"), which, perhaps, emphasizes the role of chance variation too strongly. Estimates can be "significant" (chance not a plausible explanation) because a large number of observations are involved, but the results do not reflect an important biological or physical measurement. However, a confidence interval approach is complicated when more than one estimate is involved. In many cases, as will be seen, several estimates can be assessed simultaneously with a significance test where the analogous confidence region is difficult to construct and to interpret. Of course, a significance test and a confidence interval can both be presented. However, if one approach must be chosen, a confidence interval allows a simple and more comprehensive assessment of the influence of random variation on a single estimated quantity.

Lack of precision, incurred when a sample represents a fraction of the population sampled, must be taken into account to assess realistically a factor's influence on the risk of a disease. To evaluate the impact of random variation associated with the estimate $\hat{b}$, both a significance test and a confidence interval require an estimate of the variance of $\hat{b}$, which is estimated by

$$\text{variance } (\hat{b}) = 1/n_{11} + 1/n_{12} + 1/n_{21} + 1/n_{22}. \tag{7.8}$$

For the behavior type data (Table 7.3), the variance of the estimate of b is

$$\text{variance } (\hat{b}) = 1/178 + 1/1411 + 1/79 + 1/1486 = 0.020. \tag{7.9}$$

For reasons beyond the scope of this presentation, the variance of the logarithm of the number of observations in a specific cell of a contingency table is approximately variance $[\pm\log(n_{ij})] \approx 1/n_{ij}$. This estimate of the variance is based on the assumption that the number of observations occurring in a specific cell, at least approximately, represents an independent sample from a Poisson distribution. Risk measures based on the log-odds can be broken into a sum of independent terms of the form $\pm\log(n_{ij})$, and, therefore, the variance of these risk measures is a sum of the variances associated with each of these terms. For example, since $\hat{a} = \log(n_{21}/n_{22}) = \log(n_{21}) - \log(n_{22})$, then the variance of $\hat{a}$ is

$$\text{variance } (\hat{a}) = \text{variance } [\log(n_{21})] + \text{variance}[-\log(n_{22})]$$

$$= 1/n_{21} + 1/n_{22}. \tag{7.10}$$

The estimated variance of the estimated regression coefficient $\hat{b}$ [expression (7.8)] follows the same pattern.

To test the null hypothesis that the risk factor is unrelated to the disease outcome (H_0: $b = 0$), the test statistic

$$X^2 = \frac{\hat{b}^2}{\text{variance } (\hat{b})} \tag{7.11}$$

has an approximate χ^2 distribution with one degree of freedom when the null hypothesis is true. The test of $b = 0$ is equivalent to testing a number of other hypotheses including: odds ratio $= 1.0$, $P(D|F) = P(D|\bar{F})$ or $P(F|D) = P(\bar{F}|D)$. These expressions all indicate the same property, namely that the disease outcome and the risk factor are statistically independent, or $P(D|F) = P(D)$. For the WCGS data, $X^2 = 0.864^2/0.020 = 37.325$, yielding a p-value less than 0.001, indicating that the A/B behavior type is associated with CHD incidence.

An approximate $(1 - \alpha)\%$ confidence interval based the estimate $\hat{b}$ has the bounds

$$\text{upper bound} = \hat{b} + z_{1-\alpha/2}\sqrt{\text{variance}(\hat{b})} \tag{7.12}$$

and

$$\text{lower bound} = \hat{b} - z_{1-\alpha/2}\sqrt{\text{variance}(\hat{b})} \tag{7.13}$$

when $\hat{b}$ has an approximate normal distribution. The value $z_{1-\alpha/2}$ is, as usual, the $(1 - \alpha/2)$ percentile from a standard normal distribution. A $(1 - \alpha)\%$ confidence interval for the odds ratio is then $(e^{\text{lower}}, e^{\text{upper}})$. The approximate 95% confidence interval based on $\hat{b} = 0.864$ from the behavior type data is $(0.589, 1.139)$. The approximate 95% confidence interval for the odds ratio or is then $(e^{0.589} = 1.803, e^{1.139} = 3.123)$, indicating the precision of the estimate $\hat{or} = 2.373$.

Using a linear model to represent the log-odds is related to describing the probabilities from a 2×2 table with a logistic function. The logistic function, which has historically been used in a variety of contexts to study biological phenomena, is formally

$$f(x) = \frac{1}{1 + e^{-x}}. \tag{7.14}$$

The function $f(x)$ is an "s-shaped" curve where large negative values of x yield $f(x)$ near 0, large positive values of x yield $f(x)$ near 1, and a value of $x = 0$ produces $f(0) = 0.5$. The logistic curve is always greater than 0 and less than 1, which makes it ideal for representing probabilities, also bounded between 0 and 1.

In symbols, the logistic probabilities applied to a 2×2 table are

$$P(D|F = 0) = \frac{1}{1 + e^{-a}} \text{ and } P(D|F = 1) = \frac{1}{1 + e^{-(a+b)}}, \tag{7.15}$$

where a and b are the quantities previously defined in terms of log-odds. In other words, the same parameters (a, b) describe the relationships within a contingency table using either the log-odds or logistic probabilities as measures of risk. A logistic relationship among the probabilities from a contingency table implies a linear relationship among the log-odds and conversely. To illustrate,

$$\text{log-odds} = \log\left(\frac{P(D|F=1)}{P(\bar{D}|F=1)}\right) = \log\left(\frac{1/(1+e^{-(a+b)})}{e^{-(a+b)}/(1+e^{-(a+b)})}\right)$$

$$= \log(e^{(a+b)}) = a + b. \tag{7.16}$$

The odds ratio is most easily interpreted when the frequency of the disease is low (less than 0.1 in both the risk-factor and non-risk-factor groups) since, in this case, the estimated odds ratio is approximately equal to a simpler measure of association between risk factor and disease, the relative risk [i.e., $or \approx$ relative risk $= P(D|F)/P(D|\bar{F})$]. Relative risk is a natural measure of risk to apply to prospective data when one group is "exposed" and another is "unexposed" and is discussed in detail elsewhere (e.g., [Refs. 4, and 5]). However, the odds ratio is a valid measure of association regardless of the frequency of the outcome variable.

A summary of the logistic regression analysis of the association between behavior type and coronary disease in the WCGS data is shown in Table 7.4. The logistic probabilities are estimated as $\hat{P}(D|F=0) = 0.050$ and $\hat{P}(D|F=1) = 0.112$, which can be calculated from the logistic function using $\hat{a}$ and $\hat{b}$ or directly from the data.

The 2 × 2 × 2 Case

When an association is detected in a 2×2 table, a natural question is: How is this relationship influenced by other variables? The WCGS data show a strong association between behavior type and coronary disease, but an important question remains: Could this association be, at least in part, due to the influence of other risk factors? For example, systolic blood pressure level is related to coronary disease as well as behavior type and could influence the observed association. A $2 \times 2 \times 2$ contingency table sheds some light on the influence of another variable on the risk factor-disease relationship under investigation. The role of systolic blood pressure as a possible confounding influence can be

Table 7–4. CHD by A/B

Variable	Term	Coefficient	Std. error	p-value	$\hat{or}$
Constant	$\hat{a}$	−2.934	0.115	—	—
A/B	$\hat{b}$	0.864	0.140	<0.001	2.373

−2LogLikelihood = 1740.334; number of model parameter = 2.

Table 7-5. CHD by A/B by systolic blood pressure

	Blood pressure $\geqslant 140$			Blood pressure < 140		
	CHD	No CHD	Total	CHD	No CHD	Total
Type A	69	319	388	109	1,092	1,201
Type B	27	278	305	52	1,208	1,260
Total	96	597	693	161	2,300	2,461

$or_1 = 2.227$; $or_2 = 2.319$.

explored from the $2 \times 2 \times 2$ Table 7.5. Another version of these data in terms of the log-odds is given in Table 7.6.

The influence of behavior type is measured by $\hat{b}_1 = \hat{l}_{11} - \hat{l}_{12} = 0.801$ for individuals with blood pressure $\geqslant 140$ and by $\hat{b}_2 = \hat{l}_{21} - \hat{l}_{22} = 0.841$ for blood pressure < 140. These two quantities do not differ in principle from the log-odds measure previously described for a 2×2 table but are calculated twice, once in each blood pressure subtable. In the case of a $2 \times 2 \times 2$ table, measures of risk associated with the blood pressure can also be estimated in each of the two behavior type categories. The two log-odds measures of blood pressure risk are $\hat{c}_1 = \hat{l}_{11} - \hat{l}_{21} = 0.773$ for type A individuals and $\hat{c}_2 = \hat{l}_{12} - \hat{l}_{22} = 0.814$ for type B individuals. The failure of these two measures ($\hat{b}$'s or $\hat{c}$'s) to be equal in each of the subtables brings up a fundamental concern in the analysis of contingency table data. One of two possible situations exists:

1. The influence of the risk factor under study is the same in both subtables, and the observed differences arise only because of the influence of random variation (no interaction), or
2. The influence of the risk factor under study is different in each subtable (interaction present).

The first possibility suggests that the two estimates should be combined to produce a single summary measure of the association between risk

Table 7-6. CHD by A/B by systolic blood pressure: A summary

Blood pressure	Behavior type	CHD	No CHD	Log-odds	Notation
$\geqslant 140$	A	69	319	-1.531	l_{11}
$\geqslant 140$	B	27	278	-2.332	l_{12}
< 140	A	109	1,092	-2.304	l_{21}
< 140	B	52	1,208	-3.145	l_{22}

factor and disease. The second indicates quite the opposite. As noted before, if a variable behaves differently in each subtable, then a combined estimate of the influence will likely be misleading—interactions restrict "combinability."

In symbolic terms, for the case of a $2 \times 2 \times 2$ table, an interaction measure using the log-odds is

$$\text{interaction} = b_1 - b_2 = (l_{11} - l_{22}) - (l_{21} - l_{22}) = l_{11} - l_{12} - l_{21} + l_{22}, \quad (7.17)$$

or, similarly,

$$\text{interaction} = c_1 - c_2 = (l_{11} - l_{21}) - (l_{12} - l_{22}) = l_{11} - l_{12} - l_{21} + l_{22}. \quad (7.18)$$

The expression $l_{11} - l_{12} - l_{21} + l_{22}$ quantifies the amount of interaction associated with two risk factors on a log-odds scale and is occasionally used as the definition of interaction. An estimate of the magnitude of the interaction associated with behavior type and blood pressure is $\hat{b}_1 - \hat{b}_2 = \hat{c}_1 - \hat{c}_2 = \hat{l}_{11} - \hat{l}_{12} - \hat{l}_{21} + \hat{l}_{22} = -1.531 + 2.332 + 2.304 - 3.145 = -0.040$.

A critical issue is whether the data provide evidence of a nonrandom ("real") interaction. Testing the null hypothesis that $l_{11} - l_{12} - l_{21} + l_{22} = 0$ is equivalent to testing the hypothesis that $b_1 = b_2$ or $c_1 = c_2$. A statistical test to evaluate the magnitude of the estimated interaction effect requires an expression for the variance. Along the lines discussed for the 2×2 contingency table, the variation of the estimated interaction effect is estimated by

$$\text{variance(interaction)} = \sum_{i=1}^{2} \sum_{j=1}^{2} \sum_{k=1}^{2} 1/n_{ijk}, \quad (7.19)$$

where n_{ijk} represents a cell frequency in the $2 \times 2 \times 2$ table. For example, the estimated degree of interaction associated with blood pressure and behavior type is -0.040 and the estimated variance associated with this estimate is

$$\text{variance(interaction)} = \frac{1}{69} + \frac{1}{319} + \frac{1}{27} + \frac{1}{278} + \frac{1}{109} + \frac{1}{1092} + \frac{1}{52} + \frac{1}{1208}$$

$$= 0.088. \quad (7.20)$$

The test statistic

$$X^2 = \frac{(\hat{l}_{11} - \hat{l}_{12} - \hat{l}_{21} + \hat{l}_{22})^2}{\text{variance(interaction)}} \quad (7.21)$$

has an approximate χ^2 distribution with one degree of freedom when no interaction exists and provides a rigorous assessment of the importance of the estimated interaction effect. Continuing the WCGS example, $X^2 = 0.018$ and a p-value $= 0.892$ formally indicates no evidence of an interaction between the risk factors blood pressure and behavior type in the analysis of CHD risk.

A linear model underlying the log-odds approach to describing relationships in a $2 \times 2 \times 2$ table is

$$l_{11} = a + b_2 + c_2 + d, \tag{7.22}$$

$$l_{12} = a + c_2, \tag{7.23}$$

$$l_{21} = a + b_2, \text{ and} \tag{7.24}$$

$$l_{22} = a, \tag{7.25}$$

where d represents the magnitude of the interaction effect (i.e., $d = l_{11} - l_{12} - l_{21} + l_{22}$). The values b_2 and c_2 represent the direct effects of behavior type and blood pressure as defined earlier. Notice the parameters b_1 and c_1 are redundant since $b_1 = b_2 + d$ and $c_1 = c_2 + d$ (four parameters uniquely establish four log-odds values; see Figure 7.2).

Another view of the parameter d is

$$e^d = \frac{or_1}{or_2}, \tag{7.26}$$

where or_1 is the odds ratio from the first 2×2 subtable and or_2 is the odds ratio from the second 2×2 subtable. For the blood pressure and behavior type data, $or_1 = 2.227$ and $\hat{or}_2 = 2.319$ yielding $e^d = 0.960$. When $d = 0$ ($e^{0.0} = 1.0$), the odds ratios are identical in both subtables; otherwise the magnitude of e^d reflects the degree of interaction in terms of the ratio of odds ratios.

Table 7.7 summarizes the estimates of these four components and describes the relationships among the variables coronary disease, blood pressure, and behavior type in terms of the logistic model.

The application of the logistic model to a $2 \times 2 \times 2$ table can be geometrically interpreted as two straight lines on a log-odds scale, each

Table 7—7. CHD by A/B by systolic blood pressure

Variable	Term	Coefficient	Std. error	p value	Odds ratio
Constant	$\hat{a}$	-3.145	0.142	—	—
A/B	$\hat{b}_2$	0.841	0.174	<0.001	2.319
Blood pressure	$\hat{c}_2$	0.814	0.246	<0.001	2.256
Interaction	$\hat{d}$	-0.040	0.297	0.892	0.960

$-2\text{LogLikelihood} = 1709.934$; number of model parameter $= 4$.

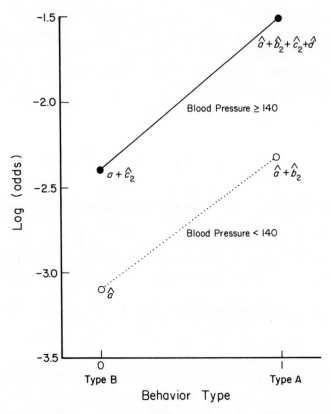

Figure 7–2. Log-odds associated with CHD risk by behavior type and by systolic blood pressure (<140 and ⩾140).

depicting the influence of the risk factor at each level of the other variable. The parameter d reflects the degree to which these two lines are not parallel. Figure 7.2 shows the lines for behavior type for the two levels of blood pressure estimated from the WCGS data and reflects CHD risk. It should be noted that the same estimated odds ratios (last column in Table 7.7) could have been calculated directly from the tabled data, indicating that the model is saturated. There are four log-odds values, and four parameters define the logistic model. For example, $\hat{b}_2 = 0.841$ giving $\hat{or} = e^{\hat{b}_2} = 2.319$, which is identical to $\hat{or}_2 = (109)(1208)/(52)(1092) = 2.319$.

When no interaction exists (i.e., $d = 0$; that is, $or_1 = or_2$), an additive linear model (nonsaturated) represents the relationships in a $2 \times 2 \times 2$

table, again in terms of the log-odds

$$l_{11} = a + b + c, \tag{7.27}$$

$$l_{12} = a + c, \tag{7.28}$$

$$l_{21} = a + b, \text{ and} \tag{7.29}$$

$$l_{22} = a. \tag{7.30}$$

This statistical structure is additive since each log-odds is a sum of no more than three component parameters $(a, b, \text{ and } c)$. Note that $l_{11} - l_{12} - l_{21} + l_{22} = 0$ by definition of the additive model. The values b and c take the place of the previous values b_1, b_2, c_1, and c_2. An iterative procedure [expression (6.33)] or computer program is necessary to estimate the values of a, b, and c from a $2 \times 2 \times 2$ table. Using such a program, the maximum likelihood estimates (see Appendix for a description) from the WCGS data are $\hat{a} = -3.136$, $\hat{b} = 0.827$, and $\hat{c} = 0.786$. "Data" and the log-odds based on these estimates are given in Table 7.8.

The no-interaction model requires that the influence of the risk factor be exactly the same in both subtables or $b_1 = b_2 = b$ and $c_1 = c_2 = c$. The odds ratio associated with behavior type is $\hat{or}_{A/B} = e^{\hat{b}} = e^{0.827} = 2.286$, which is an evaluation of the CHD risk associated with behavior type adjusted for the influence of blood pressure. A type A individual has odds of a coronary event 2.286 times greater than a type B individual in both blood pressure status groups ($\geqslant 140$ or < 140). Similarly, $\hat{or}_{bp} = e^{\hat{c}} = e^{0.786} = 2.195$ is the estimated odds ratio for CHD risk of individuals with blood pressure equal to or exceeding 140 relative to those with values less than 140 for both behavior types. Also $\hat{or}_{A/B} \hat{or}_{bp} = (2.286)(2.195) = 5.018$ is a measure of the CHD risk associated with simultaneous possession of both risk factors (type A with blood pressure $\geqslant 140$) relative to an individual with neither risk factor (type B with blood pressure < 140). In terms of

Table 7–8. CHD by A/B by systolic blood pressure: Expected values based on the additive model

Blood pressure	Behavior type	CHD	No CHD	Log-odds	Notation
$\geqslant 140$	A	69.48	318.52	-1.523	$\hat{l}_{11}$
$\geqslant 140$	B	26.55	278.45	-2.350	$\hat{l}_{12}$
< 140	A	108.59	1,092.41	-2.309	$\hat{l}_{21}$
< 140	B	52.47	1,207.53	-3.136	$\hat{l}_{22}$

the additive model, the log-odds associated with possessing both risk factors relative to possessing neither factor is $\hat{l}_{11} - \hat{l}_{22} = \hat{a} + \hat{b} + \hat{c} - \hat{a} = 1.613$ and the odds ratio $= e^{\hat{b}+\hat{c}} = e^{1.613} = 5.018$. In general, the odds ratio derived from a logistic regression coefficient, when no interaction is present, is a measure of the contribution of a specific factor to the risk of disease, "free" from the influences of other risk factors in the model.

A summary of the no-interaction model is given in Table 7.9. A comparison of the estimated values from the additive (no-interaction) model with the analogous values in Table 7.7 (saturated model) shows no important differences.

The influence of interaction can be formally evaluated by contrasting the likelihood values (see Appendix) associated with each model. A likelihood value is a relative measure of the goodness-of-fit of a specific model. The value of likelihood decreases with each parameter added to a model. This reduction is likely to be small when the added parameter is unrelated to the disease under study and substantial if the added parameter is related to the disease. The difference between two likelihood values is, therefore, an assessment of the comparative strength of two models to "explain" the data. For the WCGS data the two likelihood values are 1709.954 for the no-interaction model (the parameter d set equal to zero) and 1709.934 for the saturated model (the parameter d not equal to zero) showing that the descriptive power of the logistic model is essentially unchanged by assuming that no interaction exists (i.e., $d = 0$). The difference between two likelihood values has an approximate χ^2 distribution when the difference observed arises from random variation alone. The degrees of freedom are equal to the difference in the number of parameters necessary to describe each model. Using this χ^2 test verifies that setting $d = 0$ in the logistic model has essentially no impact $(L_{d=0} - L_{d=0} = X^2 = 1709.954 - 1709.934 = 0.020$ with a p-value of $0.887)$. Contrasting likelihood values to

Table 7-9. CHD by A/B by systolic blood pressure

Variable	Term	Coefficient	Std. error	p-value	$\hat{or}$
Constant	$\hat{a}$	-3.136	0.124	—	—
A/B	$\hat{b}$	0.827	0.138	<0.001	2.286
Blood pressure	$\hat{c}$	0.786	0.141	<0.001	2.195

-2LogLikelihood $= 1709.954$; number of model parameters $= 3$.

evaluate the descriptive worth of two competing models is an important statistical tool and is used repeatedly in the following sections.

When there is no interaction, the factors influencing the outcome act additively on the log-odds scale and multiplicatively on the odds scale. No interaction, therefore, means that each factor contributes to the risk of a disease separately and the overall odds ratio can be expressed as a product of a series of specific odds ratios each strictly associated with each risk factor (i.e., $or = \Pi\, or_i$); or, conversely, the overall risk can be factored into a set of individual component parts (or_i). Under these additive conditions, risk factors are said to have "independent" influences on the risk of disease.

To evaluate the role of systolic blood pressure, the logistic model with blood pressure not included is helpful. The additive model with the parameter c set equal to zero gives results identical to those in Table 7.4. The difference in the likelihood values for the model including blood pressure and the model excluding blood pressure reflects the contribution of the blood pressure variable to the additive model describing the risk of coronary disease. That is, $L_0 = 1740.344$ (blood pressure excluded) and $L_1 = 1709.954$ (blood pressure included) gives $L_0 - L_1 = 30.390$ with one degree of freedom producing a p-value less than 0.001, showing that blood pressure is important in the description of CHD risk. This likelihood approach to evaluating a single variable is not basically different from the statistical test of the parameter $c = 0$. As indicated earlier, an estimated coefficient squared divided by its variance $[X^2 = \hat{c}^2/\text{variance}(\hat{c}) = 32.4]$ has an approximate χ^2 distribution with one degree of freedom when the expected value of the coefficient is zero. The usefulness of employing likelihood measures to evaluate hypotheses stems from the fact that combinations of risk factors can be assessed simultaneously by comparing models containing several risk factors with a model excluding these factors, resulting in a rigorous statistical test.

A Note on the Power to Detect Interaction Effects

The power of a statistical test to detect an interaction can be relatively low compared to tests of direct effects. In terms of the WCGS data, the probability of identifying a blood-pressure–behavior-type interaction is less than the probability that such variables as blood pressure and behavior type will be identified as important risk factors. In the case of a $2 \times 2 \times 2$ contingency table, the reason for a relatively less powerful test is easily seen. Recall that the variance of the estimated measure of interaction is

$$\text{variance(interaction)} = \sum\sum\sum 1/n_{ijk}, \tag{7.31}$$

where n_{ijk} represents a cell frequency in the $2 \times 2 \times 2$ table. From the previous example [expression (7.20)] the estimated measure of an interaction associated with blood pressure and behavior type is -0.040, and the estimated variance of this estimate is

$$\text{variance(interaction)} = \frac{1}{69} + \frac{1}{319} + \frac{1}{27} + \frac{1}{278} + \frac{1}{109} + \frac{1}{1092} + \frac{1}{52} + \frac{1}{1208}$$

$$= 0.088. \tag{7.32}$$

This variance involves all eight cells of the contingency table, and its value is primarily determined by the cells with the lowest frequency, in this case 27 and 52. Therefore, the variance of the interaction is necessarily larger than $1/27 + 1/52 = 0.057$. Since the measure of an interaction involves all cells in the table, the variance is largely determined by the cells with the fewest observations, which can lead to unreliable estimates (large variances) of the interaction measure and a resulting loss of statistical power. Estimates of the direct effects do not necessarily involve the low-frequency cells producing more reliable estimates (lower variances) and increased power. In more complex situations the investigation of interactions also suffers from problems of low power for much the same reasons as illustrated in the $2 \times 2 \times 2$ case. Failure of a statistical test to reject the null hypothesis of no interaction provides some justification for employing an additive model, but the power of this test is often low. Therefore, an analysis based on the proposition that the risk factors are additive simplifies the interpretation but also is potentially biased.

It is important to detect interaction effects when they exist. It is not as critical to eliminate interaction terms from the logistic model when the data can support an additive model. In other words, a type I error is not as important as a type II error when it comes to testing for an interaction. For a test of the interaction, it is probably a good idea to increase the level of significance (say, $\alpha = 0.2$) to increase the power. Increasing α to attain more statistical power (decreasing the type II error) is a conservative strategy in the sense that relatively minor losses occur, such as some loss of efficiency and increased complexity of the model, if interaction terms are unnecessarily included in the model. Mistakenly eliminating interactions, however, can substantially disrupt the validity of any conclusions ("wrong model bias").

Interactions can also occur among combinations of more than two variables. A failure of interaction effects to be the same at levels of other variables is called a second-order interaction (the interactions interact). These higher-order interactions are rarely considered in epidemiologic applications, for at least three reasons. Like the two factor interactions, the estimation of higher-order interactions is unreliable without large sample sizes and well-distributed data (no sparse cells). These interactions are also usually highly correlated (collinear) with lower-order terms of the logistic model, which also makes estimation unreliable. Higher-order interactions are usually difficult to interpret, and experience indicates that they add little to the description of many disease–risk situations.

Some argue that one solution to the "issue" of interactions is to find a measurement scale to minimize interactions effects. A better goal is a clear understanding of the nature of the interaction, and, therefore, deeper insight into the way the variables investigated are related to each other as well as with a disease outcome.

The 2 × K Case

A $2 \times K$ table can be effectively analyzed using log-odds measure of risk. As before, underlying the log-odds approach is the assumption that risk factor influence can be described by a series of multiplicative effects. The previous approach to a $2 \times K$ table describes a series of proportions as a straight line (Chapter 6), implying an additive relationship between a probability and the level of the risk factor. WCGS data relating coronary heart disease to the amount smoked ($k = 4$ levels) are given in Table 7.10 to illustrate the estimation and testing of a multiplicative influence of a risk factor.

A logistic model that exactly duplicates the information contained in a $2 \times K$ contingency table (saturated model) in terms of log-odds (l_i; $i = 1, 2, \ldots, k$) is, for $k = 4$,

$$l_0 = a, \, l_1 = a + b_1, \, l_2 = a + b_2, \text{ and } l_3 = a + b_3 \qquad (7.33)$$

or

$$\text{log-odds} = l_i = a + b_1 x_1 + b_2 x_2 + b_3 x_3, \qquad (7.34)$$

Table 7–10. CHD by smoking

Cigarettes/day	0	1–20	21–30	30$^+$	Total
CHD	98	70	50	39	257
No CHD	1,554	735	355	253	2,897
Total	1,652	805	405	292	3,154

where x_1, x_2, and x_3 are three binary variables $(0, 1)$, called dummy variables or design variables, identifying each level of the risk factor. For example, the dummy variables $x_1 = 0$, $x_2 = 1$, and $x_3 = 0$ produce a value log-odds $= l_2 = a + b_2$, which measures the risk from smoking 21–30 cigarette per day. The values $x_1 = x_2 = x_3 = 0$ establish a baseline of comparison (i.e., log-odds $= l_0 = a$, measures the risk among nonsmokers).

> Aside: In Chapter 6 it was noted that the values of the k-level variable in a $2 \times K$ table can have at least three forms—numeric, ordered, and nominal. Each variable type suggests a specific analytic approach. In using a logistic model to analyze categorical data similar issues arise. Categories that can be characterized numerically generate values that are typically used directly in the regression analysis, implying a specific relationship among the values. However, nominal values have no specific ordering, and usually no logical numeric coding is possible. The presence or absence of a nominal variable is incorporated into a logistic regression equation with a binary indicator variable. For example, if two races are being considered, say white and black, one is coded 0 and the other 1. The logistic regression coefficients and the odds ratios are then relative to the variable coded zero. If the odds ratio is 2 and the whites are coded as 0 and blacks as 1, then the odds are two times greater among blacks as compared to whites. The principle of using an indicator variable can be extended. If more than two categories are desired (e.g., whites, blacks, Hispanics, and Asians), then a series of indicator or dummy variables is used. For k categories, $k - 1$ indicator variables, each taking on the values 0 or 1, allow the analysis to include a series of categorical variables in a regression model. Again a "baseline" category is established by setting the associated $k - 1$ dummy variables equal to zero. The other categories are identified by a single dummy variable that takes on the value 1 while the remaining dummy variables are set to zero. For example, if blacks, Hispanics, and Asians are to be compared relative to the whites, then $k = 4$,
>
> Whites: $x_1 = 0$, $x_2 = 0$, and $x_3 = 0$;
> Blacks: $x_1 = 1$, $x_2 = 0$, and $x_3 = 0$;
> Hispanics: $x_1 = 0$, $x_2 = 1$, and $x_3 = 0$;
> Asians: $x_1 = 0$, $x_2 = 0$, and $x_3 = 1$.

Like the binary case, the resulting logistic regression coefficients and the odds ratios measure the role of each category relative to the category with all dummy variables set equal to zero. Any number of categories can be identified with this scheme, allowing the assessment of a risk-factor using a logistic model without requiring a numeric value or even requiring that the risk categories be ordered.

The model describing four categories of smoking exposure and CHD risk is not restricted in any way, so the saturated linear model can produce any pattern of log-odds necessary to describe the relationship of disease response to the differing levels of the risk factor. A logistic model that does not imply a particular ordering in the l_i values is said to be unconstrained. Estimates of the model parameters are (notation is given in Table 6.2)

$$\hat{a} = \log(n_{11}/n_{21}), \ \hat{b}_1 = \log(n_{12}/n_{22}) - \hat{a},$$
$$\hat{b}_2 = \log(n_{13}/n_{23}) - \hat{a}, \ \hat{b}_3 = \log(n_{14}/n_{24}) - \hat{a}, \qquad (7.35)$$

giving the estimates from the WCGS smoking data shown in Table 7.11.

The odds ratios ($\hat{or}_{0i} = e^{\hat{b}_i}$) measure the multiplicative risk for each smoking category relative to a baseline (nonsmokers). For example, smoking more than 30 cigarettes a day produces an odds = 2.444 ($e^{0.894}$) times greater than the odds among nonsmokers. The odds ratios associated with increasing levels of smoking show an increasing risk of CHD (increasing from 1.5 to 2.2 to 2.4; see Figure 7.3). This pattern is a property of the data and not the model; any pattern, as mentioned, could have emerged.

One reason to construct a $2 \times K$ table is to explore the question of whether or not a risk factor has a specific pattern of influence on the risk of disease. Does the risk, for example, of a coronary event increase multiplicatively with increases in the level of smoking categories? Multiplicative relationships translate into additive relationships of logarithms. In terms of a logistic model, the log-odds generated by an additive relationship are described by the straight line

$$\text{log-odds} = l_i = a + bF_i, \qquad (7.36)$$

where F_i represents one of the k numeric levels of the risk factor and l_i represents the log-odds resulting from the ith level of the risk factor. The choice of the F_i values brings a degree of subjectivity to the analysis

Table 7-11. CHD by smoking

Variable	Term	Coefficient	Std. error	p-value	$\hat{or}$
Constant	$\hat{a}$	−2.764	0.104	—	—
Smoking (1–20)	$\hat{b}_1$	0.412	0.163	<0.001	1.510
Smoking (21–30)	$\hat{b}_2$	0.804	0.183	<0.001	2.233
Smoking (30+)	$\hat{b}_3$	0.894	0.201	<0.001	2.444

−2LogLikelihood = 1751.695; number of model parameter = 4.

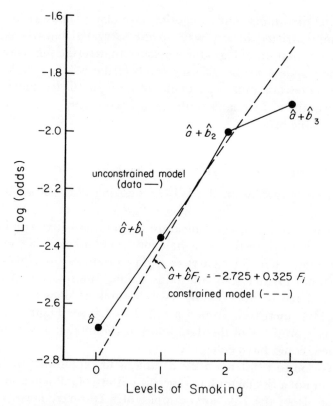

Figure 7-3. Log-odds associated with CHD risk by amount smoked (unconstrained and constrained models).

that will influence the results. For the WCGS example the values $F_0 = 0$, $F_1 = 1$, $F_2 = 2$, and $F_3 = 3$ are chosen to reflect the four smoking levels. Other equally spaced F_i values reflecting each category would give the same analysis (i.e., same p-values and likelihoods but different values a and b). For this straight-line model the log-odds must follow a linearly increasing or decreasing pattern, making the model constrained.

Computer-generated (maximum likelihood) estimates for the parameters of the constrained model from the smoking data are $\hat{a} = -2.725$ and $\hat{b} = 0.325$ (see Figure 7.3). The likelihood value reflecting the fit of the two-parameter constrained model is $L_0 = 1753.045$ (degrees of freedom = 2). The previous unconstrained model has a likelihood of $L_1 = 1751.695$ (degrees of freedom = 4). The difference in likelihood statistics has an approximate χ^2 distribution with 2 degrees of freedom when the fit of the models being compared differs strictly because of sampling variation $(L_0 - L_1 = X^2 = 1.350,\ p\text{-value} = 0.509)$. The comparison shows that using a single line representing the smoking–CHD relationship does not differ in any important way from the saturated, unconstrained model (again see Figure 7.3). The straight-line model adequately and more simply describes the relationship between CHD and smoking. Consequently, smoking levels can be represented as increasing multiplicatively the risk of a CHD event. Note that

$$\hat{l}_i = \hat{a} + \hat{b}F_i \text{ implies that } \hat{or}_{0i} = (e^{\hat{b}})^{F_i}, \qquad (7.37)$$

where $\hat{or}_{0i}$ is the odds ratio associated with the ith level of the risk factor relative to a baseline. For the smoking data then,

$$\hat{or}_{0i} = (e^{\hat{b}})^{F_i} = (e^{0.325})^{F_i} = (1.384)^{F_i}, \qquad (7.38)$$

where the baseline is the nonsmoking group $(F_0 = 0)$ and the other values of F_i are shown in Table 7.12. The linear constrained model translates into logistic probabilities (also given in Table 7.12) since

$$\hat{p}_i = \frac{1}{1 + e^{-(-2.735 + 0.325F_i)}}, \qquad (7.39)$$

which provides an alternative expression of the relationship between smoking exposure group and CHD risk. For example, based on a linear constrained model, smoking 30 or more cigarettes a day produces an odds of a CHD event 2.651 times greater than a the odds among nonsmokers and a probability of a CHD event of 0.147.

The $2 \times 2 \times K$ Case

When a logistic model is used to explore the relationships in a set of data, there are two typical ways to begin: the simplest model or the most complex model. In the first case, variables are added to the model until a useful description is achieved ("forward"). In the second case, variables are removed from the most complex model until a simpler but satisfactory statistical structure is found ("backward"). In this section

Table 7–12. CHD by smoking: Straight-line model

F	0	1	2	3
	$\hat{or}_{00}$	$\hat{or}_{01}$	$\hat{or}_{02}$	$\hat{or}_{03}$
Odds ratio	1.000	1.384	1.915	2.651
$\hat{p}_i$	0.061	0.082	0.111	0.147

Table 7–13. CHD by smoking by A/B

	Type A					Type B				
Cigarettes/day	0	1–20	21–30	30$^+$	Total	0	1–20	21–30	30$^+$	Total
CHD	70	45	34	29	178	28	25	16	10	79
No CHD	714	353	185	159	1,411	840	382	170	94	1,486
Total	784	398	219	188	1,589	868	407	186	104	1,565

the most complicated (most parameters) model will serve as a starting point for analyzing the risk of a disease at k levels of a categorical risk factor at two levels of another variable. The most complicated model (saturated model) for $k = 4$ levels of one variable and two levels of another is given by

$$\text{log-odds} = a + b_1 x_1 + b_2 x_2 + b_3 x_3 + cC + d_1 Cx_1 + d_2 Cx_2 + d_3 Cx_3, \quad (7.40)$$

where x_i is, as before, a dummy variable indicating the categories of a four-level risk factor, while $C = 1$ produces the log-odds when another factor is present and $C = 0$ produces the log-odds when that factor is absent. The terms $d_i Cx_i$ measure the interaction between the k-level risk factor and the two-level risk factor. All direct influences and all possible interactions are included in this statistical structure, yielding an eight-parameter saturated model. To be concrete, let $x_i =$ smoking level using four smoking categories and $C =$ the two levels of behavior type (B coded 0, A coded 1). The WCGS data for four smoking levels and the two behavior categories are given in Table 7.13. The logistic model produces estimates for the eight parameters for the saturated logistic model, as shown in Table 7.14.

This model is a starting point, but the results are not much different from the data themselves since the contingency table produces eight

Table 7–14. CHD by A/B by smoking (saturated)

	Term	Coefficient	Std. error	p-value	$\hat{or}$
Constant	$\hat{a}$	−3.401	0.192	—	—
Smoking (1–20)	$\hat{b}_1$	0.675	0.282	0.017	1.963
Smoking (21–30)	$\hat{b}_2$	1.038	0.324	0.001	2.824
Smoking (30+)	$\hat{b}_3$	1.160	0.384	0.003	3.191
A/B	$\hat{c}$	1.079	0.229	<0.001	2.941
Interaction	$\hat{d}_1$	−0.412	0.347	0.235	0.662
Interaction	$\hat{d}_2$	−0.410	0.395	0.299	0.664
Interaction	$\hat{d}_3$	−0.540	0.452	0.232	0.583

−2LogLikelihood = 1713.694; number of model parameter = 8.

log-odds values and the model employs eight parameters. Although a saturated model is not a very useful summary of a set of data, it produces a baseline against which to compare the efficacy of reduced models (models with fewer parameters) that are simpler representations of the relationships under study. One such reduced model postulates no interactions exist between the k-level factor (smoking) and the dichotomous factor (behavior type). That is, when the two risk factors do not interact, the model becomes strictly additive and is

$$\text{log-odds} = a + b_1 x_1 + b_2 x_2 + b_3 x_3 + cC. \tag{7.41}$$

Note that this model is a special case of the saturated model formed by setting the interaction coefficients to zero $(d_i = 0)$. The maximum likelihood estimates of the five parameters of the no interaction model are given in Table 7.15.

Geometrically, the no interaction model is represented by two parallel lines (Figure 7.4). The pattern is not constrained to either increase or decrease with increasing levels of smoking, but the distance between type A and type B individuals differs by a constant amount (represented by c in the model) on a log-odds scale for all four levels of smoking exposure. That is, the pattern of risk associated with smoking is exactly the same for both type A and type B individuals.

Formally, the difference between the saturated model and the no interaction model is evaluated by comparing the respective likelihood values $(L_0 - L_1 = X^2 = 1716.069 - 1713.694 = 2.375$ with three degrees of freedom and the p-value $= 0.498)$. The comparison shows no persuasive evidence that smoking and behavior type interact implying that smoking and behavior type risk factors are usefully represented as additive influences on a log-odds scale (multiplicatively on an odds scale). For example, the A-type $(C = 1)$ individuals who smoke more than 30 cigarettes per day $(x_1 = 0, x_2 = 0, x_3 = 1)$ have an odds ratio of $\hat{or} = e^{(\hat{b}_3 + \hat{c})} = (2.170)(2.259) = 4.904$ relative to B-type individuals

Table 7-15. CHD by A/B by smoking (no interaction)

Variable	Term	Coefficient	Std. Error	p-value	$\hat{or}$
Constant	$\hat{a}$	-3.223	0.139	—	—
Smoking (1–20)	$\hat{b}_1$	0.401	0.164	0.014	1.493
Smoking (21–30)	$\hat{b}_2$	0.761	0.185	<0.001	2.141
Smoking (30+)	$\hat{b}_3$	0.775	0.203	<0.001	2.170
A/B	$\hat{c}$	0.815	0.141	<0.001	2.259

-2LogLikelihood $= 1716.069$; number of model parameters $= 5$.

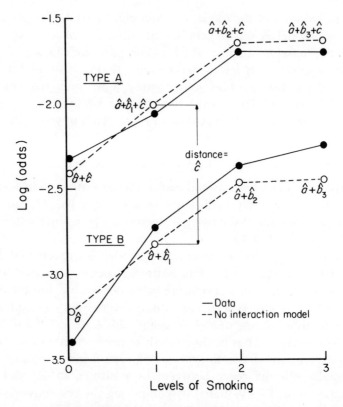

Figure 7-4. Log-odds associated with CHD risk by amount smoked and by behavior type (unconstrained and additive model)

$(C = 0)$ who are nonsmokers $(x_1 = x_2 = x_3 = 0)$. Figure 7.4 contrasts the no interaction model with the data (saturated model).

A further step in building an appropriate model to understand the relationships of the three variables recorded in the $2 \times 2 \times K$ contingency table is to postulate a model that is linearly constrained. When the influence from the k-level factor is linearly related to the risk of disease, the model is

$$\text{log-odds} = a + bF_i + cC + dF_iC, \qquad (7.42)$$

where in this case F_i is a numeric (or coded) value representing the ith level of a risk factor. Note that the interaction term F_iC is included. Continuing the smoking–behavior-type data, as before, $F_i = 0, 1, 2,$ or 3 for levels of smoking and C is again a binary variable $(1, 0)$ representing the dichotomous risk factor, behavior type (A, B).

Geometrically, the log-odds in this model [expression (7.42)] represent the relationships in the $2 \times 2 \times K$ contingency table as two straight lines with different slopes and intercepts: one line for each level of the dichotomous variable C. In terms of the example, a straight line for type A individuals and a straight line for type B individuals reflects the log-odds risk of disease associated with the four levels of smoking. Explicitly this statistical structure is

$$\text{when } C = 0 \text{ (type B), then log-odds} = a + bF_i. \qquad (7.43)$$

and

$$\text{when } C = 1 \text{ (type A), then log-odds} = (a+c) + (b+d)F_i = A + BF_i. \qquad (7.44)$$

These two linear relationships do not differ in principle from the straight-line logistic model used in the previous section to analyze the $2 \times K$ contingency table since these data can be viewed as two separate $2 \times K$ contingency tables. The estimates of the four parameters of the constrained model are given in Table 7.16.

Using the estimated parameters, equations for the two straight lines are: $\text{log-odds} = \hat{a} + \hat{b}F_i = -3.305 + 0.423F_i$ (type B individuals) and $\text{log-odds} = \hat{A} + \hat{B}F_i = -2.300 + 0.233F_i$ (type A individuals). Contrasting this constrained model with the unconstrained saturated model ($L_0 - L_1 = X^2 = 1715.859 - 1713.694 = 2.165$ with four degrees of freedom produces a p-value of 0.705) shows that different straight lines describing the response in CHD risk from increased levels of smoking for each behavior type are an excellent summary (Figure 7.5).

A further refinement of this constrained statistical structure is possible by postulating that the response to the k levels of one risk factor is the same at both levels of the dichotomous risk factor. This no-interaction model is achieved by setting $d = 0$ in the previous model [expression (7.42)], giving an additive three-parameter expression or

$$\text{log-odds} = a + bF_i + cC. \qquad (7.45)$$

Table 7–16. CHD by A/B by smoking (constrained)

Variable	Term	Coefficient	Std. error	p-value	$\hat{or}$
Constant	$\hat{a}$	-3.305	0.164	—	—
Smoking	$\hat{b}$	0.423	0.108	<0.001	1.52
A/B	$\hat{c}$	1.005	0.198	<0.001	2.733
Interaction	$\hat{d}$	-0.190	0.130	0.144	0.827

$-2\text{LogLikelihood} = 1715.859$; number of model parameters = 4.

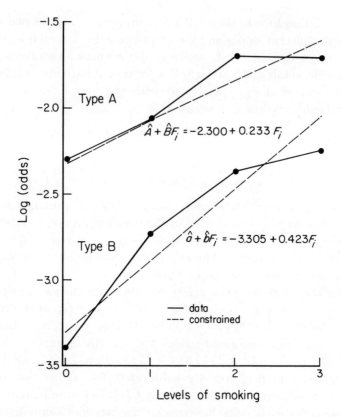

Figure 7–5. Log-odds associated with CHD risk by amount smoked and by behavior type (constrained model).

Again, the data are described by two straight lines, one for each level of the dichotomous risk factor, but the lines have identical slopes, namely b. Using this model, computer estimates of the three parameters are given in Table 7.17.

The comparison of the likelihoods of the two constrained models shows that describing the contingency table data (Table 7.13) with two

Table 7–17. CHD by A/B by smoking (constrained: no interaction)

Variable	Term	Coefficient	Std. error	p-value	$\hat{or}$
Constant	$\hat{a}$	-3.171	0.129	—	—
Smoking	$\hat{b}$	0.290	0.060	<0.001	1.336
A/B	$\hat{c}$	0.808	0.141	<0.001	2.244

$-2\text{LogLikelihood} = 1717.972$; number of model parameter $= 3$.

parallel lines is not misleading and provides an adequate description of CHD risk ($L_0 - L_1 = X^2 = 1717.912 - 1715.859 = 2.053$ with one degree of freedom, producing p-value $= 0.151$). This three-parameter description of the relationships among smoking, behavior type, and CHD allows a particularly simple expression for the multiplicative role of these factors in the risk of coronary disease (see Figure 7.6). The two estimated parallel lines are: log-odds $= \hat{a} + \hat{b}F_i = -3.171 + 0.290F_i$ for type B individuals and log-odds $= \hat{A} + \hat{b}F_i = -2.363 + 0.290F_i$ for type A individuals. The no interaction constrained model translates into odds ratios:

$$\text{for } C = 0 \text{ (type B)}, \; \hat{or}_{0i} = (1.336)^{F_i} \tag{7.46}$$

and

$$\text{for } C = 1 \text{ (type A)}, \; \hat{or}_{0i} = 2.244(1.336)^{F_i}, \tag{7.47}$$

where $\hat{or}_{0i}$ is again the odds ratio associated with the ith level of

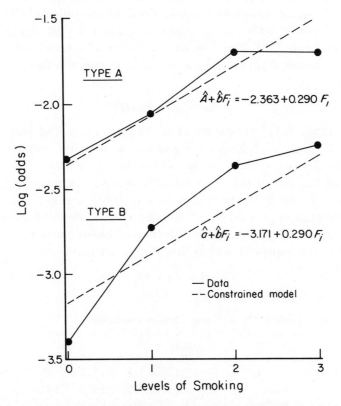

Figure 7-6. Log-odds associated with CHD risk by amount smoked and by behavior type (constrained and additive model).

Table 7–18. CHD by smoking by behavior type: Parallel straight-line model

Levels	0	1	2	3
	$\hat{or}_{00}$	$\hat{or}_{01}$	$\hat{or}_{02}$	$\hat{or}_{03}$
Type A	2.244	2.998	4.005	5.351
Type B	1.000	1.336	1.785	2.385

smoking relative to the nonsmokers for each of the behavior types. This structure gives the odds ratio estimates shown in Table 7.18. These estimated odds ratios succinctly summarize the role of behavior type and smoking in the risk of a coronary event.

Trend in the Odds Ratios

To a large extent the analysis of trend in a set of odds ratios is contained in the previous discussion, but it is worth focusing specifically on this aspect of logistic regression analysis. Data on smoking and CHD along with a series of odds ratios estimated under different conditions are given in Table 7.19. The directly calculated odds ratios and the odds ratios estimated from the logistic model do not substantially differ. The model

$$\text{log-odds} = a + bF_i \tag{7.48}$$

summarizes, as before, the trend in the odds ratios and produces the values $\hat{or}$ unadjusted. Both the direct and unadjusted estimates show a definite increasing trend in the odds ratios with increasing levels of smoking but fail to take into account influences from other possibly confounding variables. For example, a variable such as blood pressure may have an impact on the observed trend attributable to increased smoking. To account for the influence of blood pressure, a term is added to the logistic model so that the model becomes

$$\text{log-odds} = a + bF_i + dD, \tag{7.49}$$

Table 7–19. Odds ratios: Smoking and CHD

F_i	0	1	2	3
CHD	98	70	50	39
No CHD	1554	735	355	253
$\hat{or}$ direct	1	1.510	2.233	2.444
$\hat{or}$ unadjusted	1	1.384	1.915	2.651
$\hat{or}$ adjusted	1	1.378	1.900	2.619

where $D = 0$ (blood pressure < 140) and $D = 1$ (blood pressure $\geqslant 140$). The extended model yields an estimate of the coefficient associated with the trend in disease risk from smoking adjusted for the influence of blood pressure, $\hat{b} = 0.321$. Comparison of the unadjusted and adjusted regression coefficients shows that blood pressure measured as a binary variable has little influence on the increasing risk of a coronary event associated with the amount smoked [i.e., $\hat{b}$ (unadjusted) $= 0.325$ and $\hat{b}$ (adjusted) $= 0.321$]. The lack of difference in these coefficients is, of course, reflected in the similarity of the estimates of the unadjusted and the adjusted odds ratios (Table 7.19). The formal test of trend is the usual test of the coefficient b. A χ^2 statistic for trend is, again, $X^2 = (\hat{b}/S_{\hat{b}})^2$ and X^2 has a χ^2 distribution with one degree of freedom when no trend exists $(H_0: b = 0)$.

Adjustment for the influence of any number of variables follows the same pattern. The impact of each variable is accounted for by the logistic model, and the coefficient for trend yields an adjusted odds ratio when these variables are included in the model. More exactly, the model

$$\text{log-odds} = a + bF_i + cC + dD + \cdots \qquad (7.50)$$

yields an estimate of b adjusted for the influence of the other variables in the expression and produces an unconfounded description of the trend in risk associated with the variable represented by F_i.

The $2 \times 2 \times 2 \times K$ Case

Of course, any number of variables can be used to form a contingency table. This section describes a logistic model employed to summarize relationships among three discrete risk variables and a disease outcome. Interest is again focused on defining the role of behavior type (two levels) in the risk of a coronary event while accounting for the influences from smoking ($k = 4$ levels) and blood pressure. As before, the blood pressure variable is defined by two levels (< 140 and $\geqslant 140$). These three risk variables produce a $2 \times 2 \times 2 \times 4$ contingency table of WCGS data in (Table 7.20). These data, in a slightly different format, are given in the introduction to this chapter (Table 7.1).

A saturated model containing 16 parameters can be estimated from the data in Table 7.20. The likelihood value serves as a point of comparison for reduced models. The likelihood value is the minimum possible, since a saturated model fits the data perfectly so that a reasonable goodness-of-fit measure will be at its minimum. For the

Table 7-20. CHD by smoking by A/B by blood pressure

	Type A and blood pressure ≥ 140				
Cigarettes/day	0	1—20	21—30	30⁺	Total
CHD	29	21	7	12	69
No CHD	155	76	45	43	319
Total	184	97	52	55	388

	Type A and blood pressure < 140				
Cigarettes/day	0	1—20	21—30	30⁺	Total
CHD	41	24	27	17	109
No CHD	559	277	140	116	1,092
Total	600	301	167	133	1,201

	Type B and blood pressure ≥ 140				
Cigarettes/day	0	1—20	21—30	30⁺	Total
CHD	8	9	3	7	27
No CHD	171	62	31	14	278
Total	179	71	34	21	305

	Type B and blood pressure < 140				
Cigarettes/day	0	1—20	21—30	30⁺	Total
CHD	20	16	13	3	52
No CHD	669	320	139	80	1,208
Total	689	336	152	83	1,260

WCGS data, this minimum is likelihood = 1667.138 with 16 degrees of freedom.

A basic question to be addressed is: To what extent can the 16-parameter saturated model be reduced and still maintain a faithful but simpler representation of the relationships among the four variables (A/B, smoking, blood pressure, and CHD)? A "minimum" model that accounts for influences from the three risk factors involves four parameters, no interaction among the risk factors, and smoking levels constrained to produce the same linear response in CHD risk for the four levels of the other two risk variables. This four-parameter logistic model is

$$\text{log-odds} = a + bF_i + cC + dD, \qquad (7.51)$$

where F_i is one of the coded levels of smoking (again, 0, 1, 2, and 3), $C = 0$ or 1 indicates the behavior type (B, A), and $D = 0$ or 1 indicates the level of blood pressure (<140, $\geqslant 140$). The estimates of the four parameters for this model are given in Table 7.21.

Geometrically the model represents the data as four parallel straight lines on a log-odds scale (one for each of four blood-pressure–behavior-type categories), each describing a linear increase in CHD risk from increased smoking. The distance between these lines results from the differing influences of blood pressure and behavior type on the risk of a coronary event. The four parallel lines along with the data (saturated model) are shown in Figure 7.7.

The utility of this four-parameter model compared to the saturated model can be evaluated by contrasting likelihood values (reduced versus saturated; $L_0 - L_1 = X^2 = 1688.422 - 1667.138 = 21.284$ with 12 degrees of freedom giving p-value $= 0.046$). This much simpler statistical structure is not an extremely accurate reflection of the relationships among the risk factors and the log-odds associated with a coronary event. The difference between these two descriptions of the data illustrates the typical tradeoff between lack of fit and simplicity of the model. Although the simpler model is not ideal, it gives an approximate measure of the magnitude of the influences of the three risk factors on CHD producing Table 7.22.

The odds ratios in this table are derived from combinations of the parameter estimates $\hat{b}$, $\hat{c}$, and $\hat{d}$ using the relationship

$$\hat{or} = e^{\hat{b}F_i + \hat{c}C + \hat{d}D} = (1.331)^{F_i}(2.157)^{C}(2.179)^{D}, \qquad (7.52)$$

which identifies the risk associated with the 15 different levels of the risk factors relative to the baseline category (nonsmokers, type B with blood

Table 7–21. CHD by A/B by smoking by blood pressure (no interaction and constrained)

Variable	Term	Coefficient	Std. error	p-value	$\hat{or}$
Constant	$\hat{a}$	-3.365	0.136	—	—
Smoking	$\hat{b}$	0.286	0.060	<0.001	1.331
A/B	$\hat{c}$	0.769	0.142	<0.001	2.157
Blood pressure	$\hat{d}$	0.779	0.139	<0.001	2.179

-2LogLikelihood $= 1688.422$; number of model parameter $= 4$.

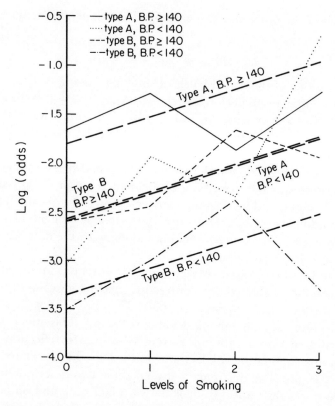

Figure 7–7. Log-odds associated with CHD risk by systolic blood pressure (<140 and ≥140), by amount smoked, and by behavior type (constrained and additive model).

pressure <140). Note that the highest risk is about 11 times the baseline when each factor has a separate (multiplicative) influence. Type A individuals with blood pressure <140 have about the same log-odds pattern as type B individuals with blood pressure ≥140, which is expected since the logistic model coefficients $\hat{c}$ and $\hat{d}$ are about equal. Table 7.22 begins, using the three-parameter logistic model, to

Table 7–22. CHD by A/B by systolic blood pressure: Odds ratio

Blood pressure	Behavior type	$F = 0$	$F = 1$	$F = 2$	$F = 3$
≥140	A	4.702	6.259	8.331	11.090
≥140	B	2.179	2.901	3.861	5.140
<140	A	2.158	2.872	3.823	5.089
<140	B	1.000	1.331	1.772	2.358

address the questions suggested by the analogous table present at the beginning of this chapter (Table 7.1).

Goodness-of-fit: Discrete Case

For contingency table data, the goodness-of-fit of a logistic model can be assessed in typical fashion by generating a series of expected values based on the model ($\hat{n}_k$) and comparing these values to the observed data (n_k) with a χ^2 statistic. The expected value in each cell in the table results from a combination of parameters of the model. These parameters generate a logistic probability that, multiplied by a marginal

Table 7-23. Goodness of fit—various summaries

Outcome	Type	b.p.	F_i	n_k	$\hat{n}_k$	$n_k - \hat{n}_k$	$(n_k - \hat{n}_k)/\sqrt{\hat{n}_k}$	$(n_k - \hat{n}_k)^2/\hat{n}_k$
CHD	A	$\geqslant 140$	0	29	25.722	3.278	0.646	0.418
CHD	A	$\geqslant 140$	1	21	17.251	3.749	0.903	0.815
CHD	A	$\geqslant 140$	2	7	11.625	−4.625	−1.357	1.840
CHD	A	$\geqslant 140$	3	12	15.239	−3.239	−0.830	0.689
No CHD	A	$\geqslant 140$	0	155	158.278	−3.278	−0.261	0.068
No CHD	A	$\geqslant 140$	1	76	79.749	−3.749	−0.420	0.176
No CHD	A	$\geqslant 140$	2	45	40.375	4.625	0.728	0.530
No CHD	A	$\geqslant 140$	3	43	39.761	3.239	0.514	0.264
CHD	A	< 140	0	41	42.027	−1.027	−0.158	0.025
CHD	A	< 140	1	24	27.428	−3.428	−0.655	0.428
CHD	A	< 140	2	27	19.663	7.337	1.655	2.738
CHD	A	< 140	3	17	20.062	−3.062	−0.684	0.467
No CHD	A	< 140	0	559	557.973	1.027	0.043	0.002
No CHD	A	< 140	1	277	273.572	3.428	0.207	0.043
No CHD	A	< 140	2	140	147.337	−7.337	−0.604	0.365
No CHD	A	< 140	3	116	112.938	3.062	0.288	0.083
CHD	B	$\geqslant 140$	0	8	12.422	−4.422	−1.255	1.574
CHD	B	$\geqslant 140$	1	9	6.411	2.589	1.023	1.046
CHD	B	$\geqslant 140$	2	3	3.968	−0.968	−0.486	0.236
CHD	B	$\geqslant 140$	3	7	3.141	3.859	2.177	4.741
No CHD	B	$\geqslant 140$	0	171	166.578	4.422	0.343	0.117
No CHD	B	$\geqslant 140$	1	62	64.589	−2.589	−0.322	0.104
No CHD	B	$\geqslant 140$	2	31	30.032	0.968	0.177	0.031
No CHD	B	$\geqslant 140$	3	14	17.859	−3.859	−0.913	0.834
CHD	B	< 140	0	20	23.018	−3.018	−0.629	0.396
CHD	B	< 140	1	16	14.778	1.222	0.318	0.101
CHD	B	< 140	2	13	8.771	4.229	1.428	2.039
CHD	B	< 140	3	3	6.256	−3.256	−1.302	1.694
No CHD	B	< 140	0	669	665.982	3.018	0.117	0.014
No CHD	B	< 140	1	320	321.222	−1.222	−0.068	0.005
No CHD	B	< 140	2	139	143.229	−4.229	−0.353	0.125
No CHD	B	< 140	3	80	76.744	3.256	0.372	0.138
Total	—	—	—	3154	3154	0.0	0.0	22.126

frequency, produces a value that is exactly the frequency expected under the model. The data on blood pressure (two levels), behavior type (two levels), and smoking (four levels) produce the 32 ($k = 1$, $2, \ldots, 32$) expected values based on the four-parameter logistic model shown in Table 7.23. The logistic probabilities are estimated using

$$\hat{p}_{disease} = \frac{1}{1 + e^{-(\hat{a} + \hat{b}F_i + \hat{c}C + \hat{d}D)}} \tag{7.53}$$

and $\hat{n}_k$ is either $n\hat{p}_{disease}$ individuals with CHD events or $n(1 - \hat{p}_{disease})$ individuals with no occurrences of CHD. For example, $\hat{n}_4 = n\hat{p}_{disease} = (n_D + n_{\bar{D}})\hat{p}_{disease} = 55(0.277) = 15.239$ is the number of expected CHD events and $\hat{n}_8 = 55 - 15.239 = 39.761$ is the number of expected non-CHD among 55 study subjects who are type A individuals with blood pressures greater than or equal to 140 and who smoke more than 30 cigarettes per day. The corresponding observed values are $n_4 = 12$ and $n_8 = 43$. All 32 values are similarly calculated. A χ^2 goodness-of-fit (the sum of the last column) statistic yields $X^2 = 22.126$ (12 degrees of freedom) and a p-value of 0.036. The four-parameter model, as seen in Table 7.23 (columns 8 or 9), is a reasonable representation of the data for most cells. Only a few categories are seriously misrepresented by the additive, constrained logistic model ($\hat{p}_{disease}$). The similarity between the classic χ^2 approach and the comparison of the likelihood statistics is typical (22.126 versus 21.284 both with degrees of freedom of 12). The two methods are likely to be similar for large sample sizes and usually do not substantially differ when applied to small data sets.

SUMMARIZING A SERIES OF 2 × 2 TABLES

As already noted, one way to deal with the confounding influence of a variable is to stratify a set of data into a series of more or less homogeneous groups based on values of the confounding variable (discussed in Chapter 2). This process can produce a series of 2 × 2 tables (one table per stratum). For example, a series of strata formed on the basis of age might each contain a set of individuals classified by the presence or absence of a coronary event as well as behavior type (A or B). To combine properly information from a series of 2 × 2 tables, three issues are important:

1. Interaction: Is the association between risk factor and disease the same for all tables (strata)?;

2. Association: If the association is the same, is it substantial?—not likely a result of random variation;
3. Estimation: If the association is the same and it is not likely random, then what is the magnitude of the risk–disease association?

These issues have been traditionally addressed without using a multivariate statistical model. Three approaches to answering these questions are briefly reviewed in the following sections, and, additionally, the parallel multivariate logistic model approach applied to the same issues is presented.

Test of Homogeneity

A single summary of the relationships among a number of 2×2 tables only makes sense when the relationships summarized are the same for all tables (no interaction). In terms of an odds ratio, if a series of 2×2 tables reflects the same degree of association between risk factor and disease outcome (random fluctuations from a common overall value), then a single summary odds ratio serves as an accurate measure of that association. A method by Woolf [Ref. 6] is one way to assess homogeneity among a series of odds ratios. The null hypothesis conjectures that the odds ratio estimates calculated from each of k tables differ only because of random variation, or

$$H_0: or_1 = or_2 = \cdots = or_k = or,$$

where or_i is the odds ratio associated with the ith 2×2 table. A summary odds ratio ($\hat{or}_W$), derived from a weighted average of the logarithms of the stratum-specific odds ratios ($\hat{or}_i$), is

$$\log(\hat{or}_W) = \frac{\sum\limits_{i=1}^{k} w_i \log(\hat{or}_i)}{\sum\limits_{i=1}^{k} w_i} \qquad (7.54)$$

(W for Woolf, who first presented the estimate) with the weights w_i given by

$$w_i = \frac{1}{\text{variance}[\log(\hat{or}_i)]} = \left(\frac{1}{a_i + \frac{1}{2}} + \frac{1}{b_i + \frac{1}{2}} + \frac{1}{c_i + \frac{1}{2}} + \frac{1}{d_i + \frac{1}{2}}\right)^{-1}. \qquad (7.55)$$

The intuitive rationale for these weights is that reliable estimates (small variance) have relatively large weight and unreliable estimates (large variance) have relatively small weight in determining the overall summary value. Instead of the odds ratios, the logarithms of the odds ratios produce estimates with approximately normal distributions (see Appendix). The estimate of the odds ratio from each table ($\hat{or}_i$) can have one of several forms (again see Appendix). Here the odds ratio is estimated by

$$\hat{or}_i = \frac{(a_i + \frac{1}{2})(d_i + \frac{1}{2})}{(b_i + \frac{1}{2})(c_i + \frac{1}{2})}. \tag{7.56}$$

The question of whether the individual odds ratios (or_i) systematically differ from the overall odds ratio (or) is addressed by the Woolf test for homogeneity using a χ^2 test statistic

$$X_W^2 = \sum_{i=1}^{k} w_i [\log(\hat{or}_i) - \log(\hat{or}_W)]^2. \tag{7.57}$$

The statistic X_W^2 has an approximate χ^2 distribution with $k - 1$ degrees of freedom when the 2×2 tables are homogeneous with respect to the odds ratio (H_0 is true); large values indicate that the odds ratios are not likely to be the same in all or some of the k strata.

The WCGS data serve once again to illustrate. Table 7.24 shows study participants divided into five age groups to examine the relationship between behavior type and CHD. These data consist of five 2×2 tables, which generate the odds ratio measures of association between behavior type and CHD in each strata given in Table 7.25. Using the example data, $\log(\hat{or}_W) = 0.773$ ($\hat{or}_W = 2.166$) and

$$X_W^2 = 6.966(0.695 - 0.773)^2 + \cdots + 6.811(1.023 - 0.773)^2 = 0.773. \tag{7.58}$$

The test of homogeneity ($X_W^2 = 0.773$ with four degrees of freedom; p-value $= 0.942$) shows no reason to infer that the odds ratios differ among the five age categories—no evidence of interaction.

Table 7–24. WCGS: Age by behavior type by CHD

	Type A		Type B		
	CHD	No CHD	CHD	No CHD	Total
Age	a_i	b_i	c_i	d_i	n_i
< 40	20	241	11	271	543
40—44	34	462	21	574	1,091
45—49	49	337	21	343	750
50—54	38	209	17	184	448
54$^+$	37	162	9	114	322
Total	178	1,411	79	1,486	3,154

Table 7-25. WCGS: Odds ratios by age

Age	$\hat{or}_i$	$\log(\hat{or}_i)$	variance[$\log(\hat{or}_i)$]	w_i
<40	2.004	0.695	0.144	6.966
40–45	1.993	0.690	0.079	12.594
45–49	2.343	0.852	0.073	13.776
50–54	1.937	0.661	0.093	10.717
54+	2.781	1.023	0.147	6.811
Total	2.373	0.864	—	—

Test of Association

A second step in summarizing a series of 2×2 tables is to assess the association between the risk factor and the disease, using the data from all k tables. One such test is called the Mantel–Haenszel χ^2 test [Ref. 6] (Cochran suggested a similar test in an earlier paper [Ref. 7]). The approach argues that the cell frequencies in each 2×2 table can be estimated from the marginal frequencies if the risk factor and disease are independent (null hypothesis). That is, for each strata the observed value a_i should equal $\hat{A}_i$, except for random variation, where $\hat{A}_i$ is calculated under the hypothesis of independence and, as before [expression (5.20) or (6.2)], is

$$\hat{A}_i = \frac{(a_i + c_i)(a_i + b_i)}{n_i}. \tag{7.59}$$

The variance of a_i is estimated by

$$\text{variance}(a_i) = V_i = \frac{(a_i + b_i)(a_i + c_i)(b_i + d_i)(c_i + d_i)}{n_i^2(n_i - 1)}. \tag{7.60}$$

The Mantel–Haenszel χ^2 test statistic compares $\Sigma\, a_i$ with $\Sigma\, \hat{A}_i$ and is

$$X_{\text{MH}}^2 = \frac{\left(\sum_{i=1}^{k} a_i - \sum_{i=1}^{k} \hat{A}_i\right)^2}{\sum_{i=1}^{k} V_i} \tag{7.61}$$

(MH for Mantel—Haenszel—See appendix).

The Mantel—Haenszel χ^2 statistic combines information from each table resulting in a test statistic that measures the overall association between risk factor and disease outcome as long as the odds ratios are homogeneous (no interaction). The value X_{MH}^2 has an approximate χ^2 distribution with one degree of freedom when risk factor and disease are unrelated in all k strata. Continuing the WCGS example, since $\Sigma\, a_i = 178$ and $\Sigma\, \hat{A}_i = 134.684$, $X_{\text{MH}}^2 = (178 - 134.684)^2/57.444$

$= 32.663$ (p-value < 0.001), producing strong evidence that behavior type and CHD are associated.

Estimation of a Common Odds Ratio

The third step in summarizing a series of 2×2 tables is to estimate the common measure of association. A popular estimate that provides an overall measure of association is the Mantel–Haenszel summary odds ratio [Ref. 6] given by

$$\hat{or}_{MH} = \frac{\sum_{i=1}^{k} a_i d_i / n_i}{\sum_{i=1}^{k} b_i c_i / n_i}. \qquad (7.62)$$

When a series of odds ratios is homogeneous, then $\hat{or}_{MH}$ estimates the common value. For the age and behavior type data, the Mantel–Haenszel summary odds ratio is

$$\hat{or}_{MH} = \frac{(20)(271)/543 + \cdots + (37)(114)/322}{(241)(11)/543 + \cdots + (162)(9)/322} = 2.214. \qquad (7.63)$$

The estimated odds ratio 2.214 summarizes, using information from each age stratum ("adjusted for the influence of age"), the risk of CHD for the two behavior types. The Woolf summary odds ratio $\hat{or}_W = 2.166$ [expression (7.48)] is also an estimate of the odds ratio common to the fine 2×2 tables.

Logistic Regression Approach

The Woolf test of interaction, the Mantel–Haenszel test of association, and the Mantel–Haenszel summary odds ratio have analogous measures derived from logistic regression models. In most situations, the results are similar from these rather different approaches.

Four basic logistic models that relate CHD outcome to the risk factors age and behavior type are

1. Model (saturated):

$$\text{log-odds} = a + bF + c_1 x_1 + c_2 x_2 + c_3 x_3 + c_4 x_4 + d_1 F x_1 + d_2 F x_2 + d_3 F x_3 + d_4 F x_4.$$

The variable F represents type A (when $F = 1$) and type B (when $F = 0$) behavior; x_1, x_2, x_3, and x_4 represent dummy variables to account for the five age categories. The likelihood associated with this saturated 10-parameter model is likelihood $= 1702.156$. Three relevant reduced models and parameter estimates are given in Tables 7.26–7.28.

Table 7-26.

log-odds $= a + bF + c_1x_1 + c_2x_2 + c_3x_3 + c_4x_4$

Variable	Term	Coefficient	Std. error	p-value	Odds ratio
Constant	$\hat{a}$	-2.461	0.192	—	—
A/B	$\hat{b}$	0.793	0.141	<0.001	2.210
Age	$\hat{c}_1$	-0.112	0.232	0.629	0.894
Age	$\hat{c}_2$	0.510	0.225	0.023	1.665
Age	$\hat{c}_3$	0.793	0.236	<0.001	2.211
Age	$\hat{c}_4$	0.921	0.246	<0.001	2.512

-2LogLikelihood $= 1703.010$; number of model parameters $= 6$.

Table 7-27.

log-odds $= a + c_1x_1 + c_2x_2 + c_3x_3 + c_4x_4$

Variable	Term	Coefficient	Std. error	p-value	Odds ratio
Constant	$\hat{a}$	-2.894	0.192	—	—
Age	$\hat{c}_1$	-0.132	0.231	0.569	0.877
Age	$\hat{c}_2$	0.531	0.224	0.018	1.700
Age	$\hat{c}_3$	0.838	0.234	<0.001	2.311
Age	$\hat{c}_4$	1.013	0.246	<0.001	2.753

-2LogLikelihood $= 1736.578$; number of model parameter $= 5$.

Table 7-28.

log-odds $= a + bF$

Variable	Term	Coefficient	Std. error	p-value	$\hat{or}$
Constant	$\hat{a}$	-2.934	0.115	—	—
A/B	$\hat{b}$	0.864	0.140	<0.001	2.373

-2LogLikelihood $= 1740.344$; number of model parameter $= 2$.

2. Additive model (behavior type and age—no interaction).

$$\text{log-odds} = a + bF + c_1x_1 + c_2x_2 + c_3x_3 + c_4x_4$$

3. Model (age only).

$$\text{log-odds} = a + c_1x_1 + c_2x_2 + c_3x_3 + c_4x_4$$

4. Model (behavior type only).

$$\text{log-odds} = a + bF$$

Some summary results of applying these four models to the WCGS data are shown in Table 7.29.

To test for possible interaction effects (different odds ratios among some or all of the five age categories), two likelihoods are contrasted. The likelihood calculated from the saturated model ($L_1 = 1702.156$) is compared to the likelihood from the model with the interaction terms ignored ($L_2 = 1703.010$), producing a difference of $L_2 - L_1 = X^2 = 0.854$, which measures the lack of homogeneity among the five odds ratios. The contrast of the fit of the logistic models shows no evidence of an interaction (p-value = 0.931). This result is similar to the Woolf homogeneity χ^2 value, and these two approaches are likely to be similar in general.

A Mantel–Haenszel-like test of the association between behavior type and CHD can be conducted in the context of a logistic model. The difference between the model containing the risk factors behavior type and age (model 2) and the model containing only age (model 3) measures the degree of association between behavior type and CHD outcome while accounting for the influence of age. These two models produce a difference in likelihoods analogous to the X^2_{MH}. The difference $L_3 - L_2$ has a χ^2 distribution with one degree of freedom when the risk variable is unrelated to the outcome. Both the Mantel–Haenszel and the logistic model approaches require that no interactions exist among the k tables. For the age–behavior-type data, $L_3 - L_2 = X^2 = 1736.578 - 1703.010 = 33.568$ (p-value <0.001), which is not very different from the X^2_{MH} calculated to assess the same association. Like the tests of the interaction effects, these two tests of association will also be similar in general.

Last, when the five 2×2 tables show no interactions, the strictly additive logistic model (model 2) produces an estimate of the strength of the risk-factor–disease association unbiased by confounding influences from age. For the WCGS data, $\hat{b}$ is 0.793 and the estimated odds ratio is $\hat{or} = e^{0.793} = 2.210$, which is almost identical to $\hat{or}_{MH} = 2.214$. Both estimates are a measure of the relative role of A/B

Table 7–29. Comparison of model

Model	L_i	−2LogLikelihood	$\hat{b}$	Std. error	$\hat{or}$	Parameters
A/B + age + interactions	L_1	1702.156	0.715	0.386	2.045	10
A/B + age	L_2	1703.010	0.793	0.141	2.210	6
Age only	L_3	1736.578	—	—	—	5
A/B only	L_4	1740.344	0.864	0.140	2.373	2

Table 7–30. Summary of two approaches for combining 2×2 tables

	No model	Logistic model
Homogeneity	$X^2_W = 0.773$	$X^2 = 0.854$
Association	$X^2_{MH} = 32.663$	$X^2 = 35.568$
Odds ratio	$\hat{or}_{MH} = 2.214$	$\hat{or} = 2.210$

behavior type in determining the risk of CHD independent of the influence of age. The logistic model odds ratio estimate from the additive model and the Mantel–Haenszel summary odds ratio estimate will usually be similar. Note that both estimates require homogeneity of the odds ratios (no interactions) among the k tables to summarize usefully the behavior-type–CHD association. The maximum likelihood estimate $\hat{or} = e^{\hat{b}}$ from the additive logistic model is very slightly more efficient (smaller variance) than $\hat{or}_{MH}$. A summary of these two approaches is given in Table 7.30.

8 The Analysis of Continuous Data: Logistic Model II

Three basic features of the logistic regression model are: the appropriateness of binary outcome variables, estimation of adjusted odds ratios, and the effective analysis of both continuous and discrete variables as risk factors. This chapter focuses on the last property. The logistic model capitalizes on the actual measurement to attain the maximum amount of information from a measured risk factor, whether the variable is discrete or continuous. There is no need to distribute continuous data into a series of sometimes arbitrary categories. Application of a logistic model uses risk factors measured in their original units, producing a less arbitrary and more powerful analysis.

Simple Logistic Regression

The logistic model, as before, is expressed in terms of either the log-odds of disease or the probability of disease. Again, the log-odds is assumed to be a linear function of the risk factor magnitude or

$$\text{log-odds} = l_x = a + bx, \tag{8.1}$$

where l_x represents the logarithm of the odds of disease occurrence for a specific continuous value x of the risk factor. The coefficient b measures the change (additive) in risk of disease associated with a one unit change in the risk factor on the log-odds scale; e^b measures the change (multiplicative) in the risk of disease associated with a one unit change in the risk factor on the odds scale. Expression (8.1) is functionally the same as the model used in the purely discrete case [expression (7.1)], but when the risk factor represented by x is a continuous variable, the application and interpretation of the logistic model takes on a somewhat different character.

To illustrate logistic regression using a binary disease outcome and a single continuous risk factor, a person's body weight (x) is assessed as a risk factor for the onset of coronary heart disease. Computer estimates (maximum likehood estimates) produce values of the logistic parameters a and b from the WCGS data as given in Table 8.1. The estimated models relating body weight and the risk of a coronary event are then

$$\hat{l}_x = -4.215 + 0.0104x \quad \text{or} \quad \hat{p}_x = \frac{1}{1 + e^{-(-4.215 + 0.0104x)}}. \quad (8.2)$$

For example, the log-odds that a CHD event occurs to a 200-pound man ($x = 200$) participating in the WCGS is $\hat{l}_{200} = -2.135$ based on the linear log-odds form of the logistic model; the probability of a CHD event is $\hat{p}_{200} = (1 + e^{2.135})^{-1} = 0.106$ based on the estimated logistic model. This probability refers to about 7.5 years of WCGS data collection and represents about a 7.5-fold increase over a value for 1 year (a more typical unit of time).

The importance of the variable x in influencing the probability of disease can be statistically evaluated in the usual way, using the estimated standard error ($S_{\hat{b}}$) of the estimated coefficient $\hat{b}$. That is, the quantity

$$X^2 = (\hat{b}/S_{\hat{b}})^2 = (0.0104/0.003)^2 = 12.018 \quad (8.3)$$

has an approximate χ^2 distribution with one degree of freedom when the risk factor is unrelated to the disease. The variance estimate $S_{\hat{b}}^2$ is typically a byproduct of the maximum likelihood estimation process. Formally, this χ^2 statistic provides a test of the null hypothesis that the coefficient represented by b is zero (i.e., H_0: $b = 0$). The logistic regression coefficient $\hat{b} = 0.0104$ shows clear evidence of an association (p-value < 0.001) between body weight and the probability of a coronary event.

The odds ratio associated with the risk factor ($e^{\hat{b}} = \hat{or}$) measures the increase in odds for a one unit change in the risk factor. For the present example (Table 8.1), $\hat{b} = 0.0104$ and the estimated odds ratio is then $\hat{or} = e^{0.0104} = 1.0104$. At first glance it might be concluded that this odds ratio is essentially 1.0 and not biologically meaningful, but it is important to keep in mind that the coefficient b measures risk in the units associated with the risk factor (in the WCGS case pounds). The

Table 8-1. CHD by weight

Variable	Term	Coefficient	Std. error	p-value	$\hat{or}$
Constant	$\hat{a}$	−4.215	0.512	—	—
Weight	$\hat{b}$	0.0104	0.003	<0.001	1.010

−2LogLikelihood = 1768.938; number of model parameters = 2.

odds ratio e^b reflects the multiplicative increase in risk for a one unit change in the risk factor or, in terms of the illustrative data, a one pound gain of weight multiplies the odds of coronary disease by a factor of 1.0104. For example, if a person gains 20 pounds in weight, the risk of a coronary event increases $20\hat{b}$ on the log-odds scale and increases the odds of a CHD event by a factor of $e^{\hat{b}20} = (1.0104)^{20} = 1.231$. In general, a t unit increase in the risk factor from x_0 to $x_1 = x_0 + t$ produces a change in the odds to $\text{odds}_1 = \text{odds}_0 (e^b)^t$ and the odds ratio for an increase of t units is then $\text{odds}_1/\text{odds}_0 = e^{bt}$.

An important property of the simple logistic model is seen at this point. The change in risk of disease associated with an increase in a risk factor is the same regardless of the level of the risk factor. A 300-pound man multiplies his risk by a factor of 1.231 for a 20-pound gain in weight as does a 150-pound man. The property that the log-odds is a linear function of the risk variable is a mathematical property of the simple logistic model and may or may not be biologically reasonable. More complicated logistic models can be formulated to reflect non-linear relationships. For the risk factor weight, it is perhaps more realistic to postulate that a gain of 20 pounds would increase the risk to a 300-pound man less than the risk to a 150-pound man. Such a logistic model is easily created, and an example of a nonlinear logistic model is presented [expression (8.14)].

An approximate 95% confidence interval for the regression coefficient $(\hat{b} \pm 1.96S_{\hat{b}})$ is almost always helpful in evaluating the strength of an association. Based on the estimate $\hat{b} = 0.0104$, the 95% confidence interval is (0.005, 0.016); the approximate 95% confidence interval for the odds ratio is then $(e^{\text{lower}}, e^{\text{upper}}) = (1.005, 1.016)$. For a gain of 20 pounds, similarly, the approximate 95% confidence interval is $(e^{20(\hat{b} \pm 1.96S_{\hat{b}})}) = (1.095, 1.385)$ based on estimated odds ratio $\hat{or} = e^{20\hat{b}} = 1.231$.

The analysis of weight and CHD illustrates another point that is generally true for a logistic model applied to human disease. The range of the logistic probabilities is rather restricted and almost linear. For example, for $x = 100$ pounds, $p_x = 0.040$, for $x = 150$ $p_x = 0.066$, and for $x = 200$ pounds, $p_x = 0.106$, showing the rate of increase in the probability of disease over this range as more or less linear (see Figure 8.1). A greater range in the probability of disease is not likely for most epidemiologic data since low-frequency diseases are usually under study and the associated risk factors do not strongly influence the frequency.

A related and traditional approach to assessing observed differences between two groups is a t test. In terms of body weight and its influence

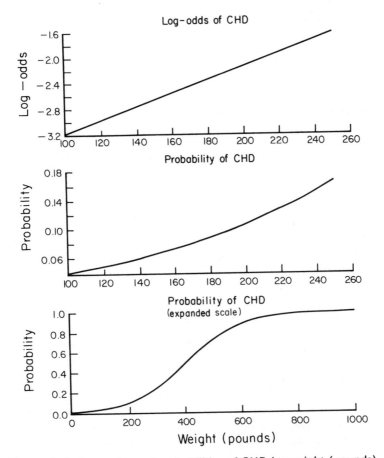

Figure 8–1. Log-odds and probabilities of CHD by weight (pounds).

on CHD, the mean weight of individuals who developed coronary heart disease can be compared with those who did not. The relevant data are given in Table 8.2.

The difference of a little less than 5 pounds in mean weight between these two groups is small in biological terms but is not likely produced by sampling variation (p-value < 0.001). Similar results were seen in the logistic analysis of the same data. The logistic regression approach and the two-sample procedure show essentially the same strength of association between body weight and CHD ($t = 3.503$ from the t analysis and $z = \sqrt{12.018} = 3.467$ from the logistic analysis). The similarity of these two analytic approaches to evaluating a risk factor is typical. The basic difference is that the t test requires the values represented by x be normally distributed where the logistic approach

Table 8-2. *t* test: Weight by CHD

	Sample size	Mean	Standard error
CHD	257	174.463	21.010
No CHD	2,897	169.554	21.574
Difference	—	4.909	1.401

t statistic = 3.503; *p* value < 0.001.

requires the log-odds to have a linear relationship with the risk factor x. The logistic model, however, is a more sophisticated structure based on postulating a specific relationship between risk factor and disease. This simple logistic model is naturally extended to the case of several risk factors, as will be explored.

The Bivariate Case

The single risk factor model is modified readily to include a second risk factor. A logistic model in terms of log-odds of disease for a value of x of one risk factor and a value of y for the other risk factor is

$$\text{log-odds} = a + bx + cy. \tag{8.4}$$

To illustrate this bivariate model, the variable x represents the age of an individual, the variable y represents the number of cigarettes smoked by that individual, and, again, the occurrence or non-occurrence of CHD among the 3,154 WCGS participants is the disease outcome. The number of cigarettes smoked is not a strictly continuous variable and is recorded with considerable digit preference (Figure 8.2). Estimates for the bivariate model parameters where x = age (years) and y = number of cigarettes smoked per day (as reported) are given in Table 8.3.

Table 8-3. CHD by smoking and age—no interaction

Variable	Term	Coefficient	Std. error	*p*-value	$\hat{or}$
Constant	$\hat{a}$	−6.360	0.563	—	—
Age	$\hat{b}$	0.0764	0.011	<0.001	1.079
Smoking	$\hat{c}$	0.0239	0.004	<0.001	1.024

−2LogLikelihood = 1705.860; number of model parameters = 3.

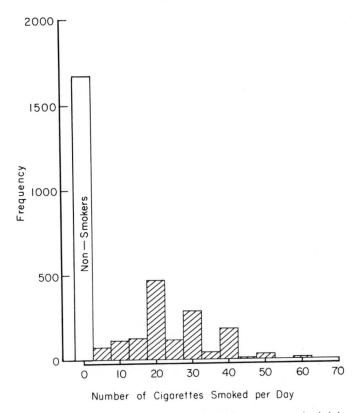

Figure 8-2. Histogram of the frequency of cigarettes smoked (cigarettes per day).

As shown in Figure 8.3 (first panel, top), this logistic model defines the relationship between smoking and the risk of disease by straight lines with slope $\hat{c}$. The influence of age is to increase the overall level of risk by an amount $\hat{b}x$. The lines in Figure 8.3 show the increase in the risk of disease from smoking for the individuals aged 40, 50, and 60. These lines are parallel since the model dictates a linear influence of smoking with the same slope (c) for each value of age (no interaction).

The question immediately arises as to whether the additive model is an adequate representation of the relationship between age, smoking, and CHD. To explore the possibility of an interaction between two continuous risk factors, an interaction term is added to the postulated model. Such a model, again in terms of log-odds, is

$$\text{log-odds} = a + bx + cy + dxy. \tag{8.5}$$

The coefficient d measures the influence of any interaction effects. If d

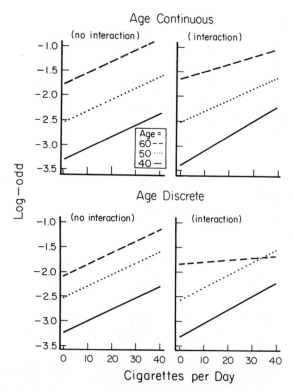

Figure 8–3. Four logistics models describing the relationship of smoking exposure to the risk of CHD for 40, 50, and 60 years of age.

is inconsequential, then the interaction between variables x and y can be ignored and the additive model provides a potentially useful summary of the data. A statistical test of the coefficient d presents no new issues; $X^2 = (\hat{d}/S_{\hat{d}})^2$ has an approximate χ^2 distribution with one degree of freedom when no interaction exists (i.e., H_0: $d = 0$). It is reasonable to delete the interaction term (set $d = 0$) from the model when its influence cannot be differentiated clearly from chance variation (p-value > 0.20, say). The parameter estimates for the interaction model from the smoking and age data are given in Table 8.4.

Figure 8.3 (top) also shows the interaction model where the risk from smoking increases at a different rate depending on the subjects age (lines of smoking risk are not parallel). The magnitude of the interaction influence measured as $\hat{d}$ is evaluated by $X^2 = (-0.0071/0.007)^2 = 1.029$ produces a p-value of 0.310.

An analogous statistical test compares the likelihoods generated by the two models. That is, the model including the interaction term yields

Table 8-4. CHD by smoking and age—interaction

Variable	Term	Coefficient	Std. error	p-value	$\hat{or}$
Constant	$\hat{a}$	−6.884	0.776	—	—
Age	$\hat{b}$	0.0872	0.016	<0.001	1.091
Smoking	$\hat{c}$	0.0580	0.035	0.093	1.060
Interaction	$\hat{d}$	−0.00071	0.007	0.310	0.999

−2LogLikelihood = 1704.878; number of model parameters = 4.

a likelihood of $L_1 = 1704.878$, and, when the possibility of an interaction is excluded ($d = 0$), the likelihood increases to $L_0 = 1705.860$. The difference has an approximate χ^2 distribution with one degree of freedom ($L_0 - L_1 = X^2 = 1705.860 - 1704.878 = 0.982$ and the p-value is 0.322) when $d = 0$. The similarity of the two tests is expected, particularly for data sets with a large number of observations.

Instead of treating age as a continuous variable, age can be divided into three categories (set at 35–44, 45–54, and 55+ years) to illustrate the logistic model with both continuous (smoking) and categorical (age) predictor variables. The three age categories are identified by two binary variables, x_1 and x_2. These two dummy variables indicate three unordered age strata, and the additive logistic model is

$$\text{log-odds} = a + b_1x_1 + b_2x_2 + cy. \tag{8.6}$$

Note that $x_1 = 0$ and $x_2 = 0$ indicate the age stratum 35−44 years, which serves as baseline for comparisons; $x_1 = 1$ and $x_2 = 0$, the age stratum 45−54 years; and $x_1 = 0$ and $x_2 = 1$, the age stratum 55+ years. The estimates of the four model parameters are shown in Table 8.5.

The interaction model is a bit more complicated but not different in principle from the previous interaction models and is given by

$$\text{log-odds} = a + b_1x_1 + b_2x_2 + cy + d_1x_1y + d_2x_2y. \tag{8.7}$$

Table 8-5. CHD by smoking and age (discrete)—no interaction

Variable	Term	Coefficient	Std. error	p-value	$\hat{or}$
Constant	$\hat{a}$	−3.245	0.137	—	—
Age 45–54	$\hat{b}_1$	0.708	0.150	<0.001	2.029
Age 55+	$\hat{b}_2$	1.153	0.201	<0.001	3.168
Smoking	$\hat{c}$	0.0235	0.002	<0.001	1.024

−2LogLikelihood = 1710.557; number of model parameters = 4.

Table 8-6. CHD by smoking and age (discrete)—interaction

Variable	Term	Coefficient	Std. error	p-value	$\hat{or}$
Constant	$\hat{a}$	−3.319	0.175	—	—
Age 45–54	$\hat{b}_1$	0.735	0.218	<0.001	2.087
Age 55$^+$	$\hat{b}_2$	1.469	0.268	<0.001	4.346
Smoking	$\hat{c}$	0.027	0.00278	<0.001	1.02
Interaction	$\hat{d}_1$	−0.00162	0.009	0.860	0.998
Interaction	$\hat{d}_2$	−0.0228	0.013	0.080	0.978

−2LogLikelihood = 1706.868; number of model parameters = 6.

The WCGS data produce the six estimated parameters for the interaction model given in Table 8.6.

Comparison of the two likelihoods $(L_0 = 1710.557$ and $L_1 = 1706.868$ gives $L_0 - L_1 = X^2 = 3.689$ with $4 - 2 = 2$ degrees of freedom, yielding a p-value $= 0.158)$ shows no persuasive evidence, but perhaps an indication, of an interaction between smoking and age with regard to coronary heart disease when age is treated as an unordered categorical variable. Categorizing age into three groups causes some loss of statistical efficiency and requires a somewhat more complicated model. Additionally, categorizing continuous data can influence the analytic results (e.g., $\hat{c}_{discrete} = 0.027$ and $\hat{c}_{continuous} = 0.058$), emphasizing the importance of the definition and measurement of risk variables in general. Figure 8.3 shows the results of both the additive and interaction models applied to the age and smoking WCGS data where age is measured as a three level categorical variable.

A bivariate logistic regression analysis of the influence of body weight and cholesterol on the probability of coronary disease provides an opportunity to explore the consequences of an interaction. Employing both variables in their natural units (weight = pounds and cholesterol = mg per 100 ml) produces the parameter estimates for a bivariate interaction logistic model [expression (8.5)] given in Table 8.7.

Table 8-7. CHD by weight and cholesterol—interaction

Variable	Term	Coefficient	Std. error	p-value	$\hat{or}$
Constant	$\hat{a}$	−13.21	2.58	—	—
Cholesterol	$\hat{b}$	0.0373	0.010	<0.001	1.038
Weight	$\hat{c}$	0.0450	0.015	0.003	1.046
Interaction	$\hat{d}$	−0.000142	0.000058	0.014	0.999

−2LogLikelihood = 1684.702; number of model parameters = 4.

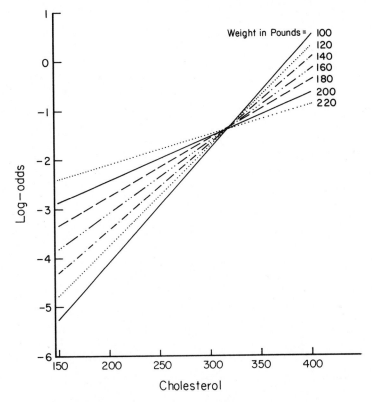

Figure 8-4. Log-odds measure of risk of CHD by levels of cholesterol for a series of selected weights based on estimated logistic parameters.

The test of the coefficient $\hat{d}$ ($z = 2.448$ and p-value $= 0.014$) yields no evidence to justify excluding a weight–cholesterol interaction term from the model (i.e., $d \neq 0$). A similar result is achieved by comparing the respective likelihoods (i.e., $L_{d=0} - L_{d\neq0} = X^2 = 1690.221 - 1684.702 = 5.519$ and $z^2 = (2.448)^2 = 5.992$). The estimated log-odds plots (Figure 8.4) and the plot of the estimated logistic functions (Figure 8.5) both show the modeled influence of the interaction effect. The lines representing risk associated with cholesterol for different weights are not parallel on the log-odds scale. For example, say a person increases his cholesterol value by 50% over a value of 225 mg per 100 ml. If no interaction exists, then the increased risk of disease is the same regardless of the individual's weight. Since weight and cholesterol interact, the risk from a 50% increase in cholesterol depends on weight. A 50% increase for a 190-pound individual produces, via the logistic model, an increased probability of CHD from

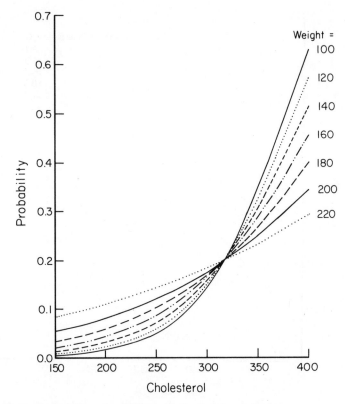

Figure 8-5. Probability of a CHD event by levels of cholesterol for a series of selected weights based on estimated logistic probabilities.

0.088 to 0.235, whereas a 50% cholesterol increase for a person weighing 250 pounds produces a smaller increase in CHD risk, from 0.174 to 0.205. The interaction between cholesterol and weight implies that, in the context of the logistic model, the risk to heavier individuals is less affected by increases in cholesterol levels. In geometric terms, the slope of the line describing the increase in log-odds of disease with increasing values of cholesterol decreases in magnitude with higher weights (the slope associated with cholesterol risk is slope = $\hat{b} - \hat{d} \times$ weight = $0.0373 - 0.000142 \times$ weight—see Figure 8.4). A direct consequence of an interaction is that the risk factor coefficients (linear effects; $\hat{b}$ and $\hat{c}$) in the logistic model no longer measure the isolated effects of the risk variables but reflect a more complex combination of influences.

A formal expression derived from the cholesterol–weight logistic model that defines the impact of an interaction on the calculation and interpretation of the odds ratio is

$$\hat{or} = e^{(\hat{b} + \hat{d} \times \text{weight})} \times (\text{difference in cholesterol levels})$$

or, specifically,

$$\hat{or} = e^{(0.0373 - 0.000142 \times \text{weight})} \times (\text{difference in cholesterol levels}), \tag{8.8}$$

where the odds ratios reflecting the risk from differences in cholesterol levels are compared for individuals with the same weight. The expression shows that the odds ratio is related to the difference in cholesterol, as expected, but the magnitude of the odds ratio is also influenced by the value of *weight*. Therefore, an interpretation of $\hat{or}$ is conditional on the weight of the individuals being compared. To be specific, $\hat{or} = 4.950$ for two men weighing 150 pounds and $\hat{or} = 2.435$ for two men weighing 200 pounds for the same 100 mg per 100 ml difference in their cholesterol levels. Only when $d = 0.0$ (no inter-action) are inferences concerning cholesterol "free" from considera-tions of weight.

Logistic Coefficients: General Considerations

A general additive multivariate logistic model (i.e., without interaction terms) is

$$\text{log-odds} = a + \sum_{i=1}^{k} b_i x_i \quad \text{or} \quad p_x = \frac{1}{1 + e^{-(\text{log} - \text{odds})}} \tag{8.9}$$

and the odds for two sets of x values $(x_1, x_2, \ldots, x_k$ and $x'_1, x'_2, \ldots, x'_k)$ are

$$\frac{p_x}{1 - p_x} = e^{a + \Sigma b_i x_i} \quad \text{and} \quad \frac{p_{x'}}{1 - p_{x'}} = e^{a + \Sigma b_i x'_i}, \tag{8.10}$$

giving the associated odds ratio as

$$\text{odds ratio} = \frac{p_x / (1 - p_x)}{p_{x'} / (1 - p_{x'})}$$

$$= e^{\Sigma b_i (x_i - x'_i)} = e^{b_1 (x_1 - x'_1)} e^{b_2 (x_2 - x'_2)} e^{b_3 (x_3 - x'_3)} \cdots e^{b_k (x_k - x'_k)}. \tag{8.11}$$

If one risk variable in the set is increased by one unit while the other variables are unchanged $(x_1 = x'_1 + 1$ while $x_2 = x'_2, \ x_3 = x'_3, \ldots, \ x_k = x'_k)$, then

$$\text{odds-ratio} = e^{b_1}. \tag{8.12}$$

That is, the coefficient b_1 or e^{b_1} expresses the influence of one unit difference in the variable x_1 on the risk of disease while the other $k - 1$ variables are equal or held constant. In effect, the logistic model allows two hypothetical individuals or groups to be compared that differ with respect to one variable and have identical values for the other $k - 1$ risk factors. The odds ratio is, in this way, adjusted for the presence of the other risk factors. Like a randomized experiment, the regression coefficient measures the impact from a specific variable since the influence of the other measured variables are "equalized" between the two groups compared. Experimental data remain superior in the sense that randomization likely equalizes all confounding variables between compared groups, whereas a logistic model allows for adjustment only for confounding influences from measured variables entered in the logistic model and, of course, the adjustment depends on the validity of the additive model [Expression (8.9)].

"Centering"

Problems arise when highly correlated risk variables are used in a logistic regression analysis. High correlation means that two variables are essentially indistinguishable in their influence on the disease outcome, making it difficult to produce accurate estimates of the regression coefficients associated with each variable. In other words, separation of individual influences on the outcome by means of a regression coefficient becomes difficult (unreliable) when the two variables are themselves almost identical. This phenomenon is called collinearity, and the topic is discussed in detail in textbooks on regression analysis (e.g., [Ref. 1]). Collinearity in the context of logistic regression and a method for potentially improving the precision of the estimated coefficients associated with collinear variables will be illustrated with the WCGS data.

The size of an individual is reflected by a body-mass index, often defined as weight (kilograms) divided by a function of height (meters^2). The body-mass index ($q = \text{kg/m}^2$) calculated from the WCGS data is seen to be related to the probability of CHD by the following linear logistic analysis. The model is

$$\text{log-odds} = a + bq, \tag{8.13}$$

which gives the parameter estimates displayed in Table 8.8.

Clearly, the body-mass index is associated with CHD (p-value < 0.001). However, the data suggest (not shown) that for high values of body-mass index risk increases more slowly than for low or

Table 8-8. CHD by body-mass index

Variable	Term	Coefficient	Std. error	p-value	$\hat{or}$
Constant	$\hat{a}$	−4.509	0.606	—	—
q	$\hat{b}$	0.085	0.0241	<0.001	1.088

−2LogLikelihood = 1769.426; number of model parameters = 2.

intermediate values. One way to incorporate this nonlinearity of response into the analysis is to modify the simple logistic model by adding a quadratic term. The model becomes

$$\text{log-odds} = a + bq + cq^2. \tag{8.14}$$

Parenthetically, a quadratic term in a logistic equation describes a special type of interaction. The risk variable can be viewed as interacting with itself, which means that the level of risk associated with the outcome variable depends on the level of the risk factor itself. The estimated parameters of the quadratic model are shown in Table 8.9.

The addition of the quadratic term changes strikingly the results observed from the linear logistic model. The coefficient measuring the effects of the body-mass index on the risk of CHD changes from 0.085 to 0.373, and the precision, as reflected by the standard error, changes from 0.0241 to 0.276 (a more than tenfold increase!). These changes are predominantly due to the high correlation between q and q^2. The correlation is $r = 0.995$, and it is this collinearity that disrupts the estimation process.

If the body-mass index is transformed by subtracting the overall mean value from each observed value ($q_i - \bar{q}$, where $\bar{q} = \text{mean} = 24.52$), the logistic analysis becomes considerably more reliable. This "centered" variable remains useful for estimating the risk–disease association when a quadratic term is added to the model. Two inconsequential changes occur. The constant term in the model is different, and the units of measurement are relative to the mean. The transformed risk values have mean zero, causing extreme individuals to have

Table 8-9. CHD by body-mass index—quadratic term included

Variable	Term	Coefficient	Std. error	p-value	$\hat{or}$
Constant	$\hat{a}$	−8.217	3.58	—	—
q	$\hat{b}$	0.373	0.276	0.177	1.452
q^2	$\hat{c}$	−0.0055	0.0053	0.295	0.995

−2LogLikelihood = 1768.227; number of model parameters = 3.

Table 8–10. CHD by body-mass index—centered

Variable	Term	Coefficient	Std. error	p-value	$\hat{or}$
Constant	$\hat{a}$	−2.443	0.066	—	—
$(q - \bar{q})$	$\hat{b}$	0.085	0.0241	<0.001	1.089

−2LogLikelihood = 1769.212; number of model parameters = 2.

either positive or negative values. The logistic analysis using a "centered" body-mass index values gives the parameter estimates in Table 8.10.

Note that the estimate of the influence of body mass on the risk of CHD is the same in both logistic analyses ($\hat{b} = 0.085$, with standard error = 0.241 for both the transformed and nontransformed data). More important, the estimates are not highly affected when q^2 is added to the model using the "centered" data. The estimates for the quadratic model parameters using the "centered" data are given in Table 8.11.

Precision is less affected when the risk factors (body mass and body mass squared) are "centered" and no longer highly correlated ($r = 0.359$). The estimated coefficient measuring the influence of body mass is $\hat{b} = 0.101$ with a standard error of 0.029, only slightly increased over the additive model. The reduction in correlation between risk factor variables (q and q^2) has the desired effect of producing an analysis less disrupted by collinearity. The small price for the improved estimates is the use of transformed measurements rather than natural units. Centering a risk variable can, but may not always, increase the precision of a variable used in a logistic regression analysis.

Figure 8.6 shows the curves associated with both the linear (first row) and quadratic (second row) models relating body mass to CHD. The log-odds, odds ratio (relative to $q_0 = \bar{q} = 24.52$), and the probability of a coronary event are shown in each column based on a logistic model.

Table 8–11. CHD by body-mass index—centered with quadratic term included

Variable	Term	Coefficient	Std. error	p-value	$\hat{or}$
Constant	$\hat{a}$	−2.412	0.072	—	—
$(q - \bar{q})$	$\hat{b}$	0.101	0.0293	<0.001	1.106
$(q - \bar{q})^2$	$\hat{c}$	−0.00545	0.0053	0.302	0.995

−2LogLikelihood = 1768.050; number of model parameters = 3.

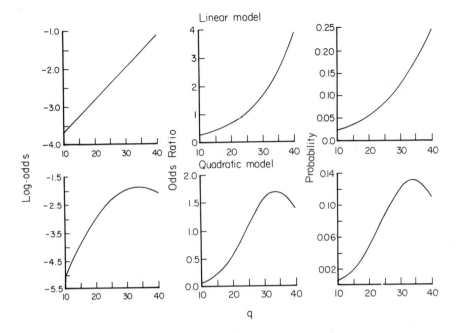

Figure 8–6. Two logistic models (linear and quadratic) showing the relationship of a body-mass index to the risk of CHD for three measures (log-odds, odds ratio, and probability) of association.

The differences in the shape of the curves associated with these two models shows the importance of selecting a model to describe appropriately the risk factor and disease relationship.

The WCGS Additive Model

The no-interaction model is, perhaps, the simplest description of the influence of a series of risk factors. All variables are entered into the analysis only as additive influences and the log-odds is expressed, as shown earlier, as

$$\text{log-odds} = a + \sum_{i=1}^{k} b_i x_i. \tag{8.15}$$

For the WCGS data, eight risk factors ($k = 8$) employed in the additive model produce the nine estimated parameters (eight risk factor coefficients and a constant term) shown in Table 8.12.

Using all eight risk factors in a logistic analysis substantially improves the summary model (reduces the likelihood) over the situation

Table 8-12. Full model—no interaction

Variable	Term	Coefficient	Std. error	p-value	$\hat{or}$
Constant	$\hat{a}$	-13.55	2.32	—	—
Age	$\hat{b}_1$	0.0648	0.012	<0.001	1.067
Height	$\hat{b}_2$	0.0160	0.033	0.629	1.016
Weight	$\hat{b}_3$	0.00782	0.0038	0.044	1.008
Systolic bp	$\hat{b}_4$	0.0177	0.0064	0.005	1.018
Diastolic bp	$\hat{b}_5$	-0.0015	0.011	0.989	1.000
Cholesterol	$\hat{b}_6$	0.0111	0.0015	<0.001	1.011
Smoking	$\hat{b}_7$	0.0209	0.0043	<0.001	1.021
A/B	$\hat{b}_8$	0.653	0.145	<0.001	1.922

-2LogLikelihood $= 1580.738$, number of model parameters $= 9$.

where no risk factors are considered. That is, $L_0 = 1781.224$ when all risk factors are ignored, and $L_1 = 1580.738$ when all risk factors are included. The reduction $L_0 - L_1 = X^2 = 200.486$ (p-value < 0.001) is attributable to the inclusion of these eight risk factors in describing CHD risk. The overall influence of all risk factors simultaneously entered into an analysis is rarely of interest. More important questions focus on the relative role of each risk factor in determining the probability of disease occurrence.

The relative impact of each variable is related to the corresponding coefficient in the logistic regression equation. However, direct comparison of the coefficients (b_i's) does not account for the fact that variables are often measured in different units. For example, age in the WCGS data is not four times more important than height in determining the risk of CHD because the age coefficient is about four times larger. Three common ways to evaluate the relative role of each variable in a logistic regression equation are: the use of standardized coefficients (two methods) and the comparison of specific likelihoods. These methods allow the influence from variables measured in different units, such as age and height, to be directly compared.

Method 1

To make the regression coefficients commensurate (comparable units), they can be multiplied by the standard deviation of the associated variable. For example, a 1-year increase in age results in an increase of 0.0648 in the log-odds of disease. Since the estimated standard deviation of the distribution of ages is 5.524 (Table A.1), the quantity $(0.0648)(5.524) = 0.358$ is an estimate of the increase in the log-odds for a one standard deviation increase in age. Similarly, all values $\hat{b}_i S_i$ estimate the change in the log-odds of disease for a one standard deviation increase in the ith risk factor. These standardized coefficients have the same units (response in log-odds per standard deviation of the risk factor), producing comparable measures of response directly reflecting the role of each variable in the risk of disease.

Method 2

When a specific variable is deleted from the logistic regression analysis (keeping the rest of the variables in the equation), the increase in the likelihood based on $k - 1$ variables is attributable specifically to the influence of the deleted variable. This fact produces another technique to evaluate the role of each variable in a logistic equation. The difference between the likelihood for the k-variable model (L_k) and the likelihood for the model with the variable x_i excluded (L_{k-1}) measures the role of the removed variable. The difference $L_{k-1} - L_k$ directly measures the magnitude of the contribution of the variable x_i that is not reflected by the other variables in the logistic model. The unique contributions of each variable to the regression analysis provide a series of commensurate measures of each risk factor's relative influence on the probability of disease.

Method 3

The third approach consists of dividing the regression coefficient $\hat{b}_i$ by its standard error. The quantity $\hat{b}_i / S_{\hat{b}_i}$ also measures the role of the risk factor x_i in the logistic model. Similar to the likelihood measure, these standardized values are unitless and produce commensurate measures of risk associated with each individual risk factor. One further note: standardizing a coefficient by its standard error and the difference between likelihoods are both related to a χ^2 distribution (as already discussed), and these two measures are not likely to substantially differ in a specific analysis, particularly when large sample sizes are involved.

Table 8.13 illustrates the three methods applied to the WCGS data using the eight-variable additive logistic model. The three approaches give essentially the same results. Cholesterol makes the strongest contribution to CHD risk, followed by roughly equal contributions from age, smoking, and behavior type. Weight and systolic blood pressure play lesser roles in the logistic equation, while the variables diastolic blood pressure and height have essentially no influence on CHD risk.

Table 8-13. Comparisons of three commensurate coefficients

Variable	Term	S_i	$\hat{b}_i S_i$	$L_7 - L_8$	$X^2 = (\hat{b}_i/S_{\hat{b}_i})^2$
Age	$\hat{b}_1$	5.524	0.358	28.522	29.160
Height	$\hat{b}_2$	2.529	0.040	0.234	0.235
Weight	$\hat{b}_3$	21.100	0.165	4.015	4.235
Systolic bp	$\hat{b}_4$	15.112	0.267	7.512	7.649
Diastolic bp	$\hat{b}_5$	9.727	-0.015	0.001	0.019
Cholesterol	$\hat{b}_6$	43.420	0.482	57.727	54.760
Smoking	$\hat{b}_7$	14.518	0.303	23.057	23.624
A/B	$\hat{b}_8$	0.500	0.327	21.226	20.281

Confounder Bias in the WCGS Data

The definition of confounding is essentially the same whether the analysis involves continuous or discrete variables (defined previously in Chapters 2, 6, and 7). Confounder bias in the context of logistic regression is most naturally measured in terms of the changes in the regression coefficients or the odds ratios. The impact of confounding bias on a specific variable (x_i) is seen by the changes in the coefficient (b_i) caused by excluding one of more other risk factors from an additive logistic model. This "before–after" comparison yields the measure of confounder bias $B_i - b_i$, where B_i is the logistic coefficient when one or more confounding variables are eliminated from the model and b_i is the logistic coefficient when the confounding variables are included in the model. Again, implicit in this definition is the assumption that no interaction exists (additive model) among the variables considered.

The additive model applied to the WCGS data provides a look at the issue of confounder bias. Consider the behavior type variable. The logistic coefficient associated with behavior type when no other risk factors are considered is 0.864. The confounder bias from the other seven variables (change in the value 0.864) is seen in Table 8,14, where the rows contain the logistic regression coefficients for a series of models that include the variables given by the columns. The confounder bias influencing the A/B behavior type regression coefficient ranges from 0.864 to 0.653 (column 1 of Table 8.14).

Confounder bias for a specific measure of association is a somewhat arbitrary quantity since its magnitude depends on both the variables included in the model and the order in which they are entered into the logistic equation. For example, if the cholesterol variable is added to the model first rather than sixth, the coefficient associated with behavior type changes from 0.864 to 0.819 (confounder bias = 0.045) rather than the observed change of 0.752 to 0.715 (confounder bias = 0.037).

Table 8.14. Confounding and the A/B association with CHD

A/B	Age	Ht	Wt	SBP	DBP	Chol	Cigs
0.864	—	—	—	—	—	—	—
0.799	0.069	—	—	—	—	—	—
0.791	0.071	0.039	—	—	—	—	—
0.780	0.070	−0.013	0.012	—	—	—	—
0.751	0.062	0.008	0.007	0.020	—	—	—
0.752	0.062	0.006	0.007	0.022	−0.005	—	—
0.715	0.030	0.006	0.021	0.021	−0.006	0.012	—
0.653	0.065	0.016	0.008	0.018	−0.002	0.011	0.021

The same table can be expressed in terms of the odds ratios, and the impact of confounding on the measure of behavior type is given in Table 8.15.

The WCGS example data illustrate that confounding bias is generally a function of the combined influences of all the risk factors entered into the equation $(B_i - b_i = 0.653 - 0.864 = -0.211)$. Extreme examples can be constructed such that two risk factors do not cause confounding bias when treated individually, but when they are considered together confounding occurs [Ref. 2]. It is problematic whether this dependency on only a joint influence occurs in actual data. However, it is important to keep in mind that confounding bias is a function of all risk factors and its magnitude cannot be inferred from analyses dealing with each variable separately (sometimes called the marginal analyses).

Goodness-of-fit: Continuous Case

Assessing the fit of a logistic model when some or all of the risk factors are continuous is not straightforward. In the discrete case an expected

Table 8–15. Odds ratios: Confounding and the A/B association with CHD

A/B	Age	Ht	Wt	SBP	DBP	Chol	Cigs
2.373	—	—	—	—	—	—	—
2.223	1.071	—	—	—	—	—	—
2.206	1.074	1.040	—	—	—	—	—
2.181	1.073	0.987	1.012	—	—	—	—
2.119	1.064	1.008	1.007	1.020	—	—	—
2.121	1.064	1.006	1.007	1.022	0.995	—	—
2.044	1.030	1.006	1.021	1.021	0.994	1.012	—
1.921	1.067	1.016	1.008	1.018	0.999	1.011	1.021

number based on the model was calculated and compared to the observed number for each category of data. In the continuous case no natural categories exist leading to a variety of proposals for measures of "fit" (see [Ref. 3]). A common approach is to form somewhat arbitrary categories and apply a χ^2 statistic much like the previously discussed discrete case.

One strategy uses categories based on levels of risk estimated from the logistic model under investigation. Traditionally ten groups are formed, each containing approximately one-tenth of the data. The members of the first group are all subjects with the lowest probability of the event estimated by the logistic model, while the second group makes up the next 10% of the subjects with respect to risk and so forth until the tenth group consists of all individuals above the 90th percentile of the estimated logistic risk probabilities. The percentile groups are sometimes called "deciles of risk." Once the groups are formed, the average logistic probability per group is calculated. That is, the logistic probabilities for each one-tenth of the data are summed and divided by the number of members of that group or for the kth decile group the average probability is

$$\bar{p}_k = \frac{1}{n_k} \sum_{j=1}^{n_k} \hat{p}_j \tag{8.16}$$

where $n_k \approx n/10$, when n represents the total observed number of individuals. To be perfectly clear, the value $\hat{p}_j$ is the estimated probability of disease based on the estimated logistic coefficients ($\hat{b}_i$'s), the values of an individual's risk factors, and the logistic model, producing one estimate per study subject. The expected number of events in the kth group is then $\hat{e}_k = n_k \bar{p}_k = \Sigma \hat{p}_j$. Also for each of the ten groups the observed number of events is recorded, symbolized by o_k. A similarly expected number of nonevents can be calculated and compared to the observed number in each decile. The pairs of observed and expected counts generated for each decile of risk (20 pairs) are compared with the usual χ^2 statistic or, in symbols,

$$X^2 = \sum \frac{(\text{observed} - \text{expected})^2}{\text{expected}} \tag{8.17}$$

and, specifically,

$$X^2 = \sum_{i=1}^{10} \frac{(o_i - \hat{e}_i)^2}{\hat{e}_i} + \sum_{i=1}^{10} \frac{[(n_i - o_i) - (n_i - \hat{e}_i)]^2}{n_i - \hat{e}_i} = \sum_{i=1}^{10} \frac{(o_i - \hat{e}_i)^2}{n_i \bar{p}_i (1 - \bar{p}_i)}. \tag{8.18}$$

The test statistic X^2 has an approximate χ^2 distribution with eight degrees of freedom when the logistic model is "correct."

Once again the WCGS data will serve as an example. The full, additive model produces the components for assessing the fit shown in Table 8.16.

Each row in the table describes a "decile of risk" for the 3,154 subjects. For example, the observed number of coronary events for the fourth decile is 9 among the 315 individuals in that group, and the expected number based on the additive logistic model is $\hat{e}_4 = n_4 \bar{p}_4 = 315(0.0444) = 13.986$. The corresponding values for the individuals who did not experience a coronary event are 306 and 301.014, respectively. The summary χ^2 statistic for this percentile-type grouping strategy is $X^2 = 12.090$ (degrees of freedom = 8) producing a p-value of 0.147, showing no strong evidence of a lack of fit of the additive model.

Binary Variable Bias

Sometimes it is not possible to measure a continuous variable precisely; instead, a variable is recorded in terms of broad categories. For example, a survey question may not accurately assess the total amount of alcohol consumed by an individual, but reliable information on whether or not an individual consumes any alcoholic beverage might be obtained. Using a binary variable (did or did not drink alcoholic beverages) in place of the underlying continuous variable (total amount of alcohol consumed) is preferable to ignoring entirely the influence of alcohol on the risk–disease relationship. Including a confounding variable reduces the confounder bias to zero, excluding

Table 8-16. Fit of the additive logistic model to the WCGS data

k	$\bar{p}_k$	CHD		no CHD		
		o_k	$\hat{e}_k$	$n_k - o_k$	$n_k - \hat{e}_k$	n_k
1	0.0155	1	4.898	315	311.102	316
2	0.0252	5	7.938	310	307.062	315
3	0.0343	14	10.805	301	304.196	315
4	0.0444	9	13.986	306	301.014	315
5	0.0564	17	17.766	298	297.234	315
6	0.0708	17	22.302	298	292.698	315
7	0.0886	24	27.909	291	287.091	315
8	0.1154	43	36.351	272	278.649	315
9	0.1568	48	49.392	267	265.608	315
10	0.2800	79	89.040	239	228.960	318
summary	0.0890	257	280.706	2,897	2,873.294	3,154

the variable produces the maximum confounder bias and employing a binary "substitute" produces a bias somewhere between these two extremes.

To illustrate "binary variable bias" in concrete terms, a bivariate linear regression model is used. A linear bivariate regression model expressed as

$$y_i = a + b_1 x_{1i} + b_2 x_{2i} + e_i \qquad (8.19)$$

is one choice for summarizing the relationship between a continuous outcome symbolized by y (e.g., cholesterol), a predictor variable described by x_1 (e.g., total calories) and a potential confounder represented by x_2 (e.g., age). The symbol e_i, as before, represents one of a series of normally distributed, independent error terms with constant variance [variance$(e_i) = \sigma^2$]. In the context of this linear regression model, the variable x_2 is a confounder when the coefficient b_1 depends on whether the analytic equation includes the variable x_2, as previously discussed. The same linear regression model, but without the variable x_2, is represented as

$$y_i = A + B_1 x_{1i} + e_i. \qquad (8.20)$$

An expression of the confounder bias in terms of the estimated regression coefficients $\hat{B}_1$ and $\hat{b}_1$ is

$$\text{confounder bias} = \hat{B}_1 - \hat{b}_1 = \hat{b}_2 s_2 r_{12}/s_1, \qquad (8.21)$$

where s_i represents the standard deviation associated with the variable x_i and r_{12} is the product–moment correlation coefficient measuring the association between the variables x_1 and x_2.

When $r_{12} \neq 0$ and $\hat{b}_2 \neq 0$, then $\hat{b}_1$ will incur at least some confounder bias whenever x_2 is not included in the analysis ($\hat{B}_1 \neq \hat{b}_1$). That is, the value $\hat{b}_1$ depends on whether x_2 is included in the regression model. In this case, x_2 is usually retained in the analysis to remove the confounder bias. If x_2 is unrelated to y, $\hat{b}_2 = 0$ or, if x_2 is unrelated to x_1, $r_{12} = 0$, then x_2 is not a confounder ($\hat{B}_1 = \hat{b}_1$); the coefficient $\hat{b}_1$ is free from confounder bias.

Binary variable bias occurs when the value x_2 is measured as the presence or absence of a risk factor rather than as a continuous variable. That is, x_2 is replaced by x_2^* where, for the sake of illustration, $x_2^* = 1$ if x_2 exceeds the mean value of the x_2 distribution and $x_2^* = 0$ otherwise. In this case,

$$r_{12}^* \approx r_{12}\sqrt{2/\pi}, \qquad (8.22)$$

where r_{12} is again the product–moment correlation coefficient for the continuous variables x_1 and x_2 and r_{12}^* represents the point biserial correlation coefficient measuring the association between the continuous variable x_1 and the binary variable x_2^*. The expression relating the two correlations shows that employing a binary "substitute" variable reduces (biases downward) the observed correlation between x_1 and x_2 ($r_{12}^* < r_{12}$).

The bias introduced by using x_2^* instead of x_2 in a bivariate regression model is approximately

$$\text{binary variable bias} = \hat{b}_1^* - \hat{b}_1 \approx (\text{confounder bias}) \frac{1 - 2/\pi}{1 - 2r_{12}^2/\pi}, \quad (8.23)$$

where $\hat{b}_1$ is the coefficient associated with x_1 when x_2 is treated as a continuous variable. The coefficient $\hat{b}_1^*$ is the same coefficient when x_2 is treated as a binary variable. Only when $r_{12} = 1$ is the binary variable bias equal to the confounder bias; otherwise some reduction in confounder bias is achieved when a binary version of a continuous variable is used in the linear regression analysis. The maximum possible reduction is $1 - 2/\pi = 0.363$ when $r_{12} = 0$.

The bivariate linear regression model illustrates that, when x_2 is a confounder, some bias occurs when a categorical measure replaces an underlying continuous variable, but using such a variable is an improvement over leaving the confounding variable out of the analysis entirely. This bias is most extreme in the binary case and decreases as the number of categories describing the continuous variable increases.

A similar binary variable bias is also incurred when the logistic regression model is used to study a set of risk factors. Again, it is better to use a "substitute" variable than no variable at all. The confounder bias incurred from blood pressure in evaluating the role of body weight in the risk of coronary disease is substantial. When the influence of blood pressure is ignored, the risk of a CHD event reflected by the logistic regression coefficient is $\hat{b}_{\text{weight}} = 0.0104$. When blood pressure is included in the regression equation, the confounding influence is removed and the coefficient is reduced by almost half, to $\hat{b}'_{\text{weight}} = 0.0054$. In terms of an odds ratio applied to a gain of 50 pounds, $\hat{or} = 1.682$ ignoring blood pressure as a risk factor, compared to taking blood pressure into account $\hat{or}' = 1.311$. If blood pressure is measured as a binary variable and used in the logistic model, the regression coefficient associated with weight is $\hat{b}''_{\text{weight}} = 0.0069$. The binary variable bias in terms of the odds ratios for a 50-pound difference in body weight is $\hat{or}'' = 1.415$, compared to $\hat{or}' = 1.311$. As shown for the linear regression model, the binary variable reduces the confounder bias but does not remove it completely. To summarize, see Table 8.17.

Table 8-17. Binary variable bias of blood pressure: Summary

Blood pressure	Excluded	Binary	Included
$\hat{b}_{weight}$	0.0104	0.0069	0.0054
$\hat{or}_{50^+}$	1.682	1.415	1.311

Case–Control Sampling

The odds ratio measure of association is central to epidemiologic analyses. One reason for the reliance on this measure is its usefulness in describing associations for a variety of sampling designs (e.g., cohort, cross-sectional, and case–control data).

Cohort sampling produces two groups of a predetermined number of individuals, one exposed and one not exposed to a risk factor. Subsequent numbers of cases of disease are then recorded for each group. Cohort data would look like those in Table 8.18, and the odds ratio is estimated by $(ad)/(bc)$. The sample sizes n_1 and n_2 are considered fixed. The ratio a/b estimates the odds of disease associated with the exposed group, and c/d estimates the odds of disease associated with the unexposed group. The estimated odds ratio is, then,

$$\hat{or} = \frac{a/b}{c/d} = \frac{ad}{bc}. \tag{8.24}$$

The ratios a/c and b/d are related to the sample sizes n_1 and n_2 and have no importance as measures of association.

Case–control sampling also produces two groups, but the number of cases (diseased individuals) and controls (nondiseased individuals) are determined by the investigator. For example, 100 cases (n_1 cases) of prostatic cancer could be collected in a specific hospital and 200 noncancer cases (n_2 controls) sampled from the same hospital population to make up a case–control sample of 300 individuals. The number of individuals exposed to a risk factor is ascertained for each group. The data would look like those in Table 8.19, and the odds ratio is also

Table 8-18. Data collected by exposure

	Disease	No disease	Total
Exposed	a	b	n_1
Not exposed	c	d	n_2

Table 8–19. Data collected by disease

	Disease	No disease.
Exposed	a	b
Not exposed	c	d
Total	n_1	n_2

estimated by the quantity $(ad)/(bc)$ but for different reasons. Here the odds of being exposed to the risk factor among the cases are estimated by a/c, and the odds of being exposed among the controls are estimated by b/d. However, the odds ratio remains

$$\hat{or} = \frac{a/c}{b/d} = \frac{ad}{bc}. \tag{8.25}$$

The ratios a/b and c/d have relatively little meaning since they are again influenced largely by the numbers of cases and controls selected.

The fact that the odds ratio is the same for both cohort and case–control sampling designs suggests that the coefficients in a simple logistic regression analysis will also be the same for both types of data.

The following demonstrates that, for a simple logistic regression analysis, case–control sampling produces the same assessments of risk as cohort data. Consider the simple logistic equation where p_x represents the probability of the disease for a specific value of a variable represented as x or, as before,

$$p_x = \frac{1}{1 + e^{-(a+bx)}} \text{ and, therefore, } \log\left(\frac{p_x}{1 - p_x}\right) = a + bx. \tag{8.26}$$

Let $s_1 = P(\text{sampled}|\text{case})$ and $s_0 = P(\text{sampled}|\text{control})$. Recall that Bayes' theorem (slightly complicated by the presence of event C) applied to arbitrary events A, B, and C states

$$P(A|BC) = \frac{P(B|AC)P(AC)}{P(BC)}, \tag{8.27}$$

then, specifically

$$P(\text{disease}|x \text{ and sampled}) = \frac{s_1 p_x}{s_1 p_x + s_0(1 - p_x)}, \tag{8.28}$$

where $A =$ disease, $B =$ sampled, and $C =$ value of the variable x. The log-odds is

$$\text{log-odds} = \log\left(\frac{P(\text{disease}|x \text{ and sampled})}{P(\text{no disease}|x \text{ and sampled})}\right), \tag{8.29}$$

and it follows that

$$\text{log-odds} = \log\left(\frac{s_1 p_x/[s_1 p_x + s_0(1 - p_x)]}{s_0(1 - p_x)/[s_1 p_x + s_0(1 - p_x)]}\right)$$

$$= \log\left(\frac{s_1}{s_0}\frac{p_x}{1 - p_x}\right) = A + \log\left(\frac{p_x}{1 - p_x}\right), \qquad (8.30)$$

giving

$$\text{log-odds} = A + a + bx = a' + bx. \qquad (8.31)$$

Expression (8.31) shows that the coefficient b associated with the level of risk x, is not influenced by the case–control sampling. The coefficient b, as before, indicates the change in risk of the disease measured in log-odds for a one unit change in x for either cohort or case–control sampling. Only the constant term in the logistic model (a) is affected by the sampling process.

Similarly, regression coefficients from a multiple logistic analysis are not influenced by case–control sampling of data. Only the constant term is affected by the sampling scheme. The constant term has no useful interpretation since it is made up of an unknown mixture of two elements (the probabilities s_0 and s_1 as well as the frequency of the disease in the sampled population). However, the constant term in the logistic model does not play an important role and can be ignored in the study of a series of risk factors. Therefore, the properties of a logistic regression apply equally to case–control data, adding flexibility to this analytic technique and, more importantly, providing a powerful tool for investigating rare diseases. Texts are completely devoted to the analysis of case–control data (e.g., [Refs. 4 and 5]).

9 Life Tables: An Introduction

Life tables (of sorts) date back to third-century Roman records of the age at death. The development of the formal life table is usually attributed to Edmund Halley (1693) and John Graunt (1662). By the end of the nineteenth century, life tables were routinely computed as part of a generally emerging awareness of the importance of mortality statistics. The first official U.S. (death registration states) life table published in 1900 showed the expected length of life for white males as 46.6 years and for white females as 48.7 years.

A life table is a systematic way to keep track of the mortality experience of a group. A cohort life table is constructed from the mortality records of individuals followed from the birth of the first to the death of the last member of a group. Such life tables are constructed from animal and insect data. For human populations, it is obviously not practical to construct a life table by following a cohort of individuals from birth until all have died. Instead a life table is constructed from current mortality rates. These rates do not apply to past populations and undoubtedly will not apply to future populations. Nevertheless, patterns of mortality can be seen from a current life table, and the comparison of life tables calculated for different groups is a basic strategy for analyzing certain types of epidemiologic data.

Complete, Current Life Table: Construction

The word *complete* when applied to a life table means that ages are not grouped but recorded in 1-year intervals. The actual construction of a complete life table is rather mechanical and embraces seven basic elements:

Age interval (x to $x + 1$): Each age interval consists of 1 year (age denoted by x) except the last age interval, which is left open ended (e.g., 90+ years).

Number alive (l_x): The number of individuals alive at exactly age x. The number l_x is the life table population at risk for the interval x

to $x + 1$. The number alive at age 0 (l_0) is set at some arbitrary value, such as 100,000, and called the radix.

Deaths(d_x): The number of individuals who died between the ages of x and $x + 1$.

Probability of death (q_x): The conditional probability that an individual who is alive at age x dies before age $x + 1$. That is, $q_x = d_x/l_x$. The probability of death within a specific age interval is related to a hazard rate and is distinct from the probability of dying before a specific age x, which is expressed in terms of a survival curve.

Years lived (L_x): The cumulative time lived by the entire cohort between the ages of x and $x + 1$. Each individual alive at age x contributes to the total time lived by all individuals either 1 year or the proportion of the year lived if the person died in the interval. The value L_x is the life table person-years of risk for the interval x to $x + 1$.

Total time lived (T_x): The total time lived beyond age x by all individuals alive at age x is $T_x = L_x + L_{x+1} + L_{x+2} + \cdots$. The value T_x is primarily a calculational step in the life-table construction.

Expectation of life (e_x): The average number of additional years expected to be lived by those individuals alive at age x and $e_x = T_x/l_x$.

The following relationships are direct consequences of these definitions:

1. Number dying in the interval x to $x + 1 = d_x = q_x l_x = l_x - l_{x+1}$;
2. Number surviving at age $x + 1 = l_{x+1} = p_x l_x = l_x - d_x$;
3. Probability of dying in the interval x to $x+1 = q_x = (l_x - l_{x+1})/l_x = d_x/l_x$;
4. Probability of surviving from x to $x+1 = p_x = 1 - q_x = (l_x - d_x)/l_x = l_{x+1}/l_x$.

These definitions apply to a complete life table, using age intervals of 1 year.

The total person-years at risk for the interval x to $x + 1$ includes 1 year of survival for each person who did not die during the interval. Individuals who die contribute the proportion of the year they were alive to the total time lived. The average time contributed by those who died in the interval x to $x + 1$ is represented by $\bar{a}_x$. The value $\bar{a}_x$ is close to 0.5 for all ages except the first few years of life. For years 0 to 4 the values of $\bar{a}_x$ are: $\bar{a}_0 = 0.09$, $\bar{a}_1 = 0.43$, $\bar{a}_2 = 0.45$, $\bar{a}_3 = 0.47$, and $\bar{a}_4 = 0.49$ (determined empirically by Chiang [Ref. 1]). These values make logical sense—the distribution of survival times in the first year of life is skewed towards the beginning of the interval since most deaths in the interval 0 to 1 year are within the first month. Therefore, the average contribution of time lived by those who died to the total years lived is low for the interval 0 to 1. For ages 2 to 4, the mean $\bar{a}_x$ shows slightly earlier deaths within the interval, but these $\bar{a}_x$ values are much closer to 0.50. For all other age intervals the average value of $\bar{a}_x$ is essentially 0.5 years.

The value $\bar{a}_x$ takes on importance in calculating the person-years of life for a life table since

$$L_x = (l_x - d_x) + \bar{a}_x d_x \tag{9.1}$$

estimates the life table person-years of risk for the age interval x to $x + 1$. Using L_x, the life-table age-specific mortality rate becomes d_x/L_x, providing a link to observed age-specific mortality rates. This life-table person-years calculation does not differ from the person-years calculation in Chapter 1 [expression (1.5)].

The starting point for construction of a life table is a set of age-specific probabilities of death (q_x). These probabilities can be derived by equating the life-table age-specific mortality rates to the age-specific mortality rates from the population of interest, or

$$\text{life-table mortality rate} = \frac{d_x}{L_x} = R_x = \text{observed mortality rate,} \tag{9.2}$$

where R_x is the age-specific rate for age x calculated from observed mortality data. A value for q_x follows from R_x since

$$\text{life-table mortality rate} = \frac{d_x}{(l_x - d_x) + \bar{a}_x d_x} = \frac{q_x}{1 - (1 - \bar{a}_x)q_x} = R_x \tag{9.3}$$

and solving for q_x gives

$$q_x = \frac{R_x}{1 + (1 - \bar{a}_x)R_x}. \tag{9.4}$$

A set of observed mortality rates (R_x) produce a set of life-table probabilities (q_x). The probabilities q_x generate the rest of the life-table functions $(l_x, d_x, L_x, T_x,$ and $e_x)$ with one exception.

The person-years of life (L_x) for the last interval cannot be calculated directly since a value for $\bar{a}_x$ is not generally available. The individuals who are present at the start of the last interval all die $(q_{x'} = 1.0)$ so that $l_{x'} = d_{x'}$, where x' symbolizes the final age interval (e.g., if the last interval is $90+$, then $x' = 90$). Therefore, again equating the observed mortality rate with the life-table mortality rate for this last age interval gives

$$\frac{d_{x'}}{L_{x'}} = \frac{l_{x'}}{L_{x'}} = R_{x'} \tag{9.5}$$

and then solving for $L_{x'}$ yields

$$L_{x'} = \frac{l_{x'}}{R_{x'}}. \tag{9.6}$$

Therefore, an observed set of age-specific mortality rates is all that is needed to calculate a complete life table.

Specifically, consider the age interval 65 to 66 for white males, 1980, California:

1. $$q_{65} = \frac{R_{65}}{1 + 0.5R_{65}} = \frac{0.0284}{1 + 0.5(0.0284)} = 0.0280,$$

    since $R_{65} = \dfrac{2097}{73832} = 0.0284$ (note: $\bar{a}_{65} = 0.5$),

2. $d_{65} = l_{65}q_{65} = 69728(0.0280) = 1953,$
3. $L_{65} = l_{65} - d_{65} + 0.5d_{65} = 69728 - 1953 + 0.5(1953) = 68752,$
4. $T_{65} = L_{65} + L_{66} + \cdots + L_{90+}$
   $= 68752 + 66757 + \cdots + 9126 + 41616 = 1011356,$

and

5. $$e_{65} = \frac{T_{65}}{l_{65}} = \frac{1011356}{69728} = 14.504.$$

These five steps are repeated for each age interval, starting at age 0, resulting in the entire current life table from a set of mortality rates (R_x) and an arbitrary starting value (l_0).

Two example life tables are given in Tables 9.1 and 9.2 for male and female residents of California for the year 1980. The expected number of years of life remaining after the age x is an effective summary of the entire mortality pattern described by a life table (e_x; last column in Tables 9.1 and 9.2). The expectation of life is not more than a special mean value and is calculated in the same way as most mean values, where

$$\text{mean years remaining} = e_x = \frac{\text{total years lived beyond age } x}{\text{number of individuals age } x} = \frac{T_x}{l_x}. \tag{9.7}$$

Perhaps the most common single summary value calculated from a life table is the expectation of life at birth (e_0). For the California data, $e_0 = 69.61$ years for males and $e_0 = 76.93$ years for females, based on 1980 mortality patterns.

Table 9-1. California 1980 population of white males

$x-x+1$	Population	Deaths	R_x^*	q_x	d_x	l_x	L_x	T_x	e_x
0-1	129,602	2,166	1,671.3	0.01647	1,647	100,000	98,518	6,960,692	69.61
1-2	117,753	123	104.5	0.00104	103	98,353	98,295	6,862,175	69.77
2-3	115,003	73	63.5	0.00063	62	98,251	98,217	6,763,880	68.84
3-4	113,314	60	53.0	0.00053	52	98,188	98,161	6,665,663	67.89
4-5	110,822	41	37.0	0.00037	36	98,137	98,118	6,567,502	66.92
5-6	110,548	55	49.8	0.00050	49	98,076	98,100	6,469,384	65.95
6-7	106,857	42	39.3	0.00039	39	98,051	98,032	6,371,308	64.98
7-8	112,184	58	51.7	0.00052	51	98,013	97,988	6,273,276	64.00
8-9	116,423	44	37.8	0.00038	37	97,962	97,944	6,175,288	63.04
9-10	132,952	52	39.1	0.00039	38	97,925	97,906	6,077,344	62.06
10-11	134,266	48	35.7	0.00036	35	97,887	97,869	5,979,438	61.09
11-12	128,938	60	46.5	0.00047	46	97,852	97,829	5,881,569	60.11
12-13	125,502	52	41.4	0.00041	41	97,806	97,786	5,783,740	59.13
13-14	128,212	82	64.0	0.00064	63	97,766	97,735	5,685,954	58.16
14-15	132,775	129	97.2	0.00097	95	97,703	97,656	5,588,219	57.20
15-16	143,600	233	162.3	0.00162	158	97,608	97,529	5,490,563	56.25
16-17	151,840	290	191.0	0.00191	186	97,450	97,357	5,393,034	55.34
17-18	157,365	400	254.2	0.00254	247	97,264	97,141	5,295,677	54.45
18-19	159,476	415	260.2	0.00260	252	97,017	96,891	5,198,535	53.58
19-20	171,235	416	242.9	0.00243	235	96,765	96,648	5,101,644	52.72
20-21	173,682	418	240.7	0.00240	232	96,530	96,414	5,004,996	51.85
21-22	172,656	436	252.5	0.00252	243	96,298	96,177	4,908,582	50.97
22-23	176,544	400	226.6	0.00226	217	96,056	95,947	4,812,405	50.10
23-24	175,732	410	233.3	0.00233	223	95,838	95,726	4,716,458	49.21
24-25	174,780	409	234.0	0.00234	223	95,615	95,503	4,620,731	48.33
25-26	173,214	393	226.9	0.00227	216	95,391	95,283	4,525,228	47.44
26-27	169,980	400	235.3	0.00235	224	95,175	95,063	4,429,944	46.55
27-28	168,369	366	217.4	0.00217	206	94,951	94,848	4,334,881	45.65
28-29	157,189	330	209.9	0.00210	199	94,745	94,646	4,240,033	44.75
29-30	162,394	346	213.1	0.00213	201	94,547	94,446	4,145,387	43.84
30-31	161,191	329	204.1	0.00204	192	94,345	94,249	4,050,941	42.94
31-32	154,874	355	229.2	0.00229	216	94,153	94,045	3,956,692	42.02
32-33	162,136	338	208.5	0.00208	196	93,937	93,840	3,862,647	41.12
33-34	163,065	305	187.0	0.00187	175	93,742	93,654	3,768,807	40.20
34-35	127,624	267	209.2	0.00209	196	93,567	93,469	3,675,153	39.28
35-36	128,890	296	229.7	0.00229	214	93,371	93,264	3,581,684	38.36
36-37	127,933	302	236.1	0.00236	220	93,157	93,047	3,488,420	37.45
37-38	127,923	334	261.1	0.00261	242	92,937	92,816	3,395,373	36.53
38-39	109,718	281	256.1	0.00256	237	92,695	92,576	3,302,557	35.63
39-40	108,168	325	300.5	0.00300	277	92,458	92,319	3,209,981	34.72
40-41	104,314	338	324.0	0.00324	298	92,180	92,031	3,117,662	33.82
41-42	100,059	342	341.8	0.00341	314	91,882	91,725	3,025,630	32.93
42-43	97,330	344	353.4	0.00353	323	91,569	91,407	2,933,905	32.04
43-44	92,394	356	385.3	0.00385	351	91,246	91,070	2,842,497	31.15
44-45	91,741	431	469.8	0.00469	426	90,895	90,682	2,751,427	30.27
45-46	92,331	438	474.4	0.00473	428	90,469	90,255	2,660,745	29.41
46-47	88,150	522	592.2	0.00590	532	90,041	89,775	2,570,491	28.55
47-48	90,475	559	617.9	0.00616	551	89,509	89,233	2,480,716	27.71
48-49	90,095	650	721.5	0.00719	639	88,958	88,638	2,391,483	26.88
49-50	97,275	696	715.5	0.00713	630	88,318	88,003	2,302,845	26.07
50-51	98,008	734	748.9	0.00746	654	87,688	87,361	2,214,841	25.26

Table 9-1. (*Continued*)

$x-x+1$	Population	Deaths	R_x^*	q_x	d_x	l_x	L_x	T_x	e_x
51–52	93,134	825	885.8	0.00882	768	87,034	86,650	2,127,480	24.44
52–53	94,496	875	926.0	0.00922	795	86,267	85,869	2,040,830	23.66
53–54	93,239	1,010	1,083.2	0.01077	921	85,472	85,011	1,954,960	22.87
54–55	96,443	1,126	1,167.5	0.01161	981	84,551	84,060	1,869,949	22.12
55–56	97,763	1,197	1,224.4	0.01217	1,017	83,569	83,061	1,785,889	21.37
56–57	96,823	1,272	1,313.7	0.01305	1,077	82,552	82,014	1,702,829	20.63
57–58	96,189	1,334	1,386.9	0.01377	1,122	81,475	80,914	1,620,815	19.89
58–59	98,518	1,553	1,576.4	0.01564	1,257	80,353	79,724	1,539,901	19.16
59–60	96,154	1,564	1,626.6	0.01613	1,276	79.096	78,458	1,460,177	18.46
60–61	88,552	1,472	1,662.3	0.01649	1,283	77,820	77,820	1,381,719	17.76
61–62	83,814	1,684	2,009.2	0.01989	1,522	76,537	75,776	1,304,541	17.04
62–63	81,464	1,763	2,164.1	0.02141	1,606	75,014	74,211	1,228,766	16.38
63–64	76,317	1,871	2,451.6	0.02422	1,778	73,408	72,519	1,154,554	15.73
64–65	75,505	2,032	2,691.2	0.02656	1,902	71,630	70,679	1,082,035	15.11
65–66	73,832	2,097	2,840.2	0.02801	1,953	69,728	68,752	1,011,356	14.50
66–67	69,480	2,121	3,052.7	0.03007	2,038	67,776	66,757	942,604	13.91
67–68	65,690	2,130	3,242.5	0.03191	2,098	65,738	64,689	875,847	13.32
68–69	62,557	2,256	3,606.3	0.03542	2,254	63,640	62,513	811,159	12.75
69–70	57,412	2,327	4,053.2	0.03973	2,439	61,386	60,166	748,646	12.20
70–71	53,926	2,205	4,088.9	0.04007	2,362	58,947	57,766	688,479	11.68
71–72	50,402	2,376	4,714.1	0.04606	2,606	56,585	55,282	630,713	11.15
72–73	47,213	2,342	4,960.5	0.04840	2,613	53,979	52,673	575,431	10.66
73–74	42,931	2,233	5,201.4	0.05070	2,604	51,366	50,064	522,759	10.18
74–75	39,611	2,300	5,806.5	0.05643	2,751	48,762	47,386	472,694	9.69
75–76	36,306	2,408	6,632.5	0.06420	2,954	46,011	44,534	425,308	9.24
76–77	33,386	2,251	6,742.3	0.06523	2,808	43,057	41,653	380,774	8.84
77–78	30,141	2,102	6,973.9	0.06739	2,712	40,249	38,892	339,121	8.43
78–79	26,432	2,272	8,595.6	0.08241	3,094	37,536	35,990	300,229	8.00
79–80	26,264	2,093	7,969.1	0.07664	2,640	34,443	33,123	264,239	7.67
80–81	21,846	1,958	8,962.7	0.08578	2,728	31,803	30,439	231,117	7.27
81–82	18,868	1,947	10,319.1	0.09813	2,853	29,075	27,648	200,677	6.90
82–83	16,653	1,802	10,820.9	0.10265	2,692	26,222	24,876	173,029	6.60
83–84	14,825	1,751	11,811.1	0.11153	2,624	23,530	22,218	148,153	6.30
84–85	13,137	1,689	12,856.8	0.12080	2,525	20,906	19,643	125,935	6.02
85–86	11,350	1,622	14,290.7	0.13338	2,452	18,380	17,155	106,292	5.78
86–87	9,442	1,426	15,102.7	0.14042	2,237	15,929	14,811	89,137	5.60
87–88	8,047	1,198	14,887.5	0.13856	1,897	13,692	12,744	74,327	5.43
88–89	6,091	1,072	17,599.7	0.16176	1,908	11,795	10,841	61,583	5.22
89–90	5,382	897	16,666.7	0.15385	1,521	9,887	9,126	50,742	5.13
90+	17,346	3,487	20,102.6	1.00000	8,366	8,366	41,616	41,616	4.97

*Rate per 100,000 person years of risk.

Expectations of life from birth are compared among countries and among groups within a country. The U.S. life expectancy e_0 has steadily increased over the last 80 years, and the difference between males and females has also increased, as Table 9.3 shows.

The expectation of life has a geometric interpretation related to the

Table 9-2. California 1980 population of white females

$x-x+1$	Population	Deaths	R_x^*	q_x	d_x	l_x	L_x	T_x	e_x
0-1	123,342	1,635	1325.6	0.01310	1,310	100,000	98,821	7,693,461	76.93
1-2	111,520	64	57.4	0.00057	57	98,690	98,658	7,594,641	76.95
2-3	109,200	41	37.5	0.00038	37	98,633	98,613	7,495,983	76.00
3-4	108,749	22	20.2	0.00020	20	98,596	98,586	7,397,370	75.03
4-5	105,698	41	38.8	0.00039	38	98,576	98,557	7,298,784	74.04
5-6	105,801	37	35.0	0.00035	34	98,538	98,521	7,200,227	73.07
6-7	101,630	37	36.4	0.00036	36	98,504	98,486	7,101,706	72.10
7-8	106,850	32	29.9	0.00030	29	98,468	98,453	7,003,220	71.12
8-9	110,410	32	29.0	0.00029	29	98,438	98,424	6,904,767	70.14
9-10	127,237	33	25.9	0.00026	26	98,410	98,397	6,806,342	69.16
10-11	128,916	33	25.6	0.00026	25	98,384	98,372	6,707,945	68.18
11-12	124,123	32	25.8	0.00026	25	98,359	98,347	6,609,573	67.20
12-13	119,672	28	23.4	0.00023	23	98,334	98,322	6,511,227	66.22
13-14	123,652	48	38.8	0.00039	38	98,311	98,292	6,412,905	65.23
14-15	127,869	68	53.2	0.00053	52	98,273	98,247	6,314,613	64.26
15-16	139,122	98	70.4	0.00070	69	98,220	98,186	6,216,366	63.29
16-17	146,318	93	63.6	0.00064	62	98,151	98,120	6,118,180	62.33
17-18	150,163	132	87.9	0.00088	86	98,089	98,046	6,020,059	61.37
18-19	152,382	121	79.4	0.00079	78	98,003	97,964	5,922,014	60.43
19-20	162,203	138	85.1	0.00085	83	97,925	97,883	5,824,050	59.47
20-21	162,313	118	72.7	0.00073	71	97,842	97,806	5,726,167	58.52
21-22	162,709	104	63.9	0.00064	62	97,771	97,739	5,628,360	57.57
22-23	167,087	96	57.5	0.00057	56	97,708	97,680	5,530,621	56.60
23-24	168,874	121	71.7	0.00072	70	97,652	97,617	5,432,940	55.64
24-25	168,959	119	70.4	0.00070	69	97,582	97,548	5,335,324	54.68
25-26	168,414	110	65.3	0.00065	64	97,513	97,481	5,237,776	53.71
26-27	165,167	141	85.4	0.00085	83	97,450	97,408	5,140,295	52.75
27-28	164,403	123	74.8	0.00075	73	97,366	97,330	5,042,887	51.79
28-29	154,062	137	88.9	0.00089	86	97,294	97,250	4,945,557	50.83
29-30	158,102	135	85.4	0.00085	83	97,207	97,166	4,848,307	49.88
30-31	157,975	134	84.8	0.00085	82	97,124	97,083	4,751,141	48.92
31-32	153,534	134	87.3	0.00087	85	97,042	97,000	4,654,058	47.96
32-33	160.016	157	98.1	0.00098	95	96,957	96,910	4,557,058	47.00
33-34	160,299	127	79.2	0.00079	77	96,862	96,824	4,460,149	46.05
34-35	125,826	144	114.4	0.00114	111	96,785	96,730	4,363,324	45.08
35-36	126,747	158	124.7	0.00125	120	96,675	96,614	4,266,594	44.13
36-37	125,960	155	123.1	0.00123	119	96,554	96,495	4,169,980	43.19
37-38	127,942	161	125.8	0.00126	121	96,436	96,375	4,073,485	42.24
38-39	109,358	169	154.5	0.00154	149	96,314	96,240	3,977,110	41.29
39-40	106,481	196	184.1	0.00184	177	96,166	96,077	3,880,870	40.36
40-41	103,828	171	164.7	0.00165	158	95,989	95,910	3,784,793	39.43
41-42	99,325	205	206.4	0.00206	198	95,831	95,732	3,688,883	38.49
42-43	96,380	228	236.6	0.00236	226	95,633	95,520	3,593,151	37.57
43-44	93,276	256	274.5	0.00274	261	95,407	95,276	3,497,631	36.66
44-45	92,873	258	277.8	0.00277	264	95,146	95,014	3,402,355	35.76
45-46	92,183	246	266.9	0.00267	253	94,882	94,755	3,307,341	34.86
46-47	88,595	274	309.3	0.00309	292	94,629	94,483	3,212,586	33.95
47-48	91,046	323	354.8	0.00354	334	94,337	94,170	3,118,103	33.05
48-49	89,588	384	428.6	0.00428	402	94,003	93,802	3,023,934	32.17
49-50	97,274	398	409.2	0.00408	382	93,601	93,409	2,930,132	31.30

Table 9-2. (Continued)

$x-x+1$	Population	Deaths	R_x^*	q_x	d_x	l_x	L_x	T_x	e_x
50–51	98,371	449	456.4	0.00455	425	93,218	93,006	2,836,722	30.43
51–52	95,717	474	495.2	0.00494	458	92,794	92,565	2,743,716	29.57
52–53	99,570	557	559.4	0.00558	515	92,335	92,078	2,651,152	28.71
53–54	101,653	687	675.8	0.00674	618	91,820	91,511	2,559,074	27.87
54–55	105,815	675	637.9	0.00636	580	91,202	90,912	2,467,563	27.06
55–56	108,657	737	678.3	0.00676	613	90,622	90,316	2,376,651	26.23
56–57	106,689	784	734.8	0.00732	659	90,009	89,680	2,286,336	25.40
57–58	106,142	842	793.3	0.00790	706	89,350	88,997	2,196,656	24.58
58–59	107,384	929	865.1	0.00861	764	88,644	88,263	2,107,659	23.78
59–60	103,981	1,007	968.4	0.00964	847	87,881	87,457	2,019,396	22.98
60–61	97,063	964	993.2	0.00988	860	87,034	86,604	1,931,939	22.20
61–62	93,115	1,033	1,109.4	0.01103	951	86,174	85,698	1,845,335	21.41
62–63	90,046	1,070	1,188.3	0.01181	1,007	85,223	84,720	1,759,637	20.65
63–64	86,916	1,141	1,312.8	0.01304	1,098	84,216	83,667	1,674,917	19.89
64–65	85,726	1,282	1,495.5	0.01484	1,234	83,118	82,501	1,591,250	19.14
65–66	86,996	1,387	1,594.3	0.01582	1,295	81,884	81,237	1,508,749	18.43
66–67	83,258	1,400	1,681.5	0.01668	1,344	80,589	79,917	1,427,513	17.71
67–68	79,961	1,428	1,785.9	0.01770	1,403	79,245	78,544	1,347,595	17.01
68–69	78,039	1,485	1,902.9	0.01885	1,467	77,842	77,109	1,269,052	16.30
69–70	74,389	1,617	2,173.7	0.02150	1,642	76,375	75,554	1,191,943	15.61
70–71	70,163	1,614	2,300.4	0.02274	1,700	74,733	73,883	1,116,389	14.94
71–72	67,599	1,816	2,686.4	0.02651	1,936	73,033	72,065	1,042,506	14.27
72–73	65,045	1,813	2,787.3	0.02749	1,954	71,097	70,120	970,441	13.65
73–74	60,676	1,905	3,139.6	0.03091	2,137	69,143	68,074	900,320	13.02
74–75	57,975	1,889	3,258.3	0.03206	2,148	67,006	65,931	832,246	12.42
75–76	54,912	1,995	3,633.1	0.03568	2,314	64,857	63,700	766,315	11.82
76–77	51,217	2,089	4,078.7	0.03997	2,500	62,543	61,293	702,615	11.23
77–78	48,251	1,993	4,130.5	p.04047	2,430	60,043	58,828	641,322	10.68
78–79	43,234	2,344	5,421.7	0.05279	3,041	57,613	56,093	582,494	10.11
79–80	47,158	2,399	5,087.2	0.04961	2,707	54,572	53,218	526,401	9.65
80–81	39,462	2,318	5,874.0	0.05706	2,960	51,865	50,385	473,183	9.12
81–82	36,295	2,416	6,656.6	0.06442	3,151	48,905	47,330	422,798	8.65
82–83	31,875	2,360	7,403.9	0.07140	3,267	45,755	44,121	375,468	8.21
83–84	30,470	2,535	8,319.7	0.07987	3,394	42,488	40,791	331,347	7.80
84–85	27,904	2,540	9,102.6	0.08706	3,404	39,094	37,392	290,556	7.43
85–86	24,712	2,458	9,946.6	0.09475	3,382	35,690	34,000	253,163	7.09
86–87	21,302	2,383	11,186.7	0.10594	3,423	32,309	30,597	219,164	6.78
87–88	19,402	2,120	10,926.7	0.10361	2,993	28,886	27,389	188,567	6.53
88–89	14,905	1,993	13,371.4	0.12533	3,245	25,893	24,270	161,177	6.22
89–90	13,873	1,900	13,695.7	0.12818	2,903	22,648	21,196	136,907	6.05
90+	47,650	8,131	17,064.0	1.00000	19,745	19,745	115,710	115,710	5.86

*Rate per 100,000 person years of risk.

survive curve (see the next section). The expectation of life (e_0) is approximately equal to the area under the survival curve. In Chapter 10 this interpretation is discussed further [expression (10.36)].

The crude mortality rate associated with a life table is the total

Table 9-3. United States life expectancy for white males and females (1900-80)

Year	1900	1910	1920	1930	1940	1950	1960	1970	1980
Male	46.6	48.6	54.5	59.7	62.1	66.5	67.4	68.0	70.7
Female	48.7	52.0	55.6	63.5	66.6	72.2	74.1	75.6	78.1

Source: Vital Statistics of the United States, 1983, U.S. Department of Health and Human Services.

number of persons who died divided by the total number of person-years lived by the entire life-table population or

$$\text{crude mortality rate} = \frac{\Sigma\, d_x}{T_0} = \frac{l_0}{T_0}. \qquad (9.8)$$

The crude mortality rate is the reciprocal of the expectation of life at birth or

$$\text{crude mortality rate} = \frac{l_0}{T_0} = \frac{1}{e_0} \qquad \text{or} \qquad e_0 = \frac{1}{l_0/T_0}. \qquad (9.9)$$

Referring to the life table for males (Table 9.1), the crude mortality rate is $100,000/6,960,692 = 0.0144$, or $1,437$ deaths per $100,000$ person-years of life and $1/0.0144 = 69.607$ years of life are expected to be lived by a newborn male infant who experiences the exact 1980 age-specific mortality rates. A life table formally shows the expected relationship that survival time (average expected lifetime) is inversely related to risk (average rate of death).

Three assumptions are implicit in constructing and interpreting a life table. The life-table structure requires that the same number of births occur each year (l_0 constant). The deaths are assumed to be uniformly distributed within each interval for ages greater than four (thus resulting in $\bar{a}_x = 0.5$), and no population growth occurs (the number of births is equal to the number of deaths each year, and no immigration or emigration occurs). When a population conforms to these three properties, it is called a stationary population. Although stationary human populations do not exist, in most cases changes are sufficiently slow so that postulating that a group of individuals has an approximately stationary structure is not unreasonable, making a life table a useful tool to describe human mortality experience.

Life Table Survival Curve

A fundamental summary statistic derived from a life table is an estimate of a survival curve (introduced in Chapter 1), that is, the probability of surviving beyond a specific point in time. In symbols, $S(x)$ represents the probability of surviving beyond age x. Two identical ways of computing $S(x)$ from a life table are:

$$S(x) = \frac{l_x}{l_0} \tag{9.10}$$

or

$$S(x) = \prod_{i=0}^{x-1} (1 - q_i) = \prod_{i=0}^{x-1} p_i. \tag{9.11}$$

The equivalence of these two calculations comes from the fact that

$$S(x) = \prod_{i=0}^{x-1} p_i = \frac{l_1}{l_0} \frac{l_2}{l_1} \frac{l_3}{l_2} \frac{l_4}{l_3} \cdots \frac{l_{x-1}}{l_{x-2}} \frac{l_x}{l_{x-1}} = \frac{l_x}{l_0}, \tag{9.12}$$

since $p_i = l_{i+1}/l_i$ is the probability of surviving from age i to age $i + 1$ given that the individual is alive at the beginning of the interval. Also note that $S(0) = 1$, which is a property of survival curves in general.

The survival curves for the male (solid line) and female (dotted line) 1980 California populations are displayed in Figure 9.1 (top). A small

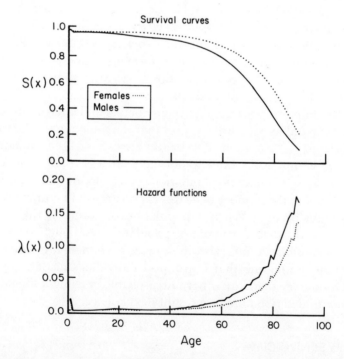

Figure 9-1. Survival curve and hazard function from the life table for white males and females, California, 1980.

decrease in $S(x)$ caused by high rates of infant mortality in the first year of life is followed by a slight and gradual decrease in the probability of survival until about ages 60 or 70, where the $S(x)$ curve begins to fall rapidly. This pattern is often observed in modern human populations. The probability of living more than 90 years is given by the values $S(90) = 0.084$ for males and $S(90) = 0.197$ for females (females are 2.4 times more likely than males to live beyond the age of 90).

Life Table Hazard Function

The slope of the survival curve or the derivative of $S(x)$ at the point x $[dS(x)/dx]$ measures the impact of mortality on a population at a specific age x. The slope indicates the rate of change (intensity of mortality) of the curve representing the probability of surviving beyond a particular point. Analogous to the definition of a mortality rate [expression (1.2)], if the instantaneous slope of the survival curve is measured relative to the proportion surviving up to age x, then the previous definition of a hazard rate emerges, given as

$$\lambda(x) = -\frac{dS(x)/dx}{S(x)}, \tag{9.13}$$

where $\lambda(x)$ represents the hazard rate and the negative sign makes it a positive quantity. A hazard rate applied to mortality data is the instantaneous rate of death, relative to being alive at age x.

To estimate the hazard rate from a life table, it is necessary to make a series of approximations to calculate this theoretical quantity. The slope of the survival curve at the midpoint of the interval x to $x + 1$ is approximately $S(x + 1) - S(x)$, and the value of the survival curve at $x + \frac{1}{2}$ is approximately $[S(x + 1) + S(x)]/2$. These two approximations are exact if the survival curve is a straight line. Combining these two quantities gives an approximate expression for the hazard rate at age $x + \frac{1}{2}$ of

$$\lambda(x + \tfrac{1}{2}) = -\frac{dS(x + \tfrac{1}{2})/dx}{S(x + \tfrac{1}{2})} \approx -\frac{S(x + 1) - S(x)}{[S(x + 1) + S(x)]/2}. \tag{9.14}$$

This expression in terms of the number of persons alive at age x (l_x) is

$$\lambda(x + \tfrac{1}{2}) \approx -\frac{l_{x+1} - l_x}{(l_{x+1} + l_x)/2} = -2\frac{p_x - 1}{p_x + 1} = \frac{2q_x}{p_x + 1}, \tag{9.15}$$

where $p_x = l_{x+1}/l_x$.

Since $\log(p) \approx 2(p - 1)/(p + 1)$ for $p > 0.7$, then

$$\lambda(x + \tfrac{1}{2}) \approx -\log(p_x), \tag{9.16}$$

which provides a useful approximation of the hazard rate for most life tables based on human mortality. An expression for the hazard rate at age x is the average of the hazard rates at age $x - \frac{1}{2}$ and $x + \frac{1}{2}$ or

$$\lambda(x) \approx \frac{-[\log(p_{x-1}) + \log(p_x)]}{2}. \tag{9.17}$$

A further simplification is achieved by using yet another approximation, that of $\log(p) \approx p - 1$ for $p > 0.9$, giving

$$\lambda(x + \tfrac{1}{2}) \approx -\log(p_x) \approx q_x \tag{9.18}$$

and, as before,

$$\lambda(x) \approx \frac{q_{x-1} + q_x}{2} \tag{9.19}$$

for age intervals with low probabilities of death. Similar to a mortality rate, a hazard rate is conceptually an instantaneous quantity and must be approximated when the survival curve $S(x)$ is not specified.

Another estimate for the hazard rate $\lambda(x + \frac{1}{2})$ can be derived by noting that a hazard rate is an instantaneous age-specific rate. An average age-specific rate from a life table is estimated by

$$\text{rate} = \frac{d_x}{l_x - 0.5d_x}. \tag{9.20}$$

For a small interval (say, 1 year), the age-specific life-table mortality rate is approximately equal to the hazard rate at the middle of an age interval or

$$\lambda(x + \tfrac{1}{2}) \approx \text{rate} = \frac{d_x}{l_x - 0.5d_x}. \tag{9.21}$$

Two other versions of this expression are used. They are

$$\lambda(x + \tfrac{1}{2}) \approx \frac{q_x}{1 - 0.5q_x} = \frac{2q_x}{p_x + 1}. \tag{9.22}$$

The last expression is the same as the previous expression for the hazard rate [expression (9.15)] derived from different considerations. Again, if d_x is small relative to l_x ($p_x \approx 1$), then $\lambda(x + \frac{1}{2}) \approx q_x$. In general, an approximate life-table hazard rate is

$$\lambda(x + n_x/2) \approx \frac{d_x}{n_x(l_x - 0.5d_x)}, \tag{9.23}$$

where n_x represents the interval length. The accuracy of this expression as an approximation for a hazard rate decreases as the interval length n_x increases for most situations.

The hazard functions (a series of hazard rates) are plotted in Figure 9.1 (bottom) for the California 1980 life tables for males and females. Detail of the mortality pattern is clearly seen from these hazard functions. For example, an inconsistency in the rise of the hazard function for the older age groups is obvious and undoubtedly due to the lack of reliability in reporting of age for older individuals (about 80 years or so).

The shape of the curve observed for the 1980 California life-table populations is typical of most human populations over the entire age span. After the first year of life, the next 60 years are characterized by an essentially level hazard function followed by a sharp increase. However, hazard functions in other contexts take on a variety of shapes. A population subject to only accidental (random) deaths, for example, would have a mortality pattern with a constant hazard function (a horizontal line). A hazard function and a survival curve are related—higher rates of mortality imply lower probabilities of survival. The exact mathematical relationship is described in Chapter 11, and complete discussions are found in technical texts on survival analysis (e.g., [Ref. 2]).

Life tables can be constructed from small sets of data. The principles are the same as those described, but the issue of sampling variation should not be ignored. The values q_x, l_x, etc. are estimated quantities subject to sampling variation, which usually requires reporting their associated standard errors. Huge numbers of individuals make up the California life-table data sets so the precision of the estimates is not much of an issue. For a life table based on a small number of individuals, however, the variability of the estimated quantities should be taken into account. Expressions for the variances of life-table estimates are based on assuming that the probabilities of death can be modeled by binomial distributions (these expressions are presented in detail elsewhere [Ref. 1]). A life table based on small numbers of observations illustrates where 11 individuals failed to respond to a specific treatment ("died") [Ref. 2]. The survival times, amount of time to remission (in weeks), are 5, 5, 8, 8, 12, 23, 27, 30, 33, 43, 45. A life table, based on 10-week intervals, summarizing these data is given in Table 9.4.

The size of the sample used to construct this life table is small, making the variability of the estimates an issue, and, once again, categorizing a continuous variable (survival time) is not an ideal way

Table 9-4. Life table for a small set of data

Interval	Midpoint	"Deaths"	Population	q_x	p_x	l_x	$S(x)$	$\lambda(x+5)$
0–10	5	4	11	0.364	0.636	1.000	1.000	0.044
10–20	15	1	7	0.143	0.857	636	0.636	0.015
20–30	25	2	6	0.333	0.667	545	0.545	0.040
30–40	35	2	4	0.500	0.500	364	0.364	0.067
40–50	45	2	2	1.000	0.000	182	0.182	0.200

to proceed. Small sets of survival data are better analyzed by other approaches (presented in Chapters 10 and 11).

Proportional Hazard Rates—An Example

An instructive application of a life table involves an actuarial-like calculation showing the consequences of lowered hazard rates in a specific population. Suppose a hazard rate is reduced uniformly by a set proportion c [i.e., $\lambda(t) = c\lambda_0(t)$, where $\lambda_0(t)$ is a known or estimated hazard function]; construction of a life table based on such a hazard function describes the resulting mortality experience. Figure 9.2 (top) shows three hypothetical hazard functions based on the 1980 California, white male population mortality rates [$\lambda_0(t)$, top line], where c is set at 0.75, 0.50, and 0.25. The logarithms of the hazard rates clearly show the detail of these curves (Figure 9.2, bottom). Note that the logarithms of a set of proportional hazard rates produce parallel lines. The associated life table can be used to describe the impact of the lower hazard rates.

To summarize the life tables constructed from the three reduced hazard functions, the proportion of individuals alive at ages 65, 75, and 85 years along with the expected length of life from birth for the "proportional populations" are shown in Table 9.5.

It is unlikely that a decrease in mortality would be exactly proportional throughout the life span (i.e., proportional hazards rates); nevertheless, some idea of the impact of decreasing mortality risk is gained by life-table summary values. The percentage of older individuals increases markedly as the age-specific mortality decreases. For example, about 46% of the 1980 California males are older than 75 years, but, when the mortality is reduced by a factor of 4 ($c = 0.25$), this value increases to an estimated 84%. The expected length of life at birth is correspondingly increased from 69.6 to 87.4 years.

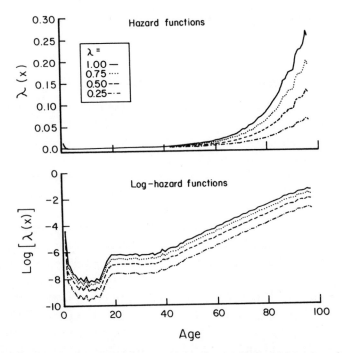

Figure 9–2. Hazard functions and the logarithm of the hazard functions for three hypothetical patterns of mortality based on the white, male mortality rate, California 1980.

The effects on a population of an increasing or decreasing hazard rate are not always clear. As the illustration shows, a hazard rate can be related to more easily interpreted measures of the impact of risk using life-table summaries. A decrease in hazard rate becomes a less abstract expression of risk when translated, for example, into an increase in the number of individuals exceeding a specific age or into an increase in the expected years of remaining life.

Table 9–5. Influence of three hypothetical hazard rates on the 1980 California male population

Hazard	% ≥ 65 years	% ≥ 75 years	% ≥ 85 years	Expectation
1.00λ	69.7	46.0	18.3	69.6
0.75λ	78.7	58.7	30.0	74.7
0.50λ	85.3	70.2	45.1	79.8
0.25λ	92.3	83.8	67.4	87.4

LIFE TABLES: THREE APPLICATIONS OF LIFE-TABLE TECHNIQUES

Life-Table Method for Calculating a Survival Probability

The evaluation of the treatment of chronic disease usually involves the assessment of survival (or, perhaps, remission) times. The probability of surviving 5 years after receiving a treatment is a frequent measure of efficacy. Survival data can be collected and recorded in a sequence of intervals to form a series of cohort tables (one for each year of follow-up, for example). It is this follow-up pattern of data collection that allows an efficient estimate of the 5-year survival probability or, in general, an estimate of the survival curve associated with the sampled population. The set of follow-up data in Table 9.6 concerns the survival of six cohorts of kidney cancer patients, illustrating this type of data [Ref. 3].

The complete display of the data set is presented to show the cohorts formed as each year new patients are added to the sample. The interval x to $x + 1$ denotes the years survived since the kidney cancer was diagnosed. The column labeled l_x contains the count of the individuals

Table 9-6. Calculation of a survival probability: Data

Year	x to $x+1$	l_x	d_x	u_x	w_x
1946	0–1	9	4	1	—
	1–2	4	0	0	—
	2–3	4	0	0	—
	3–4	4	0	0	—
	4–5	4	0	0	—
	5–6	4	0	0	4
1947	0–1	18	7	0	—
	1–2	11	0	0	—
	2–3	11	1	0	—
	3–4	10	2	2	—
	4–5	6	0	0	6
1948	0–1	21	11	0	—
	1–2	10	1	2	—
	2–3	7	0	0	—
	3–4	7	0	0	7
1949	0–1	34	12	0	—
	1–2	22	3	3	—
	2–3	16	1	0	15
1950	0–1	19	5	1	—
	1–2	13	1	1	11
1951	0–1	25	8	2	15

alive at the beginning of the time interval x to $x + 1$. The number of deaths in each interval is represented by d_x. The possibility exists that patients are "lost to follow-up" during the time period covered by the study. The count of patients lost during an interval is symbolized by u_x. The last column in the table contains the counts of patients withdrawn from study. Individuals are said to be withdrawn when they are no longer relevant to further calculations. For example, consider the 1950 cohort of 19 patients. Five patients died the first year, and one the second year; two were lost, one each year, and the remaining 11 individuals produced information about the first and second year of survival but cannot be used in calculations for the third year or beyond since they were only observed for a maximum of 2 years. The 11 ($w_2 = 11$) members of this cohort alive at the end of the second year are said to be withdrawn after 2 years and are not part of subsequent calculations. They either survived or died after 1951, but this information is not part of the collected data. The times of these four possible events (l_x, d_x, u_x, and w_x) are recorded to the nearest year in the kidney cancer follow-up data. A summary table that combines the survival experience of all kidney cancer patients for the six cohorts (Table 9.6) is given in Table 9.7. Note that

$$l_{x+1} = l_x - d_x - u_x - w_x. \qquad (9.24)$$

If the entire cohort was entered into the study on the first day and followed for at least 5 years and no one was lost, then a 5-year survival probability would be the number who lived 5 years divided by the number who started the study. For most survival data, however, individuals die, are lost, or withdrawn from follow-up at different times during the study period. It is also likely that, during the course of collecting a set of follow-up data, individuals will die from causes other than the one being investigated. Somewhat pragmatically, these

Table 9–7. Calculation of a survival probability from tabled data: Summary data

$x - x + 1$	l_x	d_x	u_x	w_x
0–1	126	47	4	15
1–2	60	5	6	11
2–3	38	2	0	15
3–4	21	2	2	7
4–5	10	0	0	6
5–6	4	0	0	4

individuals are usually classified as lost (i.e., u_x is increased), which introduces no bias if these deaths are completely unrelated to the disease under study. The sequential pattern of follow-up data collection makes it necessary to piece together the followup information.

Notice that 15 individuals in the 1951 cohort were withdrawn after 1 year. If the exact time these patients were observed was known, then the total person-years of risk would be the sum of their observed individual survival times. When this information is not available, estimates of survival time must be adjusted to compensate for the incomplete nature of the data. One approach is to assume that each person withdrawn during an interval, on the average, contributes one-half an interval of time ($\bar{a}_x = 0.5$) to the total survival time. That is, it is postulated that individuals come into the study uniformly throughout the follow-up period, implying they will be withdrawn uniformly from observation. If this is the case, then attributing one-half an interval's time to each person withdrawn is "on the average" correct. A similar assumption is usually made about individuals lost from follow-up. An estimate of the probability of death (q_x) that accounts for the two types of incomplete information is made by reducing the number of persons beginning the interval (l_x) to compensate for those individuals lost (u_x) and withdrawn (w_x) during the interval. Specifically,

$$l'_x = l_x - 0.5u_x - 0.5w_x, \qquad (9.25)$$

where l'_x is the "effective" persons at risk in the interval and the probability of death within an interval is then estimated by

$$q_x = \frac{d_x}{l'_x}. \qquad (9.26)$$

The adjusted persons at risk (l'_x) better reflects the underlying situation.

An alternate view of this adjustment comes from noting that the observed number of deaths is understated since lost and withdrawn individuals are not followed for, on the average, half an interval and deaths occurring during that time will not be recorded. An estimate of this additional number of "deaths" is $0.5(u_x + w_x)q_x$. Adding these "deaths" to the number of observed deaths gives an estimate of the probability of death as

$$q_x = \frac{d_x + 0.5(u_x + w_x)q_x}{l_x}, \qquad (9.27)$$

and solving for q_x produces the same result as before ($q_x = d_x/l'_x$).

Employing the value q_x to estimate the proportion of deaths among those who were lost or withdrawn implies that these individuals do not differ in their mortality experience from those who continued to be followed. This assumption may not be tenable in some situations. For example, it might be that lost individuals are more likely to have survived or, perhaps, more likely to have died; a suitable q_x should be used under these conditions. A more subtle implication of employing l'_x is the implicit assumption that mortality experience is unrelated to the probability that an individual is withdrawn from follow-up.

Analogous to the life-table calculation of the survival curve, the survival probabilities are

$$\hat{P}_k = \prod_{x=0}^{k-1} p_x, \tag{9.28}$$

where, as before, $p_x = 1 - q_x$. The value $\hat{P}_k$ is the probability of surviving up to the kth time interval. Applying these estimates to the kidney cancer data gives Table 9.8.

The 5-year survival probability is

$$\hat{P}_5 = (0.597)(0.903)(0.934)(0.879)(1.000) = 0.442$$

(standard error $= 0.060$). The variance of these estimates comes from the expression

$$\text{variance}(\hat{P}_k) = P_k^2 \sum_{i=0}^{k-1} \frac{q_x}{l'_x p_x}. \tag{9.29}$$

The variance estimate is often referred to as "Greenwood's formula" after Major M. Greenwood, an early biostatistician, and is used to test hypotheses or construct confidence intervals for specific estimated survival probabilities.

Another estimate of the 5-year survival probability is the number of individuals who survived 5 years divided by those who began the study at least 5 years previously. Only the 1946 cohort can be used to estimate this 5-year survival probability since the other cohorts contain

Table 9-8. Calculation of a 5-year survival rate from tabled data: Calculations

Interval	d_x	l'_x	q_x	p_x	$\hat{P}_x$	Πp_x	Std. error
0–1	47	116.5	0.403	0.597	$\hat{P}_0$	1.000	—
1–2	5	51.5	0.097	0.903	$\hat{P}_1$	0.597	0.045
2–3	2	30.5	0.066	0.934	$\hat{P}_2$	0.539	0.048
3–4	2	16.5	0.121	0.879	$\hat{P}_3$	0.503	0.051
4–5	0	7.0	0.000	1.000	$\hat{P}_4$	0.442	0.060
5–6	0	2.0	0.000	1.000	$\hat{P}_5$	0.442	0.060

individuals with less than 5 years of follow-up time. The 5-year survival probability is then $4/9 = 0.444$, with a standard error of 0.166 (assuming the lost individual survived). Using all available data rather than a single cohort produces a more precise estimate of the 5-year survival probability (ratio of standard errors $= 0.166/0.060 = 2.7$ in the kidney cancer example). However, the cost of this increased precision is possible bias from the assumption that the mortality experience over time is similar enough among cohorts that combining data for all years reflects the overall mortality experience of all observed individuals.

Another important summary of survival data is an estimate of the mean time individuals survived. This calculation is complicated by the fact that the time of death is not known for all participating individuals. For the data recorded on the 126 kidney cancer patients, the mean survival time is 3.523 years. Mean survival time calculations are discussed in Chapter 10.

Survival patterns experienced by different groups can be summarized and compared using specific survival probabilities. Two such groups from the WCGS data are those with high values of the body-mass index (greater than the 75th percentile) and those with smaller body-mass values (less than the 75th percentile). The data and the calculated "survival" probabilities are (here "survival" means free from a coronary event) given in Tables 9.9 and 9.10.

The comparison of these survival probabilities shows a lower probability (higher risk) of "survival" for those individuals with high body-mass indexes. For example, the 5-year survival probability of 0.940 for high values of body-mass index is less than the 0.961 observed for individuals with "normal" values of the body-mass index. The

Table 9–9. WCGS body mass > 75th percentile

$x-x+1$	l_x	d_x	w_x	q_x	$\hat{P}_x$	Std. error
0–1	871	6	0	0.0069	1.000	—
1–2	865	8	21	0.0094	0.993	0.0028
2–3	836	16	19	0.0194	0.984	0.0043
3–4	801	9	23	0.0114	0.965	0.0063
4–5	769	11	14	0.0144	0.954	0.0072
5–6	744	12	19	0.0163	0.940	0.0082
6–7	713	18	46	0.0261	0.925	0.0092
7–8	649	9	195	0.0163	0.901	0.0106
8–9	445	5	431	0.0218	0.886	0.0115
9–10	9	0	9	0.0000	0.867	0.0141

Table 9-10. WCGS body mass < 75th percentile

$x-x+1$	l_x	d_x	w_x	q_x	$\hat{P}_x$	Std. error
0–1	2283	9	4	0.0039	1.000	—
1–2	2270	20	24	0.0089	0.996	0.0013
2–3	2226	23	50	0.0104	0.987	0.0024
3–4	2153	18	41	0.0084	0.977	0.0032
4–5	2094	18	37	0.0087	0.967	0.0037
5–6	2039	27	61	0.0134	0.961	0.0042
6–7	1951	14	99	0.0074	0.947	0.0048
7–8	1838	22	502	0.0139	0.940	0.0051
8–9	1314	12	1271	0.0177	0.927	0.0057
9–10	31	0	31	0.0000	0.911	0.0073

standard errors for these estimates indicate that this difference is not likely to have occurred by chance variation. For the > 75th percentile group the approximate 95% confidence interval is (0.924, 0.956) and for the < 75th percentile group it is (0.953, 0.969) based on "Greenwood's" variance [expression (9.29)]. A plot of these two sets of survival probabilities is given in Figure 9.3.

The WCGS follow-up times are recorded exactly (to the nearest day); so the probability that a coronary event does not occur ("survival") can be calculated without assumptions about the indiv-

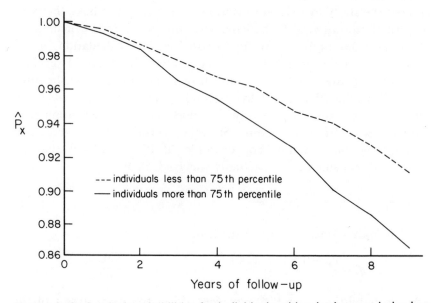

Figure 9-3. Survival probabilities for individuals with a body-mass index less than and greater than the 75th percentile (WCGS data).

iduals lost or withdrawn during the follow-up years. Instead of using 0.5 years of risk, the exact total time contributed by individuals lost or withdrawn can be directly calculated and produces the exact number persons at risk. The difference between the exact and approximate approaches is inconsequential in this example. The 9-year probability using the exact follow-up times is 0.869 for individuals with body-mass indexes in the upper quartile and 0.913 for the "normal" body-mass individuals, compared to the approximate ($\bar{a}_x = 0.5$) values 0.867 and 0.911, respectively. In other study settings, however, individuals lost or withdrawn from follow-up may have different outcome experiences, necessitating careful selection of an adjustment method when exact values are not available.

Three assumptions about the structure of the sampled population are made to calculate a survival curve using life-table techniques. First, all lost and withdrawn subjects are assumed to contribute, on the average, half the survival information of an individual followed for a complete year (or complete time interval). Second, the data collected for a number of cohorts are combined to maximize the number of observations available in each time interval to calculate the probability of death. To give an unbiased estimate of survival probabilities, all cohorts must experience the same pattern of mortality during the follow-up period (again, the absence of interaction permits the data to be combined). In terms of the kidney cancer data, the individuals who entered the study in 1947, for example, are assumed to have the same pattern of mortality as the patients who entered in 1951, which allows the data from both groups to be used in the calculation of the probability of surviving the first year after diagnosis. The third assumption is that the lost and withdrawn individuals have the same probability of death as the individuals remaining in the follow-up data set. This conjecture is probably the most tenuous when applied to individuals lost from observation. Situations certainly arise where other assumptions make sense. For example, if it is assumed that all individuals classified as lost actually survived, then

$$q'_x = \frac{d_x + 0.5 w_x q'_x}{l_x} \quad \text{or} \quad q'_x = \frac{d_x}{l_x - 0.5 w_x} \tag{9.30}$$

or, if all individuals lost in fact died, then

$$q''_x = \frac{d_x + 0.5(u_x + w_x q''_x)}{l_x} \quad \text{or} \quad q''_x = \frac{d_x + 0.5 u_x}{l_x - 0.5 w_x}. \tag{9.31}$$

The probabilities q'_x and q''_x represent the extremes in terms of the impact of the lost individuals on the calculation of the q_x. These two extremes applied to the kidney cancer data yield 5-year survival probabilities of $\hat{P}'_5 = 0.454$ if all lost patients survive and $\hat{P}''_5 = 0.387$ if all lost patients die.

Life-Table Measures of Specific Causes of Death

Hundreds of causes of death act simultaneously within human populations. Two approaches based on life-table methods provide an opportunity to isolate the individual impact of specific causes on the pattern of human mortality. These methods help resolve two questions:

1. What is the age structure throughout the life span associated with specific causes of death, taking into account other causes?
2. How does the probability of death from a specific cause change when other causes are "eliminated" from the population?

The first question is answered by applying a multiple cause life table (also called a multiple decrement life table). The second question is addressed by a competing risk analysis.

Multiple-Cause Life Table

A multiple-cause life table is similar to the single-cause life table but is used to describe simultaneously the mortality patterns of a number of diseases in a population. The goal of such a table is to organize and display the age structure of individuals dying of specific causes. The mechanics of constructing these age distributions are defined and illustrated by a set of data consisting of California resident males who died during 1980. The causes of death come from death certificates, classified according to the ninth revision of the International Classification of Diseases (ICD9) [Ref. 4]. These deaths are classified into four categories—death from lung cancer (ICD9, code 162), deaths from ischemic heart disease (ICD9, codes 410 to 414), deaths from motor vehicle accidents (ICD9, codes E810 to E819), and deaths from all other causes. Also necessary is a series of age-specific population counts—the 1980 U.S. Census counts of California male residents are used. The following life-table construction is abridged, which means that the lengths of the age intervals are not consistently 1 year. Most age intervals are 5-year lengths (represented as n_x; for example, $n_{60} = 5$ years).

The basic components required to construct a multiple-cause life table are the total number of deaths, the age-, cause-specific numbers of deaths and the age-specific midyear populations. That is,

D_x = total number of recorded deaths in the age interval x to $x + n_x$,
$D_x^{(i)}$ = number of recorded deaths from ith cause in the age interval x to
$x + n_x$, and
P_x = total number of individuals at risk ages x to $x + n_x$ at midyear.

These quantities for male residents of California (1980) are given in
Table 9.11.

Average age-specific mortality rates calculated from Table 9.11 are
$R_x = D_x/P_x$ for the age interval x to $x + n_x$ and, similar to the single-
cause, complete life table,

$$q_x = \frac{n_x R_x}{1 + 0.5 n_x R_x} \tag{9.32}$$

is again the conditional probability of death, where n_x is the length of
interval starting at age x. These probabilities are an extension of those
calculated in the single-cause life table [expression (9.4)] applied to age
intervals with widths of n_x years. The value q_x is, as before, the
conditional probability of death between ages x and $x + n_x$ for

Table 9–11. Deaths from four causes: California, males, 1980

Age	P_x Population	$D_x^{(1)}$ Lung cancer	$D_x^{(2)}$ IHD	$D_x^{(3)}$ Motor	$D_x^{(4)}$ All other
0–1	193,310	1	2	3	2,507
1–4	515,150	1	3	58	375
5–9	843,750	0	2	90	195
10–14	915,240	0	1	80	248
15–19	1,091,684	3	1	523	1,162
20–24	1,213,068	4	6	965	1,507
25–29	1,132,811	3	13	627	1,665
30–34	1,008,606	12	63	437	1,547
35–39	776,545	36	136	277	1,371
40–44	629,452	85	306	201	1,510
45–49	578,420	225	567	197	2,115
50–54	578,795	445	1,050	150	3,163
55–59	573,119	786	1,807	147	4,663
60–64	467,607	1,059	2,528	129	5,603
65–69	378,259	1,297	3,328	97	7,014
70–74	269,849	1,266	3,815	89	7,423
75–79	175,580	941	3,793	99	7,508
80–84	95,767	557	3,452	44	6,202
85+	78,832	430	5,249	61	8,222
Total	11,515,844	7,151	26,122	4,274	64,000

individuals alive at age x. For example, the probability of death for individuals age 60 before age 65 is

$$q_{60} = \frac{5(0.0199)}{1 + 0.5(5)0.0199} = 0.0949, \text{ where } R_{60} = \frac{9319}{467607} = 0.0199. \quad (9.33)$$

To "fine tune" these calculations, the 0.5 in the denominator is sometimes replaced by better estimates of the average time lived by those who died. The use of values other than 0.5, however, has little impact on the final calculations for data covering the entire life span.

To compute the cause-specific conditional probabilities of death, the q_x values are distributed proportionally (prorated) by the observed numbers of death. Since

$$q_x^{(i)} = \frac{n_x D_x^{(i)}}{P_x + 0.5n_x D_x} \quad \text{and} \quad q_x = \frac{n_x D_x}{P_x + 0.5n_x D_x}, \quad (9.34)$$

then

$$q_x^{(i)} = \frac{D_x^{(i)}}{D_x} q_x. \quad (9.35)$$

Continuing the illustration for the age interval 60 to 65, the probability of dying from lung cancer between ages 60 and 65 for individuals age 60 is

$$q_{60}^{(lung)} = \frac{1059}{9319} 0.0949 = 0.0108. \quad (9.36)$$

The value $q_x^{(i)}$ is the age-, cause-specific conditional probability of death before age $x + n_x$ for those alive at age x. These conditional probabilities for the illustrative data are given in Table 9.12.

Since all causes of death are included, $q_x = \Sigma \, q_x^{(i)}$. The $q_x^{(i)}$ values calculated from the California mortality data indicate that the cause-specific conditional probabilities for lung cancer $(q_x^{(1)})$ increase rapidly after age 40 until about age 70 and then increase less rapidly in the older ages. The same probabilities for ischemic heart disease (IHD) $(q_x^{(2)})$ also increase sharply at about age 70 but are generally associated with older individuals (shifted to the right). The conditional probabilities describing deaths from motor vehicle accidents $(q_x^{(3)})$, however, increase until ages 20 to 25, decrease and remain fairly constant until age 70 and then sharply increase again. The cause-specific probabilities for three causes of death are shown in Figure 9.4 (smoothed).

Again parallel to the single-cause life table, an arbitrary number of individuals (l_0) can be distributed according to the conditional probabilities of death to produce the distribution of the number of life-

Table 9–12. Conditional probabilities: California, males, 1980

Age	q_x Total	$q_x^{(1)}$ Lung cancer	$q_x^{(2)}$ IHD	$q_x^{(3)}$ Motor	$q_x^{(4)}$ All others
0–1	0.01292	0.00001	0.00001	0.00002	0.01289
1–4	0.00339	0.00001	0.00002	0.00045	0.00291
5–9	0.00170	0.00000	0.00001	0.00053	0.00115
10–14	0.00180	0.00000	0.00001	0.00044	0.00135
15–19	0.00771	0.00001	0.00000	0.00239	0.00530
20–24	0.01018	0.00002	0.00002	0.00396	0.00618
25–29	0.01014	0.00001	0.00006	0.00275	0.00731
30–34	0.01016	0.00006	0.00031	0.00216	0.00763
35–39	0.01165	0.00023	0.00087	0.00177	0.00878
40–44	0.01656	0.00067	0.00241	0.00158	0.01190
45–49	0.02648	0.00192	0.00484	0.00168	0.01804
50–54	0.04069	0.00377	0.00889	0.00127	0.02677
55–59	0.06256	0.00664	0.01527	0.00124	0.03941
60–64	0.09492	0.01079	0.02575	0.00131	0.05707
65–69	0.14397	0.01591	0.04082	0.00119	0.08604
70–74	0.20896	0.02101	0.06330	0.00148	0.12317
75–79	0.29891	0.02279	0.09187	0.00240	0.18185
80–84	0.42235	0.02294	0.14217	0.00181	0.25543
85+	1.00000	0.03080	0.37595	0.00437	0.58888

Table 9–13. Deaths from four causes: California, males, 1980

Age	l_x Total	$d_x^{(1)}$ Lung cancer	$d_x^{(2)}$ IHD	$d_x^{(3)}$ Motor	$d_x^{(4)}$ All other
0–1	1,000,000	5	10	15	12,885
1–4	987,084	8	23	444	2,869
5–9	983,740	0	12	524	1,136
10–14	982,069	0	5	429	1,329
15–19	980,305	13	4	2,339	5,197
20–24	972,751	16	24	3,849	6,012
25–29	962,850	13	55	2,651	7,040
30–34	953,091	56	296	2,054	7,272
35–39	943,412	217	821	1,673	8,280
40–44	932,421	624	2,248	1,476	11,091
45–49	916,982	1,760	4,435	1,541	16,543
50–54	892,703	3,362	7,933	1,133	23,896
55–59	856,379	5,689	13,078	1,064	33,748
60–64	802,800	8,659	20,671	1,055	45,814
65–70	726,601	11,560	29,663	865	62,517
70–74	621,996	13,066	39,374	919	76,611
75–79	492,026	11,214	45,203	1,180	89,476
80–84	344,954	7,913	49,042	625	88,111
85+	199,263	6,137	74,913	871	117,343

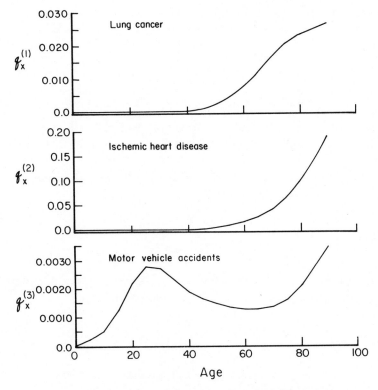

Figure 9–4. Cause-specific probabilities of death for three specific causes (lung cancer, ischemic heart disease, and motor vehicle accidents) for California males, 1980.

table "deaths" for a population with a pattern of age-specific mortality described by the estimated $q_x^{(i)}$ values. The cohort constructed from the California data is shown in Table 9.13.

The life-table deaths given in Table 9.13 come from applying the relationship

$$d_x^{(i)} = l_x q_x^{(i)} \tag{9.37}$$

where, as before, l_x represents the number of persons alive at the beginning of age interval x. For example, the number of persons age 60 who die from lung cancer between age 60 to 65 is

$$d_{60}^{(\text{lung})} = 802800(0.0108) = 8659. \tag{9.38}$$

An additional table calculated by accumulating the deaths in each cause-specific category is also a useful description of the life-table population. These sums represent the number of individuals who reach age x and will ultimately die of a specific cause. In symbols,

$$W_x^{(i)} = d_x^{(i)} + d_{x+n_x}^{(i)} + \cdots + d_{x'}^{(i)} \tag{9.39}$$

and to illustrate

$$W_{60}^{(\text{lung})} = 8659 + 11560 + \cdots + 7913 + 6137 = 58550 \tag{9.40}$$

is the number of individuals who reach age 60 who will eventually die of lung cancer. Again for the California data, see the values in Table 9.14.

The cumulative numbers of deaths provide the values necessary to estimate the probability of death before age x for each cause. That is, for the ith cause

$$F_x^{(i)} = 1 - \frac{W_x^{(i)}}{W_0^{(i)}} \tag{9.41}$$

is the probability of dying before age x. Among individuals dying of lung cancer, the probability of dying before age 60 is

$$F_{60}^{(\text{lung})} = 1 - \frac{58550}{70313} = 0.1673, \tag{9.42}$$

Table 9–14. Expected number of deaths after age x: California, males, 1980

Age	$W_x^{(1)}$ Lung cancer	$W_x^{(2)}$ IHD	$W_x^{(3)}$ Motor	$W_x^{(4)}$ All other
0–1	70,313	287,809	24,707	617,171
1–4	70,308	287,799	24,691	604,285
5–9	70,301	287,776	24,248	601,416
10–14	70,301	287,765	23,723	600,280
15–19	70,301	287,759	23,295	598,951
20–24	70,287	287,755	20,955	593,754
25–29	70,271	287,731	17,106	587,742
30–34	70,259	287,676	14,455	580,702
35–39	70,202	287,380	12,401	573,430
40–44	69,985	286,558	10,728	565,151
45–49	69,360	284,311	9,251	554,059
50–54	67,601	279,876	7,711	537,516
55–59	64,239	271,943	6,577	513,620
60–64	58,550	258,865	5,513	479,872
65–69	49,891	238,194	4,459	434,058
70–74	38,330	208,531	3,594	371,540
75–79	25,264	169,157	2,676	294,929
80–84	14,050	123,955	1,496	205,454
85+	6,137	74,913	871	117,343

or about 17% of the lung cancer deaths occur before age 60. Table 9.15 shows cumulative probabilities of death (F_x values) for the California 1980 data.

The age structure for each cause of death throughout the life span is apparent from the F_x values and the patterns for separate causes of death can be contrasted. For example, 78% of all motor vehicle accident deaths occur by age 60, while 17% of lung cancer deaths occur before age 60. These cumulative distributions are shown in Figure 9.15, and a few representative summary values are given in Table 9.16.

The cumulative distributions reveal the distinct pattern of mortality associated with three specific causes. Motor vehicle accidents, expectedly, have the greatest impact at the younger ages, while, perhaps less expectedly, the ischemic heart disease is associated with the older ages, producing a median age at death of 78.8 years.

Lifetime Probability of Death

A multiple-cause life table allows a direct calculation of the lifetime probability of death from a specific cause, which is occasionally a useful summary of risk. The probability of dying from a specific cause is

Table 9–15. Cumulative distributions for four causes of death: California, males, 1980

Age	$F_x^{(1)}$ Lung cancer	$F_x^{(2)}$ IHD	$F_x^{(3)}$ Motor	$F_x^{(4)}$ All other
0–1	0.00000	0.00000	0.00000	0.00000
1–4	0.00007	0.00004	0.00062	0.02088
5–9	0.00018	0.00012	0.01859	0.02553
10–14	0.00018	0.00016	0.03980	0.02737
15–19	0.00018	0.00017	0.05716	0.02952
20–24	0.00037	0.00019	0.15184	0.03794
25–29	0.00060	0.00027	0.30764	0.04768
30–34	0.00078	0.00046	0.41494	0.05909
35–39	0.00158	0.00149	0.49809	0.07087
40–44	0.00467	0.00435	0.56580	0.08429
45–49	0.01355	0.01216	0.62555	0.10226
50–54	0.03858	0.02757	0.68792	0.12906
55–59	0.08640	0.05513	0.73379	0.16778
60–64	0.16730	0.10057	0.77685	0.22246
65–69	0.29045	0.17239	0.81954	0.29670
70–74	0.45486	0.27545	0.85453	0.39799
75–79	0.64069	0.41226	0.89171	0.52213
80–84	0.80018	0.56932	0.93946	0.66710
85+	0.91272	0.73971	0.96476	0.80987

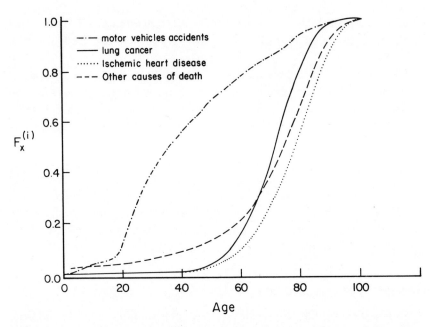

Figure 9-5. Cumulative distributions of age at death for three specific causes (lung cancer, ischemic heart disease, and motor vehicle accidents) for California males, 1980.

estimated by the number of people who died of that cause divided by the number of persons who could have died (those at risk). The table of the expected numbers of deaths after a specific age contains this information (Table 9.14). The first row in the table contains the total number of individuals ultimately dying from each cause over the entire life span. Since 1,000,000 males make up the 1980 California life-table "population at risk" (sum of the first row of Table 9.14), then

P(dying from lung cancer) $= 70,313/1,000,000 = 0.070$
P(dying from ischemic heart disease) $= 287,809/1,000,000 = 0.288$
P(dying from motor vehicle accident) $= 24,707/1,000,000 = 0.025$

P(dying from other causes) $= 617,170/1,000,000 = 0.617$

Table 9-16. Median age (as well as 25th and 75th percentiles) at death

	Median	25th percentile	75th percentile
Lung cancer	71.98	64.45	78.77
Ischemic heart disease	78.82	69.34	86.40
Motor vehicle accidents	36.40	24.20	58.09
Other causes	75.03	63.16	83.79
All causes	74.64	63.37	83.86

are the lifetime probabilities of dying from any one of the three specific causes.

Each row in the table allows the estimation of the lifetime probability associated with individuals of a specific age. For example, for males age 60, the lifetime probability of dying of lung cancer is $58,550/802,800 = 0.073$, where 802,800 is the number of individuals alive at the beginning of the age interval 60–65 (the sum of the row age 60–65) and 58,550 is the number who died of lung cancer after age 60. Three cause-specific conditional probabilities for the 1980 California data are:

P(dying from lung cancer after age 60) $= 58,550/802,800 = 0.073$
P(dying from ischemic heart disease after age 60) $= 258,865/802,800 = 0.322$
P(dying from motor vehicle accident after age 60) $= 5,513/802,800 = 0.007$

P(dying from other causes after age 60) $= 479,872/802,800 = 0.598$.

The cumulative probability of death from a multiple-cause life table is related to the lifetime probability of death from a specific cause. The probability $1 - F_x^{(i)}$ is the conditional probability of death after age x among those who ultimately die of cause i. The lifetime probability of death from a specific cause i is the conditional probability of death from cause i for all individuals who reach age x. That is, the first probability is P(death after age x|death from cause i) and the second is P(death from cause i|death after age x). Specifically, $1 - F_{60}^{(\text{lung})} = P$(death after 60|death from lung cancer) $= 58,550/70,313 = 0.833$ and P(death from lung cancer|death after 60) $= 58,550/802,800 = 0.073$.

Competing Risks

British statistician William Farr (1875) was among the first to discuss the problem of estimating the risk of one disease while other risks are operating in the studied population. This problem was also explored by the early French mathematicians Bernoulli and D'Alembert and later by a British actuary Makeham. The issues are neatly summarized by the following simple example given by J. Berkson and L. Elveback [Ref. 5]:

> Two marksmen shoot at a range of targets under conditions in which, if a target is struck, it instantly drops from view so that it cannot be struck again. Represent the striking rate of marksman 1, that is the probability of a hit when he is firing alone, as Q_1 and similarly the rate of marksman 2 when he is firing alone as Q_2. The probability when one risk operates alone is called the net risk or rate and is represented by upper case Q; when it operates together with another risk it is called the crude risk or rate and is represented by lower case q.

Suppose N targets are exposed and marksman 1 shoots first, followed by marksman 2:

Rate for 1 is $q_1 = Q_1$;
Rate for 2 is $q_2 = (1 - Q_1)Q_2$;
Total rate is $q = q_1 + q_2 = Q_1 + Q_2 - Q_1Q_2$.

Suppose marksman 2 shoots first, followed by marksman 1, then:

Rate for 2 is $q_2 = Q_2$;
Rate for 1 is $q_1 = (1 - Q_2)Q_1$;
Total rate is $q = q_1 + q_2 = Q_1 + Q_2 - Q_1Q_2$.

It is seen that the total crude rate with both marksmen shooting is the same, whichever marksmen shoots and assuming independence of the net probabilities Q_1 and Q_2, this will be true in general. Regardless of the ordering of the shooting or whether the two marksmen shoot together, the total crude rate is given by the "total rate," which, of course, can be derived as the complement of the product of the probabilities, $P_1 = 1 - Q_1$ and $P_2 = 1 - Q_2$, of not being struck (survival rate).

If, from independent trials, we know Q_1, the net rate of marksman 1, and have a record of q, the crude rate when both shot together, we can derive the net rate Q_2 from "total rate":

$$Q_2 = \frac{q - Q_1}{1 - Q_1}. \tag{9.43}$$

Rarely are the net probabilities Q_1 or Q_2 known, but, rather, the crude probabilities q_1, q_2, and q can be estimated from collected data. Manipulation of these crude probabilities, under specific conditions, allows estimation of the net probabilities from observed data.

For the following discussion of competing risks, it is assumed that only two causes of death are of interest and only a single age interval is considered (simply 0 to 1). These two assumptions do not affect the principles underlying the competing risk argument (mathematicians say, "there is no loss of generality") and simplify the notation.

The formal definitions of the two central probabilities are:

Crude probability: q_i = the probability an individual who is alive at the start of the interval dies from cause i in the presence of cause j, sometimes called the mixed probability of death.

Net probability: Q_i = the probability an individual who is alive at the start of the interval dies from cause i when cause j is not present, sometimes called the pure probability of death.

The marksman example shows a relationship between the net and crude probabilities [expression (9.43)], but is not much use unless one of the net probabilities is known. To estimate the net probabilities further statistical structure is needed. First, assume that the net probabilities are described by exponential functions, where λ_1 and λ_2 are hazard rates associated with causes 1 and 2, respectively, and where

$$Q_1 = 1 - e^{-\lambda_1} \quad \text{and} \quad Q_2 = 1 - e^{-\lambda_2} \tag{9.44}$$

and, second, that the probability of surviving the interval is

$$P(\text{surviving}) = P_1 P_2 = (1 - Q_1)(1 - Q_2) = (e^{-\lambda_1})(e^{-\lambda_2}) = e^{-\lambda_1 + -\lambda_2} = e^{-\lambda},$$
$$\tag{9.45}$$

where $\lambda = \lambda_1 + \lambda_2$. That is, cause 1 and cause 2 are statistically independent. Cause 2 can be thought of as a specific cause of death and cause 1 as all the other causes combined. Then, the net probability Q_1 describes the likelihood of death as if death from cause 2 was not possible (cause 2 "removed"). The exponential survival model will be explored in more detail in the next chapter.

Expression (9.45) for the probability of surviving the interval is valid only when cause 1 and 2 are statistically independent. Although death from cause 1 is mutually exclusive of death from cause 2, it is still important that the mechanisms underlying these two events act independently. In terms of the marksman example, independence means that the hits and misses of one marksman do not influence the accuracy of the other marksman and conversely. Equivalently, cause of death 1 is assumed not to be related in any way to cause of death 2. Independence of causes of death is certainly not a realistic assumption for some diseases, particularly chronic diseases. The influence of non-independence of diseases on the estimate of the net probabilities has not been extensively studied.

These two assumptions (exponential survival and independence) make it possible to estimate the risk from one cause while the other cause is "removed" from consideration (net probability). To estimate the net probability of death, a bit of algebra relates the crude and net probabilities. Consider $q = $ crude probability of death in the interval, death from either from cause 1 or 2, then

$$P(\text{death}) = q = 1 - P_1 P_2 = 1 - e^{-\lambda}. \tag{9.46}$$

Note that the crude probability has the same form as both net probabilities. Furthermore,

$$(1 - q)^{\lambda_i/\lambda} = e^{-\lambda_i} = P_i, \quad \text{giving } Q_i = 1 - P_i = 1 - (1 - q)^{\lambda_i/\lambda}. \tag{9.47}$$

This basic relationship [expression (9.47)] allows the estimation of the net probabilities since the ratio of the two hazard rates λ_i/λ is estimated by d_i/d, where d_i represents the number of deaths from cause i and $d = d_1 + d_2$ represents the total number of deaths from both causes in the time interval being considered. The estimated net probability of death from cause i is, then,

$$\hat{Q}_i = 1 - \left(1 - \frac{d}{l}\right)^{d_i/d}, \qquad (9.48)$$

where l individuals are at risk from both causes of death at the beginning of the interval.

The assumption that the net probabilities are a simple exponential function may not be appealing in some situations [expression (9.44)]. An alternative estimate of the net probability can be derived from intuitive considerations that do not involve an exponential risk model. Individuals at risk can be classified into three categories: (1) died of cause 1, (2) died of cause 2, or (3) lived through the interval. A death from cause 2 can be considered as a person "lost to follow-up" with respect to calculations for cause 1. When cause 2 is "removed," deaths from cause 1 are undercounted since the former "lost to follow-up" are then at risk. That is, the direct estimate of the net probability is too small since a proportion of the individuals who would have died of cause 2 and are "lost" can now die of cause 1. Those who would have died of cause 2 are exposed to risk, on the average, for half the interval so that $0.5d_2$ represents the additional number of individuals at risk when cause 2 is "removed." The value $0.5d_2Q_1$ estimates the number of deaths from cause 1 among the individuals who would have died from cause 2 if it were present. Therefore, "correcting" the number of deaths d_1 gives

$$\hat{Q}'_1 = \frac{d_1 + 0.5d_2\hat{Q}'_1}{l} \qquad (9.49)$$

and solving for the net probability Q'_1 yields

$$\hat{Q}'_1 = \frac{d_1}{l - 0.5d_2}. \qquad (9.50)$$

The probability $\hat{Q}'_1$ is another estimate of the net probability of death from cause 1 among l individuals at risk. The net probability $\hat{Q}'_1$ is greater than crude probability q_1 since additional individuals are at risk and die of cause 1 when cause 2 is "removed." In general,

$$\text{net probability} = \hat{Q}'_i = \frac{d_i}{l - 0.5d_j} \geq \frac{d_i}{l} = \hat{q}_i = \text{crude probability.} \qquad (9.51)$$

For most applications of competing risk calculations the crude probability and the net probability differ by very little. Expression (9.51) indicates why. For $\hat{Q}'_i$ and $\hat{q}_i$ to differ substantially, the

Table 9-17. Competing risks: Exponential versus intuitive methods

	q_1	$q_2 = 0.05$	0.10	0.15	0.20
Exponential	0.05	0.0513	0.1027	0.1541	0.2056
Intuitive	0.05	0.0513	0.1026	0.1538	0.2051
Exponential	0.10	0.0527	0.1056	0.1585	0.2116
Intuitive	0.10	0.0526	0.1053	0.1579	0.2105
Exponential	0.15	0.0543	0.1087	0.1633	0.2182
Intuitive	0.15	0.0540	0.1081	0.1622	0.2162
Exponential	0.20	0.0559	0.1112	0.1686	0.2254
Intuitive	0.20	0.0556	0.1111	0.1667	0.2222

competing cause of death must be a fairly large proportion of the individuals at risk (d_j has to be large relative to l), which is not usually the case for human mortality data.

Although the exponential and intuitive estimates come from different considerations, they differ little in value $(\hat{Q}_i \approx \hat{Q}'_i)$ for most situations. Table 9.17 illustrates the similarity of the two expressions. If $q < 0.1$, then $Q_i - Q'_i < 0.001$, showing why Q_i and Q'_i are essentially equal when applied to questions concerning competing risks among human diseases. The net probability of death from a specific cause, if other causes of death act independently, can also be estimated by considering other causes as censored survival times. The topic of censored data is developed in the next two chapters. It should simply be noted that many of the methods applicable to censored data can be applied in the context of competing risks.

Applications

The estimation of the net probabilities (exponential and intuitive) are illustrated by a subset of data from a large study of the effects of smoking on coronary heart disease mortality (Hammond and Horn [Ref. 6] and reported in [Ref. 5]). A small part of these smoking and CHD data are given in Table 9.18.

As expected, the net probabilities of death from CHD for smokers and nonsmokers increase, but moderately, when competing causes of death are "removed." The increase in net risk for CHD among smokers and nonsmokers can be expressed as a difference or as a ratio (Table 9.18), providing an estimate of the "pure" impact of smoking on CHD risk. Some controversy exists over which is the "best" expression for the increased risk from smoking. The issues surrounding the choice of a ratio versus a difference as an expression of risk are basically semantic and are discussed elsewhere (see [Ref. 5 or 7]).

Table 9-18. Competing risks: Deaths after 44 months of follow-up for ages 60–65

	Nonsmokers	Smokers
$CHD = d_1$	552	921
$Other = d_2$	714	1,095
Population	20,278	21,594
Crude	0.0272	0.0427
Exponential	0.0277	0.0438
Intuitive	0.0277	0.0438

Difference 0.0155 (crude); 0.0161 (net)
Ratio 1.567 (crude); 1.579 (net).

Occasionally the argument is put forth that cancer increases in the last three or four decades, at least in part, are due to the decrease in mortality from infectious diseases. This thought is based on the idea that deaths from infectious diseases operate early in life, thereby eliminating a proportion of individuals who would die of cancer later in life. Data for the years 1900 to 1950 that reflect on this question are given in Table 9.19.

Using competing risk estimates, the net probabilities show no reason to believe that the decreasing mortality from infectious disease plays a role in the observed increase in cancer mortality. Comparison of the crude and net probabilities (multiplied by 100,000) for cancer deaths shows essentially identical values for all six decades. That is, under the conditions for a competing risk calculation, "removing" infectious disease as a competing cause of death does not change the national mortality pattern of cancer deaths over the years 1900 to 1950.

The expression for net probabilities can be used when specific causes of death are available and the results summarized with life-table

Table 9-19. Competing risks: Total cancer and infectious disease deaths by year for the U.S.

Year	1900	1910	1920	1930	1940	1950
Infection	240,077	225,565	191,958	137,971	90,239	60,370
Cancer	48,700	70,414	88,793	119,985	158,943	208,109
Total deaths	1,308,056	1,356,535	1,382,887	1,394,611	1,422,161	1,472,842
Population	76,094	92,407	106,466	123,188	132,122	151,683
Crude	64.00	76.20	83.40	97.40	120.30	137.20
Intuitive*	64.10	76.29	83.48	97.45	120.34	137.23

Note: the crude cancer mortality rate is $(d_{cancer}/\text{population}) \times 100,000$, and population is given in thousands.
*Net probabilities multiplied by 100,000

Table 9-20. Expectation of life for specific competing causes of death "eliminated," California, 1980

Age	No causes*	CVD*	IHD*	Lung cancer*	Motor*
0	70.92	80.63	73.79	71.80	71.81
20	52.41	62.61	55.33	53.31	53.19
40	34.49	44.71	37.49	35.41	34.68
60	18.16	28.01	20.08	18.96	18.22
80	7.07	16.56	8.07	7.18	7.07

*Cause of death eliminated (cause j).

functions. The exponential-based expression for a net probability of death from cause i at age x using life-table deaths is

$$Q_{x,i} = 1 - (1 - q_x)^{d_x^{(i)}/d_x}, \qquad (9.52)$$

where $d_x^{(i)}$ represents life-table deaths from ith cause in the interval x to $x + 1$ and $d_x = d_x^{(i)} + d_x^{(j)}$ represents the total life-table deaths. The net probabilities $Q_{x,i}$ reflect the impact of mortality at age x from cause i with the cause j "removed" and can be used to calculate other life-table functions, particularly the expectation of life. For example, if all deaths from cardiovascular disease (CVD deaths = cause j) are "eliminated" and a life table based on the remaining causes of death (all non-CVD deaths = cause i) is computed, then an estimate of the years of life lost attributable to cardiovascular disease is found by comparing the "net" expectation of life with the expectation calculated when all causes of death are operating. That is, the life-table functions are based on the net probabilities $Q_{x,i}$ rather than the crude probabilities q_x. Table 9.20 gives the expectation of life for 1980 California males for five selected ages. Also included are the expectations of life when three other causes of death (ischemic heart disease, lung cancer, and motor vehicle accidents) are each "removed." The impact of cardiovascular disease on the total mortality picture is clear. The life-table competing-risk calculations indicate that the expectation of life would be increased about 10 years if cardiovascular disease was "removed" as a risk of death and a 1–4-year increase would result if ischemic heart disease was "removed." Almost no impact on the expectation of life is observed when lung cancer or motor vehicle accidents are "removed" as causes of death.

10 Estimates of Risk from Follow-up Data

Follow-up data consists of a variety of outcomes such as relapse of disease, occurrence of tumors, and other types of "failures" and generally involves individuals observed for different periods of time. The study of a therapeutic treatment is a common source of follow-up data where the outcome is death. For simplicity the terminology used in the following, by and large, pertains to mortality and disease incidence. A basic characteristic that separates follow-up data from other data is that the outcome is not always observed in all subjects. When death is the endpoint of a follow-up study, for example, some of the sampled individuals typically will be alive at the end of the study period. The lack of knowledge of the exact time of death biases direct measurement of the survival experience. Special techniques exist, however, to compensate for the incomplete nature of follow-up data and to combine a series of differing follow-up times into summary measures of risk. Two approaches are described: one parametric and the other nonparametric.

Parametric Model of Survival Time

A simple and often useful parametric model postulates that survival probabilities are characterized by an exponential function. More specifically, the probability that an individual will be alive after a time t is

$$P(\text{surviving from time} = 0 \text{ until time} = t) = S(t) = e^{-\lambda t}. \quad (10.1)$$

The parameter λ represents the hazard rate for a population with an exponential survival structure. The survival curve $S(t) = e^{-\lambda t}$ is a parametric model of the relationship between time and risk with the potential of providing a compact description of a set of follow-up data. This model was briefly introduced earlier in the context of competing risk calculations [expression (9.44)].

An exponential pattern of survival derives from the proposition that the number of deaths in a specific population at risk is proportional only to the number of members of that population. That is, deaths occur at random among the individuals at risk. Proportionality translates into the mathematical expression that

$$\text{decrease in population size} = \frac{dl_t}{dt} = -\lambda l_t, \tag{10.2}$$

which implies that the rate of decrease at a time t is governed by a constant hazard rate λ and the population size l_t. This expression was used earlier in the context of nearest-neighbor analysis [expression (5.8)]. It directly follows that

$$l_t = l_0 e^{-\lambda t}, \tag{10.3}$$

where l_0 is the size of the population at risk when $t = 0$, or, expressed in terms of a survival curve,

$$l_t/l_0 = S(t) = e^{-\lambda t}. \tag{10.4}$$

The parameter λ in this model does not depend on the time t. Exponential survival implies, for example, that the age of a person is unrelated to the hazard rate. The survival of an individual is a function of time but the hazard rate is the same regardless of the age considered. Clearly, this is an unrealistic description of a human population when the full spectrum of ages (e.g., 0 to 100 years) is considered. But over short periods of time, or under specific conditions, rates are sometimes essentially constant, and an exponential survival model adequately reflects the mortality or disease experience of a human population.

The fact that the probability of living beyond a fixed point in time does not depend on "age" can be seen from the following:

$$P(\text{surviving 0 to } t_0) = e^{-\lambda t_0} \quad \text{and} \quad P(\text{surviving 0 to } t_1) = e^{-\lambda t_1},$$
$$\text{where } t_0 < t_1. \tag{10.5}$$

The probability that an individual survives beyond time t_1 given the individual has survived to t_0 is

$$P(\text{surviving to } t_1|\text{surviving to } t_0) = \frac{e^{-\lambda t_1}}{e^{-\lambda t_0}} = e^{-\lambda(t_1 - t_0)}, \tag{10.6}$$

showing that the difference $t_1 - t_0$ is the sole determinant of the probability of surviving to at least t_1, given that the person is alive at t_0 and the probability of survival is not influenced by the actual values of t_1 and t_0. For example, the probability of surviving an additional 10 weeks for a person followed 65 weeks is the same as the probability of surviving 10 weeks for an individual followed 5 weeks; the probability of survival depends only on the difference $t_1 - t_0 = 10$ weeks when the value λ is constant. Furthermore, since the probability of survival is not related to the previous amount of follow-up time, then all individuals alive a specific time are expected to survive the same amount of additional time. A patient followed 65 weeks, for example, has the same expected time of continued survival as a person followed 5 weeks when the distribution of survival times is exponential.

To demonstrate that an "exponential" population has a constant average mortality rate, recall the definition of a rate:

$$\text{average mortality rate} = \frac{\text{number who died}}{\text{total time at risk}}. \qquad (10.7)$$

The number of deaths among N individuals between times t_0 and t_1 is

$$\text{deaths} = N(e^{-\lambda t_0} - e^{-\lambda t_1}) \qquad (10.8)$$

and the total time at risk is

$$\text{total time at risk} = N \int_{t_0}^{t_1} e^{-\lambda x} \, dx = N \frac{e^{-\lambda t_0} - e^{-\lambda t_1}}{\lambda}. \qquad (10.9)$$

The average mortality rate for the time interval $[t_0, t_1]$ is then given by

$$\text{average mortality rate} = \frac{N(e^{-\lambda t_0} - e^{-\lambda t_1})}{N(e^{-\lambda t_0} - e^{-\lambda t_1})/\lambda} = \lambda. \qquad (10.10)$$

That is, the average mortality rate is constant, and, not surprisingly, the average mortality rate and the hazard rate are identical or

$$\text{hazard rate} = \frac{-dS(t)/dt}{S(t)} = \lambda = \text{average mortality rate.} \qquad (10.11)$$

The exponential parametric survival time model yields a simple relationship between the average mortality rate and the probability of death. Since

$$P(\text{death in the interval } [t_0, t_1]) = e^{-\lambda t_0} - e^{-\lambda t_1} \qquad (10.12)$$

and when the mortality rate λ is small, $e^{-\lambda t_i} \approx 1 - \lambda t_i$, giving

$$P(\text{death in the interval } [t_0, t_1]) \approx \lambda(t_1 - t_0). \qquad (10.13)$$

The probability of death in an interval is approximately equal to the rate of mortality multiplied by the time at risk [e.g., if $t_1 - t_0 = 1$ year, then $P(\text{death during one year}) \approx \lambda$]. A parallel result was noted in Chapter 1 derived without a parametric model [expression (1.12)].

Age Adjustment of Rates

Two traditional procedures for age adjustment of mortality and incidence rates were discussed in Chapter 1 [expressions (1.42) and

(1.43)]. A less common method, with advantages over the two more usual approaches, is based on modeling the survival experience of individuals within an interval by an exponential function. That is, it is assumed that the probability of surviving a specific interval (x_{i-1}, x_i) for all individuals who started the interval is

$$P(\text{surviving to } x_i | \text{alive at } x_{i-1}) = p_i = e^{-\lambda_i(x_i - x_{i-1})} = e^{-\lambda_i X_i}, \quad (10.14)$$

where $X_i = x_i - x_{i-1}$. The value λ_i is the mortality rate associated with the ith age interval, which is assumed, at least approximately, constant within each interval. However, these constant mortality rates can vary from interval to interval. The probability of surviving over a series of age intervals, x_0 to x_1, x_1 to x_2, ..., x_{k-1} to x_k, is then

$$P = \prod_{i=1}^{k} p_i = \prod_{i=1}^{k} e^{-\lambda_i X_i} = e^{-\sum_{i=1}^{k} \lambda_i X_i}. \quad (10.15)$$

The cumulative probability, symbolized by P, summarizes the combined influence of a series of age-specific rates (λ_i's). This summary value is "age adjusted" in the sense that comparisons in terms of values of P among different populations are not influenced by differences in age distributions. For most diseases the mortality or incidence rates λ_i are small so that the survival probability for a period x_0 to x_k is approximately $P \approx 1 - \Sigma \lambda_i X_i$.

A simple illustration comes from the hypothetical data given in Chapter 1 (Table 1.16), where $\hat{\lambda}_1 = 0.001$, $\hat{\lambda}_2 = 0.002$, $\hat{\lambda}_3 = 0.004$, and $\hat{\lambda}_4 = 0.008$ represents four age-specific rates that are identical for two populations (I and II). The probability of surviving from age 40 to 80 (P) is based exclusively on the four age-specific rates. That is,

$$\hat{P} = e^{-10(0.001 + 0.002 + 0.004 + 0.008)} = e^{-0.150} = 0.861 \quad (10.16)$$

estimates the probability of living from age 40 to 80 in the two hypothetical populations. This value is the same for both groups because the age-specific rates are the same for both groups. The estimate of the probability P is unaffected by the differing age distributions in the populations at risk.

Consider again (Table 1.19) the data describing the incidence of breast cancer among women residents of the San Francisco Bay Area (1977–83), where breast cancer rates are to be compared between whites and blacks. The race-, age-, and stage-specific incidence rates from these data are shown in Table 10.1.

The probability of being diagnosed with a specific stage of breast cancer $(1 - \hat{P})$ reflects the risk for individuals throughout a specific age range from a series of age-specific rates. Unlike the direct and indirect

Table 10–1. Breast cancer by race, age, and stage: Incidence rates per 100,000 (1977–83)

Age	White		Black	
	Local	Regional	Local	Regional
40–49	87.89	66.55	56.90	56.60
50–59	126.96	96.97	81.18	91.62
60–69	185.46	118.04	109.58	90.04
70–79	211.17	119.11	143.06	94.57
79 +	207.80	102.72	138.41	119.54
Crude rate	125.87	88.86	73.74	72.56
$\hat{P}$	0.941	0.961	0.962	0.967
$1 - \hat{P}$	0.059	0.039	0.038	0.033

methods of rate adjustment, the comparison of groups on the basis of $\hat{P}$ or $1 - \hat{P}$ does not require the choice of a standard population. The addition of the estimated age-specific rates each multiplied by the length of the age intervals produces an "age-adjusted" value with a probabilistic interpretation. For the race–cancer example, the value $1 - \hat{P}$ is an estimate of the probability of breast cancer among women for the specified age range. The probability that a white female age 40 will be diagnosed with breast cancer (local stage) before age 80 in the San Francisco Bay Area is estimated by $1 - \hat{P} = 0.059$. The corresponding value for blacks is 0.038. The difference between these two probabilities is not biased by differences in age distributions (Table 1.18).

Although it is not much of an issue when the cumulative probability $\hat{P}$ is calculated from large numbers of observations such as the breast cancer example, when $\hat{P}$ is estimated from smaller sets of data the variance of this estimated quantity is important. If the mortality or disease rates are small (less than 0.10 or so), then the variance is approximately

$$\text{variance}(\hat{P}) = \text{variance}(1 - \hat{P}) \approx \sum_{i=1}^{k} \frac{X_i^2 d_i}{l_i^2}, \qquad (10.17)$$

where d_i is the number of deaths in a population of l_i individuals at risk at the beginning of the ith interval of length X_i and k is the number of age-specific rates combined to estimate the "age-adjusted" probability P. Applying the variance expression to the estimated value from the hypothetical data for population I (Table 1.16) gives

$$\hat{P}_I = 0.861 \text{ with variance}(\hat{P}_I) = 0.00075, \qquad (10.18)$$

producing an approximate 95% confidence interval of (0.807, 0.914). The same calculation applied to population II rates gives a different result since the variance, unlike $\hat{P}$, depends on the distribution of ages in population at risk. That is, $\hat{P}_{II} = 0.861$ but the variance is 0.00022 producing a smaller confidence interval, (0.832, 0.890).

Censored and Truncated Data

A measurement is censored when its exact value is unknown but it is known that the value exceeds a specific limit. A censored survival time results from the nature of the sampling process or study design. If a study is continued until all individuals die, complete survival times are available and no data are censored. For most follow-up studies, however, the survival time is known only for those individuals who die during the study period. All that is known about the remaining study subjects is that they were alive at the end of the period of observation (i.e., beyond a specific point). The exact time of death is censored

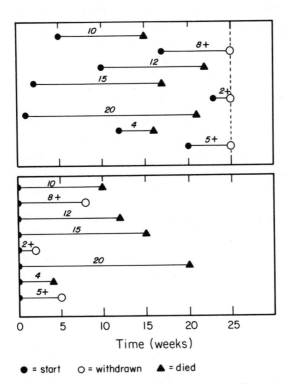

Figure 10–1. Eight hypothetical survival times shown by time entered the study and by length of follow-up.

(missing). Individuals with censored survival experience would contribute additional survival time to the total observed if the study has continued. Figure 10.1 shows two views of the same set of hypothetical survival times for eight individuals (three censored) collected over a 25-week period. The survival times are: 5^+, 4, 20, 2^+, 15, 12, 8^+, and 10. The "+" is a notational convention indicating those individuals who did not die during the study period and are said to be censored (withdrawn) from observation (i.e., 5^+, 2^+, and 8^+).

For contrast, a truncated observation is a measurement that is missing completely. When the sampling process is conducted so that some observations will never be included in the sample, the data are truncated. A classic example of truncated data occurs in genetic studies, where a sample is derived from a list of affected individuals (index cases). A series of families is identified from a list of cases, such as a registry of patients with a specific disorder. Every family sampled will necessarily have one or more affected individuals. Families that do not contain an affected individual will not be identified and sampled, producing a set of truncated data. Such a sample is truncated because the nature of the sampling process excludes relevant individuals who belong to families without an index case. For both censored and truncated data, the analysis must account for the missing information to produce an unbiased summary description.

Mean Survival Time: Parametric Estimate

The exponential model is completely defined by one parameter, and, if it is realistic to assume that an exponential structure underlies a set of collected data, then it is relatively simple to estimate this single parameter. Consider a data set concerning 10 individuals with acute

Table 10-2. Lung cancer follow-up data

Person	Status	Days
1	Died	2
2	Withdrawn	72
3	Died	51
4	Withdrawn	60
5	Died	33
6	Died	27
7	Died	14
8	Died	24
9	Died	4
10	Withdrawn	21
Total	Died = 7	308

lung cancer [Ref. 1] who were followed for different lengths of time (days) until their death or withdrawal from observation, as seen in Table 10.2.

An estimated average mortality rate is the number of observed deaths divided by the observed total time at risk. Using the lung cancer follow-up data, the mortality rate λ is estimated by

$$\text{rate} = \hat{\lambda} = \frac{d}{\sum_{i=1}^{n} t_i} = \frac{7}{308} = 0.0227, \tag{10.19}$$

where d is the number of deaths among the n individuals in the sample and t_i is the follow-up time for both complete and censored observations (7 complete and 3 censored survival times, yielding a total time at risk of 308 days). An estimate of the variance of the estimate $\hat{\lambda}$ is

$$\text{variance}(\hat{\lambda}) = \frac{\hat{\lambda}^2}{d}, \tag{10.20}$$

giving an estimated standard error for $\hat{\lambda} = 0.0227$ of $S_{\hat{\lambda}} = 0.0086$. The estimates $\hat{\lambda}$ and variance$(\hat{\lambda})$ can be derived from maximum likelihood considerations (again see the Appendix for a brief discussion). A natural estimate of the exponential survival curve is then $\hat{S}(t) = e^{-\hat{\lambda} t}$ and for the lung cancer data, $\hat{S}(t) = e^{-0.0227t}$.

It is worth noting that the transformed estimate $\log(\hat{\lambda})$ has an approximate variance of $1/d$. Removing the dependence of the variance on the parameter λ improves the use of the normal distribution as a way of testing conjectures about the mortality rate (λ) and the construction of confidence intervals. For the lung cancer data, $\log(\hat{\lambda}) = \log(0.0227) = -3.784$, and an approximate 95% confidence interval for $\log(\hat{\lambda})$ is therefore $-3.784 \pm 1.96\sqrt{1/7}$, giving $(-4.525, -3.043)$ and $(e^{-4.525}, e^{-3.043}) = (0.011, 0.048)$ is then an approximate 95% confidence interval for the hazard rate λ.

Also of interest is the mean survival time, which is estimated by the total observed time lived by all individuals at risk divided by the number who died (the reciprocal of $\hat{\lambda}$) or

$$\bar{t} = \frac{1}{\hat{\lambda}} = \frac{\sum_{i=1}^{n} t_i}{d}. \tag{10.21}$$

For the lung cancer data, $\bar{t} = 308/7 = 44$ days. Mean survival time is related to the reciprocal of a rate, as similarly noted for a life table [expression (9.9)].

The denominator used to calculate the mean survival time is the number of deaths rather than the total number of persons under observation (deaths $d = 7$, not individuals $n = 10$). The reason relates to the fact that the total survival time is biased (too small) since $\Sigma\, t_i$ includes individuals who did not die (censored) during the follow-up period. For the lung cancer example, the three patients who were withdrawn from observation would have added more survival time to the total time at risk if the follow-up period had been longer.

A constant hazard rate implies that at any point in time all living individuals have the same expected amount of life remaining. The expected amount of time remaining to a specific individual is a function only of the hazard rate λ. It is, therefore, consistent to assign to all individuals withdrawn from observation (number $= n - d$) the same additional amount of lifetime (represented as T). These "complete" survival times $(t_i + T)$ are then used to estimate the mean survival time as if no censoring occurred. The lung cancer "complete data" adjusted for the censored survival times are given in Table 10.3. The mean survival time based on "complete" survival times, like most mean values, is the total time divided by all individuals observed. Using these "complete data" to calculate the mean survival time gives

$$\bar{t} = \frac{\Sigma\, t_i + (n - k)\bar{t}}{n} = \frac{308 + 3\bar{t}}{10}, \tag{10.22}$$

where $\bar{t}$ estimates the expected survival time T and solving for $\bar{t}$ produces the same estimate as before:

$$\bar{t} = \frac{\Sigma\, t_i}{d} = \frac{308}{7} = 44 \text{ days.} \tag{10.23}$$

This estimate [expression (10.23)] only makes sense if the survival

Table 10–3. Lung cancer follow-up data with adjustment for individuals withdrawn from follow-up

Person	Status	Days
1	Died	2
2	Adjusted	$72 + T$
3	Died	51
4	Adjusted	$60 + T$
5	Died	33
6	Died	27
7	Died	14
8	Died	24
9	Died	4
10	Adjusted	$21 + T$
Total	Died $= 7$	$308 + 3T$

experience of the population sampled can be, at least approximately, described by an exponential survival curve. An estimate of the variance of the estimated mean survival time $\bar{t}$ is given by

$$\text{variance}(\bar{t}) = \frac{\bar{t}^2}{d} \tag{10.24}$$

and for $\bar{t} = 44$ days, $S_{\bar{t}} = 44/\sqrt{7} = 16.630$.

Mean Survival Time: Nonparametric Estimate

To understand the calculation of the mean survival time without a parametric model, consider for the moment the situation where each individual studied is followed until death (i.e., no censored survival times). A hypothetical data set of complete survival times might look like: 5, 4, 20, 2, 15, 12, 8, and 10 (weeks). The basis for describing the survival experience nonparametrically is again the probability of surviving a specific time interval.

The Kaplan–Meier or product-limit nonparametric estimate of the probability of survival is based on constructing time intervals so that only one death occurs in each. Therefore, the probability of death is simply calculated. If q_i represents the probability of death in the ith interval, then q_i is estimated by one divided by the number of individuals at risk in that interval. If several individuals have identical survival times, then the probability of a single death is multiplied by the number of deaths. Each of n intervals (one for each death) is characterized by an estimate of q_i, and these probabilities, along with the probabilities of surviving the interval $(p_i = 1 - q_i)$, derived from the hypothetical data are given in Table 10.4.

The quantity of most interest is the probability of surviving from the start of the first interval until the end of the kth interval. This survival

Table 10–4. Hypothetical follow-up data: No censoring

i	Interval	$\hat{q}_i$	$\hat{p}_i$	$\hat{P}_k = \Pi\,\hat{p}_i$	$S_{\hat{P}_i}$
1	0–2	1/8	7/8	7/8	0.117
2	2–4	1/7	6/7	6/8	0.153
3	4–5	1/6	5/6	5/8	0.171
4	5–8	1/5	4/5	4/8	0.177
5	8–10	1/4	3/4	3/8	0.171
6	10–12	1/3	2/3	2/8	0.153
7	12–15	1/2	1/2	1/8	0.117
8	15–20	1/1	0/1	0/8	—

probability (P_k) is estimated by the product of the probabilities of surviving each interval, called the product-limit estimate, and is

$$\hat{P}_k = \prod_{i=1}^{k} \hat{p}_i. \qquad (10.25)$$

Little difference exists between the product-limit survival probabilities and the similar values computed from a life table. The life-table estimates are based on fixed interval widths, where the product-limit estimates are not; otherwise the resulting survival probabilities estimate the same survival curve and play the same role in the analysis of survival data.

For the complete follow-up case

$$\hat{P}_k = \frac{n-1}{n}\frac{n-2}{n-1}\frac{n-3}{n-2}\cdots\frac{n-k}{n-k+1} = \frac{n-k}{n} = 1 - \frac{k}{n}, \qquad (10.26)$$

which is identical to calculating the survival probability directly. That is, k individuals died before or during the kth interval, resulting in an estimate of the probability of death before k complete intervals of time have passed of k/n, and the probability of surviving beyond the kth interval is $1 - k/n$. The observed number of deaths has a binomial distribution under the assumption that the probability of death is the same for a series of independent individuals within the study period. The usual variance associated with a binomial distribution can be applied to $\hat{P}_k$, giving an estimated variance of $\hat{P}_k(1 - \hat{P}_k)/n$ for a set of follow-up data with complete survival times. For the illustrative data, the probability of surviving 12 weeks (intervals 1, 2,...,6) is $\hat{P}_6 = 1 - 6/8 = 2/8 = 0.250$, and the estimated variance of $\hat{P}_6$ is 0.0234. The value $\hat{P}_6$ is also $(7/8)(6/7)(5/6)(4/5)(3/4)(2/3) = 5{,}040/20{,}160 = 0.250$.

The mean survival time in the complete follow-up case is simply the total time lived divided by the number of observed individuals $(n = d)$ and, as usual,

$$\bar{t} = \frac{\sum_{i=1}^{n} t_i}{n}. \qquad (10.27)$$

This same expression written in terms of the estimated survival probabilities $\hat{P}_i$ is

$$\bar{t} = \sum_{i=1}^{n} t_i(\hat{P}_{i-1} - \hat{P}_i), \text{ where } P_0 = 1. \qquad (10.28)$$

Expression (10.28) is more complicated but is useful when complete follow-up times are not available since, as will be seen, the P_i values can be estimated in an unbiased way from censored survival data. The mean survival time for the hypothetical data is $\bar{l} = 76.0/8 = 9.5$ weeks. Also when no individuals are censored or lost, the variability of the mean survival time is measured by the usual estimate for the standard error of a mean $(S_{\bar{l}} = S_t/\sqrt{n})$. For the example data, $S_{\bar{l}} = 2.138$. Product-limit estimation applied to complete data leads to familiar results, and, when survival times are censored, this approach [expressions (10.25) and (10.28)] continues to produce unbiased values for the survival probabilities and for mean survival time where standard methods fail.

The product-limit calculations of survival probabilities from incomplete survival data follow the same pattern as described for the complete data. The probability of death in a specific interval is calculated in the identical manner. All individuals who were not withdrawn or lost contribute to the calculation of the probability of death for that interval. Individuals withdrawn or lost from follow-up are included in the calculations only when they are known to be at risk for the entire interval. Otherwise, they are excluded from further calculations. Suppose three individuals in the previous data set did not die during the follow-up period, producing the same hypothetical data as shown in Figure 10.1 (5^+, 4, 20, 2^+, 15, 12, 8^+, and 10; for $n = 8$ individuals with $d = 5 =$ deaths). The probability estimates associated with these survival times are given in Table 10.5.

For these censored data the survival probabilities are calculated in the identical manner as the complete follow-up case $(\hat{P}_k = \Pi \, \hat{p}_i)$. For the hypothetical survival data, the probability of surviving three intervals (12 weeks), for example, is $\hat{P}_3 = 0.429$. That is, $\hat{P}_4 = (6/7)(3/4)(2/3) = 36/84 = 0.429$.

The product-limit estimate of the survival probability $\hat{P}_k$ is subject to sampling variability, which can be estimated by Greenwood's expression for the approximate variance of a survival probability, and is [repeated in a slightly different form; expression (9.29)]

$$\text{variance}(\hat{P}_k) = \hat{P}_k^2 \sum_{i=1}^{k} \frac{\hat{q}_i^2}{\hat{p}_i}. \tag{10.29}$$

Table 10-5. Hypothetical follow-up data: Censoring

i	Interval	$\hat{q}_i$	$\hat{p}_i$	$\hat{P}_k = \Pi \hat{p}_i$	$S_{\hat{P}}$
1	0–4	1/7	6/7	0.857	0.132
2	4–10	1/4	3/4	0.643	0.210
3	10–12	1/3	2/3	0.429	0.224
4	12–15	1/2	1/2	0.214	0.188
5	15–20	1/1	0/1	0.000	—

For example, $\hat{P}_3 = 0.429$, and an estimate of the variance is

$$\text{variance}(\hat{P}_3) = 0.429^2 \left(\tfrac{1}{7}\tfrac{1}{6} + \tfrac{1}{4}\tfrac{1}{3} + \tfrac{1}{3}\tfrac{1}{2}\right) = 0.050. \qquad (10.30)$$

Greenwood's expression for the variance of a survival probability involves a cumulative sum, which slightly complicates the calculation. An alternative, simpler approximation is [Ref. 2]

$$\text{variance}(\hat{P}_k) = q_k \hat{P}_k^2 (1 - \hat{P}_k). \qquad (10.31)$$

Mean Survival Time from Censored Data

When censored values are present, the direct calculation of a mean produces an estimate that is likely too small, as already noted. The previous expression for the mean, however, gives an unbiased estimate of the mean survival time as

$$\bar{t} = \sum_{i=1}^{d} t_i (\hat{P}_{i-1} - \hat{P}_i), \text{ where } \hat{P}_0 = 1. \qquad (10.32)$$

Expression (10.32) is sometimes given in a different form as

$$\bar{t} = \sum_{i=1}^{d} \hat{P}_{i-1}(t_i - t_{i-1}), \text{ where } t_0 = 0. \qquad (10.33)$$

Both expressions produce identical estimated mean values. The value d is again the number of deaths observed or categories in a sample of n individuals $(d \leqslant n)$. If the data do not contain censored values $(d = n)$, then $\hat{P}_{i-1} - \hat{P}_i = 1/n$ and the expressions for $\bar{t}$ reduce to the usual computation of a mean value. When censored values are present, the mean $\bar{t}$ is a weighted average of the observed survival times. Expression (10.33) has a clear geometric interpretation. It is an estimate of the area under the survival curve which is the sum of a series of rectangles whose areas are each the height times the width or $\hat{P}_{i-1}(t_i - t_{i-1})$.

Table 10-6. Calculation of the mean from censored survival data

i	t_i	q_i	$\hat{P}_i$	$\hat{P}_{i-1} - \hat{P}_i$	$t_i(\hat{P}_{i-1} - \hat{P}_i)$	$t_i - t_{i-1}$	$\hat{P}_{i-1}(t_i - t_{i-1})$
1	4	0.143	0.857	0.143	0.571	4	4.000
2	10	0.250	0.643	0.214	2.143	6	5.143
3	12	0.333	0.429	0.214	2.571	2	1.286
4	15	0.500	0.214	0.214	3.214	3	1.286
5	20	0.000	0.000	0.214	4.286	5	1.071
Mean	—	—	—	—	12.786	—	12.786

The estimated mean survival time from the hypothetical data (5^+, 4, 20, 2^+, 15, 12, 8^+, and 10) is 12.786 weeks, as shown in Table 10.6. Figure 10.2 shows the estimated survival curve associated with these censored data. Note that $\bar{t}$ is the total area under the product-limit survival curve estimate.

The approximate variance of $\bar{t}$ is somewhat complicated, but is usually produced by "package" programs for survival analysis (e.g., SPSS and SAS or see [Ref. 3]). An approximate variance for the mean value estimated from censored data is given by

$$\text{variance}(\bar{t}) = \sum_{i=1}^{d} \frac{q_i^2}{p_i} A_i^2, \text{ where } A_i = \sum_{j=1}^{i} \hat{P}_{j-1}(t_j - t_{j-1}) - \bar{t}. \quad (10.34)$$

For the hypothetical data, $S_{\bar{t}} = 2.108$. More complete descriptions of the properties of this variance are given elsewhere (see [Ref. 3]). Incidentally, if no censoring is present, the estimate of the variance of the estimated mean [expression (10.34)] reduces to $\text{variance}(\bar{t}) = (1/n^2) \Sigma (t_i - \bar{t})^2$, indicating a slight bias since the denominator should be $n(n-1)$ to yield the usual unbiased estimate of the variance of $\bar{t}$.

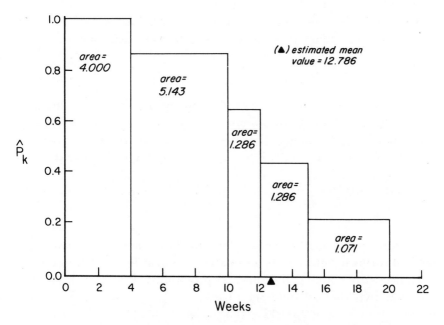

Figure 10–2. Survival curve for the hypothetical eight data values.

Table 10-7. Kidney cancer data: Survival probabilities

Interval	$\hat{P}_i$
0–1	0.597
1–2	0.539
2–3	0.503
3–4	0.442
4–5	0.442

Survival probabilities from almost any survival curve can be used to estimate the mean survival time. The kidney cancer data (Table 9.7) provide an example. The survival probabilities for 6 years of follow-up data (Table 9.8) are given in Table 10.7. These data based on $n = 126$ patients give an estimated mean survival time $\bar{t} = \Sigma\,\hat{P}_i = 3.523$ years since $t_i - t_{i-1} = 1$. The standard error of $\bar{t}$ is 0.236.

The lung cancer data provide another example. The survival probabilities calculated from the ten survival times given previously (Table 10.2) are shown in Table 10.8, and the estimated mean survival time is $\bar{t} = 34.550$ days with a standard error of 8.165. This calculation is slightly complicated by the fact that the longest survival time (72 days) is a censored value (to be discussed).

The expected number of years to be lived from birth calculated from a complete life table is an application of the mean survival time expression. That is,

$$\bar{t} = \Sigma\,P_{i-1}(t_i - t_{i-1}) \approx e_0 - 0.5, \tag{10.35}$$

where e_0 is the expected years of life from birth. The approximation occurs because of the indeterminate last age interval in a life table. For the complete life table, the age interval width is 1 year or $(t_x - t_{x-1}) = x - (x-1) = 1$ (except the last interval); therefore,

$$\bar{t} \approx \Sigma\,P_x = \Sigma\,\frac{l_x}{l_0} = \frac{1}{l_0}\,\Sigma\,(L_x - 0.5 d_x) = \frac{T_0 - 0.5 l_0}{l_0}, \text{ giving } \bar{t} \approx e_0 - 0.5.$$

$$\tag{10.36}$$

An alternative to the mean is the median time of survival. The median survival times can be estimated by linear interpolation within the interval containing the survival probability $\hat{P} = 0.50$. From the censored hypothetical data set (Table 10.5), the estimated median survival time is $10 + 2(0.643 - 0.5)/(0.643 - 0.429) = 11.336$ weeks.

Table 10-8. Lung cancer data:
Survival probabilities

Interval	$\hat{P}_i$
0–2	0.900
2–4	0.800
4–14	0.700
14–24	0.583
24–27	0.467
27–33	0.350
33–51	0.233
51–72	0.000

Goodness-of-fit

Most analyses require a fundamental choice:

Should a parametric model be used with advantages in efficiency but possible losses due to "wrong model bias," or should a nonparametric approach be selected that can incur some loss of efficiency but does not require a sometimes problematic statistical structure?

Specifically this question might be: Does a sample of follow-up data come from a population with exponential survival structure? The answer to such questions clearly dictates subsequent analytic directions. A first step in deciding between parametric and nonparametric methods of analysis is the investigation of the goodness-of-fit of possible parametric choices. One type of goodness-of-fit procedure, involving the comparison of two cumulative distributions, can be formalized with a statistical test (e.g., χ^2 or Kolomogorov test [Ref. 4]), but a simple graphic display often provides sufficient information to choose satisfactorily between parametric and nonparametric approaches. The following is a description of a general graphic technique, but it is only one of the many possibilities for dealing with the question of whether a data set supports a specific parametric model.

Goodness-of-fit: Cumulative distributions

Two cumulative distributions must first be defined. A population cumulative distribution describes the probability that a sampled value is less than a specified value x by

$$Q^* = F(x) = P(X \leq x), \tag{10.37}$$

where F represents a parametric function. The function F is based primarily on theoretical considerations. For example, the population cumulative distribution function associated with the exponential model is $F(t) = 1 - S(t) = 1 - e^{-\lambda t}$. The cumulative distribution $F(t)$ could represent the probability of death before time t.

The analogous sample cumulative distribution function is

$$Q_i = \frac{\text{the number of observations} \leqslant x_i}{n} = \frac{i}{n}, \tag{10.38}$$

where $x_1, x_2, \ldots, x_n$ is an ordered sample of n independent observations. Goodness-of-fit is measured by comparing the theoretically derived population distribution function with the sample-derived cumulative distribution function. That is, Q^* is compared to Q_i at each observed value x_i. If the theoretically derived and the empirically derived cumulative distribution functions are similar, the parametric form $F(x)$ may be helpful as a description of the data. Conversely, if these two distributions differ, the parametric representation will likely be misleading.

Normal Distribution Case

The two types of cumulative distribution functions and their comparison are illustrated with a sample of 20 observations thought to be normally distributed. An ordered sample of data, in terms of standardized values $\hat{z}_i = (x_i - \bar{x})/s$, is given in Table 10.9 (column 1). Also shown are the sample cumulative distribution probabilities (Q_i, column 2) associated with the $\hat{z}_i$ values.

Cumulative values from the sample should be similar to cumulative values derived from a standard normal distribution when the sampled population is normally distributed. For example, if 95% of the sampled values are less than $\hat{z}_i$, the value $\hat{z}_i$ should be near 1.645, since 95% of a normal distribution is less than 1.645. In symbols, this comparison of percentiles is

$$\hat{z}_i \text{ versus } z_i^* = F^{-1}(Q_i), \tag{10.39}$$

where $\hat{z}_i$ is a directly observed sample value and z_i^* is calculated from the theoretically derived normal distribution. The expression $F^{-1}(Q_i)$ represents a percentile of a population cumulative distribution. Given a probability, the F-inverse function produces the associated percentile. The notation is a bit complex but indicates a familiar process. For example, if $Q_i = 0.25$, using the normal population cumulative distribution, $z_i^* = F^{-1}(0.25) = -0.674$ or $P(X < -0.674) = 0.25$. From the data, $\hat{z}_1 = -1.49$ and $z_1^* = F^{-1}(0.05) = -1.645$ (this value, as

Table 10-9. Values for goodness-of-fit plots

$\bar{z}_i$	Q_i	$z_i^* = F^{-1}(Q_i)$	$Q_i^* = F(\hat{z}_i)$
−1.49	0.05	−1.645	0.068
−1.21	0.10	−1.282	0.113
−1.19	0.15	−1.036	0.117
−1.06	0.20	−0.841	0.145
−1.01	0.25	−0.674	0.156
−0.87	0.30	−0.524	0.192
−0.68	0.35	−0.385	0.248
−0.63	0.40	−0.253	0.264
−0.07	0.45	−0.125	0.472
0.01	0.50	0.000	0.504
0.01	0.55	0.125	0.504
0.04	0.60	0.253	0.516
0.07	0.65	0.385	0.528
0.15	0.70	0.524	0.560
0.15	0.75	0.674	0.560
0.26	0.80	0.841	0.603
0.42	0.85	1.036	0.663
0.76	0.90	1.282	0.776
1.33	0.95	1.645	0.908
1.47	1.00	—	0.929

usual, comes from a table of standard normal probabilities or a computer program). The comparison of $\hat{z}_i$ with z_i^* (column 1 versus column 3 in Table 10.9) is shown in Figure 10.3 (left side) and is called a percentile plot. On a percentile plot, if the observed $\hat{z}_i$ values represent a random sample from a normal distribution, the points $(\hat{z}_i, z_i^*)$ will fall near a 45° line, differing from this line only because of random variation.

A parallel process involves comparing theoretical cumulative normal probabilities derived from the $\hat{z}_i$ values with those directly derived from the sample. The logic is that, when the sampled population is normal, a probability calculated from $\hat{z}_i$ based on the theoretical normal cumulative distribution (Q_i^*) should be similar to the probability associated with $\hat{z}_i$ based on the sample cumulative distribution (Q_i). For $\hat{z}_1 = -1.49$, the cumulative probability based on the normal distribution is 0.068 (i.e., $Q_1^* = P(Z < -1.49) = 0.068$). The probability based on the sample cumulative distribution associated with −1.49 is 0.05 ($Q_1 = 1/n = 1/20 = 0.05$). The comparisons of Q_i with Q_i^* (column 2 versus column 4 in Table 10.9) for the 20 observations are shown in Figure 10.3 (right side). Again the points (Q_i, Q_i^*) will form an approximate straight line (45°) when the distribution sampled is normal.

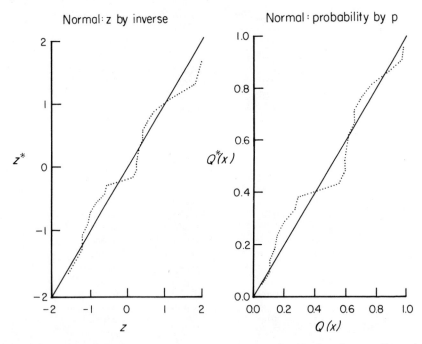

Figure 10–3. Goodness-of-fit plots for the normal distribution (percentile and probabilities).

Note that the two types of plots differ only in scale—the percentiles z_i and z_i^* are measured in standard deviations, while probabilities Q_i and Q_i^* must lie between 0 and 1. These plots of percentiles or probabilities provides an evaluation of the goodness-of-fit of any distribution where $F(x)$ can be defined.

Expenential Distribution Case

The exponential case is straightforward since the theoretical distribution function F is expressed by

$$Q^* = F(t) = 1 - S(t) = 1 - e^{-\lambda t} \text{ (probability)}, \qquad (10.40)$$

and it follows that F^{-1} is

$$F^{-1}(Q) = t^* = \frac{-\log(1 - Q)}{\lambda} \text{ (percentile)}. \qquad (10.41)$$

The hazard rate λ is usually unknown, but the estimated value $\hat{\lambda} = 1/\bar{t}$ allows estimates of the probabilities and percentiles associated with exponentially distributed data as the following Table 10.10 illustrates.

Table 10-10. Values for goodness-of-fit plots

t_i	Q_i	$t_i^* = F^{-1}(Q_i)$	$Q_i^* = F(t_i)$
0.94	0.05	1.126	0.042
3.68	0.10	2.313	0.154
5.25	0.15	3.567	0.213
5.48	0.20	4.898	0.221
8.81	0.25	6.314	0.331
11.95	0.30	7.829	0.420
12.31	0.35	9.455	0.429
13.28	0.40	11.212	0.454
14.16	0.45	13.122	0.475
15.80	0.50	15.214	0.513
16.54	0.55	17.527	0.529
18.86	0.60	20.112	0.577
20.38	0.65	23.043	0.605
22.19	0.70	26.427	0.636
22.84	0.75	30.428	0.647
32.38	0.80	35.326	0.771
40.68	0.85	41.641	0.843
50.66	0.90	50.541	0.901
55.10	0.95	65.755	0.919
67.70	1.00	—	0.954

Table 10.10 contains (column 1) a set of computer-generated random "exponential data," ordered from low to high. The percentiles t_i and t_i^* are compared in the same manner as in the normal distribution case. For example, $t_{16} = 32.38$ with $Q_{16} = 16/20 = 0.80$. The percentile associated with 0.80 for an exponential distribution is $t_{16}^* = F^{-1}(0.80) = -\log(0.20)/0.0456 = 35.326$, when λ is estimated by $\hat{\lambda} = 1/\bar{t} = 1/21.95 = 0.0456$. Figure 10.4 (left side) shows the comparison of the sample percentile (t_i, column 1) with the corresponding theoretically derived percentile (t_i^*, column 3) for the 20 data values. A goodness-of-fit comparison can also be made between the probabilities Q_i and Q_i^*. For example, $Q_{16}^* = 1 - e^{-0.0456(32.38)} = 0.771$ (theoretical) and $Q_{16} = 0.80$ (empirical). Figure 10.4 (right side) shows the comparison for the 20 observations in Table 10.10 (Q_i, column 2, versus Q_i^*, column 4).

Aside: Percentile plots are a general technique that allows an evaluation of the goodness-of-fit of a set of data to a theoretical model by the comparison of cumulative distributions. A simple graphic technique that applies specifically to the exponential survival distribution also involves plotting a function of the cumulative distribution. If the survival curve is $S(t) = e^{-\lambda t}$, then

$$\log[-\log\{S(t)\}] = \log(\lambda) + \log(t). \qquad (10.42)$$

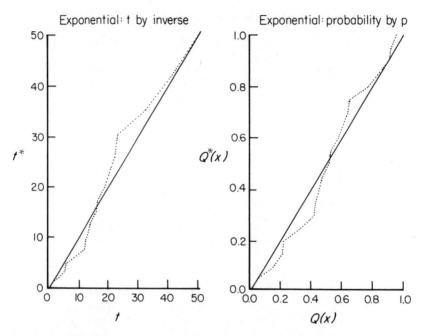

Figure 10–4. Goodness-of-fit plots for the exponential distribution (percentile and probabilities).

That is, when the individual survival times are sampled from an exponential distribution, plotting $\log\{-\log[S(t)]\}$ against the logarithm of the survival time will deviate from a straight line only because of random variation. Values for $S(t)$ can be estimated using a product-limit or a life table estimate. The "log-log" transformation suggests a more general survival model given by

$$\log\{-\log[S(t)]\} = \log(\lambda) + b \log(t), \text{ then } S(t) = e^{-\lambda t^b}, \quad (10.43)$$

which is a special case of the Weibull distribution used to analyze specific types of survival data [Ref. 5].

TWO-SAMPLE DATA

Studies are designed and data collected so that the mortality or disease experience of two groups can be compared. A study to evaluate two treatments provides an example of this two-sample situation (cited in [Ref. 6]):

A clinical trial to evaluate the efficacy of maintenance chemotherapy for acute myelogenous leukemia (AML) was conducted by Embury *et al.*

Table 10-11. Maintained group

k	Interval	q_k	p_k	$\hat{P}_k = \Pi\, p_i$	$S_{\hat{P}_k}$
1	0-9	1/11	10/11	0.909	0.087
2	9-13	1/10	9/10	0.818	0.116
3	13-18	1/8	7/8	0.716	0.140
4	18-23	1/7	6/7	0.614	0.153
5	23-31	1/5	4/5	0.491	0.164
6	31-34	1/4	3/4	0.368	0.162
7	34-48	1/2	1/2	0.184	0.153
8	48+	1/1	0	0	—

at Stanford University. After reaching a state of remission through treatment by chemotherapy, the patients who entered the study were randomized into two groups. The first group received maintenance chemotherapy; the second or control group did not. The objective of the trial was to see if maintenance chemotherapy prolonged the time until relapse, that is, increased the length of remission.

Preliminary data collected during the course of the trial were as follows (in weeks):

Maintained group ($n = 11$):
9, 13, 13$^+$, 18, 23, 28$^+$, 31, 34, 45$^+$, 48, 161$^+$

Nonmaintained group ($n = 12$):
5, 5, 8, 8, 12, 16$^+$, 23, 27, 30, 33, 43, 45.

The product-limit estimates of the survival probabilities ($\hat{P}_k$ values) for these two groups (note: "survival" means time to relapse) are given in Tables 10.11 and 10.12. The estimated survival curves are shown in Figure 10.5 for both nonparametric (product-limit—$\hat{P}_k$) and parametric [exponential assumption—$\hat{S}(t)$] approaches.

Table 10-12. Nonmaintained group

k	Interval	q_k	p_k	$\hat{P}_k = \Pi\, p_i$	$S_{\hat{P}_k}$
1	0-5	2/12	10/12	0.833	0.108
2	5-8	2/10	8/10	0.667	0.136
3	8-12	1/8	7/8	0.583	0.142
4	12-23	1/6	5/6	0.486	0.148
5	23-27	1/5	4/5	0.389	0.147
6	27-30	1/4	3/4	0.292	0.139
7	30-33	1/3	2/3	0.194	0.122
8	33-43	1/2	1/2	0.097	0.092
9	43-45	1/1	0	0	—

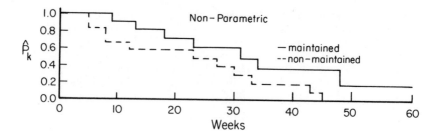

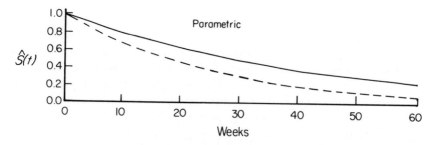

Figure 10–5. Two sample AML remission data for the maintained and non-maintained groups—non-parametric and parametric plots of the survival curves.

If the longest follow-up period ends with a patient being withdrawn, then the product-limit-derived mean value is biased (too small). That is, the final interval is undefined, and the longest survival time does not contribute, because each interval used in the calculation must contain at least one death. The maintained AML data should, therefore, be adjusted to avoid this bias since the patient who survived the longest (161 weeks) was withdrawn from observation. One conventional practice is to consider the longest survival time as always ending in a death (or in the AML case, relapse). In this way the survival time contributes to the total time at risk, and a lesser bias is incurred when this artificial endpoint is necessary. The nonparametric estimated mean survival times for these two groups are then [from expressions (10.33) and (10.34)]: for maintained = 52.645 (standard error = 19.828) and for nonmaintained = 22.708 (standard error = 4.181). This difference between mean survival times yields weak, at best, evidence of a difference between the two therapies. The large amount of variation in times to relapse associated with the maintained group interferes with assessing the observed difference of about 30 weeks.

For the leukemia data example, the one patient who survived 161 weeks dominates the comparison. The disproportionate influence is seen by comparing the mean and median survival times. The estimated median survival times, maintained = 30.415 and nonmaintained = 21.412 weeks, respectively, differ by far less than the 30-week difference between mean values since extreme survival values have little impact on the median. These median values are estimated by linear interpolation of the product-limit survival curve. Sometimes the median survival time is estimated by using the endpoint of the interval containing the 50th percentile (maintained = 31 weeks and nonmaintained = 23 weeks).

Another way to reduce the bias incurred when the longest survival time is censored involves selecting a specific time before the end of the study period so that the last survival time is complete in both groups, eliminating observations with longer survival times regardless of survival status. For example, if 35 weeks is selected (e.g., 45^+, 48, 161^+ are ignored) as a "period of observation" for the AML-maintained group, then the mean is 23.525 (standard error = 3.33). For the nonmaintained group, the mean survival time (e.g., 43 and 45 ignored) is then 17.925 (standard error = 3.44).

A parametric estimate is, in principle, more efficient than a nonparametric approach, but at the cost of making additional assumptions about the structure of the data. If the survival experience of these two groups of leukemia patients is modeled by an exponential survival curve, then parametric estimated mean survival times are: maintained = 60.429 (standard error = 22.840) and nonmaintained = 23.182 (standard error = 6.989). A parametric analysis also does not provide sufficient statistical precision to identify the observed difference in mean survival times as unlikely to be a chance occurrence. The estimated median survival time, again based on the exponential distribution, is $\bar{t} \log(2)$ and for the AML data are: maintained = 41.886 and nonmaintained = 16.068. To summarize, the estimates for the AML data are given in Table 10.13.

The tradeoff between parametric and nonparametric analyses is illustrated by these estimates. The choice between the two approaches is rarely clear and relies primarily on the judgement of the investigator, supported by goodness-of-fit analysis.

Table 10–13. Summary: Leukemia data survival times

	Mean		Median	
	Maintained	Nonmaintained	Maintained	Nonmaintained
Parametric	60.429	23.182	41.887	16.068
Nonparametric	52.645	22.708	30.415	21.412

Table 10–14. 2×2 table generated for each stratum

t_i	Died	Alive	Total
Treatment	a_i	b_i	$a_i + b_i$
Control	c_i	d_i	$c_i + d_i$
Total	$a_i + c_i$	$b_i + d_i$	n_i

Evaluation of Two-Sample Data

A formal nonparametric evaluation of differences in survival between groups is accomplished by a χ^2 procedure almost identical to the traditional Mantel–Haenszel χ^2 technique [expression (7.61)].

Similar to the product-limit (Kaplan–Meier) estimate, the data are sorted into strata based on times of each death (t_i). The process produces a set of 2×2 tables, one for each recorded death, where individuals under observation are classified as treatment or control and survived or died (i.e., d = number of deaths = number of strata—one stratum for each death if all survival times are different). Specifically, each time of death generates a standard 2×2 table of the type represented by Table 10.14. The AML data produce 15 ($d = 15$ strata) 2×2 tables (Figure 10.6 displays these 15 tables in detail), and are summarized in Table 10.15.

The analysis of an association between two binary variables (died–survived and treatment–control), while controlling for the

Table 10–15. AML follow-up data summary

i	Interval	a_i	b_i	c_i	d_i	n_i
1	0–5	0	11	2	10	23
2	5–8	0	11	2	8	21
3	8–9	1	10	0	8	19
4	9–12	0	10	1	7	18
5	12–13	1	9	0	7	17
6	13–18	1	7	0	6	14
7	18–23	1	6	1	5	13
8	23–27	0	6	1	4	11
9	27–30	0	5	1	3	9
10	30–31	1	4	0	3	8
11	31–33	0	4	1	2	7
12	33–34	1	3	0	2	6
13	34–43	0	3	1	1	5
14	43–45	0	3	1	0	4
15	45–48	1	1	0	0	2

t=5	death	alive	total
M	0	11	11
NM	2	10	12
total	2	21	23

t=18	death	alive	total
M	1	7	8
NM	0	6	6
total	1	13	14

t=33	death	alive	total
M	0	4	4
NM	1	2	3
total	1	6	7

t=8	death	alive	total
M	0	11	11
NM	2	8	10
total	2	19	21

t=23	death	alive	total
M	1	6	7
NM	1	5	6
total	2	11	13

t=34	death	alive	total
M	1	3	4
NM	0	2	2
total	1	5	6

t=9	death	alive	total
M	1	10	11
NM	0	8	8
total	1	18	19

t=27	death	alive	total
M	0	6	6
NM	1	4	5
total	1	10	11

t=43	death	alive	total
M	0	3	3
NM	1	1	2
total	1	4	5

t=12	death	alive	total
M	0	10	10
NM	1	7	8
total	1	17	18

t=30	death	alive	total
M	0	5	5
NM	1	3	4
total	1	8	9

t=45	death	alive	total
M	0	3	3
NM	1	0	1
total	1	3	4

t=13	death	alive	total
M	1	9	10
NM	0	7	7
total	1	16	17

t=31	death	alive	total
M	1	4	5
NM	0	3	3
total	1	7	8

t=48	death	alive	total
M	1	1	2
NM	0	0	0
total	1	1	2

Figure 10-6. Full display of the AML data by known times of remission for maintained and nonmaintained groups in a series of 2 × 2 tables.

confounding influence of a third variable (time), is a typical use of the Mantel–Haenszel χ^2 procedure. The difference between the analysis of a series of 2×2 tables generated by survival data and the usual application of the Mantel–Haenszel procedure is that survival data tables (strata) are not independent. Individuals who survive are included in subsequent tables, introducing a dependency among the observations. The lack of independence is not critical, and a χ^2 summary remains an accurate evaluation of survival–treatment associations. The censored survival times contribute to the time at risk until withdrawn from observation, and, like the product-limit estimator, the association between treatment and outcome is not biased by the incomplete follow-up. That is, the number at risk n_i is reduced in each stratum by the number who died (usually one) and the number who were withdrawn or lost from observation to form the individuals at risk in the next stratum (n_{i+1}).

The two-sample analysis in the context of time-dependent variables consists of testing for an association between treatment–control status and disease outcome status among the series of strata based on time of death. The expected number of deaths when no treatment effect exists for each stratum (table) is

$$\text{expected} = \hat{A}_i = (a_i + b_i)(a_i + c_i)/n_i, \tag{10.44}$$

and the estimated variance for the observed number of deaths in the treatment group (a_i) is

$$\text{variance}(a_i) = (a_i + b_i)(a_i + c_i)(b_i + d_i)(c_i + d_i)/[n_i^2(n_i - 1)]. \tag{10.45}$$

These two estimates are the same as those used for the Mantel–Haenszel χ^2 test of association [expressions (7.59) and (7.60)]. The expected values and the variances for the illustrative AML data are shown in Table 10.16.

A weighted χ^2 statistic is then calculated as

$$X^2 = \frac{\left(\sum\limits_{i=1}^{k} w_i(a_i - \hat{A}_i)\right)^2}{\sum\limits_{i=1}^{k} w_i^2 \, \text{variance}(a_i)}. \tag{10.46}$$

to combine and assess the differences $a_i - \hat{A}_i$. The value X^2 has an approximate χ^2 distribution with one degree of freedom under the null hypothesis of no association between treatment–control status and outcome. Large values of X^2, therefore, imply an association between treatment and survival. When $w_i = 1$, X^2 is formally the Mantel–Haenszel χ^2 statistic. Others have suggested alternative

Table 10–16. AML followup data

i	Interval	a_i	$\hat{A}_i$	Variance
1	0–5	0	0.956	0.476
2	5–8	0	1.048	0.474
3	8–9	1	0.579	0.244
4	9–12	0	0.556	0.247
5	12–13	1	0.588	0.242
6	13–18	1	0.571	0.245
7	18–23	1	1.077	0.455
8	23–27	0	0.545	0.248
9	27–30	0	0.556	0.247
10	30–31	1	0.625	0.234
11	31–33	0	0.571	0.245
12	33–34	1	0.667	0.222
13	34–43	0	0.600	0.240
14	43–45	0	0.750	0.188
15	45–48	1	1.000	0.000
Total	—	7	10.689	4.008

weights: $w_i = n_i$ (Gehan, [Ref. 7]) and $w_i = \sqrt{n_i}$ (Tarone and Ware, [Ref. 8]). Gehan's suggestion emphasizes the early observed values more heavily than the Mantel–Haenszel statistic, while the Tarone–Ware suggestion is intermediate. All three compare the total number of observed deaths (7 in the AML example) to the number expected when the treatment has no effect (10.689 from the AML data). The three χ^2 values for the AML data are shown in Table 10.17.

The χ^2 analysis of the AML data indicates, on the basis of borderline evidence, that the treatment may influence survival. The Mantel–Haenszel statistic is closely related to a procedure called the log-rank test (see [Ref. 6]). Both procedures give similar results for the comparison of two groups. The log-rank procedure can be generalized to situations where more than two treatments are considered, producing a series of $2 \times K$ tables.

A summary odds ratio calculated from a series of 2×2 tables measures the association between membership in a treatment–control group and disease outcome in the absence of interaction. For example, for the AML data (Table 10.15) the Mantel–Haenszel summary odds ratio is

$$\hat{or}_{MH} = \frac{\Sigma a_i d_i / n_i}{\Sigma b_i c_i / n_i} = \frac{(0)(10)/23 + \cdots + (1)(0)/2}{(11)(2)/23 + \cdots + (1)(0)/2} = 0.390, \quad (10.47)$$

which means that the estimated odds of a relapse is considerably lower $(1/.390 = 2.6$ times) in the maintained group (treatment group) compared to the nonmaintained group (control group). The Mantel–Haenszel summary odds ratio estimate is not reliable applied to survival data when only a small number of deaths occur and is biased in some situations. An alternate comparison of the risk of disease is available, which also allows adjustment for the influence of confounding variables and is the topic of the next chapter.

The Wilcoxon Test and the Gehan Generalization

A modification of the Wilcoxon test provides an alternative to the Mantel–Haenszel approach to evaluate observed differences in sur-

Table 10–17. Values for the three χ^2 tests

	w_i	χ^2	p-value
Mantel–Haenszel	1.0	3.396	0.065
Tarone–Ware	$\sqrt{n_i}$	2.981	0.084
Gehan	n_i	2.723	0.099

vival between two groups. First, consider the case without censored data.

Like the two-sample t test, the Wilcoxon two-sample test is designed to assess differences between two independent samples of observations. The Wilcoxon test, however, is nonparametric and is valid regardless of the distribution of the sampled population. For clarity, one sampled group will be called the "control" and the other the "treatment." The first step is to replace the data values (y_{ij}) by their ranks $(R_{ij};$ rank $1 =$ lowest value, rank $2 =$ next lowest, etc.), disregarding group membership. If the sample consists of n_1 control and n_2 treatment observations, then the "data" become the integers $1, 2, 3, \ldots, n$, where $n = n_1 + n_2$. A summary statistic that reflects differences between treatment and control groups is the sum of the ranks associated with the treatment observations $(R = \Sigma R_{ij})$. If there is no systematic differences between groups, the sum of the treatment ranks should be proportional to the number of treatment observations (n_2). Specifically, the expected sum of the ranks for the treatment group is

$$\text{expected sum of treatment ranks} = ER = n_2 \frac{n + 1}{2}, \qquad (10.48)$$

which is n_2 times the average rank. For example, if the treatment and control groups have the same number of observations, then the sum of the ranks for each group should be about equal when the groups differ only because of random variation $[ER = n(n + 1)/4$, where $n_1 = n_2 = n/2]$. If the two samples systematically differ, then the sum of the treatment ranks will likely be extreme (differ from the expected). The null hypothesis of no difference between treatment and control groups is assessed by comparing the observed value R with the null hypothesis generated value ER. This comparison, as usual, requires an expression for the variance of R, which is

$$\text{variance}(R) = n_1 n_2 \frac{n + 1}{12}. \qquad (10.49)$$

A seemingly different process for calculating a summary rank statistic involves counting the number of values less than each ordered observation and counting the number of values greater than each ordered observation. The sum of the differences (D_{ij}) between these counts associated with the n_2 treatment observations also serves as a test statistic $(D = \Sigma D_{ij})$. An example will make the process clear. A group of women reporting pregnancy complications $(n_2 = 9)$ is compared to a set of controls $(n_1 = 10)$ for levels of glucose determined by glucose tolerance tests. These data (ordered from low to high) are shown in

Table 10.18. Each observation produces a D_{ij} value. For the test statistic $D = \Sigma D_{ij}$, like R, extreme values lead to rejecting the null hypothesis that no difference exists between the two compared groups. Either R or D can equally be used to evaluate observed differences between the two groups since these two statistical measures are related. The exact relationship is $D = 2R - n_2(n + 1)$ and, therefore, variance$(D) = 4$ variance(R). Incidently, the relationship between D and R shows that $ED = 0$ [i.e., $ED = 2ER - n_2(n + 1) = 0$]. Also note that the D_{ij} values are symmetrically distributed around zero when the null hypothesis is true.

The sum of the pregnancy complications ("treatment") ranks is $R = \Sigma R_{ij} = 5 + 8 + 9 + 12 + 14 + 16 + 17 + 18 + 19 = 118$. The expected value of R (ER) is 90. Correspondingly, the sum of the differences in counts associated with the "treatment" is $D = \Sigma D_{ij} = -10 - 4 - 2 + 4 + 8 + 12 + 14 + 16 + 18 = 56$. A statistical significance test of either nonparametric measure is

$$z = \frac{R - ER}{\sqrt{\text{variance}(R)}} = \frac{D - 0}{\sqrt{\text{variance}(D)}}, \qquad (10.50)$$

where z has an approximately standard normal distribution when sample sizes are at least moderately large (say, both n_1 and $n_2 >$ about 10) and when no systematic differences exist between the treatment and

Table 10–18. Results from glucose tolerance tests

Group	y_{ij}	Rank $= R_i$	Lower than y_{ij}	Greater than y_{ij}	D_{ij}
No complications	100	1	0	18	−18
No complications	110	2	1	17	−16
No complications	117	3	2	16	−14
No complications	119	4	3	15	−12
Complications	120	5	4	14	−10
No complications	122	6	5	13	−8
No complications	127	7	6	12	−6
Complications	128	8	7	11	−4
Complications	132	9	8	10	−2
No complications	133	10	9	9	0
No complications	135	11	10	8	2
Complications	140	12	11	7	4
No complications	141	13	12	6	6
Complications	143	14	13	5	8
No complications	151	15	14	4	10
Complications	162	16	15	3	12
Complications	177	17	16	2	14
Complications	181	18	17	1	16
Complications	184	19	18	0	18

control groups. Tables of the exact distribution of R are available for small sample sizes [Ref. 9]. For the example data, the test using D is $z = 56/\sqrt{600} = 2.286$ producing a p-value of 0.022. The test of R is, of course, identical since the probabilities associated with D are the same as those associated with R. An alternative way to calculate the variance of D is

$$\text{variance}(D) = \frac{n_1 n_2 \sum\limits_{i=1}^{2} \sum\limits_{j=1}^{n_i} D_{ij}^2}{n(n-1)} \quad (\Sigma \Sigma D_{ij}^2 = 2280 \text{ for the example data}).$$

(10.51)

The D version of the Wilcoxon test statistic and the variance are introduced because they generalize [Ref. 7] to the comparison of two groups with censored survival times.

Gehan [Ref. 7] modified the Wilcoxon two-sample rank test to evaluate differences between samples that include censored survival times. The Gehan generalization of the Wilcoxon procedure employs the values D_{ij} rather than the ranks. The number of survival times that are known to be less than each ordered observation are counted. Similarly, the number of survival times when they are known to be greater than each ordered observation are counted and the difference D_{ij} calculated for each survival time (censored and noncensored). Information from the censored values is incorporated into the test statistic by this counting process. For example, if an individual is withdrawn from a study after 13 weeks (13^+), it is known that this person's survival time exceeds all individuals who died in less than 13 weeks. The test statistic is, as before, the sum of the differences $(D = \Sigma D_{ij})$ associated with the treatment survival times, and the expected value remains zero under the null hypothesis. Consider again the AML data ordered without regard to treatment–control status; as seen in Table 10.19. The sum of the D_{ij} values associated with the $n_2 = 11$ maintained individuals is

$$D = \Sigma D_{ij} = -14 - 10 + 7 - 6 - 3 + 11 + 5 + 9 + 17 + 16 + 18$$
$$= 50$$

and the

$$\text{variance}(D) = 11(12)(3498)/(22)(23) = 912.522,$$

producing $z = (50 - 0)/\sqrt{912.522} = 1.655$ giving a p-value of 0.097.

The Gehan test produces a somewhat higher p-value (0.097) than the "Mantel–Haenszel" procedure for assessing the association between survival and treatment (p-value = 0.065, Table 10.17) and

Table 10-19. Results from maintenance chemotherapy trial

Group	y_{ij}	Lower than y_{ij}	Greater than y_{ij}	D_{ij}
Nonmaintained	5	0	21	−21
Nonmaintained	5	0	21	−21
Nonmaintained	8	2	19	−17
Nonmaintained	8	2	19	−17
Maintained	9	4	18	−14
Nonmaintained	12	5	17	−12
Maintained	13	6	16	−10
Maintained	13$^+$	7	0	7
Nonmaintained	16$^+$	7	0	7
Maintained	18	7	13	−6
Nonmaintained	23	8	12	−4
Maintained	23	8	11	−3
Nonmaintained	27	10	10	0
Maintained	28$^+$	11	0	11
Nonmaintained	30	11	8	2
Maintained	31	12	7	5
Nonmaintained	33	13	6	7
Maintained	34	14	5	9
Nonmaintained	43	15	4	11
Nonmaintained	45	16	3	13
Maintained	45$^+$	17	0	17
Maintained	48	17	1	16
Maintained	161$^+$	18	0	18

produces results almost identical to the Gehan-weighted χ^2 test (p-value = 0.099, Table 10.17). The Gehan χ^2 test and the Gehan–Wilcoxon test are related. The numerators of the χ^2 approach $[\Sigma\, n_i (a_i - \hat{A}_i)]$ and the Wilcoxon approach (D) are identical, while the denominators are likely to be similar [i.e., $\Sigma\, n_i^2$ variance(a_i) $\approx$ variance(D)], giving similar results in assessing a treatment influence on the disease outcome or, in symbols, $z^2 \approx X^2$. Specifically, for the AML data $z^2 = (1.655)^2 = 2.739$ and $X^2 = 2.723$. In most situations, both the Gehan version of the χ^2 test and the Gehan form of the Wilcoxon rank test will give results that do not substantially differ.

11 A Model for Survival Data: Proportional Hazards

It is rarely sufficient to demonstrate that one group of individuals has a significantly longer survival time than another. Pursuit of plausible explanations for observed differences between groups is also important in understanding survival experience. Survival time, like risk, is affected by a number of interrelated factors. For example, such factors as age, severity of disease, past health status, and race provide concomitant information that improves the description of survival data. The investigation of the role of these explanatory variables usually requires postulating a statistical model that relates the time until death (survival time) to a series of measurements thought to influence an individual's survival. The analysis of these explanatory variables is conducted in much the same manner as the assessment of the risk variables in a logistic regression analysis. Of course, a statistical model linking a series of explanatory variables to survival time will, at best, approximate the unknown underlying situation. One is never assured that a mathematical structure is "biologically" correct. Alternative approaches, however, are rarely possible without large amounts of data, making a statistical model a basic tool for the investigation of a series of variables relevant to survival time. The success of a model-based approach clearly depends on choosing a model that adequately reflects the relationships within the data set. The choice of an appropriate statistical structure is an art, requiring knowledge of the mathematical properties of the model and a clear understanding of the phenomenon under investigation. One useful approach is the application of the proportional hazards model. This chapter explores this complex model in simple terms with the dual purpose of illustrating the technique and providing insight into the process of modeling survival experience. Also included are three applications of the proportional hazards model to published survival data. The analysis of multivariate survival data is a mathematically sophisticated topic, and texts are devoted entirely to the statistical analysis of failure-time data [e.g., Refs. 1–3]. This chapter is a brief introduction.

Table 11–1. Hypothetical data

Treatment A	5	8	12	22^+	37	41
Treatment B	23	40	43	51^+	53^+	62

Simplest Case

The simplest application of a proportional hazards model (sometimes called the Cox model, after the statistician D. R. Cox, who originated the analytic approach) is the comparison of two groups of individuals with varying survival times, some of which may be censored. A small hypothetical data set of twelve subjects is given in Table 11.1. These data consist two groups (A and B) of six individuals with a total of three incomplete survival times.

Before employing a proportional hazards model to evaluate treatment differences between A and B, it is useful to apply the χ^2 assessment of an association between two treatments and a disease outcome for this small data set. When the analysis involves simply two comparison groups, the "Mantel–Haenszel" approach relates to the proportional hazards model, as will be seen. The hypothetical data classified into 2×2 tables based on the nine known times of death gives Table 11.2. The same data are fully displayed in Figure 11.1. The χ^2 statistic for evaluating an association in a series of 2×2 tables is, once again,

$$X^2 = \frac{\left(\sum_{i=1}^{k}(a_i - \hat{A}_i)\right)^2}{\sum_{i=1}^{k}\text{variance}(a_i)} \quad \text{and} \quad X^2 = \frac{(2.743)^2}{1.428} = 5.269, \quad (11.1)$$

yielding a p-value of 0.022 for the $k = 9$ tables. The data show evidence

Table 11–2. Hypothetical data displayed in 2×2 tables: Summary

Time t	a_i	$a_i + b_i$	n_i	$\hat{A}_i$	$a_i - \hat{A}_i$	variance(a_i)
5	1	6	12	6/12	6/12	396/1584=0.250
8	1	5	11	5/11	6/11	300/1210=0.248
12	1	4	10	4/10	6/10	216/900=0.240
23	0	2	8	2/8	−2/8	84/448=0.188
37	1	2	7	2/7	5/7	60/294=0.204
40	0	1	6	1/6	−1/6	25/180=0.139
41	1	1	5	1/5	4/5	16/100=0.160
43	0	0	4	0/4	0	0/48
62	0	0	1	0/1	0	—
Total	5	—	—	2.257	2.743	1.428

t=5	death	alive	total
A	1	5	6
B	0	6	6
total	1	11	12

t=23	death	alive	total
A	0	2	2
B	1	5	6
total	1	7	8

t=41	death	alive	total
A	1	0	1
B	0	4	4
total	1	4	5

t=8	death	alive	total
A	1	4	5
B	0	6	6
total	1	10	11

t=37	death	alive	total
A	1	1	2
B	0	5	5
total	1	6	7

t=43	death	alive	total
A	0	0	0
B	1	3	4
total	1	3	4

t=12	death	alive	total
A	1	3	5
B	0	6	6
total	1	9	10

t=40	death	alive	total
A	0	1	1
B	1	4	5
total	1	5	6

t=62	death	alive	total
A	0	0	0
B	1	0	1
total	1	0	1

Figure 11–1. Full display of the hypothetical data by known times of death for group A and group B in a series of 2×2 tables.

of a nonrandom difference in survival associated with the two treatments A and B.

>   Aside: The estimated variance of a_i in the situation where no survival times are identical can be simplified over the previous more general variance [expression (10.43)] as

$$\text{variance}(a_i) = \frac{a_i + b_i}{n_i} \frac{c_i + d_i}{n_i}. \tag{11.2}$$

The proportional hazards model, in its simplest form, postulates that the hazard function associated with the survival in group A relates to the hazard function associated with the survival in group B by a multiplicative constant or

$$\lambda_B(t) = c\lambda_A(t) \text{ or } \frac{\lambda_B(t)}{\lambda_A(t)} = c, \tag{11.3}$$

where $\lambda_A(t)$ and $\lambda_B(t)$ represents hazard functions for groups A and B, respectively. Unlike the exponential model, these hazard rates can vary depending on time t. The constant c can be estimated from survival data. For example, continuing to use the hypothetical data, $\hat{c} = 0.168$ is the estimated constant of proportionality for the hazard rates associated with treatments A and B (Table 11.1). That is, the hazard rate in group B is estimated to be about six times less than in group A or $\lambda_B(t) = 0.168\lambda_A(t)$. The estimate of c is, like the logistic regression case, found by a maximum likelihood estimation procedure and requires a complex computer algorithm. In most cases the collected survival data are too sparse to estimate reliably the hazard functions themselves; however, the estimate of the constant c provides an efficient summary measure of the difference in survival experience between two groups. A special property of the proportional hazards model is that the estimate of the proportionality constant (c) does not require the actual form of the hazard function to be specified. That is, the comparison of the relative survival between the two groups can be analyzed without knowledge or assumptions about the functional form of the hazard functions $\lambda_A(t)$ or $\lambda_B(t)$, as long as the two are proportional.

In terms of survival curves, the property of proportionality of hazard functions translates to

$$S_B(t) = [S_A(t)]^c, \tag{11.4}$$

where $S_A(t)$ and $S_B(t)$ represent the survival curves for groups A and B. The general relationship between survival curves when the hazard functions are proportional will be dealt with in a following section [expression (11.12)].

If one survival curve is known or estimated, then the other is directly related when the hazard functions are proportional. For example, if $S_A(t_0) = 0.6$ at a specific time, then

$$\hat{S}_B(t_0) = [S_A(t_0)]^{\hat{c}} = (0.6)^{0.168} = 0.918 \tag{11.5}$$

explicitly gives the probability of survival for a member of group B in terms of the probability of survival of a member of group A. Note that $S_B(t)$ will always be greater than $S_A(t)$ since $\lambda_B(t) < \lambda_A(t)$, which is not surprising since a smaller hazard rate implies a higher probability of survival. That is, the survival curve $S_A(t)$ will always be below the survival curve $S_B(t)$ for all values of t since $\hat{c} = 0.168$.

Several methods can be used to evaluate statistically the estimate $\hat{c}$. To test the null hypothesis that the hazard functions are the same $(H_0: c = 1)$, an effective technique is to compare two likelihood statistics. The first is derived under the conditions that $\lambda_B(t) = \lambda_A(t)$ and the second under the hypothesis that $\lambda_B(t) = c\lambda_A(t)$. For the illustrative data, these two likelihoods are $L_0 = 31.997$ for $c = 1$ and $L_1 = 27.148$ for $c \neq 1$, produced as part of the maximum likelihood procedure. The difference $L_0 - L_1 = X^2 = 4.849$ has an approximate χ^2 distribution with one degree of freedom when $c = 1$, producing a p-value of 0.028.

Alternatively, a statistical test of $\hat{c}$ in terms of the $\log(\hat{c})$ is equally effective, or

$$z = \frac{\log(\hat{c})}{S_{\log(\hat{c})}} \tag{11.6}$$

and z has an approximate standard normal distribution when $c = 1$ or $\log(c) = 0$. For example, from the hypothetical data, the logarithm of $\hat{c}$ is $\log(0.168) = -1.785$ with a variance$[\log(\hat{c})] = 0.745$ (estimated as part of the maximum likelihood procedure). Therefore, $z = -1.785/\sqrt{0.745} = -2.067$, and the corresponding p-value is 0.039, again showing evidence that the survival experience is likely to differ between groups A and B.

The "Mantel–Haenszel" χ^2 test will also be similar to the difference between likelihood statistics, particularly when large sample sizes are involved (e.g., $X^2 = 5.286$ with a p-value $= 0.022$ [expression (11.1)] versus $X^2 = 4.849$ with a p-value $= 0.028$, for the hypothetical data). The fact that the likelihood and χ^2 approaches are related indicates that the proportional hazards model can be viewed as a process that stratifies the survival data on the time of death and combines information from each stratum to estimate the overall constant of proportionality relating the two hazard functions. Also similar to the "Mantel–Haenszel" χ^2 procedure, this simple proportional hazards approach is nonparametric in the sense that no need exists to specify the form of the hazard functions or survival curves to assess the relative influence of two treatments.

AML Example Data

The data introduced in Chapter 10 concerning two treatments for acute myelogenous leukemia (AML) [Ref. 4] can be analyzed using the conjecture that the hazard functions associated with treatments maintained (M) and nonmaintained (NM) are proportional. The estimated constant of proportionality is $\hat{c} = 0.398$. Therefore, $\lambda_M(t) = \hat{c}\lambda_{NM}(t) = 0.398\lambda_{NM}(t)$. The difference in likelihood statistics produces $L_{c=1} - L_{c \neq 1} = X^2 = 81.291 - 77.927 = 3.364$ with one degree of freedom and yields a p-value of 0.067. Assuming proportional hazard rates, the comparison of likelihoods produces borderline evidence of a systematic difference between these two treatments. This result is expectedly similar to the χ^2 analysis of the same data ($X^2 = 3.396$ with a p-value $= 0.065$, Table 10.18).

To explore these data further, it is assumed that the survival experience is adequately described by an exponential function for the nonmaintained group. This special case of proportional hazard functions gives

$$S_M(t) = (e^{-\lambda_{NM}t})^{0.398}, \tag{11.7}$$

where λ_{NM} is the constant hazard rate for the nonmaintained group.

Although this relationship results from a further and perhaps unrealistic assumption, it allows a simple and direct comparison of two survival experiences. For example, Figure 11.2 is based on this relationship, and the estimated parameter $\hat{\lambda}_{NM} = 1/\bar{t} = 1/23.182 = 0.043$, furthermore $\hat{\lambda}_M = 0.398(0.043) = 0.0172$. A value of λ_M estimated directly from the 11 AML observations is $1/\bar{t} = 1/60.429 = 0.0165$, which agrees closely with the estimate based on the proportional hazards model. Alternatively, the ratio of the mean survival times can be compared to the proportional hazards estimate. The exponential model produces mean survival times of 23.182 (nonmaintained) weeks and 60.429 (maintained), giving a ratio based on these estimates of 0.383. The proportional hazards ratio is, again, $\hat{c} = 0.398$; the two approaches agree, implying that the assumption of a constant hazard function for this leukemia remission data is not unreasonable.

General Case

A general expression for the proportional hazards model with k explanatory variables is written as

$$\lambda_j(t; x_{1j}, x_{2j}, \ldots, x_{kj}) = \lambda_0(t)c_j = \lambda_0(t)e^{\sum_{i=1}^{k} b_i x_{ij}}. \tag{11.8}$$

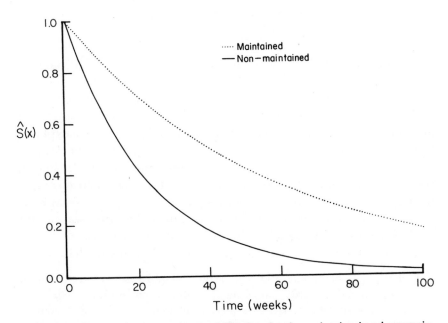

Figure 11–2. Survival curves for the AML data for the maintained and nonmaintained groups.

The value $\lambda_j(t; x_{1j}, x_{2j}, \ldots, x_{kj})$ represents the hazard rate for the jth group or person with a specific set of explanatory values at time t relative to $\lambda_0(t)$, a "baseline" hazard rate also at time t. The values x_{ij} represent a series of measures on each group or individual, and the coefficient b_i determines the influence of that measurement on the survival time. The model allows the proportionality constant c_j to be factored into a series of multiplicative components, each associated with the influence of a specific explanatory variable. The hazard rate ratio c_j can be viewed as

$$c_j = (e^{b_1 x_{1j}})(e^{b_2 x_{2j}})(e^{b_3 x_{3j}}) \cdots (e^{b_k x_{kj}}). \tag{11.9}$$

The relative contribution of each x_{ij} is measured by $(e^{b_i})^{x_{ij}}$. The value e^{b_i} is called the relative hazard for the ith explanatory variable.

A common and useful practice is to "center" the x variables so that the proportional hazards model becomes

$$\lambda_j(t; x_{1j}, x_{2j}, \ldots, x_{kj}) = \lambda_0(t) e^{\sum_{i=1}^{k} b_i(x_{ij} - \bar{x}_i)}. \tag{11.10}$$

For this form of the model, the "baseline" hazard function $\lambda_0(t)$ represents the hazard rate where all x variables are at their mean values (the "average" hazard function). Two alternative forms of the proportional hazards model are

$$\log\left(\frac{\lambda_j(t)}{\lambda_0(t)}\right) = \sum_{i=1}^{k} b_i(x_{ij} - \bar{x}_i) \quad \text{or} \quad \log[\lambda_j(t)] = \log[\lambda_0(t)] + \sum_{i=1}^{k} b_i(x_{ij} - \bar{x}_i), \tag{11.11}$$

showing more directly the way the explanatory variables (x_{ij}) relate to the ratio of hazard functions. The second part of expression (11.11) shows the proportional hazards model in a form analogous to a multivariate linear regression model with an "intercept" term that depends on follow-up time separated from a weighted sum of explanatory variables that does not depend on follow-up time. The proportional hazards model is referred to as a semi-parametric model since it contains a nonparametric component $\lambda_0(t)$ and a parametric component $\Sigma b_i(x_i - \bar{x}_i)$. The role of the explanatory (x_{ij}) variables is explored by means of estimated b_i coefficients in much the same way as the coefficients from a multivariate logistic regression analysis.

Two notable properties of the proportional hazards model are:

1. The population under study can be divided into a series of strata and the proportional hazards model used within each stratum. The most intensive stratification occurs for sets of matched cases and controls where each pair is a stratum. Nevertheless, the proportional hazards

model provides an assessment of the differences in survival for this data pattern.

2. The explanatory variables can themselves depend on time (t), and the analysis of time-dependent explanatory variables parallels the proportional hazard model under discussion (see [Ref. 1]).

The hazard function and the survival curve are related; clearly high values of the hazard function lead to low probabilities of survival, and conversely. Formally,

$$\lambda(t) = -\frac{dS(t)/dt}{S(t)} \text{ translates to } S(t) = e^{-\int_0^t \lambda(u)du}. \qquad (11.12)$$

When two hazard functions $[\lambda_j(t)$ and $\lambda_0(t)]$ are proportional such that

$$\lambda_j(t) = \lambda_0(t)e^{\Sigma b_i x_{ij}}, \qquad (11.13)$$

then

$$e^{-\int_0^t \lambda_j(u)du} = [e^{-\int_0^t \lambda_0(u)du}]^{e^{\Sigma b_i x_{ij}}}, \text{ giving } S_j(t) = [S_0(t)]^{e^{\Sigma b_i x_{ij}}}. \qquad (11.14)$$

In the special case where the survival curve is exponential [i.e., $S_0(t) = e^{-\lambda_0 t}$), then

$$S_j(t) = [e^{-\lambda_0 t}]^{e^{\Sigma b_i x_{ij}}}. \qquad (11.15)$$

Two Properties of Proportional Hazards Survival Curves

If two hazard functions are proportional, then the survival curves will not cross and will not be parallel. Consider the survival curve given by

$$S_0(t) = 1 - \frac{t}{100}, \text{ where } 0 \le t \le 100 \qquad (11.16)$$

and, as before, $\lambda_0(t) = 1/(100 - t)$; further, suppose that two groups (1 and 2) have proportional hazard functions where:

$$\lambda_1(t) = 2\lambda_0(t) \text{ and } \lambda_2(t) = 4\lambda_0(t) \text{ or } S_2(t) = [S_1(t)]^2. \qquad (11.17)$$

These two survival curves do not cross, but it is not obvious from the plots of survival curves or hazards functions that the hazard rates are proportional (Figure 11.3, top). The transformation $\log\{-\log[S(t)]\}$ is useful. For proportional hazards functions, this transformation produces survival curves that are parallel and differ because of the presence of explanatory variables. Figure 11.3 (bottom left) shows the transformed functions of $S_1(t)$ and $S_2(t)$. If the transformed values of $S_1(t)$ and $S_2(t)$ are parallel, the plot of one against the other is a single straight line (Figure 11.3, bottom right).

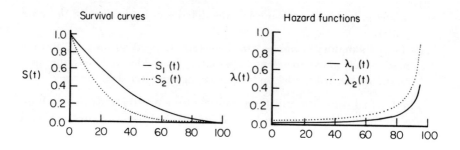

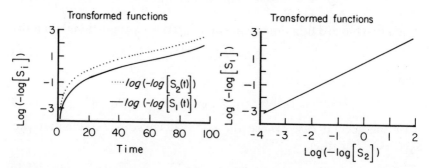

Figure 11–3. Comparisons of two hypothetical survival curves $S_1(t)$ and $S_2(t)$ based on $\lambda_0(t) = 1/(100-t)$.

The form of the proportional hazards model guarantees that the survival curves do not cross. Since

$$S_i(t; x_1, x_2, \ldots, x_k) = [S_j(t; x'_1, x'_2, \ldots, x'_k]^{e^{\Sigma b_i(x_i - x'_i)}}, \qquad (11.18)$$

then

$$e^{\Sigma b_i(x_i - x'_i)} \geqslant 1 \text{ implies } S_i(t) \leqslant S_j(t) \qquad (11.19)$$

and

$$e^{\Sigma b_i(x_i - x'_i)} \leqslant 1 \text{ implies } S_i(t) \geqslant S_j(t) \qquad (11.20)$$

for all values of t, which mathematically requires that the two survival curves do not intersect. The fact that the survival curves do not cross and a simplifying transformation exists, two properties of the proportional hazards structure which are important in the difficult task of deciding if a data set is meaningfully represented by a proportional hazards model. Clearly, a plot of the survival curves and the "log-log" transformation of the survival curves is a good place to start the goodness-of-fit evaluation of a proportional hazards model.

Proportional Hazards Model: Application I

Illustration: Lung Cancer Data

Preliminary observations from a clinical trial [Ref. 5] provide a set of lung cancer survival times as well as the ages of the patient (explanatory variable). The data are divided into two groups based on the patient's measured vital capacity. One group has 95 patients with "high" vital capacity ratios and the other 36 patients with "low" vital capacity ratios. The vital capacity group, survival time (in days) and patient's age are given in Tables 11.3 and 11.4.

Figure 11.4 (top) shows the product-limit estimates of the survival

Table 11-3. Lung cancer data: "High" vital capacity

Time	Age	Time	Age	Time	Age	Time	Age
0	74	1	74	1	63	3	78
4	66	5	40	9	65	19	51
21	73	30	62	36	68	39	50
40	56	48	64	51	72	61	58
89	64	90	41	90	69	92	76
113	73	127	64	131	51	138	75
139	56	143	50	159	60	168	74
170	71	180	69	189	56	192	68
201	64	212	58	223	70	229	76
238	63	265	65	275	63	292	55
317	65	322	55	350	54	357	73
380	51						

Time	Age	Time	Age	Time	Age	Time	Age
62	66	75	44	77	60	81	38
83	59	83	42	84	67	86	62
88	53	92	59	98	55	104	62
116	62	129	35	131	43	162	45
167	56	173	54	178	63	179	69
184	69	184	67	194	58	256	57
263	46	269	63	338	47	344	52
347	59	349	61	350	66	362	56
362	60	364	63	364	58	364	58
365	66	368	70	368	39	372	58
388	59	388	68	400	64	524	59
528	63	545	63	546	55	552	52
555	57	558	63				

Note: The first 45 survival times are complete (died within the study period) and the following 50 are censored.

Table 11-4. Lung cancer data: "Low" vital capacity

Time	Age	Time	Age	Time	Age	Time	Age
0	55	2	75	2	73	2	65
6	61	17	74	22	51	23	66
54	67	56	51	61	36	63	54
64	54	69	70	146	53	155	47
161	46	233	41	248	61	283	53

Time	Age	Time	Age	Time	Age	Time	Age
47	56	73	55	86	48	89	65
91	58	169	58	172	62	177	53
183	48	188	52	194	67	266	53
266	53	267	52	351	71	372	71

Note:: The first 20 survival times are complete (died within the study period) and the following 16 are censored.

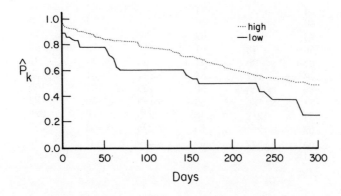

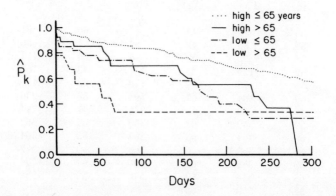

Figure 11-4. Product-limit estimates of the survival curves for two groups of lung cancer patients by vital capacity and by age.

curves associated with these two comparison groups. The "high" vital capacity group apparently has better survival experience. Figure 11.4 (bottom) shows a definite influence of age on the pattern of survival times for these patients. The two vital capacity groups subdivided by age into those less than or equal to 65 years old and those greater than 65 produce at least three distinct survival patterns. A summary of mean survival times additionally indicates that age influences survival, as can be seen in Table 11.5.

Two expected problems arise when survival data are classified into subgroups. The choice of the bounds for the categories adds an arbitrary element to the analysis that can influence final interpretations. More important, the number of observations in some categories can become small (e.g., "low", age > 65 contains only nine individuals). This reduction in sample size leads to increased variation and more difficult interpretation. The lack of clarity in Figure 11.4 comes, to a large extent, from increased variation associated with the estimated age-group-specific survival curves.

The mean ages of patients in the two groups differ ("high" = 57.63 years and "low" = 60.13 years) and age is undoubtedly related to survival, implying adjustment (via a proportional hazards model) will isolate differences between the two compared groups attributable to influences other than age. The assumption of proportional hazards allows adjustment for the influence of age and provides a systematic evaluation of "high" and "low" capacity groups while avoiding some the problems incurred by stratifying the data into several age categories. Additionally, large gains in efficiency are achieved since the entire data set, all 131 observations, is focused on the estimation of two parameters.

Application of a proportional hazards model to these lung cancer data requires making the influence of age and group membership components of the model, thus producing the potential to separate and measure each variable's influence on the observed differences in

Table 11-5. Summary: Lung cancer mean survival time

	Total	Censored	Mean	Std. error
"High," age ⩽ 65	68	41	229.5	19.3
"High," age > 65	27	9	156.7	23.8
"Low," age ⩽ 65	27	13	132.4	17.4
"Low," age > 65	9	3	120.4	46.9
Total	131	66	187.0	12.7

survival times. That is, the ratio of hazard functions is factored into a piece measuring the influence of age and a piece measuring the influence of vital capacity on survival. Such a proportional hazards model is

$$\lambda_j(t; x_{1j}, x_{2j}) = \lambda_0(t)c_j = \lambda_0(t)e^{b_1 x_{1j} + b_2(x_{2j} - \bar{x}_2)} = \lambda_0(t)(e^{b_1 x_{1j}})(e^{b_2(x_{2j} - \bar{x}_2)}),$$

(11.21)

where x_{1j} is a binary variable indicating "high" ($x_{1j} = 0$) or "low" ($x_{1j} = 1$) vital capacity groups and x_{2j} is the age of the patient. Maximum likelihood estimates and likelihood statistics associated with this model are given in Tables 11.6, 11.7, and 11.8.

Contrasting the full model (age and group included) with the model with age excluded (reduced model) shows some confounding bias. The coefficient associated with the group membership (b_1) changes from 0.637 to 0.540 when age is excluded from the model or in terms of the relative hazard the change is 1.891 to 1.716. Also, the statistical evaluation of the model excluding age shows that age has a strong influence on the observed differences in survival time. The likelihood difference $L_{b_2=0} - L_{b_2 \neq 0} = X^2 = 546.976 - 540.552 = 6.424$ has an approximate χ^2 distribution when age is not related to survival

Table 11–6. Lung cancer data: age and group included

	Term	Coefficient	Std. error	p-value	Hazard ratio
Group	$\hat{b}_1$	0.637	0.275	0.020	1.891
Age	$\hat{b}_2$	0.038	0.015	0.013	1.039

-2LogLikelihood = 540.552; number of model of parameters = 2

Table 11–7. Age excluded

	Term	Coefficient	Std. error	p-value	Hazard ratio
Group	$\hat{b}_1$	0.540	0.274	0.049	1.716

-2LogLikelihood = 546.976; number of model of parameters = 1

Table 11–8. Group excluded

	Term	Coefficient	Std. error	p-value	Hazard ratio
Age	$\hat{b}_2$	0.034	0.016	0.027	1.035

-2LogLikelihood = 545.486; number of model of parameters = 1

$(b_2 = 0)$ with degrees of freedom equal to one (the difference in the number of parameters needed to specify the two models) and yields a p-value of 0.011. Both the extent of the confounding bias and the significant χ^2 value indicate, not surprisingly, that age plays an important role in the survival of these patients and should be included in the model. The influence of the "high" versus "low" vital capacity can be similarly assessed. The comparison of the likelihoods (full versus reduced models) produces a statistical evaluation of the influence of vital capacity classification (likelihood difference $L_{b_1=0} - L_{b_1 \neq 0} = X^2 = 545.486 - 540.552 = 4.934$). This difference also has a χ^2 distribution with one degree of freedom when vital capacity is unrelated to survival (i.e., $b_1 = 0$) yielding a p-value of 0.026. Like age, the classification of individuals by vital capacity is associated with survival. The increase in the likelihood, furthermore, cannot be attributed to influences of age since a measure of the age effect is maintained in both the full and reduced models (x_{2j} is included in both models).

An alternative technique to evaluate the coefficients from the proportional hazards model is the usual calculation of an approximate standard normal value,

$$z_i = \frac{\hat{b}_i}{S_{\hat{b}_i}}, \tag{11.22}$$

which has mean $= 0.0$ and variance $= 1.0$ when the ith variable is unrelated to survival (i.e., $b_i = 0$). Age ($z_2 = 2.533$ giving a p-value $= 0.011$) and group membership ($z_1 = 2.316$ giving a p-value $= 0.021$) show the expected agreement with the likelihood approach.

Confidence intervals for the coefficients estimated from the proportional hazards model are constructed in the usual way (e.g., $\hat{b}_i \pm 1.96 S_{\hat{b}_i}$ for an approximate 95% confidence interval) and confidence intervals for the relative hazard is then ($e^{\hat{b}_{lower}}, e^{\hat{b}_{upper}}$). For example, the 95% confidence interval based on the age coefficient $\hat{b}_2 = 0.038$ is $\hat{b}_{lower} = 0.038 - 1.96(0.015) = 0.009$ and $\hat{b}_{upper} = 0.038 + 1.96(0.015) = 0.067$ and the corresponding confidence interval based on the relative hazard of $e^{\hat{b}_2} = 1.039$ is $(1.009, 1.070)$. The analogous confidence interval for the relative hazard associated with the vital capacity variable is $(1.103, 3.241)$.

This analysis implies that an appropriate proportional hazards model to represent the lung cancer data is

$$\lambda_j(t; x_{1j}, x_{2j}) = \lambda_0(t) e^{0.637 x_{1j} + 0.038(x_{2j} - 59.45)}, \tag{11.23}$$

where the mean age for all 131 patients is $\bar{x}_2 = 59.45$ years.

To explore further the survival curves associated with these data, assume that the "high" vital capacity group (Table 11.3) provides an adequate estimate of $S_0(t)$. The product-limit estimated survival curve $\hat{S}_0(t)$ given in Table 11.9 is also depicted in Figure 11.5.

"High" and "low" vital capacity groups (for the moment disregarding age) are compared by

$$\text{high capacity: } \hat{S}_0(t) \text{ versus low capacity: } [\hat{S}_0(t)]^{1.716} \qquad (11.24)$$

and plotted in Figure 11.6 (top). To show the influence of age, age 55 ($x_2 = 55$) and age 75 ($x_2 = 75$) are chosen to illustrate; the survival curves compared are

$$\text{high capacity: } [\hat{S}_0(t)]^{e^{0.038(x_2 - \bar{x}_2)}} \text{ versus low capacity: } [\hat{S}_0(t)]^{e^{0.637 + 0.038(x_2 - \bar{x}_2)}}.$$

$$(11.25)$$

This comparison is also shown in Figure 11.6 (bottom). A model representing the relationship of age and group membership to survival time uses the data with great efficiency and produces a clear and easily interpreted picture (Figure 11.4 contrasted with Figure 11.6). The price is, as usual, the insecurity that the model does not adequately represent the underlying data.

Table 11–9. Lung cancer data $-\hat{S}_0(t)$

Obs	Days	$\hat{S}_0(t)$	Obs	Days	$\hat{S}_0(t)$
1	1	0.968	23	139	0.720
2	3	0.958	24	143	0.707
3	4	0.947	25	159	0.694
4	5	0.937	26	168	0.680
5	9	0.926	27	170	0.666
6	19	0.916	28	180	0.652
7	21	0.905	29	189	0.637
8	30	0.895	30	192	0.622
9	36	0.884	31	201	0.606
10	39	0.874	32	212	0.590
11	40	0.863	33	223	0.575
12	48	0.853	34	229	0.559
13	51	0.842	35	238	0.544
14	61	0.832	36	265	0.527
15	89	0.820	37	275	0.510
16	90	0.808	38	292	0.493
17	90	0.796	39	317	0.476
18	92	0.784	40	322	0.459
19	113	0.771	41	350	0.439
20	127	0.759	42	357	0.418
21	131	0.746	43	380	0.380
22	138	0.733	—	—	—

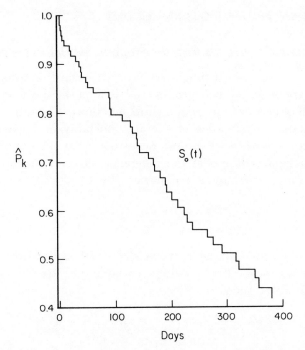

Figure 11-5. Product-limit estimates of the survival curve for lung cancer patients with "high" vital capacity, $\hat{S}_o(t)$.

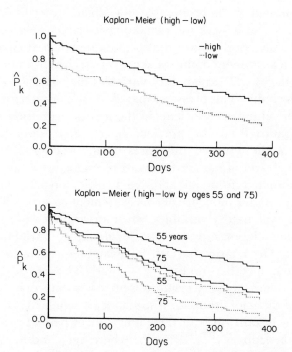

Figure 11-6. Estimates of the survival curves for two groups of lung cancer patients by vital capacity and by age based on a proportional hazards model.

Ratios of Hazard Functions from the Proportional Hazards Model

The ratio of two hazard functions (relative hazard) summarizes the survival experience of two groups and is a particularly meaningful description of two proportional hazard functions. The ratio of hazard rates is analogous to ratios of average mortality or incidence rates except that these rates are instantaneous measures of survival. For the proportional hazards model the difference in survival between two individuals or two groups is summarized by

$$\frac{\lambda_1(t; x_1, x_2, \ldots, x_k)}{\lambda_2(t; x'_1, x'_2, \ldots, x'_k)} = e^{\Sigma b_i(x_i - x'_i)} \qquad (11.26)$$

where x_i and x'_i represent different levels of the ith explanatory variable.

When two groups differ by a single variable (i.e., are identical for all but one variable), then

$$\frac{\lambda_1(t; x_1, x_2 = x'_2, x_3 = x'_3, \ldots, x_k = x'_k)}{\lambda_2(t; x'_1, x'_2, x'_3, \ldots, x'_k)}$$

$$= e^{b_1(x_1 - x'_1)} e^{b_2(x'_2 - x'_2)} \cdots e^{b_k(x'_k - x'_k)} = e^{b_1(x_1 - x'_1)} \qquad (11.27)$$

allowing survival to be compared for different levels of a single explanatory variable with the remaining variables held constant. In other words, the relative hazard associated with a particular variable represents an assessment of the influence on survival from that variable while the other $k - 1$ explanatory variables have equal values in the groups or the individuals being compared. A similar interpretation was made for the adjusted coefficients in the logistic regression model.

Hazard ratios from the previous lung cancer data provide an evaluation of the adjusted influences of age and vital capacity on survival. The ratio of hazard functions is analogous to an odds ratio measure estimated from an additive logistic model. The value e^b indicates the relative influence of a measurement on survival independent of other explanatory variables, when an additive model is used to represent the relationships between explanatory variables and the hazard rate. The relative hazard, for example, associated with vital capacity group membership is $e^{0.637} = 1.891$. That is, the hazard rate in the "low" vital capacity group is a little less than twice that of the "high" vital capacity group for a specific age. Similarly, the influence of age on the hazard rates for these lung cancer patients, regardless of group membership, is $e^{0.038(\text{age}_2 - \text{age}_1)}$ where age_1 and age_2 are compared. For example, if $\text{age}_1 = 55$ and $\text{age}_2 = 75$, then the relative hazard is $e^{0.038(20)} = 2.138$. Or, the lung cancer patients age 75 are at about twice the risk (measured by a hazard rate) as patients age 55 within each vital capacity group.

The additive nature of this proportional hazards model implies that group membership and age do not interact. Therefore, a 55-year-old member of the "high" vital capacity group compared to a 75-year-old person with "low" vital capacity yields a hazard ratio of $e^{0.637 + 0.038(20)} = 1.891(2.138) = 4.043$, illustrating a specific partitioning of the overall hazard ratio (4.043) into relative components (vital capacity group status = 1.891 and age = 2.138).

Proportional Hazards Model: Application II

Illustration: Histology-Specific Lung Cancer Data

A series of 137 patients with advanced lung cancer categorized by cancer histology [Ref. 6] provides an opportunity to apply a proportional hazards model that requires distinct categories be specified. The data consist of individual survival times (days) classified by one of four lung cancer histology categories (squamous cell, small cell, adenocarcinoma, and large cell) and by a new or standard treatment ($x_{1j} = 0$ for the standard treatment and $x_{1j} = 1$ for the new treatment). Three other explanatory variables are also recorded for each patient: a general medical status index (x_{2j}), months from diagnosis to the start of the study (x_{3j}), and age (x_{4j}). These data are given in Tables 11.10 and 11.11.

The rigorous determination of whether or not a proportional hazards model is an accurate representation of the data is not presented. Statistical tests to assess the assumption of proportionality are part of several "package" computer programs (see [Ref. 7], for example) and plotting the data can help indicate the adequacy or inadequacy of a statistical model. The relationship among survival curves, as mentioned, is the key to exploring the "fit" of the proportional hazards model.

To begin to understand the role of the explanatory variables in influencing differences in survival times among patients, a proportional hazards model is proposed that includes all five explanatory variables. The model is not fundamentally different from the one described in the previous case [expression (11.23)] except that a series of dummy variables is used to indicate histologic categories. That is, three binary variables (z_1, z_2, and z_3) are used to identify four histologic groups: $z_1 = 1$ if the cancer type is small cell with $z_2 = z_3 = 0$; $z_2 = 1$ if the

Table 11-10. Lung cancer survival by type: New treatment

	Squamous cell				Small cell				Adenocarcinoma				Large cell		
Time	x_{2j}	x_{3j}	x_{4j}	Time	x_{2j}	x_{3j}	x_{4j}	Time	x_{2j}	x_{3j}	x_{4j}	Time	x_{2j}	x_{3j}	x_{4j}
999	90	12	54	25	30	2	69	24	40	2	60	52	60	4	45
122	80	6	60	103+	70	22	36	18	40	5	69	164	70	15	68
87+	80	3	48	21	20	4	71	83+	99	3	57	19	30	4	39
231+	50	8	52	13	30	2	62	31	80	3	39	53	60	12	66
242	50	1	70	87	60	2	60	51	60	5	62	15	30	5	63
991	70	7	50	2	40	36	44	90	60	22	50	43	60	11	49
111	70	3	62	20	30	9	54	52	60	3	43	340	80	10	64
1	20	21	65	7	20	11	66	73	50	3	70	133	75	1	65
587	60	3	58	24	60	8	49	8	70	5	66	111	60	5	64
389	90	2	62	99	70	3	72	36	10	8	61	231	70	18	67
33	30	6	64	8	80	2	68	48	40	4	81	378	80	4	65
25	20	36	63	99	85	4	62	7	70	4	58	49	30	3	37
357	70	13	58	61	70	2	71	140	90	3	63	—	—	—	—
467	90	2	64	95	70	1	61	186	80	3	60	—	—	—	—
201	80	28	52	80	50	17	71	84	50	4	62	—	—	—	—
1	50	7	35	51	30	87	59	19	40	10	42	—	—	—	—
30	70	11	63	29	40	8	67	45	40	3	69	—	—	—	—
44	60	13	70	25	70	2	6	80	—	4	63	—	—	—	—
283	90	2	51	—	—	—	—	—	—	—	—	—	—	—	—
15	50	13	40	—	—	—	—	—	—	—	—	—	—	—	—

Table 11-11. Lung cancer survival by type: Standard treatment

Squamous cell				Small cell				Adenocarcinoma				Large cell			
Time	x_{2j}	x_{3j}	x_{4j}	Time	x_{2j}	x_{3j}	x_{4j}	Time	x_{2j}	x_{3j}	x_{4j}	Time	x_{2j}	x_{3j}	x_{4j}
72	60	7	69	30	60	3	61	8	20	19	61	177	50	16	66
411	60	5	64	384	60	9	42	92	70	10	60	162	80	5	62
228	60	3	38	4	40	2	35	35	40	6	62	216	50	15	52
126	60	9	63	54	80	4	63	117	80	2	38	553	70	2	47
118	70	11	65	13	60	4	56	132	80	5	50	278	60	12	63
10	20	5	49	123+	40	3	55	12	50	4	63	12	40	12	68
82	40	10	69	97+	60	5	67	162	80	5	64	260	80	5	45
110	80	29	68	153	60	14	63	3	30	3	43	200	80	12	41
314	50	18	43	59	30	2	65	95	80	4	34	156	70	2	60
100+	70	6	70	117	80	3	46	—	—	—	—	182+	90	2	62
42	60	4	81	16	30	4	53	—	—	—	—	143	90	8	60
8	40	58	63	151	50	12	69	—	—	—	—	105	80	11	66
144	30	4	63	22	60	4	68	—	—	—	—	103	80	5	38
25+	80	9	52	56	80	12	43	—	—	—	—	250	70	8	53
11	70	11	48	21	40	2	55	—	—	—	—	100	60	13	37
—	—	—	—	18	20	15	42	—	—	—	—	—	—	—	—
—	—	—	—	139	80	2	64	—	—	—	—	—	—	—	—
—	—	—	—	20	30	5	65	—	—	—	—	—	—	—	—
—	—	—	—	31	75	3	65	—	—	—	—	—	—	—	—
—	—	—	—	52	70	2	55	—	—	—	—	—	—	—	—
—	—	—	—	287	60	25	66	—	—	—	—	—	—	—	—
—	—	—	—	18	30	4	60	—	—	—	—	—	—	—	—
—	—	—	—	51	60	1	67	—	—	—	—	—	—	—	—
—	—	—	—	122	80	28	53	—	—	—	—	—	—	—	—
—	—	—	—	27	60	8	62	—	—	—	—	—	—	—	—
—	—	—	—	54	70	1	67	—	—	—	—	—	—	—	—
—	—	—	—	7	50	7	72	—	—	—	—	—	—	—	—
—	—	—	—	63	50	11	48	—	—	—	—	—	—	—	—
—	—	—	—	392	40	4	68	—	—	—	—	—	—	—	—
—	—	—	—	10	40	23	67	—	—	—	—	—	—	—	—

cancer type is adenocarcinoma with $z_1 = z_3 = 0$; and $z_3 = 1$ if the cancer type is large cell, with $z_1 = z_2 = 0$; and squamous cell carcinoma is established as the baseline for comparison by $z_1 = z_2 = z_3 = 0$. An additive proportional hazards model incorporating the five explanatory variables is

$$\lambda_j(t) = \lambda_0(t) e^{c_1 z_{1j} + c_2 z_{2j} + c_3 z_{3j} + b_1 x_{1j} + b_2(x_{2j} - \bar{x}_2) + b_3(x_{3j} - \bar{x}_3) + b_4(x_{4j} - \bar{x}_4)}. \qquad (11.28)$$

The lung cancer data analyzed using three sets of conditions produces the maximum likelihood estimates of the model parameters given in Tables 11.12, 11.13, and 11.14.

Table 11–12. Histology-specific lung cancer data: full model

	Term	Coefficient	Std. error	p-value	Hazard ratio
Indicator 1	c_1	0.884	0.268	<0.001	2.421
Indicator 2	c_2	1.170	0.296	<0.001	3.223
Indicator 3	c_3	0.372	0.280	0.184	1.450
Treatment	$\hat{b}_1$	0.385	0.205	0.061	1.470
Status	$\hat{b}_2$	−0.033	0.006	<0.001	0.968
Months	$\hat{b}_3$	0.001	0.008	0.913	1.001
Age	$\hat{b}_4$	−0.012	0.009	0.188	0.988

−2LogLikelihood = 916.335; number of model of parameters = 7

Table 11–13. Age and months excluded

	Term	Coefficient	Std. error	p-value	Hazard ratio
Indicator 1	c_1	0.848	0.264	<0.001	2.334
Indicator 2	c_2	1.134	0.293	<0.001	3.109
Indicator 3	c_3	0.361	0.279	0.195	1.435
Treatment	$\hat{b}_1$	0.334	0.199	0.094	1.400
Status	$\hat{b}_2$	−0.031	0.005	<0.001	0.970

−2LogLikelihood = 918.101; number of model of parameters = 5

Table 11–14. Age, months and histologies excluded

	Term	Coefficient	Std. error	p-value	Hazard ratio
Treatment	$\hat{b}_1$	0.239	0.182	0.190	1.270
Status	$\hat{b}_2$	−0.033	0.005	<0.001	0.967

−2LogLikelihood = 936.722; number of model of parameters = 2

The comparison of the full model to the model with the months from diagnosis (x_3) and age (x_4) variables removed (reduced model) shows that these two variables add little to the understanding of the survival times of the lung cancer patients. Comparison of the respective likelihoods (likelihood difference $= X^2 = 918.101 - 916.335 = 1.766$ with degrees of freedom $= 2$ gives a p-value $= 0.414$) yields no statistical evidence that these two explanatory variables are useful in the study of the survival of these patients. Also, only slight confounding of the influences of treatment status and histology appears associated with age and month measurements. The medical status index (x_1) is, however, worth including in any model $(z = -5.952$ with a p-value $< 0.001)$. The same is true of the variables that separate the data into histologic types. The model excluding histologic type $(c_1 = c_2 = c_3 = 0)$ substantially increases the likelihood over the three-variable model (Table 11.13), producing a likelihood difference $= X^2 = 936.722 - 918.101 = 18.621$ with three degrees of freedom yielding a p-value less than 0.001. Also, histologic type is a confounder of the treatment effect $(\hat{b}_1 = 0.334$ when histology is included and this parameter changes to $\hat{b}_1 = 0.239$ when histology is excluded). Last, the treatment variable coefficient $(b_1 = 0.334)$ indicates that treatment status is marginally important in explaining the differences in survival times between these two groups of patients. The value $z = 0.334/0.199 = 1.678$ produces a p-value of 0.094 when the medical status index and the histologic types are maintained in the model.

To explore these data further, assume that the hazard rates are at least approximately constant over the range of the follow-up period. This additional assumption yields the model

$$S_j(t) = (e^{-\lambda_0 t})e^{0.848z_{1j}+1.134z_{2j}+0.361z_{3j}+0.334x_{1j}-0.031(x_{2j}-\bar{x}_2)} \qquad (11.29)$$

as a representation of the lung cancer survival curves for specified histologies, medical status, and treatment. Under the constant hazard assumption, the expression for the proportional hazards model can be manipulated to produce adjusted estimated mean survival times for different conditions as

$$\bar{T}_k = \bar{T}_0 e^{-\Sigma b_i x_{ik}}. \qquad (11.30)$$

The value $\bar{T}_k$ is the estimated mean survival time for group k relative to an arbitrary value $\bar{T}_0$. One choice for the value $\bar{T}_0$ is the mean survival time associated with a "baseline" category. Setting T_0 to 138.57 days (the average survival time for patients with squamous cell carcinoma receiving the standard treatment with average level of

Table 11–15. Lung cancer mean survival times—no treatment and medical status influence

	Squamous	Small	Adeno	Large
Standard	138.57	52.58	46.08	118.08
New	138.57	52.58	46.08	118.08

Model: $\bar{T}_k = \bar{T}_0 e^{-(0.969z_{1k} + 1.101z_{2k} + 0.160z_{3k})}$

medical status) yields a series of estimated values for $\bar{T}_k$ under the various conditions allowed by the model. Some examples are given in Tables 11.15, 11.16, and 11.17.

A comparison of these tables and the values within each table describes the relative influence of the explanatory and treatment variables on mean survival time. These tables represent an application of the estimated relative hazard ratios applied to a baseline value (138.57 days) under the assumption that the hazard rates are at least approximately constant and illustrate one of many ways a statistical model provides a description of the issues under study.

Proportional Hazards Model: Application III

Illustration: Leukemia Survival

Data [Ref. 8] collected to investigate the relationship between survival of acute myelogenous leukemia patients, white blood cell (WBC) counts and a white cell morphologic characteristic can be explored using a proportional hazards model. The morphologic characteristic is the presence or absence of Auer rods, termed AG positive and AG negative. The survival times in weeks and the white blood cell count for AG-positive and AG-negative patients are given in Table 11.18.

These survival times are complete (no censoring; all patients died), producing 17 AG-positive and 16 AG-negative observations. A simple

Table 11–16. Lung Cancer mean survival times—treatment effect but no medical status influence

	Squamous	Small	Adeno	Large
Standard	138.57	46.68	44.85	108.69
New	177.04	59.64	57.30	138.85

Model: $\bar{T}_k = \bar{T}_0 e^{-(1.088z_{1k} + 1.128z_{2k} + 0.243z_{3k} + 0.245x_{1k})}$

Table 11-17. Lung Cancer mean survival times—both treatment and medical status influence

	Squamous	Small	Adeno	Large
Standard	130.92	52.97	43.46	137.95
New	225.96	66.48	58.63	135.93

Model: $\bar{T}_k = \bar{T}_0 e^{-(0.848z_{1k} + 1.134z_{2k} + 0.361z_{3k} + 0.334x_{1k} - 0.031(x_{2k} - x_2))}$

Note: x_{2k} is set equal to the mean score for the kth group medical status group ($\bar{x}_{2k}$).

correlation coefficient shows that the WBC count is related to survival (correlation $= -0.33$). This correlation and the generally recognized fact that WBC count is associated with the length of leukemia survival imply that the WBC count should be included in the description of the relationship between AG status and survival time. A proportional hazards model is one way to describe the influence of AG status on survival while accounting for the influence of WBC level. The full model relating WBC count and AG status to survival time (including the possibility of an interaction) is

$$\lambda_{AG}(t; x_1, x_2) = \lambda_0(t)e^{b_1x_1 + b_2x_2 + b_3x_1x_2}, \qquad (11.31)$$

Table 11-18. Survival times and white blood cell counts

	AG-positive			AG-negative	
	Weeks	WBC		Weeks	WBC
1	65	2300	1	65	3000
2	156	750	2	17	4000
3	100	4300	3	7	1500
4	134	2600	4	16	9000
5	16	6000	5	22	5300
6	108	10500	6	3	10000
7	121	10000	7	4	19000
8	4	17000	8	2	27000
9	39	5400	9	3	28000
10	143	7000	10	8	31000
11	56	9400	11	4	26000
12	26	32000	12	3	21000
13	22	35000	13	30	79000
14	1	100000	14	4	100000
15	1	100000	15	43	100000
16	5	52000	16	56	4400
17	65	100000			

and it follows that the relationship between the AG-positive and AG-negative survival curves is

$$S_{AG^-}(t; x_1, x_2) = \{S_{AG^+}(t; x_1', x_2')\}^{e^{b_1(x_1 - x_1') + b_2(x_2 - x_2') + b_3(x_1 x_2 - x_1' x_2')}}, \qquad (11.32)$$

where x_1 is an indicator (0. 1) of AG status and x_2 is the WBC count. The estimated parameters for this model under two conditions are given in Tables 11.19 and 11.20.

The relationship between WBC count and survival pattern is not the same for the AG-positive and the AG-negative groups, which means that the coefficients $\hat{b}_1$ and $\hat{b}_2$ do not exclusively characterize the roles of the two explanatory variables, AG status and WBC count. The test of the interaction coefficient (b_3) and the comparison of likelihoods (likelihood difference = $X^2 = 140.663 - 136.731 = 3.932$, degrees of freedom = 1) produce small p-values (both are 0.047), indicating a different relationship between WBC count and survival for the two types of AG status. The additive model (Table 11.20), therefore, is not useful in assessing the impact of the two explanatory variables. The presence of interaction, as usual, limits the amount of possible summarization. For these data, survival curves for a series of white blood cell counts (2500, 20,000, 50,000, and 100,000) are estimated separately (one set for AG positive and one set for AG negative) under the more restrictive condition that the hazard rates are constant. The curves plotted in Figure 11.7 for both AG^+ and AG^- are based on the

Table 11–19. Leukemia and WBC count: full model

	Term	Coefficient	Std. error	p-value	Hazard ratio
AG-status	$\hat{b}_1$	1.816	0.583	0.002	6.144
WBC	$\hat{b}_2$	0.0000415	0.000017	0.015	1.000
WBC.AG-status	$\hat{b}_3$	-0.0000209	0.0000105	0.047	1.000

-2LogLikelihood $= 136.731$; number of model of parameters $= 3$

Table 11–20. Interaction excluded

	Term	Coefficient	Std. error	p-value	Hazard ratio
AG-status	$\hat{b}_1$	1.115	0.445	0.012	3.049
WBC	$\hat{b}_2$	0.0000082	0.0000053	0.121	1.001

-2LogLikelihood $= 140.663$; number of model of parameters $= 2$

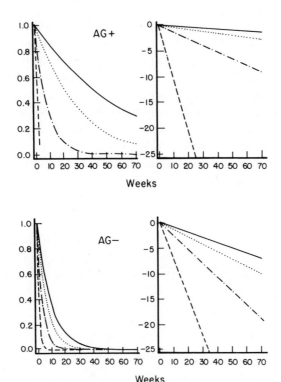

Figure 11-7. Survival curves and the logarithm of the survival curves based on the proportional hazards model for *AG*⁺ and *AG*⁻ leukemia patients.

exponential survival curve $\hat{S}_{AG^+}(t) = e^{-\hat{\lambda}t}$, where $\hat{\lambda}$ is estimated from the weeks of survival given for the AG-positive patients (the logarithms of these survival curves are also given). The lack of similarity between these curves (interaction) for the two cell characteristics is clear. Survival in the AG-positive group depends more critically on white blood cell count than the AG-negative group. That is, for a specific WBC count, the survival curve for the AG-positive patients is generally above the comparable AG-negative curve. Combining the data from the two cell types would produce an average effect, obscuring the fact that survival and white blood cell counts behave differently depending on AG status.

Dependency on Follow-up Time

A proportional hazards model does not require the relationship between follow-up time and survival to be specified in detail. The estimated relative hazard measures survival adjusted for any influences of follow-up time as long as the hazard functions are proportional. It is instructive to illustrate the situation where dependency exists between follow-up time and a survival measure that confounds the evaluation of the influence of the "treatment" variable. Two perspectives provide a brief discussion. A model showing the dependency of the odds ratio on follow-up time is presented, followed by a comparison of the logistic regression (no consideration of follow-up time) to the proportional hazard regression (accounting for the possible dependency on follow-up time) using the WCGS data.

Odds Ratio Model

A model to explore the dependency of the odds ratio on time of follow-up must describe the survival experiences for two groups of individuals. Consider two groups with exponential survival with constant hazard rates given by λ_1 and λ_2 ($\lambda_1 < \lambda_2$). The survival curves associated with these two groups are

$$S_1(t) = e^{-\lambda_1 t} \text{ and } S_2(t) = e^{-\lambda_2 t}. \tag{11.33}$$

The odds ratio measuring the relative differences in survival for these two groups at a specific follow-up time t is

$$or(t) = \frac{S_1(t)/[1 - S_1(t)]}{S_2(t)/[1 - S_2(t)]} = \frac{S_1(t)[1 - S_2(t)]}{S_2(t)[1 - S_1(t)]}. \tag{11.34}$$

To illustrate, Figure 11.8 shows $or(t)$ for $\lambda_1 = 0.1, 0.01$, and 0.001 with $\lambda_2/\lambda_1 = 3$ (note the extremely different scales on the vertical axes in Figure 11.8).

As follow-up time increases, the odds ratio increases. This increase is large (very large) for a hazard rate of about 0.1 (top of Figure 11.8). The structure of the odds ratio is such that it is forced to become large and difficult to interpret as follow-up time increases. However, for small and more typical hazard rates (in the neighborhood of 0.001), follow-up time has less impact on the odds ratio (bottom of Figure 11.8). For hazard rates in the range normally experienced by human populations, the odds ratio increases over time in an essentially linear manner with a slope proportional to the difference between the two hazard rates. That is,

$$or(t) \approx \frac{\lambda_2}{\lambda_1} [1 + 0.5t(\lambda_2 - \lambda_1)] \tag{11.35}$$

for $\lambda_i < 0.005$. The relationship between the odds ratio and follow-up time for the case of constant hazard rates is relatively simple. More

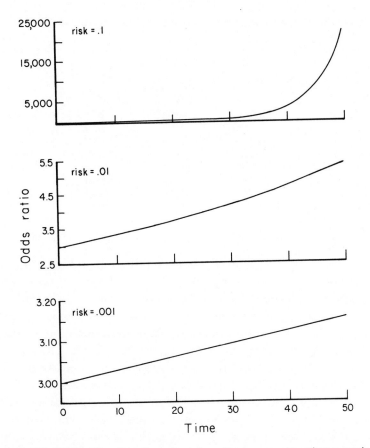

Figure 11–8. Odds ratio plotted against time for two groups that experience exponential survival ($\lambda_2/\lambda_1 = 3$).

complicated cases are easily envisioned. Postulating constant hazard rates, however, shows how the magnitude of an odds ratio depends on follow-up time. The intensity of the association between group membership and disease outcome is a function of time (t) as well as hazard rates (λ_1, λ_2), which complicates the interpretation of the odds ratio calculated as a measure of mortality risk, even in this simple case. In other words, risk measured by an odds ratio is confounded by follow-up time for exponentially distributed survival times as long as $\lambda_1 \neq \lambda_2$.

WCGS Data

The WCGS produced a prospective cohort data set that includes the time from admission to the study to the time of a coronary event or withdrawal—follow-up times for 3154 individuals. Of the participants,

Table 11-21. A comparison of the proportional hazards model and the logistic model (WCGS data)

Factor	"Cox" model $\hat{b}_i$	Std. error	Logistic model $\hat{b}_i$	Std. error
Age	0.063	0.011	0.065	0.012
Height	0.015	0.031	0.016	0.033
Weight	0.007	0.004	0.008	0.004
Systolic bp	0.014	0.006	0.018	0.006
Diastolic bp	0.008	0.010	-0.002	0.010
Cholesterol	0.009	0.001	0.011	0.002
Smoking	0.021	0.004	0.021	0.004
A/B	0.671	0.137	0.653	0.145

257 coronary events occurred, and the remaining 92% of the sample was either lost to follow-up (16%) or withdrawn from follow-up disease-free (censored) when the study ended. The proportional hazards model applied to these data shows the influence of eight risk factors on the rate of coronary events while accounting for confounding influences of time over the follow-up period. Table 11.21 gives the coefficients for the proportional hazards model compared to those produced by the multiple logistic model (Table 8.12).

The two analyses hardly differ. The multiple logistic model estimates are derived from data pooled or averaged over time, whereas the proportional hazards model takes time into account. That is, a logistic analysis does not utilize information on time of survival (follow-up); a response that occurs early in a study is given the same weight as a later response. If follow-up time is related to outcome and to the other explanatory factors, adjusting for its confounding influence is necessary. The proportional hazards model will differ from the logistic model depending on the extent to which time is a confounder. Additionally, the follow-up period must be long enough that survival times are known for a substantial proportion of the sample before a logistic and proportional hazard regression will appreciably differ. If a variable does not differ among the individuals studied, it is impossible to assess it as a factor.

Time does not significantly influence the WCGS data for a least two reasons. Coronary events occurred only among a small proportion (8%) of the study subjects (92% of the subjects "survived"), producing little information on the association of follow-up time and disease outcome. Also, the eight risk variables, measured only once at the beginning of the study, are not strongly related to time of follow-up.

Appendix A
Description of the WCGS Data Set

The Western Collaborative Group Study (WCGS) recruited middle-aged men (ages 39 to 59) from employees of ten California companies and collected data on 3,154 individuals during the years 1960–61. These subjects were selected to study the relationship between behavior pattern and the risk of coronary heart disease. A number of other risk factors were also measured to provide the best possible assessment of risk from behavior type. Analyzed here is a subset of eight of these risk factors. They are: behavior type, age, systolic blood pressure, diastolic blood pressure, cholesterol level, amount smoked, height, and weight. Behavior type was classified into two categories (called type A or type B) from a tape-recorded interview developed for the purpose and administered by trained interviewers. A precise definition of type A and type B behavior is complicated and equivocal. In general terms, type A behavior is characterized by a sense of time urgency, aggressiveness, and ambition. A type A individual is typically thought of as a competitive personality. The type B individual is essentially the converse, manifesting itself in a relaxed, noncompetitive, less hurried individual. A total of 1,589 type A and 1,565 type B individuals were identified.

The outcome variable was the presence of coronary heart disease determined by an independent medical referee. Clinical coronary disease occurred in 257 subjects during 9 years of follow-up, producing a crude incidence of CHD of about 11.1 per 1000 subjects at risk per year. The men lost to followup (504) were considered to be non-CHD cases and were about evenly split between type A and type B individuals. A total of 92.5% of all possible person-years of follow-up was completed.

Of particular note is the time of CHD event or withdrawal from the study recorded as the number of days of follow-up for each individual participating in the study. The average followup was about 7.35 years. The WCGS and data are completely described in a number of places (e.g., [Refs. 1, 2, and 3]), and a report on 22 years of follow-up has been recently published [Ref. 4].

Table A-1. List of variables in the WCGS data subset

Variable	Units	Mean	Std. deviation	Minimum	Maximum
Age	Years	46.279	5.524	39	59
Height	Inches	69.778	2.529	60	78
Weight	Pounds	169.954	21.100	78	320
Systolic blood pressure	mm Hg	128.633	15.112	98	230
Diastolic blood pressure	mm Hg	82.016	9.727	58	150
Cholesterol	mg/100 ml	226.372	43.420	103	645
Smoking	Cigarettes/day	11.601	14.518	0	99
Behavior type	A or B	—	—	—	—
Time	Days	2683.859	666.524	18	3430
CHD event	0 or 1	—	—	—	—

The ten variables employed in the text and their mean values at baseline are given in Table A.1.

The long-term follow-up of WCGS participants [Ref. 4] indicates that the relationship between behavior type and coronary heart disease is not simple. Behavior type showed a strong association with the incidence of CHD. However, no similar association was found using 22-year heart disease mortality data. The predictive association of behavior and incidence as well as the absence of an association with mortality are not likely to be totally explained by artifact or bias [Ref. 4]. An explanation may lie in the possibility that behavior type is related to recovery from nonfatal heart disease. The details of this conjecture and a discussion of the associations among a series of risk variables with coronary heart disease mortality is given elsewhere [Ref. 4]. The WCGS data illustrate a number of statistical approaches and are used to explore the original observation that behavior type is associated with coronary heart disease incidence.

Appendix B
Binomial and Poisson Distributions

The binomial and Poisson distributions are basic to many aspects of data analysis, and it is worthwhile to review some of the properties of these distributions. Complete descriptions are found in most introductory statistics texts (e.g., [Ref. 5]).

A binomially distributed variable is made up of a series of variables with two outcomes. That is,

1. The binary variable X_i is either 1 or 0 with probabilities p and $1 - p$, respectively;
2. Each X_i variable is statistically independent; and
3. The probability p is the same for all X_i.

The binomial variable X is the sum of n values of X_i or

$$X = X_1 + X_2 + \cdots + X_n. \tag{A.1}$$

More simply, X is the count of the number of times X_i equal 1. The binary character of X_i makes the X variable applicable to a wide range of data with two outcome possibilities—alive or dead, male or female, case or control, and, in general, event A or event not A.

The probabilities associated with a specific value of X, denoted as k, are given by the expression

$$P(X = k) = \binom{n}{k} p^k (1 - p)^{n-k}, \text{ where } k = 0, 1, 2, \ldots, n. \tag{A.2}$$

The term $\binom{n}{k}$ is the number of different ways k values of 1 can occur among n values of 0 and 1. The quantity $p^k (1 - p)^{n-k}$ is the probability of a specific configuration of 1's and 0's. The product is the probability that k values of X_i will equal 1 and $n - k$ values will equal 0 and, therefore, the sum X is equal to k. A direct result of these binomial probabilities is that the expected value of X for a series of n events is

$$\text{Expected binomial value} = np \tag{A.3}$$

and the variance associated with the binomial variable X is

$$\text{variance}(X) = np(1 - p). \tag{A.4}$$

To illustrate, consider the case for $n = 10$ and $p = 0.4$ shown in

Table A.2. The expected value is $np = 10(0.4) = 4$ and the variance is $np(1 - p) = 10(0.4)(0.6) = 2.4$.

A related distribution, called the Poisson distribution (named after the French mathematician Simeon Denis Poisson), can be justified from the following considerations:

$$P(X=k) = \binom{n}{k} p^k (1 - p)^{n-k} = \frac{n(n-1)(n-2) \cdots (n-k+1)}{k!} p^k \left(1 - \frac{np}{n}\right)^{n-k}$$

(A.5)

and

$$P(X = k) = \frac{1\left(1 - \frac{1}{n}\right)\left(1 - \frac{2}{n}\right) \cdots \left(1 - \frac{k+1}{n}\right)}{k!} (np)^k \left(1 - \frac{np}{n}\right)^{n-k}.$$

(A.6)

If n is large and p is small, then $(1 - np/n)^{n-k} \approx e^{-np}$, giving

$$P(X = k) = \frac{(np)^k e^{-np}}{k!} = \frac{\lambda^k e^{-\lambda}}{k!}.$$

(A.7)

Expression (A.7) describes the Poisson probabilities viewed as a limiting case of the binomial distribution. That is, the binomial distribution becomes indistinguishable from the Poisson distribution when n (the number of X_i values) is large and $P(X_i = 1) = p$ is small. The Greek letter $\lambda = np$ is the traditional associated with a Poisson distribution.

The Poisson distribution can be derived from other considerations and, like the binomial, plays a important role in analyzing discrete data. The expectation and variance are also derived from the probabilities $P(X = k)$. The expected value of a Poisson distributed variable X is

$$\text{expected Poisson value} = \lambda \tag{A.8}$$

with variance of X given by

$$\text{variance}(X) = \lambda. \tag{A.9}$$

Situations arise where the variable observed is binary, the number of occurrences n is large, and p is small, implying the Poisson distribution

Table A–2. Binomial distribution, $n = 10$ and $p = 0.4$*

k	0	1	2	3	4	5	6	7	8	9	10
$P(X = k)$	0.006	0.040	0.121	0.215	0.251	0.201	0.111	0.042	0.011	0.002	0.000

*$P(X = k) = \binom{10}{k} 0.4^k (1 - 0.4)^{10-k}$.

can be used instead of a binomial distribution as a description of a phenomenon with two outcomes. For example, the probability of k cases of leukemia occurring in a specific of geographic area (n = all possible persons at risk for leukemia and p = the probability that any one person is diagnosed with leukemia) has been modeled by a Poisson distribution (reviewed in [Ref. 6]). For the application of a Poisson distribution knowledge of p and n is unnecessary; only the parameter λ must be known or estimated to generate a set of Poisson probabilities. A partial list of phenomena that have been observed to "fit" a Poisson distributions is: deaths by horse kicks, numbers of radioactive decay particles, arrival of patients at a doctor's waiting rooms, typographical errors, numbers of individuals over 100 years old, occurrences of suicide, telephone calls arriving at a switch board, ...

Appendix C
The Odds Ratio and Its Properties

The odds ratio, central to many epidemiologic analyses, is not the simplest statistical measure of association. This section reviews some of the properties of the odds ratio measure. More complete descriptions exist elsewhere (e.g., [Ref. 7, 8, or 9]).

The odds are a ratio of two probabilities: the probability an event occurs divided by the probability the event does not occur. (The word *odds* refers to a single entity, but tradition and formal English dictate that the word be treated as plural noun.) If an event has probability p, then the odds of the event are $p/(1 - p)$. When a series of n binary outcomes are observed where a events occur and b events do not $(n = a + b)$, then the odds are estimated by a/b. For example, if a specific horse finishes among the top three fastest 30 times out of 50 races, then the odds are estimated as 3 to 2 (1.5) the horse will "show."

The odds ratio measures the relative magnitude of two sets of odds occurring under differing conditions. For example,

$$\text{odds(under conditions 1)} = \frac{p_1}{1 - p_1} \tag{A.10}$$

and are estimated by a/b, where a events occur and b events do not occur. Also,

$$\text{odds(under conditions 2)} = \frac{p_2}{1 - p_2} \tag{A.11}$$

and are estimated by c/d, where c events occur and d events do not occur. The symbols p_1 and p_2 represent the probabilities of the events being considered under conditions 1 and 2, respectively. The odds ratio is then

$$\text{odds ratio} = \frac{p_1/(1 - p_1)}{p_2/(1 - p_2)} = \frac{p_1(1 - p_2)}{(1 - p_1)p_2}. \tag{A.12}$$

An estimate of this odds ratio is given by

$$\hat{or} = \frac{a/b}{c/d} = \frac{ad}{bc}. \tag{A.13}$$

Table A-3. A 2 × 2 table

	Occurrence	No occurrence	Total
Conditions 1	a	b	$a + b$
Conditions 2	c	d	$c + d$
Total	$a + c$	$b + d$	n

The possible values of an odds ratio run from zero to infinity (∞). The odds ratio measure is symmetric about the value 1.0 in the sense that *or* represents the same degree of association as $1/or$.

Data for the calculation of an odds ratio is typically displayed in a 2×2; table given in Table A.3. Since the odds ratio is generally estimated from a sample of data, it will vary from sample to sample. An estimate of this sampling variation is

$$\text{variance}(\hat{or}) = \hat{or}^2 \left(\frac{1}{a} + \frac{1}{b} + \frac{1}{c} + \frac{1}{d} \right). \tag{A.14}$$

Figure A.1 (top left) shows a simulated distribution of 500 values of the odds ratio calculated from samples of size $n = 50$ collected under

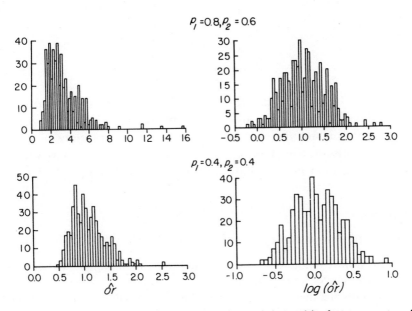

Figure A-1. Histograms of the odds ratio and log-odds for two sets of conditions.

two conditions ($p_1 = 0.8$ and $p_2 = 0.6$). The distribution of these estimated odds ratios is skewed to the right. The mean of the distribution is 3.170, showing that the directly estimated odds ratio is biased (the expected odds ratio is $(0.8)(0.4)/(0.2)(0.6) = 2.667$). To reduce this bias by producing a more symmetric distribution, the logarithm of the odds ratio is used. A simulated distribution of $\log(\hat{or})$ is also shown in figure A.1 (top right) also for $p_1 = 0.8$ and $p_2 = 0.6$. The distribution is clearly more symmetric with the mean value $= 1.037$ where $\log(or) = \log(2.667) = 0.981$ is expected. The estimated sample variance associated with the estimate $\log(\hat{or})$ is

$$\text{variance}[\log(\hat{or})] = \frac{1}{a} + \frac{1}{b} + \frac{1}{c} + \frac{1}{d}. \tag{A.15}$$

The values of $\log(or)$ range from $-\infty$ to ∞. When the mean value is 0.0, $\log(or)$ is equivalent to $-\log(or)$ as a measure of association.

Other bias-reducing transformations have been suggested for the odds ratio. Two examples are

$$\hat{or}_{\text{H}} = \frac{(a + \frac{1}{2})(d + \frac{1}{2})}{(b + \frac{1}{2})(c + \frac{1}{2})} \tag{A.16}$$

(H for Haldane's [Ref. 10] suggestion) with estimated variance

$$\text{variance}(\hat{or}_{\text{H}}) = \frac{1}{a + \frac{1}{2}} + \frac{1}{b + \frac{1}{2}} + \frac{1}{c + \frac{1}{2}} + \frac{1}{d + \frac{1}{2}} \tag{A.17}$$

and

$$\hat{or}_{\text{SS}} = \frac{ad}{(b + 1)(c + 1)} \tag{A.18}$$

(SS for small sample odds ratio) [Ref. 11]. A useful property of these two estimates is that the odds ratio remains defined when $b = 0$ or $c = 0$, which is not the case for $\hat{or}$. Simulated distributions of $\hat{or}$ and $\log(\hat{or})$ are also shown (Figure A.1, bottom) for the case where the two conditions generating the odds are not different (i.e., $p_1 = p_2 = 0.4$).

Properties

Some of the properties of or and $\hat{or}$ derived from a 2×2 table are:

1. Invariance to interchanging rows and columns, although interchanging a row only or a column only changes or to $1/or$;
2. Multiplying the rows and/or the columns by positive constants does not change the value of or;
3. The odds ratio has a probabilistic interpretation (as described);

4. The odds ratio approximates the relative risk

$$\text{relative risk} = \frac{\text{Probability of the disease with the factor present}}{\text{Probability of the disease with the factor absent}}$$

$$= \frac{P(D|\text{factor})}{P(D|\text{no factor})} \approx or$$

when the frequency of the disease is rare among those with and without the factor; and

5. The logarithm of the odds ratio produces a more or less symmetric distribution that can usually be approximated accurately with a normal distribution.

The last property is perhaps the most useful since it allows statistical tests and confidence intervals to be constructed based on the normal distribution. The exact properties of the odds ratio have been derived but are complex and difficult to compute. Using the normal distribution as an approximation is simple and sufficiently accurate for most situations.

A null hypothesis of the form H_0: $or = or_0$ can be assessed by reference to a standard normal distribution with the test statistic

$$z = \frac{\log(\hat{or}) - \log(or_0)}{\sqrt{\text{variance}[\log(\hat{or})]}}, \tag{A.19}$$

where the value for or_0 is usually chosen to be 1.0. An odds ratio of one implies that the probability of occurrence of the event under study is the same for both conditions 1 and 2 ($p_1 = p_2$). The value z has an approximate standard normal distribution with mean $= 0$ and variance $= 1$ when $or = or_0$.

An $(1 - \alpha)$-level confidence interval can also be constructed using a normal distribution as an approximation for the distribution of the logarithm of the estimated odds ratio or

$$\text{upper} = \log(\hat{or}) + z_{1-\alpha/2}\sqrt{\text{variance}[\log(\hat{or})]} \tag{A.20}$$

$$\text{lower} = \log(\hat{or}) - z_{1-\alpha/2}\sqrt{\text{variance}[\log(\hat{or})]}, \tag{A.21}$$

where $z_{1-\alpha} =$ the $(1 - \alpha)$th percentile of a standard normal distribution. The probability that the parameter $\log(or)$ is found between these upper and lower bounds is approximately $1 - \alpha$. These limits can be directly transformed to provide an α-level confidence interval of the odds ratio itself. The probability is approximately $1 - \alpha$ that the "true" odds ratio or is found in the interval $(e^{\text{lower}}, e^{\text{upper}})$.

Appendix D
Partitioning the χ^2 Statistic

Suppose the focus of an analytic technique is on a series of independent measures of association, symbolized by M_i, that take on the value 0 when no association exits (null hypothesis). A parallel series of weights w_i are defined as

$$w_i = \frac{1}{\text{variance}(\hat{M}_i)},$$

(A.22)

where $\hat{M}_i$ represents an estimate of M_i. Then, under rather general considerations,

$$X_i^2 = w_i \hat{M}_i^2$$

(A.23)

has an approximate χ^2 distribution with one degree of freedom when the null hypothesis $M_i = 0$ is true.

Three properties of the statistic M_i are:

1. A summary measure of association for k estimates of M_i is

$$\bar{M} = \frac{\sum\limits_{i=1}^{k} w_i \hat{M}_i}{\sum\limits_{i=1}^{k} w_i}$$

(A.24)

and

$$X_A^2 = \frac{\bar{M}^2}{\text{variance}(\bar{M})} = \frac{\left(\sum\limits_{i=1}^{k} w_i \hat{M}_i\right)^2}{\sum\limits_{i=1}^{k} w_i}$$

(A.25)

has an approximate χ^2 distribution with one degree of freedom when the null hypothesis is true (i.e., $M_i = 0$ for $i = 1, 2, \ldots, k$) and the k measures of association M_i are independent.

2. The total χ^2 statistic is

$$X^2 = \sum\limits_{i=1}^{k} X_i^2 = \sum\limits_{i=1}^{k} w_i \hat{M}_i^2$$

(A.26)

and has an approximate χ^2 distribution with $k - 1$ degrees of freedom when all k values of $\hat{M}_i$ are random deviations from 0 (no association exists in all k situations).

Table A-4. Partioned values of a χ^2 statistic

Summary	χ^2	Degrees of freedom
Association	$X_A^2 = \bar{M}^2/\text{variance}(\bar{M})$	1
Heterogeneity	$X_H^2 = \sum_{i=1}^{k} w_i(M_i - \bar{M})^2$	$k - 2$
Total	$X^2 = \sum_{i=1}^{k} w_i \hat{M}_i^2$	$k - 1$

3. A χ^2 statistic that measures the heterogeneity among the k measures of association is

$$X_H^2 = X^2 - X_A^2 = \sum_{i=1}^{k} w_i(\hat{M}_i - \bar{M})^2 \qquad (A.27)$$

and X_H^2 has an approximate χ^2 distribution with $k - 2$ degrees of freedom when all k measures of associations M_i are the same. Formally, X_H^2 is used to assess deviations from the null hypothesis that $M_1 = M_2 = \cdots = M_k = M$.

A summary can be found in Table A.4. The total χ^2 statistic X^2 is partitioned into two pieces, X_A^2 and X_H^2 (i.e., $X^2 = X_A^2 + X_H^2$). The χ^2 statistic X_A^2 evaluates the measure of association $\bar{M}$ resulting from combining the M_i values over k situations. This summary measure is most meaningful when each of the k components measure the same degree of association. The χ^2 statistic X_H^2 reflects the degree of heterogeneity among the k measures of association.

Application: 2 × K Table

If $\hat{M}_i = \hat{b}_i = (y_i - \bar{y})/(x_i - \bar{x})$, then $w_i = (x_i - \bar{x})^2/\text{variance}(y)$, giving

$$\bar{M} = \hat{b}_{y|x} \text{ and } X_A^2 = X_L^2 = \frac{\hat{b}_{y|x}^2}{\text{variance}(\hat{b}_{y|x})}.$$

Also, $X_H^2 = X_{NL}^2$ measures nonlinearity. Both X_L^2 and X_{NL}^2 are further defined in Chapter 6 and play key roles in connection with the analysis of a $2 \times K$ table.

Application: Mantel-Haenszel χ^2 statistic

If $M_i = (a_i - \hat{A}_i)/\text{variance}(a_i)$, then $w_i = \text{variance}(a_i)$, giving

$$\bar{M} = \frac{\sum_{i=1}^{k} a_i - \sum_{i=1}^{k} \hat{A}_i}{\sum_{i=1}^{k} \text{variance}(a_i)} \text{ and } X_A^2 = X_{MH}^2 = \frac{\left(\sum_{i=1}^{k} a_i - \sum_{i=1}^{k} \hat{A}_i\right)^2}{\sum_{i=1}^{k} \text{variance}(a_i)},$$

which is the Mantel-Haenszel χ^2 statistic used in Chapters 6, 10, and 11 to assess the association reflected in a series of 2×2 tables.

Appendix E
Maximum Likelihood Estimation

Once a statistical model is postulated, estimates of specific parameters are necessary before it becomes a useful tool in the analysis of a data set. A statistically optimum estimation technique is the method of maximum likelihood.

> Aside: Maximum likelihood estimation is one of the many statistical contributions of British geneticist/statistician Ronald Aylmer Fisher (1890–1962). R. A. Fisher ranks among the great scientists of the twentieth century. He began his career in genetics and went on to develop much of modern statistics to solve genetic and agricultural problems. His temperament was sometimes controversial, but his dominance in fields of genetics and statistics is never questioned. His work provided the research world with the confidence interval, experimental design, analysis of variance, as well as a large number of concepts in theoretical statistics. At the same time he laid down much of the mathematical foundation for Darwin's theory of evolution. Fisher's early books, *Statistical Methods for Research Workers* (1925) and *The Genetical Theory of Natural Selection* (1930), were revolutionary in their impact and remain classics today.

In simple terms, a maximum likelihood estimate of a parameter is that value that is most likely for the sampled data. In a sense, things are turned around. The data are considered fixed, and questions are asked about the possible values of the parameter. That is, for a specific set of observations, which of all possible values of the parameter is the most likely to have produced the observed data? An example illustrates. Consider a model consisting of a single parameter that determines the values of variables X and Y. The probability that $X = 1$ is p and $X = 0$ is $1 - p$. Similarly, it is postulated that the same parameter is associated with Y [i.e., $P(Y = 1) = p$ and $P(Y = 0) = 1 - p$]. Additionally, X and Y are statistically independent, giving the statistical structure shown in Table A.5. Say the data in Table A.6 were observed. The probability that such a sample occurred is related to a likelihood function or

$$\text{likelihood function} = K(p^2)^{36}[p(1 - p)]^{14}[(1 - p)p]^{34}[(1 - p)^2]^{16}. \quad (A.28)$$

where K is an unimportant constant value. This likelihood value is an

Table A–5. Model

	$X = 1$	$X = 0$	Total
$Y = 1$	p^2	$(1 - p)p$	p
$Y = 0$	$p(1 - p)$	$(1 - p)^2$	$1 - p$
Total	p	$1 - p$	1

Table A–6. Data

	$X = 1$	$X = 0$	Total
$Y = 1$	36	14	50
$Y = 0$	34	16	50
Total	70	30	100

extremely small number, which nevertheless reflects the probabilities associated with the model for any parameter p for the observed data set. Each value of p produces a different likelihood. The maximum likelihood principle states that the estimate of p will be that value which maximizes the likelihood (denoted as $\hat{p}$). The data (36, 14, 34, and 16) are fixed, and the value of p is varied until the maximum value of the likelihood is found. Estimation reduces to searching for this value. Rather than dealing with extremely small likelihood values, it is conventional to take the logarithm of the likelihood for ease of manipulation. The value of p that maximizes the logarithm of the likelihood, maximizes the likelihood. A few values of the loglikelihood [expression (A.28)] for different parameters p are given in Table A.7.

The loglikelihood is a continuous function of p and is shown in Figure A.2. The maximum value occurs at $p = 0.6$, giving a maximum likelihood estimate of $\hat{p} = 0.6$, using the illustrative data and model [expression (A.28)]. This estimate can also be found by employing techniques from calculus. In fact, the maximum likelihood estimate for this simple case is identical to the natural estimate of the number of times X or Y equals one divided by the total number of observations or $\hat{p} = 120/200 = 0.6$.

Table A–7. Loglikelihood values

p	0.2	0.3	0.4	0.5	0.6	0.7	0.8	0.9
Loglike-lihood	-177.71	-139.74	-117.55	-105.36	-101.33	-105.84	-122.26	-163.58

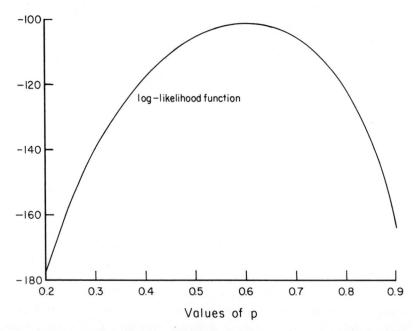

Figure A–2. The logarithm of the likelihood function for the binomial data for a range of the possible values of the parameter p.

The mechanics of finding maximum likelihood estimates becomes more tedious as the number of parameters in the model increases but the process does not change in principle. Consider a two-parameter situation. Twin births are either monozygotic (m) or dizygotic (d). Although zygosity of a twin pair is not generally recorded, twin births can be categorized by the sex of the pair: male–male, male–female, and female–female. A model describing the relationship between zygosity and sex of the twin pair and an application of the maximum likelihood estimation technique produces an estimate of the frequency of the two zygotic types of twins. The following model is postulated:

$$P(\text{male–male pair which is monozygotic}) = p \text{ and}$$
$$P(\text{male–male pair which is dizygotic}) = p^2$$

and the probability of a male–male twin pair is a mixture of these two zygotic types or

$$P(\text{male–male}) = pm + p^2d, \tag{A.29}$$

where $m = 1 - d$ is the frequency of monozygotic twin pairs. Similarly the probabilities associated with the other two types of twin pairs are

$$P(\text{female–male}) = 2p(1 - p)d \text{ and}$$
$$P(\text{female–female}) = (1 - p)m + (1 - p)^2d. \tag{A.30}$$

Table a–8 Maximum likelihood estimation: Data and model

Pair type	Male-male	Female-male	Female-female	Total
Model	$pm + p^2 d$	$2p(1-p)d$	$(1-p)m + (1-p)^2 d$	1.0
Observed number	32	41	36	109

The complete twin model along with a data set of 109 twin pairs is given in Table A.8. The likelihood function associated with this twin model depends on two parameters (p and d) and is given by

$$\text{likelihood} = K[p(1-d) + p^2 d]^{32}[2p(1-p)d]^{41}[(1-p)(1-d) + (1-p^2)d]^{36}.$$

(A.31)

This two-dimensional likelihood function is shown in Figure A.3 (four views). A search of the likelihood function indicates that the maximum occurs at $p = 0.482$ and $d = 0.753$. Therefore, the values that maximize the likelihood associated with the specific data (32, 41, and 36) are the maximum likelihood estimates $\hat{p} = 0.482$ and $\hat{d} = 0.753$. No other pair of values produces a larger value of likelihood function or logarithm of the likelihood function for the observed data. These two values $\hat{p}$ and $\hat{d}$ are the most likely among all possible values of p and d for the given set of twin data.

Likelihood function – Twin data (four views)

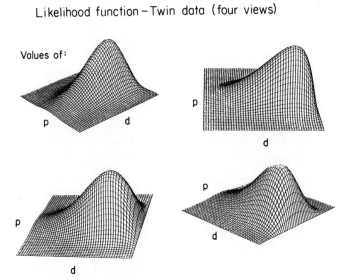

Figure A–3. Four views of the bivariate loglikelihood function for the estimates of the two parameters (p, d) from the twin data.

The maximum likelihood estimates for multiparameter models are typically estimated by computer techniques. The definition of the maximum likelihood estimate, however, is the same. To estimate k parameters of a model, say $\theta_1, \theta_2, \theta_3, \ldots, \theta_k$, the maximum likelihood estimate of the k values is such that likelihood$(\theta_1, \theta_2, \theta_3, \ldots, \theta_k)$ is maximum or

$$\text{likelihood}(\hat{\theta}_1, \hat{\theta}_2, \hat{\theta}_3, \ldots, \hat{\theta}_k) > \text{likelihood}(\theta_1, \theta_2, \theta_3, \ldots, \theta_k)$$

for all possible values of the set of k parameters. The interpretation is also the same; the estimates $\hat{\theta}_1, \hat{\theta}_2, \hat{\theta}_3, \ldots, \hat{\theta}_k$ are that set of parameters that makes the sampled data most likely to have occurred.

The maximum likelihood process also produces an estimate of the variation associated with the estimated parameters. The variance of a maximum likelihood estimate is related to the likelihood function and is calculated by sometimes rather complicated manipulations. Estimated variances, however, are part of most maximum likelihood estimation computer programs, making these estimated variances widely available. For example, the estimates $\hat{p} = 0.482$ and $\hat{d} = 0.753$ from the twin data have estimated variances of 0.00143 and 0.00862, respectively. A measure of the reliability is always an important part of the interpretation of an estimated value.

Another property of maximum likelihood estimation is that a function of a maximum likelihood estimate is itself a maximum likelihood estimate. It is often the case that maximum likelihood estimates are expressed in different forms or are used to estimate other relevant quantities. For example, if an estimate of the proportion of male–male pairs is desired, the maximum likelihood estimate is $\hat{p}\hat{m} + \hat{p}^2\hat{d} = 0.482(0.247) + 0.482^2(0.753) = 0.294$, or the number of male–male pairs is estimated by $109(0.294) = 32.046$ and is also the maximum likelihood estimate. In general, if $\hat{\theta}$ is a maximum likelihood estimate, then $f(\hat{\theta})$ is also a maximum likelihood estimate (e.g., if $\hat{b}$ is a maximum likelihood estimate, so is $e^{\hat{b}}$). A more extensive description of the theory and practice of maximum likelihood estimation is part of a mathematical statistics course (e.g., see [Ref. 12]).

Likelihood Function

The likelihood function, which is an essential part of the maximum likelihood process, is also a valuable summary of a model's "fit" to the data. Comparison of likelihood values under differing conditions allows an evaluation of different statistical models. The twin data will continue to serve as an example. The likelihood associated with the estimates $\hat{p} = 0.482$ and $\hat{d} = 0.753$ is 1.72×10^{-52}. This extremely small number is proportional to the probability of the occurrence of the observed data for these specific values of the parameters. The occurrence of the observed set of data (32 male–male pairs, 41 male–female pairs, and 36 female–female pairs) is not likely, but this probability can be compared to other similar probabilities. For example, say it is postulated that $p = 0.5$ where the observed value $\hat{p} = 0.482$ is considered a result of sampling variation (H_0: $p = 0.5$) while the proportion of dizygotic twins (d) remains 0.753. The likelihood under the condition that $p = 0.5$ is 1.53×10^{-52}—an expected decrease over the previous maximum value since the likelihood is maximum at $p = 0.482$ and any other value of p will produce some decrease. Is a decrease of this magnitude expected by chance alone? A result from mathematical statistics is helpful for comparing likelihood values. The difference between the logarithms of two likelihood values multiplied by -2 has an approximate χ^2 distribution when the two conditions being compared are identical and the observed likelihoods differ only because of random variation (null hypothesis is true). The degrees of freedom are equal to the difference in the number of estimated parameters associated with each of the models compared. For the twin data if $\hat{p} = 0.482$, then $-2\text{loglikelihood} = L_1 = 238.381$ and if $p = 0.5$, then $-2\text{loglikelihood} = L_0 = 238.616$—d remains 0.753 for both models. The difference $L_0 - L_1 = X^2 = 238.616 - 238.381 = 0.235$ has an approximate χ^2 distribution with one degree of freedom when $\hat{p}$ differs from 0.5 by chance, producing a significance probability of p-value $= 0.628$. That is, no evidence exists in the data to support the notion that the probability of a male among twin births is different from the probability of a female twin ($p = 0.5$). Additionally, suppose it is postulated that the same number of dizygotic twins are born as monozygotic twin ($d = m = 0.5$ and $p = 0.5$). The value of -2loglike- lihood associated with this conjecture is $L_0 = 247.069$. Comparison of the likelihood values gives $L_0 - L_1 = X^2 = 247.069 - 238.381 = 8.69$, which has an approximate χ^2 distribution with two degrees of freedom when the fit of the two models (i.e., likelihoods) differ by chance. An increase of 8.69 is not likely (p-value $= 0.013$), showing that the hypothesis of equally frequent sex and zygotic types is not consistent with the observed data.

In general, one set of conditions generates likelihood value L_1; a more restrictive set of conditions generates a second likelihood value L_0, and the increase $[-2\log(L_0)] - [-2\log(L_1)] = X^2$ measures the impact of the restricted set of conditions via a χ^2 distribution. The evaluation of "nested" models by comparing likelihoods is a basic tool in multivariate statistical analysis.

Problems

Chapter 1

1. A population is sampled to determine the probability of illness. A total of N days are recorded, where it is determined that an individual is ill, well, or status is unknown. That is,

y days ill + n days well + k days status unknown = N total days

$$(y + n + k = N).$$

Two possibilities for estimating the probability a person from this population is ill are:

strategy (a) Ignore the k days where the status is unknown,

strategy (b) Assume that the probability of illness is the same for days when the status is known and unknown (i.e., days where status is unknown occur at random).

Demonstrate that strategy (a) and strategy (b) are equivalent.

2. Four schemes for collecting data to estimate the average length of stay in an institution are:

a. Complete follow-up: for each individual entering an institution the length of stay is determined from beginning to end;

b. Retrospective follow-up: a series of institutionalized patients is identified at a specific time and the amount of time each person has been institutionalized is ascertained;

c. Partial follow-up: the entire stay is recorded from admission to discharge from those patients present at the start of sampling, using their admission records and observing them until they are discharged;

d. Interval follow-up: a series of institutionalized patients is followed for a specific period of time (some are discharged before and some remain institutionalized at the end of the time period).

Four sets of 1000 hypothetical observations that would result under these four sampling schemes are:

Weeks	Complete	Retrospective	Partial	Interval
0	135	332	45	344
1	271	288	180	325
2	271	198	271	208
3	180	108	240	92
4	90	48	150	31
5	36	18	72	—
6	12	6	28	—
7	4	2	11	—
8	1	0	3	—
9	0	0	0	—

Note: The underlying distribution of lengths of stay is the same in all four cases; the differences arises from the way the data were collected. Investigate the issue of length bias for these four data collecting patterns. Estimate the degree of bias in each case for the mean length of stay. How is the estimate of the variance of the distribution of lengths of stay affected by the data collection schemes?

3. Can a 1-year average mortality rate exceed the number of deaths—rate $(R_x) >$ deaths (d_x)?

Chapter 2

4. For a one-way classification of data an estimate of σ^2 is denoted S_p^2 and for a two-way classification by S^2. Usually $S^2 < S_p^2$ producing a more efficient analysis of the data while controlling the influence of an extraneous variable. However, occasionally losses are incurred by forming a two-way classification. Find a condition such that a two-way analysis is less efficient than a one-way analysis (i.e., $S^2 > S_p^2$).

Hint: $\Sigma\Sigma(y_{ij} - \bar{y}_{i.})^2 = \Sigma\Sigma(\bar{y}_{.j} - \bar{y})^2 + \Sigma\Sigma(y_{ij} - \bar{y}_{i.} - \bar{y}_{.j} + \bar{y})^2$.

5. If two hypotheses are under consideration, show that the overall type I error (one or two type I errors) is less than α if both tests are conducted at a level of $\alpha/2$.
   a. If the two tests are independent, and
   b. If the two tests are not independent.

Chapter 3

6. Derive an expression for the sample size necessary to detect a difference δ between two proportions (i.e., $\delta = p_2 - p_1$) where the sample sizes from each source differ. That is, one source yields r times more data than the other source or $n_1 = rn_2$—find n_1 where r is known.

7. If $H_0: Np_0 = 2$, generate the Poisson distribution associated with this null hypothesis.

$$\text{Note: } P(x = k) = \frac{e^{-Np_0}(Np_0)^k}{k!}.$$

Select a critical point so that $P(X > c) \approx 0.05$. If $H_1: Nrp_0 = 4$, generate the Poisson distribution under this alternative hypothesis that the relative risk is $2(r = 2)$ and compute the power [i.e., $P(X > c) = ?$]. Use the normal approximation approach to make the same calculation and compare the two results.

8. Consider the null hypothesis that the sample was collected from a normal population with mean 0.0 and variance σ^2 and the alternative that the sample was collected from a normal population with the same variance but with mean μ. Find an expression for the power curve associated with different values of μ where the test statistic is the 95th percentile. That is, H_0 is tested against H_1 using

$$\hat{P} = \bar{y} + 1.96S_Y.$$

The approximate variance of an estimated percentile is

$$\text{variance}(\hat{P}) \approx \frac{\sigma^2}{n} [1 + (\tfrac{1}{2}) z_{1-\alpha}^2].$$

Compute the efficiency of using the 95th percentile compared to using the mean value $(\bar{y})$ to detect a difference of μ between two normal populations with the same variance for set values of α and β. Define efficiency as k/n, where n is the sample size required using $\bar{y}$ and k is the sample size required when $\hat{P}$ is employed.

Chapter 4

9. When the residual values resulting from a "median polish" are subtracted from the original data, the resulting table perfectly fits an additive model, or

$$n_{ij} = n_{11} + a_i + t_j.$$

For the table

	$j = 1$	$j = 2$	$j = 3$	$j = 4$	$j = 5$
$i = 1$	10	15	18	20	40
$i = 2$	5	8	3	2	10
$i = 3$	6	10	15	17	30

find values $t_1, t_2, t_3, t_4, t_5, a_1, a_2,$ and a_3 that produce an additive relationship between the rows and the columns of the table.

Chapter 5

10. Show that when $P(X = k) = \lambda^k e^{-\lambda}/k!$,

$$P(X = i + 1) = \frac{\lambda}{i + 1} P(X = i).$$

Use this expression to generate the Poisson probabilities starting with $P(X = 0) = e^{-\lambda}$ for $\lambda = 2$.

11. Show that for $F(r) = P(R < r) = 1 - e^{-n\pi r^2/A}$, then

$$\text{median}(r) = 0.470 \sqrt{A/n}.$$

12. Consider the data:

group I: 11, 18, 21
group II: 10, 8, 12

i. t-test: compute a t statistic to evaluate the mean difference between groups I and II—find the one-sided p-value,

ii. Permutation test: list all possible mean differences (there are 20) from the data to evaluate the observed differences between groups I and II—find the one-sided p-value.

13. Demonstrate that the jackknife estimate of the mean and the variance for a sample of n observations is the same as the usual estimates $\bar{x} = \Sigma\, x_i/n$ and $S^2 = \Sigma\, (x_i - \bar{x})^2/(n - 1)$. Also show that for this case the bias must be zero.

Chapter 6

14. Show that

$$X_L^2 = \frac{\hat{b}_{y|x}^2}{\text{variance}(\hat{b}_{y|x})} = \frac{\hat{b}_{x|y}^2}{\text{variance}(\hat{b}_{x|y})}.$$

15. Demonstrate for a $2 \times K$ table that

$$X_L^2 = (n - 1)r_{xy}^2.$$

16. Show that for a $2 \times K$ table

a. $\displaystyle\sum_{i=1}^{n} (y_i - \bar{y})^2 = \frac{n_1 n_2}{n}$ when y_i takes on the values 0 and 1 only;

b. $\text{variance}(\bar{x}_2 - \bar{x}_1) = \text{variance}(\hat{b}_{x|y})$; and

c. $\dfrac{(\bar{x}_2 - \bar{x}_1)^2}{\text{variance}(\bar{x}_2 - \bar{x}_1)} = \dfrac{\hat{b}_{y|x}^2}{\text{variance}(\hat{b}_{y|x})}.$

17. Consider the following $2 \times K$ table:

	$X = 0$	$X = 1$	$X = 2$	$X = 3$	$X = 4$	Total
$Y = 0$	18	16	24	24	52	134
$Y = 1$	20	24	60	35	50	189
Total	38	40	84	59	102	323

Compute: X^2, X_L^2, and X_{NL}^2. Find the associated p-values. For the same data compute the ridit $\hat{P}$, where $Y = 1$ is the reference group—also find the associated p-value.

18. Show that if no interaction is observed between a risk factor and a disease for a $2 \times 2 \times 2$ table, then the disease-confounder and confounder–risk-factor relationships also show no interaction. That is,

$$\text{if } \hat{or}_{FD|C} = \hat{or}_{FD|\bar{C}}, \text{ then } \hat{or}_{CD|\bar{F}} = \hat{or}_{CD|F} \text{ and } \hat{or}_{CF|D} = \hat{or}_{CF|\bar{D}}.$$

19. The relationships among the variables in a $2 \times 2 \times 2$ table for a disease (D), a risk factor (F), and a confounder (C) are given by

$$or_{pooled} = \frac{1 + (or_{CD|F} - 1)P(C|F\bar{D})}{1 + (or_{CD|F} - 1)P(C|\bar{F}\bar{D})} \times or_{FD|C}$$

when no interaction exits.

Create a numeric set of data in the form of a $2 \times 2 \times 2$ table and illustrate that this expression links the relationships among F, D, and C. Demonstrate that if $or_{CD|F} = 1$, then C is not a confounder and demonstrate that if $or_{CF|\bar{D}} = 1$, then C is also not a confounder.

Chapter 7

20. If $P(D|F) = P(D)$, then events represented by F and D are statistically independent. Show statistical independence of F and D also implies that $P(D|\bar{F}) = P(D)$ for events represented by $\bar{F}$ and D where $\bar{F}$ is the complement of F or $1 - P(F) = P(\bar{F})$.

Further show that $P(D|F) = P(D)$ implies that relative risk $= P(D|F)/P(D|\bar{F}) = 1$ and odds ratio $= or = P(D|F)P(\bar{D}|\bar{F})/P(\bar{D}|F)P(D|\bar{F}) = 1$.

21. Consider the following model and data:

$$\text{log-odds} = a + bf_1 + cf_2 + df_1f_2$$

Disease by factor 1 by factor 2

	Factor 1			No factor 1		
	Disease	No disease	Total	Disease	No disease	Total
Factor 2	10	12	22	80	52	132
No factor 2	15	48	63	55	70	125
Total	25	60	85	135	122	257

Estimate the coefficients and fill in the rest of the table (these answers can be calculated *Easily* by hand)

Logistic Regression: Disease by factor 1 by factor 2

Variable	Term	Coefficient	Std. error	p-value	Odds ratio
Constant	$\hat{a}$	???	???	—	—
Factor 1	$\hat{b}$	???	???	???	???
Factor 2	$\hat{c}$	???	???	???	???
Interaction	$\hat{d}$	???	???	???	???

22. Consider the $2 \times 2 \times 2$ table for risk factors A and B:

	$B = 1$		$B = 0$	
	D	$\bar{D}$	D	$\bar{D}$
$A=1$	$P(D\|A=1, B=1)$	$P(\bar{D}\|A=1, B=1)$	$P(D\|A=1, B=0)$	$P(\bar{D}\|A=1, B=0)$
$A=0$	$P(D\|A=0, B=1)$	$P(\bar{D}\|A=0, B=1)$	$P(D\|A=0, B=0)$	$P(\bar{D}\|A=0, B=0)$

Describe the eight probabilities contained in the $2 \times 2 \times 2$ table with a strictly additive logistic model or

$$P(D|A = i, B = j) = \frac{1}{1 + e^{-(a+bi+cj)}}.$$

Express the odds ratios or_{11}, or_{01}, and or_{10} in terms of the equivalent probabilities modeled by the logistic function where

$$or_{ij} = \frac{P(D|A = i, B = j)P(\bar{D}|A = 0, B = 0)}{P(\bar{D}|A = i, B = j)P(D|A = 0, B = 0)}.$$

Show that $or_{11} = or_{01} \times or_{10}$ for the additive logistic model and that $or_{11} \neq or_{01} \times or_{10}$ for a nonadditive logistic model.

Chapter 8

23. Show that for a simple logistic regression model x_i and $x_i^* = x_i - \bar{x}$ produce the same value for the coefficient b (i.e., the value of b from the model log-odds $= a + bx$ is not influenced by the transformation). Show that the coefficient b is affected by the same transformation in the quadratic model (i.e., the value of b from the model log-odds $= a + bx + cx^2$ is influenced by the transformation).

24. Consider the linear model:

$$y_{ij} = a + b_1 x_{1j} + b_2 x_{2j} + \gamma z_j + e_{ij}.$$

If z is excluded from the model, the estimate of b_2 is potentially biased. The confounder bias is measured by

$$\text{bias} = \frac{\gamma S_z (r_{z2} - r_{z1} r_{12})}{S_2 (1 - r_{12}^2)},$$

where S_i is the standard deviation of the ith variable and r_{ij} is the correlation between variables i and j. Identify three sets of conditions where the elimination of variable z does not induce bias in the estimation of b_2 (i.e., z is not a confounding influence).

Chapter 9

25. Survival data from a clinical trial are as follows (in days):

Treatment group ($n = 12$):
4, 8, 12^+, 19, 25, 28^+, 41, 44, 57^+, 68, 73^+, 97

Control group $(n = 12)$:
2, 3, 7, 9, 15, 19^+, 33, 38, 40, 53^+, 54, 65.

The "$+$" means that the individual was withdrawn alive after being observed for a number of days.

Construct a life table for each group using 5-day intervals. Compute the probability of survival for each interval. Compare the probability of surviving 40 days for the treatment and control groups $(\hat{P}_{40})$. Compute the value of the hazard function for each interval using different approximations [e.g., $-\log(p_x)$ and q_x] and compare the results.

26. Consider the "two marksmen model" of Berkson and Elveback, where the marksmen shoot alternatively at the targets n times. Show that the net probability for marksman 1 (Q_1) is approximated by the intuitive estimate (Q_1'), particularly when the crude probabilities q_1 and q_2 are small.

27. Competing risk

	Nonfactor	Factor
Disease $= d_1$	x_1	y_1
Other $= d_2$	x_2	y_2
Population	50,000	50,000

Compute the crude, hazard base, and intuitive probabilities of disease for

a. $x_1 = 2000, x_2 = 2000, y_1 = 500, y_2 = 500$,

b. $x_1 = 1000, x_2 = 1000, y_1 = 500, y_2 = 5000$,

c. $x_1 = 200, x_2 = 20, y_1 = 100, y_2 = 10$.

Chapter 10

28. Create a small numeric example and illustrate that the following two expressions give the same estimated mean value:

$$\bar{t} = \sum_{i=1}^{k} t_i(\hat{P}_{i-1} - \hat{P}_i), \text{ where } \hat{P}_0 = 1 \text{ and } \bar{t} = \sum_{i=1}^{k} \hat{P}_{i-1}(t_i - t_{i-1}), \text{ where } t_0 = 0.$$

Demonstrate algebraically that the two ways of calculating the mean survival times are identical.

Also if no censoring occurs, show that both forms for $\bar{t}$ reduce to the usual estimate of $\bar{t} = \sum t_i/n$.

Show that "Greenwood's" formula

$$\text{variance}(\hat{P}_k) = P_k^2 \sum \frac{q_i}{n_i p_i}$$

reduces to the binomial variance of $P_k(1 - P_k)/n$ when no censoring occurs.

29. Derive an estimate for the median based on a sample from a population with exponential survival [i.e., $S(t) = e^{-\lambda t}$]. Also develop an expression for the upper and lower bounds of an approximate 95% confidence interval for this estimated median.

30. Consider the data again:

Treatment group $(n = 12)$:
4, 8, 12^+, 19, 25, 28^+, 41, 44, 57^+, 68, 73^+, 97

Control group $(n = 12)$:
2, 3, 7, 9, 15, 19^+, 33, 38, 40, 53^+, 54, 65.

a. Compute $\hat{\lambda}_1$ and $\hat{\lambda}_2$ (based on exponential survival).
b. Estimate the survival curves for each group parametrically (based on exponential survival) and nonparametrically (product-moment estimators).
c. Compute parametrically the mean survival times from group 1 and group 2 based on exponential survival and nonparametrically based on the product-moment estimators.
d. Estimate the median survival times parametrically (based on exponential survival) and nonparametrically.
e. Use the "Mantel–Haenszel" χ^2 test to evaluate the differences in survival times between treatment and control groups.
f. Use the Gehan generalization of the Wilcoxon test to evaluate differences in survival times between treatment and control groups.
g. Demonstrate with the above data that $W = \Sigma\, n_i(a_i - \hat{A}_i)$ and $z^2 \approx X^2$ for the Gehan generalization approach compared to the "Gehan" χ^2.

Chapter 11

31. Consider the lung cancer survival data

Cox Proportional Hazards Model: Lung cancer data—$S_0(t)$

	Days	$S_0(t)$		Days	$S_0(t)$
1	1	0.968	22	139	0.720
2	3	0.958	23	143	0.707
3	4	0.947	24	159	0.694
4	5	0.937	25	168	0.680
5	9	0.926	26	170	0.667
6	19	0.916	27	180	0.652
7	21	0.905	28	189	0.637
8	30	0.895	29	192	0.622
9	36	0.884	30	201	0.606
10	39	0.874	31	212	0.591
11	40	0.863	32	223	0.575
12	48	0.853	33	229	0.560
13	51	0.842	34	238	0.544
14	61	0.832	35	265	0.528
15	89	0.820	36	275	0.511
16	90	0.796	37	292	0.493
17	92	0.784	38	317	0.476
18	113	0.772	39	322	0.459
19	127	0.759	40	350	0.439
20	131	0.746	41	357	0.419
21	138	0.733	42	380	0.380

a. Show that an adequate description of survival for this group is $S_0(t) = 0.936 - 0.0015t$.

b. Write an expression for the hazard function associated with the linear model $S_0(t)$ given in (a).

c. Using this model of $S_0(t)$ create a plot that shows the differences between the "treatment" and "control" (groups = "high" and "low") groups using the coefficients estimated for these data from the proportional hazards model [see Chapter 13, expression (11.23)].

d. Similarly show the influence of age on these two groups (plot four curves) employing the linear model.

Bibliography

Chapter 1

1. Kleinbaum, D. G., Kupper, L. L., and Morgenstern, H. *Epidemiologic Research: Principle and Methods.* 1982. Van Nostrand Reinhold Co., New York.
2. Selvin, S. (1977). Three statistical models for estimating length of stay. Health Services Research **4**: 322–30.
3. Fleiss, J, L. *Statistical Methods for Rates and Proportions.* 1981. John Wiley and Sons, Inc., New York.
4. Breslow, N. E., and Day, N. E. *Statistical Methods in Cancer Research*, Volume II, *The Design and Analysis of Cohort Studies.* 1987. Oxford University Press, Oxford, U.K.
5. Cochran, W. G. *Sampling Techniques.* 1965. John Wiley and Sons, Inc., New York.
6. Owen, D. B. *Handbook of Statistical Tables.* 1962. Addison–Wesley Publishing Co., Reading, Mass.
7. McNeil, D. R. *Interactive Data Analysis.* 1977. John Wiley and Sons, Inc., New York.
8. Tukey, J. *Exploratory Data Analysis.* 1977. Addison–Wesley, Reading, Mass.
9. *Surveillance, Epidemiology End Results, Incidence and Mortality Data 1973–77.* U.S. Department of Health and Human Resources. NIH 81–2330. National Cancer Institute, Bethesda, Maryland.
10. Cox, D. R. *Analysis of Binary Data.* 1970. Methuen Co., London, U.K.

Chapter 2

1. Snedecor, G. W. and Cochran, W. G. *Statistical Methods.* 1974. The University of Iowa State Press, Ames, Iowa.
2. Ernster, V. L., Mason, L., *et al.* (1982) Effects of caffeine-free diet on benign breast disease: a randomized trial. Surgery **91**(3):263–67.
3. Robinson, R. G. (1985). Blood Pressure: A Contextual Analysis of the Effects of Race, Social Status and Stress. Ph.D dissertation. University of California, Berkeley.
4. Rivard, T. (1985). Master's thesis. University of California, Berkeley.
5. Fleiss, J. *The Design and Analysis of Clinical Experiments.* 1986. John Wiley and Sons, Inc., New York.
6. Miller, R. *Simultaneous Statistical Inference.* 1966. McGraw–Hill, New York.
7. Gardner, M. J., and Altman, D. G. *Statistics with Confidence.* 1989. The Universities Press, London, U.K.
8. Robinson, W. S. (1950) Ecological correlations and the behavior of individuals. Am. Social Rev. **15**:351–57.
9. Kasl, S. V. (1970) Mortality and the business cycle: Some questions about research strategies when utilizing macro-social models and ecologica data. Am. J. Public Health **69**:784–88.
10. Draper, N. R., and Smith, H. *Applied Regression Analysis.* 1966. John Wiley & Sons, Inc., New York.

Chapter 3

1. Johnson, N. L. *Discrete Distributions*. 1969. John Wiley and Sons, Inc., New York.
2. Fleiss, J. L. *Statistical Methods for Rates and Proportions*. 1981. John Wiley and Sons, Inc., New York.
3. Casagrande, J. T., Pike, M. C., and Smith, P. G. (1978) An improved approximate formula for calculating sample sizes for comparing two binomial distributions. Biometrics **34**:483–86.
4. Kleinbaum, D. G., Kupper, L. L., and Morgenstern, H. *Epidemiologic Research: Principle and Methods*. 1982. Van Nostrand Reinhold Co., New York.
5. Kahn, H. A., and Sempos C. T. *An Introduction to Epidemiologic Methods*. 1989. Oxford University Press, New York.
6. Cox, D. R. (1957) Note on grouping. J. American Statistical Assoc. **19**:543–49.

Chapter 4

1. Frost, W. H. (1939) The age selection of mortality from tuberculosis in successive decades. Amer. J. Hyg. **4**:91–96.
2. Levin, M. L. (1953) The occurrence of lung cancer in man. Acta Unio. Internationalis Contra Cancrum **9**:531–41.
3. Poskanzer, D., and Schwab, R. S. (1963) Cohort analysis of Parkinson's syndrome. J. Chronic Dis. **16**:961–73.
4. Ernster, V. L., Selvin, S., and Winkelstein, W. (1978) Cohort mortality for prostatic cancer among United States non-whites. Science **200**:1165–66.
5. Avila, M. H., and Walker, A. W. (1987) Age dependence of cohort phenomena in breast cancer mortality in the United States. Am. J. Epid., **126**:377–84.
6. McNeil, D. *Interactive Data Analysis*. 1977. John Wiley & Sons, New York.
7. Tukey, J. *Exploratory Data Analysis*. 1977. Addison–Wesley, Reading, Mass.
8. Selvin, S., Levin, L. I., Merrill, D. W., and Winkelstein, W., (1983) Selected epidemiologic observations of cell-specific leukemia mortality in the United States, 1969–1977. Amer. J. of Epid. **117**:140–152.

Chapter 5

1. Lilienfield, A. M. *Foundations of Epidemiology*. 1976. Oxford University Press, New York.
2. Burkitt, D. (1962) A children's cancer dependent on climatic factors. Cancer **28**:3–13.
3. Feller, W. *An Introduction to Probability Theory and Its Applications*. 1957. John Wiley and Sons, Inc. New York.
4. Ripley, B. D. *Spatial Statistics*. 1981. John Wiley and Sons, Inc., New York.
5. Selvin, S., Merrill, D. W., Schulman, J., *et al.* (1988) Transformations of maps to investigate clusters of disease. Soc. Sci. Med., **26**:215–21.
6. Schulman, J., Selvin, S., and Merrill, D. W. (1988) Density equalized map projections: A method for analyzing cluster around a fixed point Stat. Med. **7**:491–505.
7. Schulman, J. (1987) The Statistical Analysis of Density Equalized Maps. Ph.D. thesis University of California, Berkeley.

8. Knox, G. (1964) The detection of space–time interaction. Applied Stat. **13**:25–29.
9. Knox, G. (1964) Epidemiology of childhood leukemia in Northumberland and Duram. Brit. J. Prev. Soc. Med. **18**:17–24.
10. Mantel, N. (1967) The detection of disease clustering and a generalized regression approach. Cancer Res. **27**:209–20.
11. Shaw, G. M. Private communication.
12. Shaw, G. M. (1987) A Comparison of Techniques for the Detection of Spatial and Temporal–Spatial Disease Clustering. Ph.D. thesis, University of California, Berkeley.
13. Kaldor, J., Harris, J. A., Glazer, E., *et al.* (1984) Statistical association between cancer incidence and major-cause mortality and estimated exposure to emissions from petroleum and chemical plants. Environ. Health Prospect. **45**:319–332.
14. California Department of Health Services. Epidemiology study of the incidence of cancer as related to industrial emissions in Contra Costa County, California. Environmental Protection Agency. 1982 (Report No. r806393-01).
15. Efron, B. *The Jackknife, The Bootstrap and Other Resampling Plans.* 1982. Society for Industrial and Applied Mathematics. Bristol, England.
16. Diaconis, P., and Efron, B. (1983) Computer methods in statistics. Scientific American **248**:116–30.

Chapter 6

1 Everitt, B. S. *The Analysis of Contingency Table Data.* 1977. Chapman and Hall, London.
2. Bishop, M. M. Y., Feinberg, S. E., and Holland, P. W. *Discrete Multivariate Analysis: Theory and Practice.* 1975. The MIT Press. Cambridge, Mass.
3. Kahn, H. A., and Sempos, C. T. *An Introduction to Epidemioligic Methods.* 1989. Oxford Press, New York.
4. MacMahon, B., *et al.*, (1981) Coffee and cancer of the pancreas. New England J. of Medicine **304**:630–3.
5. Breslow, N. E., and Day N. E. *Statistical Methods in Cancer Research,* Vol. II. 1987. Oxford University Press, Oxford, U.K.
6. Bithell, J. F., and Steward, M. A. (1975) Prenatal irradiation and childhood malignancy: A review of Bristish data from the Oxford study. Brit. J. of Cancer **31**:271–87.
7. Bross, I. D. J. (1960) How to use ridit analysis. Biometrics **14**:18–38.
8. Conover, W. J. *Practical Nonparametric Statistics.* 1971. John Wiley & Sons, Inc., New York.
9. Selvin, S. (1977) A further note on the interpretation of ridit analysis. Am. J. of Epid. **105**:16–20.
10. Gail, M. Adjusting for covariates that have the same distribution in exposed and unexposed cohorts. In: *Modern Statistical Methods in Epidemiology.* Moolgavkar, S. H., and Prentice, R. L. (eds.). 1986. John Wiley and Sons, New York.
11. Kleinbaum, D. G., Kupper, L. L., and Morgenstern H. *Epidemiologic Research: Principle and Methods.* 1982. Van Nostrand Reinhold Co., New York.
13. Simpson, E. H. (1951) The interpretation of interaction in contingency tables. J. Roy. Statist. Soc. B **13**:238–41.

Chapter 7

1. Thomas, W. D. (1987) Statistical criteria in the interpretation of epidemiologic data. Am. J. Public Health **77**:191–94.
2. Poole, C. (1987) Beyond the confidence interval. Am. J. Public Health **77**:195–99.
3. Letters to the Editor, (1986) Am. J. Public Health **76**:237 and **76**:581.
4. Kahn, H. A., and Sempos C. T. *An Introduction to Epidemioligic Methods*. 1989. Oxford University Press, New York.
5. Kleinbaum, D. G., Kupper, L. L., and Morgenstern H. *Epidemioligic Research: Principle and Methods*. 1982. Van Nostrand Reinhold Co., New York.
6. Mantel, N., and Haenszel, W. (1959) Statistical aspects of the analysis of data from the retrospective studies of disease. J. National Cancer Inst. **22**:719–48.
7. Cochran, W. G. (1954) Some methods of strengthening the common chi-square test. Biometrics **10**:417–51.

Chapter 8

1. Draper, N. R., and Smith, H. *Applied Regression Analysis*. 1966. John Wiley & Sons, Inc., New York.
2. Kleinbaum, D. G., Kupper, L. L., and Morgenstern H. *Epidemiologic Research: Principles and Methods*. 1982. Van Nostrand Reinhold Co., New York.
3. Hosmer, D. W., and Lemeshow S. *Applied Logistic Regression*. 1989. John Wiley and Sons, Inc., New York.
4. Breslow, N. E., and Day N. E. *Statistical Methods in Cancer Research*, Vol. I. 1980. Oxford University Press, Oxford, U.K.
5. Schlesselman, J. J. *Case–Control Studies*. 1982. Oxford University Press, New York.

Chapter 9

1. Chiang, C. L. *The Life Table and Its Applications*. 1984. Robert Krieger Co., Malabar, Florida.
2. Miller, R. *Surival Analysis*. 1981. John Wiley and Sons, Inc., New York.
3. Cutler, S. J., and Ederer, E. (1958) Maximum utilization of the life table in analysis of survival. J. Chronic Diseases **6**:699–712.
4. World Health Organization. International Classification of Disease. J. of the International Statistical Classification of Disease, Injuries and Cause of Death, Geneva WHO 1968; Vol. 1, 9th revision.
5. Berkson, J. and Elveback, L. (1960) Competing exponential risks, with particular reference to the study of smoking and lung cancer. J. of the American Statistical Society **55**:415–28.
6. Hammond, E. C., and Horn, D. (1958) Smoking and death rates: report on forty-four months of follow-up on 187,783 men. J. of the American Medical Association **166**:1294–1308.
7. Sheps, M. C. (1959) An examination of some methods of comparing several rates or proportions. Biometrics **15**:87–97.

Chapter 10

1. Bartholomew, D. J. (1957) A problem in life testing. J. of Am. Stat. Assoc. **52**:350–55.
2. Peto, R., Pike, M. C., Armitage, P., Breslow, N. E., Cox, D. R., Howard, S. V., Mantel, N., McPherson, K., Peto, J., and Smith, P. G. (1977) Design and analysis of randomized clinical trials requiring prolonged observation of each patient. II. Analysis and examples. Br. J. Cancer **35**:1–39.
3. Gross, A. J., and Clark, V. A. *Survival Distributions: Reliability Applications in the Biomedical Sciences*, 1975. John Wiley & Sons, Inc., New York.
4. Snedecor, G. W., and Cochran, W. G. *Statistical Methods*. 1974. The University of Iowa State Press, Ames, Iowa.
5. Elandt-Johnson, R. C., and Johnson, N. L. *Survival Models and Data Analysis*. 1980. John Wiley and Sons, Inc., New York.
6. Miller, R. *Survival Analysis*. 1981. John Wiley and Sons, Inc., New York.
7. Gehan, E. A. (1965) A generalized Wilcoxon test for comparing arbitrary simply censored samples. Biometrika **52**:457–81.
8. Tarone, R., and Ware, J. (1977) On distribution-free tests for equality of survival distributions. Biometrica **64**:156–60.
9. Owen, D. B. *Handbook of Statistical Tables*. 1962. Addison–Wesley Publishing Co., Reading, Mass.

Chapter 11

1. Kalbfleisch, J. D., and Prentice, R. L. *The Statistical Analysis of Failure Data*. 1980. John Wiley and Sons, Inc., New York.
2. Cox, D. R., and Oakes, D. *Analysis of Survival Data*. 1984. Chapman and Hall, New York.
3. Elandt-Johnson, R., and Johnson, N. L. *Survival Models and Data Analysis*. 1980. John Wiley and Sons, Inc., New York.
4. Miller, R. *Survival Analysis*. 1981. John Wiley and Sons, Inc., New York.
5. Glaser, M. (1967) Exponential survival with covariance. American Statistical Assoc. J. **82**:561–68.
6. Prentice, R. L. (1973) Exponential survivals with censoring and explanatory variables. Biometrika **60**:279–88.
7. SUGI Supplemental Library User's Guide. 1983 Edition. SAS Institute Inc., North Carolina.
8. Feigel, P., and Zelen, M. (1965) Estimation of exponential survival probabilities with concomitant information. Biometrics **21**:826–38.

Appendices

1. Roseman, R. H., Brand, R. J., Jenkins, C. D., *et al.* (1975) Coronary heart disease in the Western Collaborative Group study. J. of the American Medical Association **223**:872–77.
2. Rosenman, R. H., Brand R., J., Sholtz, R. I., and Friedmen M. (1976) Multivariate prediction of coronary heart disease during 8.5 year follow-up in the Western Collaborative Group study. American J. of Cardiology **37**:903–10.

3. Roseman, R. H., Friedmen M., Straus R., *et al.* (1970) Coronary heart disease in the Western Collaborative Group study: A follow-up of 4.5 years. J. Chronic Diseases **23**:173–90.

4. Ragland, D. R., and Brand R. J. (1988) Coronary heart disease mortality in the Western Collaborative Group study. American J. of Epidemiology **1217**:462–75.

5. Mosteller, F., Rourke, R. K., and Thomas, G. B. *Probability with Statistical Applications.* Addison–Wesley Publishing Co., Mass.

6. Lyon, J. L., Klauber, M. R., and Gardner J. W., *et al.* (1979) Childhood leukemia associated with fallout from nuclear testing. NEng. J. Med. **300**:397–402.

7. Breslow, N. E., and Day N. E. *Statistical Methods in Cancer Research*, Volume I. 1980. Oxford University Press, Oxford U.K.

8. Fleiss, J. *The Design and Analysis of Clinical Experiments.* 1986. John Wiley and Sons, Inc., New York.

9. Kahn, H. A., and Sempos, C. T. *An Introduction to Epidemiologic Methods.* 1989. Oxford University Press, New York.

10. Haldane, J. B. S. (1956) The estimation and significance of logarithm of a ratio of frequencies. Annals of Human Genetics **20**:309–11.

11. Jewell, N. J. (1986) On the bias of commonly used measures of association for 2 × 2 tables. Biometrics **42**:351–58.

12. Kendall, M. G., and Stuart, A. *The Advanced Theory of Statistics*, Volume II. 1976. Charles Griffin and Co., London, U.K.

Index